THE ROLE OF EMOTION IN 1 PETER

Volume 173

In this book, Katherine M. Hockey explores the function of emotions in the New Testament by examining the role of emotions in 1 Peter. Moving beyond outdated, modern rationalistic views of emotions as irrational, bodily feelings, she presents a theoretically and historically informed cognitive approach to emotions in the New Testament. Informed by Greco-Roman philosophical and rhetorical views of emotions along with modern emotion theory, she shows how the author of 1 Peter uses the logic of each emotion to value and position objects within the audience's worldview, including the self and the other. She also demonstrates how, cumulatively, the emotions of joy, distress, fear, hope, and shame are deployed to build an alternative view of reality. This new view of reality aims to shape the believers' understanding of the structure of their world, encourages a reassessment of their personal goals, and ultimately seeks to affect their identity and behaviour.

KATHERINE M. HOCKEY is the inaugural Kirby Laing Postdoctoral Fellow in New Testament Studies at the University of Aberdeen. She is co-editor of *Muted Voices of the New Testament: Readings in the Catholic Epistles and Hebrews* and *Ethnicity, Race, Religion: Identities and Ideologies in Early Jewish and Christian Texts, and in Modern Biblical Interpretation.*

T0382628

SOCIETY FOR NEW TESTAMENT STUDIES

MONOGRAPH SERIES

General Editor: Edward Adams, *Kings College, London*

173

THE ROLE OF EMOTION IN 1 PETER

SOCIETY FOR NEW TESTAMENT STUDIES

MONOGRAPH SERIES

The Role of Emotion in 1 Peter

KATHERINE M. HOCKEY

University of Aberdeen

CAMBRIDGE
UNIVERSITY PRESS

University Printing House, Cambridge CB2 8BS, United Kingdom

One Liberty Plaza, 20th Floor, New York, NY 10006, USA

477 Williamstown Road, Port Melbourne, VIC 3207, Australia

314-321, 3rd Floor, Plot 3, Splendor Forum, Jasola District Centre, New Delhi - 110025, India

79 Anson Road, #06-04/06, Singapore 079906

Cambridge University Press is part of the University of Cambridge.

It furthers the University's mission by disseminating knowledge in the pursuit of education, learning and research at the highest international levels of excellence.

www.cambridge.org
Information on this title: www.cambridge.org/9781108468138
DOI: 10.1017/9781108567343

First published 2019
First paperback edition 2020

A catalogue record for this publication is available from the British Library

Library of Congress Cataloging in Publication data
Names: Hockey, Katherine M., author.
Title: The role of emotion in 1 Peter / Katherine M. Hockey,
University of Aberdeen.
Description: New York: Cambridge University Press, 2019. |
Series: Society for New Testament studies monograph series; Volume 173 |
Includes bibliographical references.
Identifiers: LCCN 2018039913 | ISBN 9781108475464 (hardback) |
ISBN 9781108468138 (paperback)
Subjects: LCSH: Bible. Peter, 1st – Criticism, interpretation, etc. |
Emotions, Biblical teaching. | Bible – Psychology.
Classification: LCC BS2795.6.P9H63 2019 | DDC 227/.9206–dc23
LC record available at https://lccn.loc.gov/2018039913

ISBN 978-1-108-47546-4 Hardback
ISBN 978-1-108-46813-8 Paperback

CONTENTS

vii

TABLE

PREFACE

This book is a revised version of my Doctoral Thesis 'Seeing Emotionally: An Investigation of the Role of Emotion in the Rhetorical Discourse of 1 Peter' undertaken at Durham University and completed in summer 2016. The Arts and Humanities Research Council (UK), to whom I am very grateful, funded my research. Unfortunately, due to being published too late in the process of this current project, I have not been able to engage with an important collection of essays on the topic of emotion and biblical interpretation: F. Scott Spencer, ed., *Mixed Feelings and Vexed Passions: Exploring Emotions in Biblical Literature* (Atlanta, GA: SBL Press, 2017). However, I recommend it to those interested in the application of various approaches to studying emotions in the biblical text beyond 1 Peter.

The completion of this book marks the end of a long process that would not have been possible without the input and support of a number of people. First, thanks must go to John Barclay who, as my Doctoral Supervisor, was and continues to be immensely generous with his time and critical insights. I have also been fortunate to have a number of other helpful discussion partners along the way such as Dorothea Bertschmann, Katie Marcar, Robbie Griggs, Madison Pierce, David Horrell, Francis Watson, and Matthew Novenson. I thank the latter two in particular for their astute questioning in the examination process and for encouraging me to pursue the publication of the thesis. Thanks must go to Paul Trebilco (former SNTSMS Editor) for recommending this book to Cambridge University Press and to the Editorial Board of Cambridge University Press for accepting this book for publication and for affording me the time to revise it. I am also grateful to Dominic Mattos and Bloomsbury T&T Clark for allowing me to re-use in this work material previously published as Katherine M. Hockey, '1 Peter 4.16: Shame, Emotion and Christian Self-Perception', in *Muted Voices of the*

New Testament: Readings in the Catholic Epistles and Hebrews (ed.
Katherine M. Hockey, Madison N. Pierce, and Francis Watson,
London: Bloomsbury T&T Clark, 2017, 27–40; see Chapter 8 in
particular).

The PhD journey, in which the majority of this research took
place, was made hugely enjoyable by the close friendship of those
who walked with me. Thank you Kayleigh, Jeanette, Tess, and
Siobhan for the fun and laughter, and for your friendship and care.
My gratitude also goes to my family – Mum, Dad, Jo, and Paul –
for their ongoing encouragement, prayers, listening ears, and wise
counsel. Lastly, I must thank my wonderful husband Joe for his
unending faith in my ability, for reminding me of the importance of
this work, for encouraging me to keep going, and for being a never-
ending source of joy!

ABBREVIATIONS

All abbreviations of primary sources follow standard Society of Biblical Literature conventions.

AB   Anchor Bible
BDAG   Bauer, W., F. W. Danker, W. F. Arndt, and F. W. Gingrich. *Greek-English Lexicon of the New Testament and Other Early Christian Literature.* 3rd ed. Chicago: University of Chicago Press, 2000
BECNT   Baker Exegetical Commentary on the New Testament
BHGNT   Baylor Handbook on the Greek New Testament
BInS   Biblical Interpretation Series
BTB   *Biblical Theology Bulletin*
BZNW   Beihefte zur Zeitschrift für die neutestamentliche Wissenschaft
CBNT   Commentaire biblique: Nouveau Testament
EH   Europäische Hochschulschriften
EKKNT   Evangelisch-katholischer Kommentar zum Neuen Testament
ESVUK   English Standard Version, Anglicised
HNT   Handbuch zum Neuen Testament
HP1   Long, A. A. and D. N. Sedley. *The Hellenistic Philosophers. Volume 1: Translations of the Principal Sources with Philosophical Commentary.* Cambridge: Cambridge University Press, 1987
HP2   Long, A. A. and D. N. Sedley. *The Hellenistic Philosophers. Volume 2: Greek and Latin Texts with Notes and Bibliography.* Cambridge: Cambridge University Press, 1987
HThKNT   Herders Theologischer Kommentar zum Neuen Testament

HTR	*Harvard Theological Review*
JBL	*Journal of Biblical Literature*
JSNT	*Journal for the Study of the New Testament*
JSNTSup	Journal for the Study of the New Testament: Supplement Series
LNTS	Library of New Testament Studies
LSJ	Liddell, H. G., R. Scott, and H. S. Jones. *A Greek-English Lexicon*. 9th ed. with revised supplement. Oxford: Clarendon, 1996
NA27	*Nestle-Aland Novum Testamentum Graece 27*. Stuttgart: Deutsche Bibelgesellschaft
NA28	*Nestle-Aland Novum Testamentum Graece 28*. Stuttgart: Deutsche Bibelgesellschaft
NABPR	National Association of Baptist Professors of Religion
NIV	New International Version
NKJV	New King James Version
NovT	*Novum Testamentum*
NovTSup	Supplements to Novum Testamentum
NRSVA	New Revised Standard Version, Anglicised
NRSVCE	New Revised Standard Version Catholic Edition
NTS	*New Testament Studies*
SBB	Stuttgarter biblische Beiträger
SBL	Society of Biblical Literature
SBLDS	Society of Biblical Literature Dissertation Series
SBLMS	Society of Biblical Literature Monograph Series
SBLSymS	Society of Biblical Literature Symposium Series
SSSP	Springer Series in Social Psychology
StUNT	Studien zur Umwelt des Neuen Testaments
WBC	Word Biblical Commentary
WUNT	Wissenschaftliche Untersuchungen zum Neuen Testament
ZMR	*Zeitschrift für Missionswissenschaft und Religionswissenschaft*
ZNW	*Zeitschrift für die neutestamentliche Wissenschaft und die Kunde der älteren Kirche*

PART I

INTRODUCTORY MATTERS

1

EMOTION STUDIES AND THE NEW TESTAMENT

This book aims to explore how emotions, specifically emotion terms, function in the discourse of 1 Peter. Since our study is concerned with how the author seeks to persuade his audience towards a particular viewpoint in order to alter behaviour, it may be categorised as a type of rhetorical analysis, even if some features of rhetorical analysis (e.g. categorisation of rhetorical species, and identification of rhetorical τόποι and figures) will here play no role.[1] Although they are often overlooked, it will show that in this letter emotions play a vital role in the persuasion of the audience, at a deep level and in highly significant ways. It will reveal that emotions are not a manipulative moving force that is separate from logical argument, but in themselves communicate logically and can be deployed to alter an audience's interpretation of events, promote systems of value, influence goals, and, consequently, shape behaviour. Therefore, the focus of this investigation will be the *emotion terms* that appear in the letter, specifically, joy (χαρά), distress (λύπη), fear (φόβος), hope (ἐλπίς), and shame (αἰσχύνη). We will not address the audience's own emotions other than as they are idealised in the text itself.

Recent progress in the study of emotions, notably in philosophy, psychology, sociology, and anthropology, has generated greater understanding about what constitutes an emotion, and revealed its interpretive and directive role. Scholars in these fields have argued persuasively that emotions are culturally constructed and can be used to shape worldviews and therefore affect our understanding of our place in the world. Subsequently, emotions influence one's conception of reality, including social structure and self-identity. To date, there has been no attempt to use these insights to explore how

---

[1] For an example of this type of approach see B. L. Campbell, *Honor, Shame, and the Rhetoric of 1 Peter*, SBLDS 160 (Atlanta, GA: Scholars Press, 1998), discussed below. For more on the rhetorical approach of this study see pp. 44–6.

3

emotions function in 1 Peter's persuasive communication. In fact, such a thoroughgoing investigation of emotions has not been undertaken for any New Testament epistle.

The Wider New Testament

In recent years, there have been only a few scholars who have analysed emotions in the New Testament.[2] One notable example is Matthew Elliott.[3] Elliott demonstrates awareness of modern and ancient theories of emotion. He outlines cognitive and non-cognitive theories of emotion; emotion in the Greco-Roman world and Jewish culture;[4] and then discusses love, joy, hope, jealousy, sorrow, fear, and anger in the New Testament. Elliott promotes a cognitive approach to emotions, and reveals that cognitive perspectives on emotion were present in the ancient world. He seeks to determine whether the New Testament has a cognitive view of emotions by examining whether the authors command emotion, categorise emotions as right and wrong, and hold their audiences responsible for their emotions. Where these are demonstrated, as they are in the New Testament, a cognitive understanding of emotions is present.[5] The problem with

---

[2] Certain emotions have been acknowledged in the scope of other arguments, but emotions themselves have not been the primary focus. Older works that address individual emotions include, J. Moffatt, *Love in the New Testament* (London: Hodder & Stoughton, 1929) and W. G. Morrice, *Joy in the New Testament* (Exeter: Paternoster Press, 1984). In both of these, 1 Peter receives only a brief mention.

[3] M. Elliott, *Faithful Feelings: Emotions in the New Testament* (Leicester: Inter-Varsity Press, 2005). Another example is S. Voorwinde, *Jesus' Emotions in the Gospels* (London: T&T Clark, 2011). Voorwinde does address the question 'what is an emotion?' However, his discussion is brief and results in the vague definition that emotions are feelings that motivate action (3). In his exegesis he gives a basic understanding of each emotion investigated by translating the Greek word to English equivalents, which shows a historical and cultural naivety towards emotions. Voorwinde does recognise that emotions are situational and implicitly assumes that they have some reasoning. But, he does not reveal how emotions are functioning as part of the discourse of the gospels other than to detail what they reveal about Jesus' own character and identity. Thus, Voorwinde's study it is not comparable to this investigation. Though it addresses emotions, it has a different type of text in view and asks different questions. In fact, it demonstrates that even Voorwinde, who seeks to take seriously emotions in the New Testament, provides only a surface-level examination with little theoretical or analytical sharpness.

[4] Though his discussion is thin, having only a few references to the ancient primary texts and relying on secondary scholarship (see 56–79). Furthermore, he gives little or no recourse to Greco-Roman views on emotion in his analysis of the New Testament. Thus, he does not show historical and cultural awareness of the emotion he is investigating.

[5] Elliott, *Faithful Feelings*, 54.

Elliott's work is not with his theoretical awareness but the extent to which this translates into critical questions asked of the text. Despite making important observations about emotions – assertions this study will echo – he does not utilise these fully in his exegesis.[6] For each emotion analysed he gives a general explanation of the emotion and its occasion; highlights the range of relevant Greek terms; and then surveys the occurrence of the emotion in groups of New Testament texts such as the gospels, 'Pauline Literature', and the 'general epistles and Revelation'. His approach tends towards the general and gives little detailed investigation of the role of the emotions in the discourse of the New Testament letters. Instead, the thrust of his work is to show that emotions are treated as cognitive in the New Testament and therefore are linked to ethics. This is a foundational concept for this present study, but the limitations of Elliott's exegesis show that there is still work to be done. It is not sufficient to note emotions and recognise that the author gives them importance; we need to understand why the author is using an emotion in a given context and what the implications of this are.

Most attention has been paid to the emotions within the field of rhetorical criticism. But, still, few works have centred on the emotions. The most prominent volume is *Paul and Pathos*.[7] This essay collection uses ancient rhetorical theory to assess how Paul sought to move his audience. The first part outlines the background and method for analysing Paul in this manner. The second part addresses πάθος in particular Pauline letters. The introductory essays helpfully highlight the importance of πάθος in ancient rhetoric, and rightly call for more attention to be paid to pathetic persuasion. However, this collection does little to utilise conceptual insights from modern theory when approaching the idea of πάθος (equated by the authors with 'emotion'). It is evident that some baggage carried by the English concept of emotion (see

---

[6] See particularly Elliott, *Faithful Feelings*, 53–5.

[7] T. H. Olbricht and J. L. Sumney, eds., *Paul and Pathos*, SBLSymS 16 (Atlanta, GA: Society of Biblical Literature, 2001). Another example is A. Harker, 'The Affective Directives of the Book of Revelation', *Tyndale Bulletin* 63 (2012): 115–30. Harker's short article highlights the importance of the affective aspects of Revelation's directives. Theoretically, it relies on Jonathan Edwards' conception of affections (Harker cites Edwards' *Treatise Concerning the Religious Affections*, 1746). Its main point is to acknowledge that the author aimed to affect his audience in order that they might have the appropriate attraction to and repulsion from the right things. See also P. von Gemünden, *Affekt und Glaube: Studien zur historischen Psychologie des Frühjudentums und Urchristentums*, StUNT 73 (Göttingen: Vandenhoeck & Ruprecht, 2009), which is not strictly interested in rhetoric, but emotion in discourse more generally.

pp. 19–25) is absorbed into a number of essays that persist in distinguishing between head and heart, emotion and reason. There are exceptions: for example, Steven J. Kraftchick acknowledges that 'emotions are part of the rational process'.[8] Nevertheless, this does not equate to recognising that emotions are themselves cognitive, which is a key tenet of this study. The generally non-cognitive standpoint pushes this collection in a certain theoretical direction.[9] Thus, the majority of exegetical essays approach emotions by looking at the relationship between author and audience, frequently exploring how the author moves the audience by arousing its emotion. This is generally considered a persuasive manoeuvre separate to the λόγος of the argument. Most essays take the same approach: they examine a passage that they think exhibits πάθος; suggest which emotion they think the author is exciting in his audience; then, give their reasoning for why Paul would want to arouse this emotion. The last stage requires relating the emotion to the behavioural outcome Paul must have desired. The problem with this approach is that it becomes conjectural, being based on the scholar's own understanding of emotions and opinion of what is most fitting. The cultural boundedness of emotions is not appreciated, and therefore emotions are analysed through English-speaking conceptual frameworks.[10] Furthermore, despite the wealth of material in ancient rhetorical handbooks that could have been accessed, the discussion linking epistolary content to emotional arousal remains basic.[11] Furthermore, no essay focuses on the emotion terms in the actual text, but instead on the projected emotions of the audience.

---

[8] S. J. Kraftchick, 'Πάθη in Paul: The Emotional Logic of "Original Argument"', in *Paul and Pathos*, ed. Thomas H. Olbricht and Jerry L. Sumney, SBLSymS 16 (Atlanta, GA: Society of Biblical Literature, 2001), 39–68, at 45.

[9] Sumney's essay is more insightful. It does acknowledge the dynamic relationship between emotions and perspective, and recognises that emotions are not irrational and are 'based to some degree on beliefs arrived at through reason'. He notes that emotions are interpretive, and that they signify the meaning of an event, but he does not utilise these insights to their full extent in his discussion. For example, the link between emotions and values or goals is never made, though this would be an obvious outcome of the statement that emotions make events meaningful; see J. L. Sumney, 'Paul's Use of Πάθος in His Argument Against the Opponents of 2 Corinthians', in *Paul and Pathos*, ed. Thomas H. Olbricht and Jerry L. Sumney, SBLSymS 16 (Atlanta, GA: Society of Biblical Literature, 2001), 147–60, esp. 147–9.

[10] For another example of this see P. Lampe, 'Affects and Emotions in the Rhetoric of Paul's Letter to Philemon: A Rhetorical-Psychological Interpretation', in *Philemon in Perspective: Interpreting a Pauline Letter*, ed. D. François Tolmie, BZNW 169 (Berlin: De Gruyter, 2010), 61–77.

[11] Martin more successfully mines Aristotle's comments in *On Rhetoric* and consequently provides a fuller and more convincing discussion of πάθος in Galatians;

Contrastingly, this study will start from the emotions present in the text. It will not suggest which emotions the audience might be caused to feel, but how 1 Peter directly addresses and uses certain emotion terms to communicate.

There are other short works that approach emotions in the New Testament from a therapeutic angle. The best example is Welborn's article 'Paul and Pain'.[12] Welborn examines Paul's innovative stance towards constructive pain in 2 Corinthians. He highlights that Paul speaks of emotions in a manner that does not map neatly on to contemporaneous philosophical opinions but is shaped by Paul's view of God's action in Christ. Consequently, Paul posits a different relationship between emotions, here pain (or distress), and the moral life. Subsequently, he suggests an alternate emotional therapy. Welborn's essay, which uses Greco-Roman philosophical theories of emotion throughout, is an excellent example of how a historical and cultural awareness of emotions can shed fresh light on New Testament texts. Welborn also rightly highlights that ancient discussion about emotions is necessarily linked to ethics, and so is not an abstract but a practical concern.[13] This study aims to follow Welborn by having the same level of cultural and historical sensitivity. Welborn's article achieves a number of important steps for the analysis of emotions in New Testament texts, but these are mostly at the level of general philosophical/theoretical views of the emotions. There are still advances that need to be made in the analysis of particular emotions, and in the understanding of the argumentative function of emotions in New Testament epistles.

One scholar who has made notable progress in studying emotion in the New Testament is Stephen Barton. In 2011 Barton published an article entitled 'Eschatology and the Emotions in Early Christianity'.[14] Barton comments that the 'study of the emotions has

---

see T. W. Martin, 'The Voice of Emotion: Paul's Pathetic Persuasion (Gal 4:12–20)', in *Paul and Pathos*, ed. Thomas H. Olbricht and Jerry L. Sumney, SBLSymS 16 (Atlanta, GA: Society of Biblical Literature, 2001), 181–202.

[12] L. L. Welborn, 'Paul and Pain: Paul's Emotional Therapy in 2 Corinthians 1.1–2.13; 7.5–16 in the Context of Ancient Psychagogic Literature', *NTS* 57 (2011): 547–70.

[13] In this regard see W. Klassen, 'Coals of Fire: Sign of Repentance or Revenge?', *NTS* 9 (1963): 337–50 for discussion on Paul's therapeutic stance towards dealing with one's enemies.

[14] S. C. Barton, 'Eschatology and the Emotions in Early Christianity', *JBL* 130 (2011): 571–91; see also S. C. Barton, 'Why Do Things Move People? The Jerusalem Temple as Emotional Repository', *JSNT* 37 (2015): 351–80 for discussion on the relationship between emotions and material objects. I will not discuss this essay as its key themes are less applicable to the current study.

attracted relatively little attention in studies of early Christianity'.[15] He states: 'Arguably, this neglect reflects a scholarly preoccupation in academic theology with matters of doctrinal, historical, and textual reconstruction. Arguably also, however, it reflects a certain myopia with respect to approaches to human perception and cognition that take seriously the expressive and cognitive resources of the emotions and the realm of the experiential.'[16] Since 2011, New Testament scholarship has not taken up Barton's challenge to extend its vision to encompass the emotions. Barton's approach is the only attempt I have discovered that takes account of the Greco-Roman histor-ical cultural setting of the emotions *and* is analytically informed by modern emotion theory. He adopts a cognitive view of emotions stating that 'emotions communicate culturally mediated moral judgements'.[17] Barton goes on to say:

> That is to say, emotions are cognitive and evaluative. This implies that study of early Christian emotions offers a window on the ethos, ethics, and identity of Christianity in a crucial formative period in a way that supplements trad-itional approaches. To put it another way, emotions as a form of rationality offer another avenue toward understanding early Christian rationality as a whole.[18]

This crucial insight has been overlooked in New Testament studies to date. Barton also recognises that emotions 'arise in the course of social relations and interactions' and therefore 'emotions are inte-gral to personal engagements in social processes'. Thus, 'the study of emotions offers additional insight into the tenor and character of early Christian social life and action'.[19] He goes on to explore grief in 1 Thessalonians, acknowledging that his essay does not answer every question raised by investigating emotions.

A second article by Barton assesses the role of emotions in moral theology.[20] This time, using Greco-Roman moral philosophy com-paratively, Barton reveals how Christian stances towards emotions

[15] Barton identifies the exception as the field of rhetorical studies, and cites *Paul and Pathos*, discussed above, as the primary example; Barton, 'Eschatology', 571.
[16] Barton, 'Eschatology', 572.
[17] Barton, 'Eschatology', 578.
[18] Barton, 'Eschatology', 578.
[19] See Barton, 'Eschatology', 579–80.
[20] S. C. Barton, '"Be Angry But Do Not Sin" (Ephesians 4:26a): Sin and the Emotions in the New Testament with Special Reference to Anger', *Studies in Christian Ethics* 28 (2015): 21–34.

can be at variance to surrounding society and, thus, emotions are integrated into Christian moral life differently.[21] He shows that Christian emotions are shaped by the 'salvific narrative of divine grace' in Christ. Therefore, emotions 'as a form of cognition' have the potential to 'be in alignment with, and an expression of, *the truth*'.[22] For the early Christians, having the appropriate moral emotions involved a process of learning, instructed by both biblical traditions and the New Testament authors themselves.[23] Hence, Barton demonstrates that investigating emotions gives insight into the moral theology of New Testament authors and New Testament therapeutic education.

Barton has argued strongly that much can be gained by analysing the place and use of emotions in the New Testament. Thus, Barton's work has been a springboard for my own. This study will build on Barton's by presenting the first full-length exploration of the role of emotions in a New Testament epistle that uses analytical tools from modern emotion theory, the cultural and historical insights gained from Greco-Roman philosophy, and the theological background of biblical tradition. In doing so, it will, to quote Barton, engage with early Christian emotions with 'greater depth and with greater analytical sophistication than has been the case hitherto'.[24]

1 Peter

Where emotion terms appear in 1 Peter they have been noted, but they have not received an informed analytical treatment. For example, in most major commentaries, e.g. Michaels', Achtemeier's, and Elliott's, emotions such as shame are given a sideways glance, whereas others like fear receive more attention. However, the comments are often thin and not thoroughly worked through, with the consequence that

---

[21] Barton also investigates anger in Biblical and Jewish tradition, noting that this also has influence on early Christian moral understanding.

[22] Barton, 'Be Angry', 33.

[23] Barton, 'Be Angry', 33–4; For more on how emotions align with belief see S. C. Barton, 'Spirituality and the Emotions in Early Christianity: The Case of Joy', in *The Bible and Spirituality: Exploratory Essays in Reading Scripture Spiritually*, ed. Andrew T. Lincoln et al. (Eugene, OR: Cascade Books, 2013), 171–93. In this same volume is a theologically illuminative, if rather analytically simple discussion of love in Galatians; see P. G. R. de Villiers, 'Love in the Letter to the Galatians', in *The Bible and Spirituality: Exploratory Essays in Reading Scripture Spiritually*, ed. Andrew T. Lincoln et al. (Eugene, OR: Cascade Books, 2013), 194–211.

[24] Barton, 'Eschatology', 573.

the specific communication contained in the emotion term is missed and, therefore, its influence on interpretation is not recognised.

There have been three notable examinations of joy in 1 Peter, specifically its relation to suffering.[25] Both Nauck and de Villiers provide short treatments, whereas Millhauer's analysis is part of his larger work *Leiden als Gnade*. Millhauer's study does not investigate the rhetorical function of joy, rather it is a tradition-historical investigation of the *Leidenstheologie* of 1 Peter. Likewise, Nauck's article focuses on tradition-historical questions. In de Villiers' essay, he provides some useful comment on the contextualisation of joy, e.g. its object in 1.6, and links joy to the argument and purpose of 1 Peter.[26] He also comments that the Christians, through 1 Peter's address, have 'obtained the proper perspective on their sufferings'.[27] However, he does not provide a full examination of *how* the author by utilising the emotion of joy has sought to achieve this, nor does he suggest the implications of employing joy in this context. It is unfair to expect these authors to give a full treatment of emotions given that the developments in emotions studies, on which my work relies, postdate them. Thus, in light of progress in other fields, a fresh reading of emotions in 1 Peter is needed.

Even in Paul Holloway's *Coping with Prejudice*, a thematic approach that utilises psychological theory, discussion of emotions is surprisingly scant.[28] Holloway does acknowledge that the fears and anxieties produced by prejudice occasioned 1 Peter, but, where such themes are encountered in the text, Holloway gives little discussion on the emotions themselves.[29] Holloway highlights 'emotion-focused' strategies as a means of coping with prejudice. This includes 'social comparisons', 'attribution of negative outcomes', and 'a restructuring of one's self concept'.[30] But, Holloway does not evaluate the rhetorical function of emotions that leads the audience

[25] W. Nauck, 'Freude im Leiden: Zum Problem einer urchristlichen Verfolgungstradition', *ZNW* 46 (1955): 68–80; J. L. de Villiers, 'Joy in Suffering in 1 Peter', in *Essays on the General Epistles of the New Testament: 11th meeting of Die Nuwe-Testamentiese Werkgemeenskap van Suid-Afrika, 1975*, ed. W. Nicol, Neotestamentica 9 (Pretoria: NTWSA, 1975), 64–86; H. Millauer, *Leiden als Gnade: Eine traditionsgeschichtliche Untersuchung zur Leidenstheologie des ersten Petrusbriefes*, EH 23 (Frankfurt: Peter Lang, 1975).

[26] de Villiers, 'Joy', 70–2, 77–9.

[27] de Villiers, 'Joy', 84.

[28] P. A. Holloway, *Coping with Prejudice: 1 Peter in Social-Psychological Perspective*, WUNT 244 (Tübingen: Mohr Siebeck, 2009).

[29] Holloway, *Coping*, 8.

[30] Holloway, *Coping*, 122–7.

to these outcomes. Consequently, Holloway's work will be a useful discussion partner when exploring the impact on the audience of the emotional content of 1 Peter; but, his work shows that a full analysis of the function of emotions in 1 Peter's rhetorical discourse is still necessary.

As noted above, due to its interest in the role of emotions in 1 Peter's communication, especially with regard to the persuasion of the audience towards certain behaviour, this investigation can be considered a type of rhetorical analysis.[31] Consequently, though their research does not focus primarily on emotions, it is necessary to discuss in this regard the works of Barth L. Campbell, Lauri Thurén, and Troy W. Martin.[32]

Barth L. Campbell's book *Honor, Shame, and the Rhetoric of 1 Peter* (1998) aims to combine the then flourishing classical rhetorical criticism of the New Testament with insights from social-scientific criticism of the New Testament to provide a fresh reading of 1 Peter. In his classical rhetorical criticism, Campbell follows Clifton C. Black II and George A. Kennedy by using five steps to analyse the text. This includes determining (1) the rhetorical unit; (2) the rhetorical situation; (3) the overriding rhetorical problem and investigating; (4) invention, arrangement, style, and evaluating; (5) the rhetorical effectiveness.[33] Thus, he studies 1 Peter 'according to the standards of Greco-Roman rhetoric'.[34] His social-scientific interests centre around the recognition that the Mediterranean world of the first century was one in which an honour/shame culture prevailed. Therefore, he aims to provide an analysis of the argument of the letter that is aware of this important cultural value system. Campbell's exegesis of 1 Peter proceeds along now familiar lines in determining the rhetorical species of the letter (for Campbell it is deliberative[35]); dividing the letter into parts of the argument (e.g. *exordium, argumentatio, peroratio*); and then making efforts to analyse the parts of the argument with reference to the τόποι and stylistic features identified in the text.

---

[31] See pp. 44–6 for more on the concerns of this study in relation to classical and modern rhetorical criticism.

[32] Troy Martin's *Metaphor and Composition in 1 Peter*, SBLDS 131 (Atlanta, GA: Scholars Press, 1992) is a structural literary analysis rather than a rhetorical analysis and therefore will not be discussed here. For a brief description and evaluation of Martin's work see Campbell, *Honor*, 19–22.

[33] See Campbell, *Honor*, 2–10.

[34] Campbell, *Honor*, 3.

[35] 'Since the major sections of the letter reflect exhortation to take future action'; Campbell, *Honor*, 30.

Campbell shows awareness of the rhetorical role of emotions only as part of the invention of the argument as one of the three artificial proofs: ἔθος, πάθος and λόγος.[36] In his analysis, he does not engage with the emotions present in the text in a critical way. Like those mentioned above, Campbell falls into the trap of only speaking about emotions as something to be aroused in the audience at particular points for particular ends. Again, such a treatment is rather unsophisticated. He repeats almost stock phrases whenever he spots a potentially pathetic aspect of the letter, e.g. 'Peter arouses a positive pathos in them', content would 'promote a healthy pathos', 'increases positive audience pathos', 'evokes positive pathos', 'seeks to arouse repugnance', and more.[37] His analysis of honour and shame is more nuanced. However, he does not treat shame as an emotion but as a social status. Thus, the same charges could be levelled at Campbell's work as those discussed above (see pp. 5–6), i.e. such an analysis of emotions remains basic and open to the conjectural cultural assumptions of the author with little attempt to ground one's understanding of emotions in appropriate theory or historical cultural frameworks.

Lauri Thurén's work, which is roughly contemporaneous with Campbell's, also tries to unpack the rhetorical argumentation of 1 Peter. Two of his works should be acknowledged: *The Rhetorical Strategy of 1 Peter* (1990) and *Argument and Theology in 1 Peter* (1995).[38] Since the latter comes closest to the aims of the current investigation but is dependent on the groundwork of the former, it is fitting to explore both works in some detail.

The aim of *Rhetorical Strategy* is to 'provide a new explanation for the disputed problem of the strategy, goal, and special character of 1 Peter'.[39] Here, Thurén is indicating how his work will add to the now classic Balch–Elliott debate over the social strategy of 1 Peter.[40] Using a modified form of George A. Kennedy's approach to rhetorical criticism combined with insights from epistolography,[41]

---

[36] Campbell, *Honor*, 8.

[37] See Campbell, *Honor*, 43, 57, 73, 77, 93, etc.

[38] L. Thurén, *The Rhetorical Strategy of 1 Peter: with Special Regard to Ambiguous Expressions* (Åbo: Åbo Akademis Förlag, 1990); L. Thurén, *Argument and Theology in 1 Peter: The Origins of Christian Paraenesis*, JSNTSup 114 (Sheffield: Sheffield Academic Press, 1995).

[39] Thurén, *Rhetorical Strategy*, 1.

[40] See pp. 260–6 for a detailed outlining of the Balch–Elliott debate, where the implications of the forthcoming work on emotions in 1 Peter for this debate will also be explained.

[41] See Thurén, *Rhetorical Strategy*, 41–78.

Thurén seeks to explain the rhetorical function of the author's deliberate use of ambiguous participles – those that could be read/ heard as either imperative or indicative – found throughout 1 Peter and how these ambiguous participles purposefully aid the author's rhetorical strategy. He concludes that the letter addresses a diverse audience simultaneously: both 'passive' and 'active' respondents.[42] Passive respondents are those who are assimilating too much; active respondents are those who are keeping to their Christian convictions but in doing so are behaving badly. Hence, this is why the letter seems to urge both conformity to surrounding culture (so Balch) and isolation from it (so Elliott).[43] Thurén goes on to argue that the ambiguous nature of the participles is helpful to the author because it allows him to structure an argument that will address the needs of both types of respondents, depending on the disposition of the hearer.[44]

Throughout his study, Thurén is keen to highlight the interactive nature of the letter's communication – the interaction between author and audience that shapes the author's approach to his argumenta- tion – and sees modern rhetorics as providing the tools by which this dynamic can be analysed best.[45] In his analysis of the purpose of the letter, Thurén concludes that the letter 'seeks to strengthen the audience's values by showing what is worth glory and what is shameful'.[46] More specifically, the author needs to strengthen the addressees' 'religious values and their motivation to live according to those values'. In order to do this, Thurén notes that the author has to overcome the paradoxical nature of the addressees' experi- ence and bring them to a place where they no longer *feel* their unjust suffering as shameful but as indicating glory.[47] Thurén is correct to highlight the importance of the audience's values and feelings (read

---

[42] See Thurén, *Rhetorical Strategy*, 112–23 for further details.

[43] Thurén, *Rhetorical Strategy*, 106–11.

[44] Thurén, *Rhetorical Strategy*, 126–63. For comments on Thurén's conclusions see p. 264 n. 29 see also Campbell, *Honor*, 23–5 for criticism of *Rhetorical Strategy* with which I broadly agree. I particularly appreciate Campbell's comments that the quality of ambiguity in communication, on which Thurén's argument rests, was not prized in the ancient world, and therefore is problematic. Dubious also is Thurén's necessary assumption that the letter would have had repeat hearings in a single community.

[45] Thurén, *Rhetorical Strategy*, 52–3; However, according to Thurén, where tech- nical terms from ancient rhetoric remain viable there is no need to replace them (54). Cf. Campbell's comments on rhetorical exigence; Campbell, *Honor*, 5–6.

[46] Hence, he categorises the letter as epideictic in genre; Thurén, *Rhetorical Strategy*, 96–7.

[47] Thurén, *Rhetorical Strategy*, 101.

emotions?)[48] for the argumentation process. His comments, however, remain brief here. At this stage, he does little to explain *how* the values and motivations of the audience are shaped or *why* emotions are connected to this process.

Nevertheless, Thurén's *Rhetorical Strategy* is helpful for this present study because it highlights the role of the audience in the process of communication. Thurén is right to acknowledge that the author would consider the position of the audience when constructing his arguments including the audience's judgements, valuations, cognitive and volitional reactions, attitudes, and convictions.[49] Thurén is clearly aware that these audience characteristics can directly affect behaviour and hence that it is necessary for the author to address them. However, despite talking about the author seeking to evoke certain reactions or the letter's content having an emotional force, Thurén does little to reveal why the author's use of emotion is important for shaping or reinforcing the audience's judgements, evaluations, goals, and subsequent behaviour. Again, in *Rhetorical Strategy*, the emotions appear as something to be aroused in the audience, rather than a communicative aspect of the text itself.

Thurén's *Argument and Theology* builds on *Rhetorical Strategy* with the conclusions reached in the latter continuing to influence his investigation. In *Argument and Theology*, Thurén aims to reveal how the paraenesis of 1 Peter is motivated. By this Thurén understands himself to be conducting a meta-level ideological analysis. Through isolating the various motivating expressions and investigating 'their function in their argumentative context', the discrete motivational material can be assessed in relation to the whole, specifically the larger motifs that appear throughout the letter, so that 'an ideological structure beyond the text' can be reconstructed.[50] Thus, where *Rhetorical Strategy* comments on the importance of the audience's values and judgements in the argumentative process but does little to expound this, *Argument and Theology* goes into detail in order to try to uncover the intricacies of the author's argumentation.

To do this, Thurén utilises S. E. Toumlin's theory of argumentation[51] to analyse the interconnectedness of the arguments and uncover the unsaid premises that allow the argument to be

---

[48] Though 'feel' (used by Thurén) is a rather fuzzy and unspecified term, I take it to convey, though somewhat subtly, a comment about the audience's emotions.

[49] See e.g. Thurén, *Rhetorical Strategy*, 43, 53, 78, 106.

[50] Thurén, *Argument*, 13.

[51] Though he recognises some limitations in Toumlin's model, he still thinks it can be usefully appropriated if its 'narrow limits are fully recognised' (45).

convincing.[52] However, Thurén wants to go beyond Toumlin's model in recognising the distinction between argumentation and persuasion: 'argumentation aims at changing or modifying the audience's thoughts, while the goal of persuasion is action'.[53] Though persuasion requires the use of convincing argument, it is not the same. Persuasion necessitates the audience's volitional assent to the speaker's will. So, '"motivation" refers to the content level of this process'.[54] Thus, Thurén concludes: 'For the persuader it is not enough to modify the receiver's opinions; it is even more important to change their attitudes toward action. Thus the volitional emotional impact is crucial.'[55] He goes on, following Brooks and Warren, to say: '[E]motions promote assent to the speaker's goal, because emotions always seek a justification and a target. After the emotion is aroused, the speaker can provide a content which defines the target for the action desired.'[56] Thus, according to Thurén, it is important 'to ask what kind of emotions the author attempts to provoke in order to elicit assent to the admonition'.[57]

By this Thurén shows that he is aware of the key role that emotions play in persuasion and that they are linked to both values and action. His use of Brooks and Warren even highlights the idea that emotions are directed at a specific target (see p. 27), though Thurén does not seem to obviously take up this concept in his analysis of 1 Peter. In his recognition of the vital role of emotions in persuasion, Thurén makes some useful steps forward, notably starting to link emotions to a person's evaluations, assent, and actions. However, having worked through Thurén's rather complex analysis of 1 Peter's motivating expressions, it does not appear that Thurén makes full use of these foundational insights. Once again, the conversation revolves around emotions being 'evoked' and the *content* of the communication remains somehow external to the emotion itself. What is not recognised here is that emotions themselves communicate meaningfully. Assessing emotions in a text does not have to be simply about asking which emotion we think might be provoked, but we can look at the emotion terms that appear *in the text* and ask what the implications of this are in each specific context.

---

[52] For more on Toumlin's theory see Thurén, *Argument*, 41–8.
[53] Thurén, *Argument*, 51.
[54] Thurén, *Argument*, 51; Thurén uses Austin's speech-act theory to explain this process further (see 51–3).
[55] Thurén, *Argument*, 53.
[56] Thurén, *Argument*, 53.
[57] Thurén, *Argument*, 54.

Having said this, because Thurén is aware of the importance of emotions for persuasion, he does include discussion of different emotions when they occur in the text in a manner that is often more insightful than the general commentaries. For example, he gives a key place to both 'positive' and 'negative' emotions,[58] and recognises that emotions such as fear and joy are not incidental aspects of the letter but form a key part of the letter's ideological structure.[59] At points, he tries to articulate, often in a propositional manner, why a particular emotion might be motivating. He does this by expressing the idea *implicit* in the text that seems to make sense of the argument. For example, regarding 1.6 he details that the claim the text makes is 'You will rejoice' (1.6a), the data that supports this is 'You will obtain salvation' (1.3–5) and therefore the implicit warrant – which shows that the data is appropriate for supporting the claim – is that 'If one receives something valuable, one begins to rejoice'.[60] Some aspects of this interpretation of 1.6 I will agree with (see pp. 116–29). However, the problem is not with Thurén's specific outlining of the argument here, but with his method. What guards against the supposed 'implicit' warrant simply being an argument that makes sense to the scholar himself but might not have been understood that way at the time? Put differently, how can we assess the argumentative function of emotions in a way that is historically and culturally attuned? For some, this may seem like an odd question since emotions appear to be universal. Surely, we understand how they motivate since we experience emotions ourselves? Therefore, simple lines of reasoning can be drawn from the emotion to our understanding of the argument. Yet, it is one of the key tenets of this investigation, following significant work done on emotions by anthropologists, that emotions are *not* universal phenomena. This will be unpacked further in the next chapter, but what it means is that we *do* need to watch what 'implicit' ideas we link with emotions because these concepts, or we might say contextualisations, may be alien to the social environment in which this use of emotion arose. Thus, the following chapter will seek to reveal a method by which such a historically and culturally sensitive reading is possible.

In addition, the following chapter will also make the claim, following cognitive psychologists, that emotions are complex processes whose elements define their function and in a sense put

---

[58] Thurén, *Argument*, 21. Campbell also does this.
[59] See Thurén, *Argument*, 221.
[60] Thurén, *Argument*, 96.

limits on what we can say about them. Emotions play a certain role in the life of the human, and we need to be aware of this before we start to investigate them in a text. Thurén, as noted above, does start to link emotions to motivation but this is not thoroughly and theoretically worked through. For example, he does not explicate how emotions and values interrelate or what this means for a person's worldview, goals, self-understanding or appreciation of the other. Therefore, in his analysis of 1 Peter, aspects of the emotion process that are significant to revealing how a specific emotion is functioning in the text are missed, as too are some of the implications for the audience. To be fair to Thurén, we must acknowledge that he is not focusing solely on the emotions but looking at a number of aspects of the argument and therefore does not have the scope to unpack the author's use of emotions in the way that I am describing. Thurén has aptly expressed the importance of emotion in persuasion but has not given a full-scale analysis of its role in 1 Peter.

Lastly, we can turn to Troy W. Martin's short essay 'The Rehabilitation of a Rhetorical Step-Child' (2007).[61] In his essay, Martin seeks to make a case for how classical rhetorical criticism can be successfully applied to 1 Peter, following lessons learned by those who have used classical rhetorical criticism to analyse Paul's letter. He dismisses the usefulness of trying to identify the species of rhetoric – though he does not deny that elements of the text may relate to such categorisations[62] – and the value of dividing the letter into parts of speech. For Martin, the fruitful application of classical rhetorical criticism lies in the area of invention, with the investigation of argumentative proofs being a key part of this. As such, Martin proceeds to briefly analyse argumentation using ἔθος, πάθος and λόγος in 1 Peter. His section on πάθος is very brief and focuses on two emotions deemed problematic: shame and fear. For Martin, the main thrust of 1 Peter's pathetic persuasion is to move the audience's emotions to their opposites – absence of shame and confidence – in order to ensure that the audience continues to walk on the right path.[63] Martin does use Aristotle to try and decipher occasions in which an emotion may be deemed fitting and how this could relate to the audience's experience. As such, he attempts to contextualise

---

[61] T. W. Martin, 'The Rehabilitation of a Rhetorical Step-Child: First Peter and Classical Rhetorical Criticism', in *Reading First Peter with New Eyes: Methodological Reassessments of the Letter of First Peter*, ed. Robert L. Webb and Betsy Bauman-Martin, LNTS 364 (London and New York: T&T Clark, 2007), 41–71.

[62] Martin, 'Rhetorical Step-Child', 46–9.

[63] See Martin, 'Rhetorical Step-Child', 64–7.

emotions, unlike either Campbell or Thurén. He does also note that moving an audience's emotional state of mind affects its conduct, with the positive emotions being beneficial in this instance. However, it is not evident from this brief excerpt that Martin has grasped the cognitive aspect of emotions or how this might influence our reading of emotions in the text. In any case, his analysis is so short that it could not be said to have exhausted all there is to say about emotions in 1 Peter. In fact, Martin even acknowledges that much is still to be done in analysing pathetic persuasion in Paul let alone in 1 Peter.[64] Therefore, there remains a need for a thorough and theoretically informed investigation of the role of emotions in the rhetoric of 1 Peter.

From the above survey of scholarship, I find Barton's approach to studying emotions in the New Testament to be the most sound. It is both theoretically informed, and historically and culturally situated in a way that is clearly lacking in the above studies of 1 Peter. Therefore, the intention of this study is to follow closely in Barton's footsteps by providing pioneering work on the use of emotions in 1 Peter. As such, this study will offer an investigation of emotion that is analytically informed by modern emotion theory (especially in relation to the cognitive features of emotion); historically and culturally attuned to the ancient world; and investigates the relationship between emotion, worldview, and action. In doing so, it will reveal the benefits of exploring emotions for our understanding of the text, and it will give a template for studying emotions in other New Testament epistles. Therefore, before outlining the methodological approach, to definitional and theoretical issues we must now turn.

---

[64] Martin, 'Rhetorical Step-Child', 61.

2

EMOTION STUDIES
Theoretical Foundations

Before outlining the methodological approach of this study, we must lay some theoretical foundations concerning emotion in order to help direct and frame our enquiry. Our concern here will be with defining what we mean by 'emotion' along with identifying the key elements of an emotion for our investigation. We will also explore why emotions should be thought of as culturally constructed and socially legitimised, tied to worldview, and useful for world construction and maintenance. Before undertaking these tasks, I will explain why I prefer to use the term 'emotion' even when approaching an ancient text. I will then go on, following Catherine Lutz, to reveal some unhelpful Western Anglo-American historical biases towards emotions that need to be discarded at the outset.

'Emotion': An Initial Problem

Mulligan and Scherer note that ordinary language words for emotions or other affective phenomena such as appetite, disgust, hope, and pain are often grouped under various classificatory terms including 'affect, affection, emotion, feeling (the noun), mood, passion, and sentiment'.[1] So, given this range, is the term 'emotion' the most appropriate? It is generally acknowledged that there has been a failure to reach an agreed definition of emotion within or across disciplines. Thus, as Dixon comments, 'some are beginning to wonder whether it is the very category of "emotion" that is the problem'.[2] For Dixon,

---

[1] K. Mulligan and K. R. Scherer, 'Toward a Working Definition of Emotion', *Emotion Review* 4 (2012): 345–57, at 347.

[2] T. Dixon, '"Emotion": The History of a Key Word in Crisis', *Emotion Review* 4 (2012): 338–44, at 338; Dixon's article, on which I am reliant, is a snapshot of his fuller work: T. Dixon, *From Passions to Emotions: The Creation of a Secular Psychological Category* (Cambridge: Cambridge University Press, 2003).

the term emotion 'has been in crisis, from a definitional and conceptual point of view, ever since its adoption as a psychological category
in the 19th century'.[3] The term, adopted from the French *émotion*,
came into English in the seventeenth to eighteenth centuries, but it
was in the mid-nineteenth century that it became an established term
for psychological states.[4] Tracking the historical course of the term
'emotion' will help us to understand the definitional issues and why
today the term has a broad meaning.

Dixon outlines the history of the term 'emotion'.[5] His main thesis
is that the emergence of the term caused other more specific terms to
be replaced in common and scientific language. Dixon's discussion
focuses on 'categories' and 'concepts'. Under categories, he explains
that until the 1830s philosophers, physicians, and theologians
separated 'passions' and 'affections'. Passions were considered
troubling, whereas affections were milder and could be viewed positively. This distinction traces back to debates between Stoicism and
Christianity. Christian thinkers (e.g. Aquinas) needed a system
that allowed negative passions (e.g. lust) to be differentiated from
positive affections (e.g. love) to avoid labelling all such phenomena
negatively.[6] So, should emotion be dispensed with in order to return
to terms such as passion or affection, particularly because we are
exploring an ancient text? I suggest this is not necessary, and could
in fact be unhelpful. The categorisation of experiences such as lust
or love under passion or affection results in moralising psychological
states. Thus, 'passion' and 'affection' will be useful when describing
ancient viewpoints in order to remain faithful to different thinkers'
philosophical and moral positions. However, to use one of these
terms for 1 Peter imposes unnecessarily an ethical standpoint on to
the letter, whereas using 'emotion', a more general term, allows the
psychological states represented in 1 Peter to speak for themselves
in their own context. Furthermore, using 'passion' or 'affection' is
confusing for the modern reader as the everyday uses of 'passion'
and 'affection' (or 'affect') have lost these historic connotations.
Moreover, the term 'affect' in psychology can be used broadly. For

---

[3] Dixon, '"Emotion"', 338.

[4] Dixon, '"Emotion"', 338.

[5] Due to the constraints of this investigation, I will not detail the major historical
trends in philosophy and psychology concerning the affective phenomena that we
term 'emotions' but more recent developments will remain the focus (see pp. 25–36).
Here, it is more important for the present investigation to understand the assumptions
that are often carried with the term 'emotion' and how these assumptions, unless
recognised, can stunt our appreciation of emotions in an ancient text.

[6] Dixon, '"Emotion"', 339.

example, psychologists speak of 'affective states', which include emotions but also moods[7] and dispositions.[8] Thus, for labelling purposes, 'emotion' is to be preferred.

However, the problem of the conceptual meaning of 'emotion' remains. With the adoption of emotion from the French *émotion* came the associated idea of 'physical disturbance and bodily movement'.[9] In French, *émotion* was a descriptive idea encompassing even crowd commotion. Thus, as Dixon explains, '[i]ncreasingly, during the 18th century, "emotion" came to refer to the bodily stirrings accompanying mental feelings'.[10] Consequently, over time, an emphasis on the visible effects and bodily manifestations accompanying mental states emerged. It was Thomas Brown, a nineteenth-century Scottish philosopher, who solidified emotion as a category of mental science. Brown defined emotions 'as noncognitive "vivid feelings" rather than as forms of thought'.[11] Consequently, emotional feelings were separated from cognitive thoughts. Many psychologists after him upheld this distinction.[12] Another nineteenth-century physician and

---

[7] Emotions can be distinguished from moods by the fact that emotions, as we will discover, have a specific object, moods do not. Moods are 'diffuse' and 'global' and 'refer to more global states' like being cheerful. They are nonintentional because it is difficult to determine a precise object of a mood. See N. H. Frijda, 'Varieties of Affect: Emotions and Episodes, Moods, and Sentiments', in *The Nature of Emotion: Fundamental Questions*, ed. Paul Ekman and Richard J. Davidson (New York and Oxford: Oxford University Press, 1994), 59–67, at 59–61. Some have also distinguished moods and emotions through differences in timespan, with emotions being more acute than moods. However, these two affective categories may interact. For example, someone in an angry mood, with the occurrence of an appropriate object, is more likely to experience a particular emotion. Conversely, an emotion or repeated emotions could cause someone to move into a particular mood; Frijda, 'Varieties of Affect', 63. See also R. Lazarus, 'The Stable and Unstable in Emotion', in *The Nature of Emotion: Fundamental Questions*, ed. Paul Ekman and Richard J. Davidson (New York and Oxford: Oxford University Press, 1994), 79–85, and other essays in §2 – 'How are Emotions Distinguished from Moods, Temperament, and Other Related Affective Constructs' – of Ekman and Davidson, eds, *The Nature of Emotion*.

[8] It is worth noting briefly what I mean by disposition because, as we will discover with 1 Peter, moving an audience towards a sustained emotional orientation turns emotions, now concretised in a text with a permanent outlook, into something more similar to a disposition. A disposition, which we might also term a trait, is enduring. It is a 'tendency to react in a particular emotional way to an adaptational encounter. To speak of trait implies frequent recurrence of the state in diverse but specifiable circumstances'; Lazarus, 'Stable and Unstable', 79. There is debate about whether such traits are learned or innate.

[9] Dixon, '"Emotion"', 340.

[10] Dixon, '"Emotion"', 340.

[11] Dixon, '"Emotion"', 340.

[12] In response to Dixon's work, Wassmann wants to correct Dixon's historical oversight by highlighting that both the 'continental tradition of thought since Kant' and

philosopher, Charles Bell, was also influential. Through Bell, bodily movements became a significant part of emotions, not just as out-wards expressions of mental states but as causes themselves. William James' and Charles Darwin's influential theories of emotion were subsequently influenced by Brown's and Bell's ideas.[13] Additionally, Wassmann sees in James' theory the influence of German psych-ology, which used *Gefühl* for emotion that had an intellectual content and *Empfindung* for feelings relating to sensation. However, despite adopting the German idea of *Gefühl* from Wunt, James made the semantic move of dissolving the distinction between *Gefühl* and *Empfindung*.[14] In fact, he 'asserted that the feeling of the bodily changes is the emotion' and thus, 'equated the meaning of the words feeling and emotion'.[15] This led, particularly in the mental sciences, to a privileging of the physical aspect of emotion and the down-grading of philosophical psychology.[16] Dixon comments:

> The founders of the discipline of psychology in the late 19th century bequeathed to their successors a usage of 'emotion' in which the relationship between mind and body and between thought and feeling were confused and unresolved, and which named a category of feelings and behaviours so broad as to cover almost all of human mental life including, as Bain (1859) had put it, all that was previously understood by the terms 'feelings, states of feeling, pleasures, pains, passions, sentiments, affections'.[17]

It is important to understand this nineteenth-century movement of separating emotional feeling from thought because it will enable us to identify some of our modern Western assumptions that are unconsciously carried into New Testament study. However, despite this conceptual confusion, continuing to use the term 'emotion' is best precisely because it has room for a range of ideas from bodily feelings to the more cognitive. To choose another term means that

---

the work of German experimental physiological psychology did retain brain activity or cognition as fundamental to emotion. She however notes that in Anglo-American psychology from the twentieth century this has been forgotten; C. Wassmann, 'On Emotion and the Emotions: A Comment to Dixon, Mulligan and Scherer, and Scarantino', *Emotion Review* 4 (2012): 385–6, at 385.

[13] Dixon, '"Emotion"', 341; Darwin is known for asserting the universality of emotions.

[14] Wassmann, 'On Emotion', 385.

[15] Mulligan and Scherer, 'Working Definition', 353.

[16] Dixon, '"Emotion"', 342.

[17] Dixon, '"Emotion"', 342–3.

one's discussion is pushed towards certain aspects of emotional experience; for example, 'feeling' tends towards the physical and 'sentiment' to the cognitive. This becomes problematic when talking about ancient rhetorical or philosophical views in which attendant physical feelings, bodily expression, and cognition are all part of a πάθος (often translated emotion). To prefer 'emotion' means that aspects of affective experience are not unduly cut off. However, it does mean we must be clear what 'emotion' means. Thus, two tasks must be tackled: first, to reveal certain unhelpful assumptions about emotions, and, second, to outline this investigation's theoretical position on emotions.

Understanding Western Anglo-American Historical Biases

First, we must identify some potential biases that have undoubtedly influenced our approach to emotions in biblical texts and contributed to the large-scale neglect of taking seriously the role of emotions in biblical discourse. In *Unnatural Emotions* Catherine Lutz has identified a number of unspoken, embedded assumptions that Western Anglo-American approaches to emotions have, often unconsciously, held.[18] Lutz warns about allowing these 'Western value orientations towards emotions' to be normative for our appreciation of emotions in other cultural contexts.[19] Though Lutz is talking about first-hand fieldwork with the Ifaluk people, her admonitions should be heard by those approaching the cross-cultural task of exploring the thought-world and communication of an ancient author. She summarises the Western Euramerican[20] standpoint as 'identifying emotions primarily with irrationality, subjectivity, the chaotic and other negative characteristics'.[21]

This understanding is exhibited in both quotidian and academic uses of the word emotion. Lutz discusses each of these characteristics in detail. However, to summarise her comments, emotions are viewed negatively in comparison 'to the positively evaluated process of

---

[18] See C. A. Lutz, *Unnatural Emotions: Everyday Sentiments on a Micronesian Atoll & Their Challenge to Western Theory* (Chicago: University of Chicago Press, 1988), 53–80.

[19] Lutz, *Unnatural*, 54.

[20] 'Euramerican' is, for Lutz, the viewpoint of an American 'of basically Protestant European, middle-class background', which is evident in 'social-science theorizing, everyday discourse, and clinical-psychological practice'; Lutz, *Unnatural*, 55.

[21] Lutz, *Unnatural*, 54–5.

thought'.[22] This is evident in the psychological opposition of 'affect' and 'cognition' and the philosophical distinction between 'passion' and 'reason'.[23] For Lutz, '[e]ncoded in or related to that contrast is an immense portion of the Western worldview of the person, of social life, and of morality'.[24] This separation of emotions and thoughts along with their embedding in the conceptualisation of the person leads to further dichotomies. Emotion indicates irrationality, impulse, vulnerability, chaos, and is subjective, physical, natural, morally suspect, feminine, and childish, whereas thoughts display rationality, intention, control, order, and are objective, cultural, ethically mature, masculine, and adult.[25] Thus, emotion is seen as inferior and negative in comparison to thought.[26]

Viewing emotions as irrational means that they are considered to hamper 'sensible, or intelligent, action'.[27] Thus, '[p]eople tend to see emotions as a disruption of, or barrier to, the rational understanding of events. To label someone "emotional" is often to question the validity, and more, the very sense of what they are saying'.[28] This leads to emotions being viewed as chaotic, and, subsequently, dangerous and weakening to the self.[29] Consequently, when emotion is devalued and rationality is ideologically esteemed, any occasion or person in which emotion is evident can be easily disregarded because it 'is the "weak" who are emotional'.[30] Moreover, the physicality of emotions is deemed more animalistic and therefore less valued than the advanced mental processing of humans. From the view of emotions as physical comes the idea that they are natural: they are not part of cultural processes but are 'aboriginally untouched by the cooking, taming, and civilizing of culture'. Subsequently, this produces the

[22] Contrastingly, emotion is viewed more positively than estrangement. However, it is the negative contrast with thought that is most dominant; Lutz, *Unnatural*, 56–8.

[23] For more on the historical philosophical stance of emotions as contrary to reason see R. C. Solomon, *The Passions: Emotions and the Meaning of Life* (Indianapolis, IN: Hackett, 1993), 9–12.

[24] Lutz, *Unnatural*, 55–6.

[25] For more on emotions as female see Lutz, *Unnatural*, 73–6.

[26] Lutz, *Unnatural*, 57. Solomon highlights how English language idioms reveal that emotions are generally understood to happen to us, for example, 'we "fall in" love' are '"paralysed" by fear' and '"struck" with jealousy', showing an assumption that emotions are separate to rational, volitional thoughts; Solomon, *Passions*, xv–i, 67–8.

[27] Lutz, *Unnatural*, 70–1.

[28] Lutz, *Unnatural*, 60.

[29] Cf. Wierzbicka who also identifies this assumption, noting that for Anglo-Americans 'composure' is seen as the normal state and emotion is a negative deviation from this norm; A. Wierzbicka, *Emotions Across Languages and Cultures: Diversity and Universals* (Cambridge: Cambridge University Press, 1999), 17–18.

[30] Lutz, *Unnatural*, 62–5.

assumption that emotions are consistent across cultures, i.e. are universal.[31]

Given these 'embedded' assumptions, it is not surprising that the role of emotions in New Testament discourse has been overlooked or devalued in modern scholarship. The privileging of rationality has led to a focus on the λόγος of the argument, with the emotional dimension seen as either superfluous to the discovery of truth, or at worst detrimental to it. Emotions may be discussed in rhetorical approaches, but they are still distinguished from the reasoning of the text and therefore appear as thin manipulative constructs. Understanding emotions to be universal has reduced the need to investigate emotions thoroughly as it assumes that the reader will automatically know what an emotion term means from her own experience. The emotions in the text can then be assessed on these terms. Lastly, overemphasising the physicality of emotion means that emotions become of little interest to those studying ancient texts. For, how can you get any reliable data about the visceral responses of the writer or audience from a textual artefact? However, many anthropologists, sociologists, psychologists, and philosophers have moved beyond these stunting views of emotion. By looking at their corrective insights we can understand that there is a great deal that investigating emotions in New Testament texts can reveal. Thus, we must proceed to outlining 'emotions' as they will be understood by this investigation.

A Working Definition of 'Emotion'

We noted above that there is no one standard definition of emotion.[32] However, it is generally agreed among psychologists that emotions contain a number of elements. The definitional problems centre around which component parts should be included and what weighting each should be given. Therefore, I will present a 'working' definition of emotion. The aim is to clarify the standpoint of this investigation rather than to delineate debates surrounding each element.

What Is an Emotion?

In this book, 'emotion' refers to a 'class of affective processes' and 'emotions' indicates that there are 'specific types or instantiations

---

[31] Lutz, *Unnatural*, 65–70.
[32] For a number of articles discussing the definition of emotion see *Emotion Review* 4 (2012) and *Social Science Information* 46 (2012): 381–443.

of that class'.[33] Thus, 'an emotion' is one type of that class. More specifically, 'emotion' does not mean simply a feeling,[34] though this is certainly part of emotion, but a mental and physiological change that someone experiences that encompasses the whole *process* of an emotion.[35] Thus emotion includes, as Moors delineates:

> (a) a cognitive component; (b) a feeling component, referring to emotional experience; (c) a motivational component, consisting of action tendencies or states of action readiness (e.g., tendencies to flee or fight); (d) a somatic component, consisting of central and peripheral physiological responses; (e) a motor component, consisting of expressive behaviour (e.g., fight and flight and facial and vocal expressions). These components correspond to functions such as: (a) stimulus evaluation or appraisal; (b) monitoring (which may serve the further function of control or regulation); (c) preparation and support of action; and (d) action.[36]

Having said this, when working with an ancient text, certain components are inaccessible. For example, we cannot ask the audience what they were physically feeling, nor observe the audience's physical expressions. Moreover, we cannot say how 1 Peter in actuality impacted its audience, only what the text idealises about its emotions. Furthermore, our starting point is not the audience itself but an emotion term that has been solidified into a literary context. Consequently, our discussion of emotion will be constrained to stimulus (object); appraisal (evaluation); and action-tendency. We will now outline each of these in more detail.

---

[33] Mulligan and Scherer, 'Working Definition', 345.

[34] I follow Mulligan and Scherer in seeing feeling as a component of emotion, but not a synonym for emotion. See Mulligan and Scherer, 'Working Definition', 345, 353–5.

[35] As Scherer comments, '[a]lthough the different subsystems or components [of emotion] operate relatively independently of each other during nonemotional states, they are recruited to work in unison during emotion episodes. I believe that emotion is an integrated process or whole'; Mulligan and Scherer, 'Working Definition', 356.

[36] This is not to say that all theorists agree on the number of components to include, or the precise nature of the components, nor the sequence of the components; A. Moors, 'Theories of Emotion Causation: A Review', *Cognition and Emotion* 23 (2009): 625–62, at 626. Cf. Mulligan and Scherer, 'Working Definition', 346, 352. Lazarus likewise determines an emotion by whether it exhibits: 'a clear, personally significant, relational content, an appraisal of personal harm, threat, challenge, or benefit, the potential for action readiness, and physiological changes'; R. S. Lazarus, 'Progress on a Cognitive-Motivational-Relational Theory of Emotion', *American Psychologist* 46 (1991): 819–34, at 822.

Elements of an Emotion

Relational and Object-Directed

Emotions are about something; put differently, they are object-directed.[37] As Solomon states: 'One is never simply angry; he/she is angry *at* someone *for* something ... One is not simply afraid, but afraid of something, even if the object of fear is something unknown.'[38] Fundamentally, emotions are elicited by and are responses to a stimulus. However, philosophers such as Nussbaum expand this to say that an emotion's identity depends on it having an object. If the object is removed, an emotion becomes senseless physiological movements.[39] Solomon further elucidates that an emotion's object is a subjective object, that is, the object as we experience it.[40] Put differently, the object is imbued with the qualities one perceives it to have, which may or may not have basis in objective fact. Consequently, emotions have an 'intentional' object. The object is intentional because 'it figures in the emotion as it is seen or interpreted by the person whose emotion it is'. Thus, emotions embody 'a way of seeing'.[41] Furthermore, that a certain object instigates an emotion indicates that, to the person, the object is of importance. In emotion, the object is 'experienced through our concerns and values'.[42] This suggests, as Lazarus asserts, that emotions are relational: 'they are about person–environment relationships'.[43] More specifically, emotions make the person aware of the object in their environment in relation to 'harms (for the negative emotions) and benefits (for the positive emotions)'.[44] Therefore, emotions are not just object-directed, but they also *say something* about that object. This has led emotion theorists to suggest that emotions have a cognitive component.

Cognitive Appraisal

From the late 1960s, psychologists such as Richard Lazarus have argued that emotions contain a cognitive component.[45] In a recent

---

[37] M. C. Nussbaum, *Upheavals of Thought: The Intelligence of Emotions* (Cambridge: Cambridge University Press, 2001), 27.
[38] Solomon, *Passions*, 111–12.
[39] Nussbaum, *Upheavals*, 27.
[40] Solomon, *Passions*, 115–16.
[41] Nussbaum, *Upheavals*, 27.
[42] Solomon, *Passions*, 116.
[43] Lazarus, 'Progress', 819.
[44] Lazarus, 'Progress', 819.
[45] R. S. Lazarus et al., 'Towards a Cognitive Theory of Emotion', in *Feelings and Emotions: The Loyola Symposium*, ed. Magda Arnold (New York: Academic Press, 1970), 207–32.

review by Agnes Moors, it is notable that in majority opinion, emotion is thought to contain cognition. What is debated is the definition of cognition (automatic or conscious) and at what stage in the emotion episode the cognitive aspect occurs.[46] This study sides with appraisal theorists (e.g. Arnold, Lazarus) and 'philosophical cognitivists' (e.g. Nussbaum, Solomon) who see cognition as an indispensable component of emotion.[47] For Lazarus, cognition occurs at the outset of an emotion when the object itself is appraised or evaluated.[48] Appraisal can be described as: '[A] process that detects and assesses the significance of the environment for well-being. Significance for well-being is best conceptualized as the satisfaction or obstruction of concerns ... "Concerns" include the individual's needs, attachments, values, current goals, and beliefs ... they include everything that an individual cares about.'[49] We can simplify this to say that the object is evaluated in terms of whether it is (potentially or presently) harmful or beneficial to the person in terms of their personal goals. In addition, for appraisal theorists, emotions can include evaluations about certainty, agency (cause), and control (coping potential, power).[50] Similarly, for philosophical cognitivists, emotion is a form of judgement about an object, assessing its salience for well-being.[51] Thus, the judgement is an evaluative judgement.[52] For Nussbaum, the judgement is propositional, that is, it contains a belief about

[46] See Moors, 'Theories', 625–56.

[47] Appraisal theory emerged in the 1960s. It is 'in essence a systemization of ancient ideas about emotion', for example, those of Aristotle. Nussbaum's work can also be viewed as a reworking of Stoic views of emotion, thus is often termed 'neo-Stoic'. Appraisal theories are also componential theories of emotion 'in that they view an emotion episode as involving changes in a number of organismic subsystems or components'; A. Moors et al., 'Appraisal Theories of Emotion: State of the Art and Future Development', *Emotion Review* 5 (2013): 119–24, at 119; cf. Solomon, *Passions*, 15. See Moors, 'Theories', 638–43, 650–2 for an outline of appraisal and philosophical cognitivist theories.

[48] However, for Lazarus, though appraisals are necessary for emotion, it is not necessary that appraisals are conscious events; they can occur unconsciously (automatically); see R. S. Lazarus, 'Cognition and Motivation in Emotion', *American Psychologist* 46 (1991): 352–67, at 361–4.

[49] Moors et al., 'Appraisal', 120.

[50] Though opinions differ, there is general agreement that appraisal includes goal relevance, goal congruence, certainty, coping potential, and agency; Moors et al., 'Appraisal', 120–1.

[51] See Nussbaum, *Upheavals*, 19 for her definition of emotion, which aligns with appraisal theorists. However, for Nussbaum, 'well-being' is equated with the idea of *eudaimonia* (human flourishing); cf. Solomon, *Passions*, xvii, 15. Solomon goes further to say that emotions are 'constitutive' judgements: they actively 'shape and structure' reality. See pp. 36–9.

[52] Solomon, *Passions*, 127.

the object.[53] If the belief about the object changes, then so will the emotion. Therefore, we can see that both appraisal theorists and philosophical cognitivists see emotions as cognitive in the sense that they receive and process information. However, emotions do not necessarily have to include more complex cognition such as 'elaborate calculation', 'computation, or even reflexive self-awareness'.[54]

Though a number of emotion theories recognise that emotions include appraisal, appraisal theorists give the evaluative component a defining role. The appraisal causes emotion and influences the 'intensity and quality' of the other components of an emotion episode.[55] Thus, different appraisals (or judgements) lead to different, distinct emotions.[56] Hence, the same object could be the cause of different emotions; it depends on how the object is being viewed. Moreover, the same appraisal will always produce the same emotion. So, the relationship between appraisal and emotion is stable, but the connection between stimuli and emotion is variable because it depends on the individual's evaluation of the object that is affected by their own concerns.[57] Furthermore, the appraisal concerns a specific object and occurs in a given context. Therefore, emotions reveal how the situation is being *interpreted*. For example, one may be startled by a gunshot. If the gunshot is interpreted as dangerous it will elicit fear. If it is seen as unjustifiable and offensive it may produce anger.[58] Consequently, this suggests that emotions have a coherent rationale in a given narrative context. Put differently, emotions have an inner logic, even if one is not aware of it or only appreciates it upon reflection.[59] If we can understand the qualities of an emotion and the person's goals we can comprehend a given emotion occurrence.

[53] This does not necessarily mean that the belief has to be true, or even consistent with other beliefs; see Nussbaum, *Upheavals*, 28, 35–6, 46–7. For Nussbaum, the judgement equates with the emotion in that it is sufficient for the emotion (see Nussbaum, *Upheavals*, 37–45, 56–64). However, I do not want to take such a reductionist approach. Though I see cognition as central, I recognise that a number of other aspects of emotion interrelate dynamically to produce the full emotion experience.

[54] Nussbaum, *Upheavals*, 23.

[55] Moors et al., 'Appraisal', 120; cf. Nussbaum, *Upheavals*, 55.

[56] Cf. Nussbaum, *Upheavals*, 28–9.

[57] Moors et al., 'Appraisal', 121. Frijda agrees that the appraisal differentiates one emotion from another. See N. H. Frijda et al., 'Relations Among Emotion, Appraisal, and Emotional Action Readiness', *Journal of Personality and Social Psychology* 57 (1989): 212–28, at 212.

[58] Lazarus, 'Progress', 821.

[59] For more on the logic of emotions, and why their 'logic' allows emotions to be analytically investigated see Solomon, *Passions*, 193–6.

That emotions contain appraisals about an object's potential to harm or benefit a person's goals indicates that emotions operate in a larger framework of norms and values.[60] First, by highlighting a particular object, emotions invest that object with value and importance. This value is specific to the object's connection with the person's flourishing.[61] Second, the appraisal of harm or benefit is dependent on a person's goals, which, in turn, are based on one's values and expectations. For, one cannot determine what is harmful or beneficial without some concept of what is important or unimportant. Therefore, an emotion's evaluation of an object is 'predicated on complex social structures and meanings'.[62] Nussbaum distinguishes between background and situational judgements. The former are 'judgements that persist through situations of numerous kinds'; the latter are 'judgements that arise in the context of some particular situation'.[63] In her explanation, her 'background judgements' sound like either dispositional states or a worldview that has a system of values and core beliefs.[64] In fact, Nussbaum even describes the background judgements as 'background judgements of value', and that they are 'closely associated with a whole network of beliefs and expectations'.[65] The 'situational judgement' tells one how 'the world is' in relation to 'what one values, thus combining one's ongoing goals and attachments with perceived reality'.[66] Though I would prefer worldview to 'background judgement', I think Nussbaum's distinction is helpful for revealing that an emotion occurrence does not stand as an isolated event, but draws on an already established system of values that a person carries into each new context. Subsequently, it also shows that the cognitive aspect of emotion requires an understanding of the environment, both 'how things work' generally and specific information about the 'demands, constraints, and resources'

[60] As Solomon argues, this is far from the common assumption that emotions 'distract us from goals' and hamper ambitions; Solomon, *Passions*, xvii.

[61] On account of this, Nussbaum describes emotions as 'localised', i.e. concerned with the person's relation to those objects, not the value of the objects generally. This is not the same as saying that emotions are egotistical, but both Nussbaum and Solomon highlight the subjective nature of emotion's judgement. They assert that it is 'my world' that the emotion gives information about. This is not necessarily objective fact but what is important to the person; Nussbaum, *Upheavals*, 30–1, 52–3. Solomon, *Passions*, 19–20.

[62] Lazarus, 'Progress', 821.

[63] Nussbaum, *Upheavals*, 69.

[64] See Nussbaum, *Upheavals*, 67–79 for her full argument.

[65] Nussbaum, *Upheavals*, 75–6.

[66] Nussbaum, *Upheavals*, 76.

of the space in which the encounter with the object happens.[67] Such understanding of the world will vary from person to person and from one culture to another. Reflexively, when we appreciate a person's values and goals we can understand why a particular emotion is fitting in a given context. If we cannot understand the person's larger motivation then an emotion occurrence can remain perplexing.

Action-Tendency

Lastly, emotion's evaluative judgement leads to a disposition (tendency) to act in a certain way. In simplistic terms, because the emotion evaluates the object as harmful or beneficial it also carries the idea that one should move towards or away from an object. Thus, emotions not only interpret the environment, they suggest how one should respond to it; they make one ready for action. Some, such as Nico Frijda, make action readiness a central aspect of emotions, with different action-tendencies defining each emotion.[68] However, Frijda does not divorce action readiness from appraisal, commenting that action readiness is 'elicited by events appraised as emotionally relevant; different states of action readiness are elicited by different appraisals'.[69] Though Lazarus would not define the emotion by the action-tendency, he would agree that each emotion 'involves its own innate action tendency'.[70] Thus, action readiness (or tendency) is considered a component of emotion that is linked to appraisal and as such is influenced by one's values and goals. The direction of motivation depends on a person's 'goal hierarchies' that she brings to the situation.[71] Though I do not want to reduce emotions to being primarily action readiness, the following investigation will take seriously the idea that emotions are drivers for action. Moreover, if emotions impact actions, we must recognise, like the ancient philosophers do, that emotions are important for shaping ethical behaviour. Thus, to have appropriate or inappropriate emotions in a certain context becomes a moral issue. In the moralising of emotions and the awareness that emotions are dependent on worldview we encounter the cultural nature of emotions.

---

[67] Lazarus, 'Progress', 820.
[68] Frijda et al., 'Relations', 213.
[69] Frijda et al., 'Relations', 213.
[70] Lazarus, 'Progress', 822.
[71] Lazarus, 'Progress', 820.

Emotions as Cultural Constructs

For some, even if all emotions are not universal, some 'basic' emotions such as fear must be. However, if we are right that emotions involve an evaluative judgement about an object, which is influenced by one's goals and values, which, in turn, depend on one's worldview, then there is scope for emotions to be shaped differently across individuals and cultures.

A number of anthropologists, linguists, and sociologists have successfully challenged universalistic assumptions about emotions. For example, Catherine Lutz, from her anthropological work with the Ifaluk people, concluded that emotions cannot be universal, but that 'emotion experience ... is more aptly viewed as the outcome of social relations and their corollary worldviews than as universal psycho-biological entities'.[72] To quote Lutz at length:

> The claim is made [in her work] that emotional experience is not precultural but pre*eminently* cultural ... As I listened to people speak the language of emotion in everyday encounters with each other on Ifaluk atoll, it became clear to me that the concepts of emotion can more profitably be viewed as serving complex communicative, moral, and cultural purposes rather than simply as labels for internal states whose nature or essence is presumed to be universal. The pragmatic and associative networks of meaning in which each emotion word is embedded are extremely rich ones. The complex meaning of each emotion word is the result of the important role those words play in articulating the full range of a people's cultural values, social relations, and economic circumstances. Talk about emotions is simultaneously talk about society – about power and politics, about kinship and marriage, about normality and deviance.[73]

Wierzbicka argues along similar lines:

> Although human emotional endowment is no doubt largely innate and universal, people's emotional lives are shaped, to a considerable extent, by their culture. Every culture offers not only a linguistically embodied grid for the conceptualization of emotions, but also a set of 'scripts' suggesting

---

[72] Lutz, *Unnatural*, 209; Lutz acknowledges that she is building on the work of Jean Briggs, Robert Levy, and Michelle Z. Rosaldo.
[73] Lutz, *Unnatural*, 5–6.

to people how to feel, how to express their feelings, how to think about their own and other people's feelings, and so on.[74]

Thus, both Lutz and Wierzbicka's studies assert with convincing evidence that emotional understanding and emotional repertoires are culturally constructed.[75]

This call to recognise the variances in emotional repertoires and emotion rules across cultures is easy to reconcile with an appraisal view of emotion. As Nussbaum states: 'If we hold that beliefs about what is important and valuable play a central role in emotions, we can easily see how those beliefs can be powerfully shaped by social norms as well as by an individual history; and we can also see how changing social norms can change emotional life.'[76] As biblical scholars, we must take these insights seriously. The New Testament texts are clearly embedded in historical, cultural, and social settings. Thus, we must expect that their use of emotion terms also is. We cannot presume our understanding of emotions is universal and consequently impose our cultural understanding of emotions on to the text, nor evaluate the validity of the emotions in the text through our cultural framework. We must attempt to understand the conceptualisation of an emotion term in its own setting, including the wider cultural framework of norms and values in which it makes sense.

We also need to understand in our interpretation of emotions, that emotions themselves are interpretative. Lutz argues that emotions are not caused by situations, but the situation is interpreted by the emotion. In this interpretive function, it is evident that emotions contain 'cultural premises'. Moreover, emotions are based on culturally established prototypical scenarios. The 'discrete emotion concepts ... have nested within them a cluster of images and propositions'. These emotional scenarios allow people of the same culture to make sense of the occurrence of an emotion in a given context, and, subsequently, the interpretation of events communicated by the emotion.[77] Therefore, an emotion's communication is only comprehensible when

---

[74] Wierzbicka, *Emotions*, 240. Cf. Nussbaum, who agrees that emotional ability is innate, but its range of expression varies across cultures so that different cultures have different 'emotional repertoires'; Nussbaum, *Upheavals*, 141. For more on the sources and areas of variation see Nussbaum, *Upheavals*, 151–65.

[75] For support for emotions as 'socio-cultural phenomena' see B. Mesquita, 'Emotions are Culturally Situated', *Social Science Information* 46 (2007): 410–15.

[76] Nussbaum, *Upheavals*, 142.

[77] In viewing emotions as communicative I am following Lutz; Lutz, *Unnatural*, 7; For more discussion on how social paradigms of emotions influence a person's

an emotion is legitimately attributed to one of the culturally under-stood scenarios. These 'scenes' are generally social. Thus, emotions also highlight the value given to certain relationships and, depending on the emotion, interpret the social relationship in a particular way.[78] Therefore, reflexively, if we grasp how an emotion is being used in a particular context we gain insight into the culture of that group, particularly its values and expectations.

On a secondary level, a person's emotional life is continu-ally shaped by social interaction. For, an emotion's 'existence and meaning are also negotiated, ignored, or validated by people in social relationships'.[79] The social moulding of emotions gives people a

> sense of how they ought to or must behave and in that way help[s] to structure people's social behavior. The force of emotion … is to a great extent the sense of moral or prag-matic compulsion, the sense that one must do what the emotion 'says' one will do … Conversely, particular moral ideas take what force they have from the commitment people learn to feel to them.[80]

Hence, people are taught socially that certain emotions are appro-priate in given situations and that the moral person will feel the right thing at the right time leading to doing the right thing on the right occasion.[81] Ole Riis and Linda Woodhead have, following William Reddy, labelled these emotion rules an 'emotional regime'.[82] They explain:

> Like with the wider social ordering with which it is bound up, an emotion regime has an internal coherence and bounded-ness … Regimes persist over time, and transcend individuals, shaping what they can feel, how they can feel it, the way they can express their feelings, and hence the forms of social rela-tionship and courses of actions that are open to them.[83]

interpretation of both her own and other's emotions see J. R. Averill, 'The Social Construction of Emotion: With Special Reference to Love', in *The Social Construction of the Person*, ed. Kenneth J. Gergen and Keith E. Davis, SSSP (New York: Springer-Verlag, 1985), 89–109.

[78] Lutz, *Unnatural*, 210–11.
[79] Lutz, *Unnatural*, 212.
[80] Lutz, *Unnatural*, 213.
[81] Cf. Wierzbicka, *Emotions*, 34; Nussbaum, *Upheavals*, 161.
[82] Though Riis and Woodhead use 'emotional regime' in a much broader sense than Reddy; see O. Riis and L. Woodhead, *A Sociology of Religious Emotion* (Oxford: Oxford University Press, 2010), 47–51.
[83] Riis and Woodhead, *Sociology*, 10.

Thus, we might expect that in 1 Peter, which exhorts people towards particular behaviour and is concerned about social relationships, both using and shaping emotions will be of importance. This can occur through which emotions are encouraged or discouraged and the context in which emotion terms are used. If we are to understand why and how the author is using emotion, we need to be aware of emotion's cultural boundedness and sociological function.

'Translating' the Emotion

The above discussion has implications for our understanding of the task of translation. We must move beyond translating one word to another and expecting that in this process we have comprehended the emotion. As Wierzbicka highlights, all cultures classify their emotions but not in the same way, and, therefore, labels cannot simply be imported across cultures.[84] When this is done, it usually results in a procrustean forcing of emotions from another culture into the English-language conceptualisation carried by the English term.[85] Lutz proposes that if emotion 'is seen as woven in complex ways into cultural meaning systems and social interaction, and if emotion is used to talk about what is culturally defined and experienced as "intensely meaningful," then the problem becomes one of translating between two different cultural views and enactments of that which is real and good and proper'.[86] Thus, it is not enough to translate one emotion term into another; we need to understand the worldview in which the emotion makes sense in order to *translate* the emotion in this broader conceptual sense. This means taking account of the 'scenarios' that are invoked for the hearer by the use of an emotion term. As Lutz explains: 'To understand the meaning of an emotion word is to be able to envisage … a complicated scene with actors, actions, interpersonal relationships in a particular state of repair, moral points of view, facial expressions, personal and social goals, and sequences of events.'[87] Wierzbicka adds: '"Emotion words" such as anger reflect, and pass on, certain cultural models; and these models, in turn, reflect and pass on values, preoccupations, and frames of reference of the society (or speech community) within which they have evolved.'[88] Consequently, the labelling of an emotion is part of a larger process of the

---

[84] Wierzbicka, *Emotions*, 24; cf. Nussbaum, *Upheavals*, 149.
[85] See Wierzbicka, *Emotions*, 26–7.
[86] Lutz, *Unnatural*, 8.
[87] Lutz, *Unnatural*, 10; cf. Wierzbicka, *Emotions*, 15.
[88] Wierzbicka, *Emotions*, 32.

social construction and use of emotions.[89] Even if we may concede to
those who argue for the universality of 'basic' emotions that similar
emotional experiences such as responses to loss are observable
across various cultures, when we come to dealing with emotions in
an ancient text these emotional experiences are already linguistically
encoded in various scenarios and, hence, we cannot get away from
their cultural locatedness. Therefore, this study will seek to be sensitive to the larger task of translation by identifying the meaning and
place of an emotion term in its historical context. This will foster a
deeper sense of what the author is communicating via the emotion.
This investigation will move beyond exchanging a Greek word for an
English term towards identifying the values, prototypical scenarios,
and concerns brought to the context by the emotion term.

We must now complete our discussion of emotion's socio-cultural
setting and function by examining emotion's relationship to world
construction and maintenance.

Emotions and World Construction and Maintenance

Berger and Luckmann have revealed how one's knowledge of reality
is socially constructed.[90] Though reality appears to the individual as
objectively ordered and is usually 'taken for granted', it has, in fact,
occurred through the group's institutionalisation of knowledge.[91]
Similarly, as part of this reality, the identity of the self is formed in
relationship with significant others and thus is a social product.[92] At
the maximum level this becomes a whole symbolic universe in which
all other realities are encompassed.[93] The symbolic universe enables
one to name, order, and make sense of objects and occurrences in one's
world. This reality has to be continually maintained from one generation to the next. Furthermore, every event that a person encounters
must be comprehensible to her within her given perspective of

---

[89] Nussbaum, *Upheavals*, 150–1, 163–4.
[90] 'Reality' is defined as a 'quality appertaining to phenomena that we recognize
as having a being independent of our own volition', and knowledge as 'the certainty
that phenomena are real and that they possess specific characteristics'; P. L. Berger
and T. Luckmann, *The Social Construction of Reality: A Treatise in the Sociology
of Knowledge* (New York: Doubleday & Company, 1966; repr., New York: Anchor
Books, 1967), 1.
[91] However, the person is unaware of this because the institutionalisation predates
them, and so things appear as the way things are; Berger and Luckmann, *Social*,
21–3, 59–60.
[92] Berger and Luckmann, *Social*, 50.
[93] Berger and Luckmann, *Social*, 96–8.

reality. When conflict arises between experience and perception the worldview needs to be legitimised if it is to remain accepted and not be problematic.[94] We have argued above that emotions are interpretative; they evaluate objects and circumstances as we encounter them. Thus, it follows that if emotions evaluate our world, particularly our relationship to other objects, they can be useful tools for shaping perceptions of reality. Put differently, they can be used to construct or enforce a symbolic universe.

So, how do emotions help to configure reality? First, we must remember that each culture has a particular emotional repertoire. This emotional repertoire orders reality through naming and conceptualising affective experience, i.e. the linking of emotion terms to prototypical emotion scenarios give the person information about how to interpret the world, particularly relational encounters. Here, we can also recall, as Riis and Woodhouse reveal, that groups have particular emotional regimes. In these regimes certain emotions are promoted in certain contexts and others discouraged. From this contextualisation of the emotional repertoire a person learns about how they should view and ultimately experience their world.[95] She learns what appropriate objects of fear, love, anger, etc. are. When this information is combined with the accepted norms, values, and goals of society, a person is informed about what to view positively and negatively, what to value, what to seek, and what to avoid.[96] Importantly, in combination, the emotions create a sense of the person's own identity and place in the world by defining her relationship to the acceptable objects of emotions. Thus, in essence, emotions enforce a map of reality. Each emotional experience highlights an object in the landscape and evaluates it in a particular way. Whether this emotional encounter is promoted as legitimate or prohibited as inappropriate places that object in a certain position with regard to the self. Together, the whole repertoire of emotions cumulatively builds a picture until the person has a cohesive view of reality. Such emotional mapping is essential for making sense of one's place within the structures of a given society. If a person has the same worldview as her fellow group member, it is likely that she will share a similar emotional understanding of the world. Consequently, if a person is to be part of a new social group

---

[94] Berger and Luckmann, *Social*, 105.
[95] Lutz notes that even our stance toward emotion 'exists in a system of power relations and plays a role in maintaining it'; Lutz, *Unnatural*, 54.
[96] Cf. Lutz, *Unnatural*, 10.

and take on its worldview then her emotional orientation will also have to be altered.[97] This means not only will she see reality differently, but she will experience it differently.

We have noted that an emotional regime is learned, and that emotions are constructed within cultural systems. As such, emotional judgements are dependent on worldview. However, this begs the question, can the process work dynamically? Is it possible for current emotions to be used to create or legitimise a new view of reality? I would suggest that it is. Lutz recognises that emotions can be used in discourse to 'theorize about events, to moralize about or judge them, and to advance one's interests by defining the situation in a particular way'.[98] I agree with this, but want to take this a stage further and propose that if an individual understands another person's emotional logic from familiarity with the culture's emotional repertoire, they can use that emotional logic to argue for a new reality.[99] This does not necessarily require changing the make-up of an emotion itself, but simply applying it differently, i.e. changing the 'scenarios' in which it should occur and altering the objects for which it is appropriate. In doing so, this new application of the emotion's logic has the capacity also to give new information to the person about what should be valued, pursued, avoided, etc. Moreover, it provides a new positioning of the self. If this is done cumulatively with a group of emotions it can give to the person a new view of reality. Objectively, to an outsider, no change has been made to the world of the person, but, subjectively, a dramatic shift has taken place. Furthermore, new emotions (if by new we mean newly applied) provide new evaluations and have the potential to lead to different actions. This is particularly the case if other legitimising arguments can add weight to the new emotionally shaped reality. It is my intention to show that this is exactly what is taking place in 1 Peter. Through his use of emotions, the author is showing the audience how to perceive reality and therefore also how to position others and the self.

Thus, we can outline our theoretical position on emotions. Emotions are intentional and object-directed; they are about something

---

[97] Berger and Luckmann note how primary socialisation requires the child to 'identify with significant others in a variety of emotional ways'. Secondary socialisation does not require this, but re-socialisation (in which one moves to a completely new view of reality) does require the same type of emotional identification; see Berger and Luckmann, *Social*, 131–2, 141, 157.

[98] Lutz, *Unnatural*, 10.

[99] This requires that the person has a shared language and understands the usual 'scenarios' for an emotion.

or someone. Emotions are evaluative judgements about the importance of the object to our well-being. As such, they interpret a situation and give information about the object's impact upon personal
goals. Consequently, emotions carry an action-tendency that helps
one to achieve the desired outcome. Subsequently, emotions influence behaviour. However, an emotion's appraisal does not occur
in isolation but relies upon a person's norms and values that themselves are supplied by their socially constructed worldview. This all
combines to mean that emotions have a logic: they make sense in a
given context and carry a rationale. If we understand the narrative in
which the emotion occurs we can appreciate both the relevance and
the communication of the emotion.

Furthermore, we have argued that emotions are not universal phenomena, but are culturally constructed and socially legitimised. Each
culture has its own emotional repertoire in which certain affective
experiences are named and are understood to refer to particular
typological scenarios. A culture's repertoire occurs through a combination of particular norms and values along with the impact of the
demands of the environment. Once an emotional repertoire has been
established an emotional regime can be utilised. This regime dictates
a culture's expectations with regard to an individual's emotional life.
In this regime, certain emotions are encouraged in given contexts and
others discouraged. Thus, because emotions help a person navigate
her world and understand her place within it, the regime also gives
a person a sense of how they should perceive reality and the self.
Emotions are particularly useful in enforcing social structures, as an
emotion's object is frequently another person. In addition, because
emotions contain an action-tendency, an emotional regime can provide behavioural expectations and boundaries. Lastly, emotions can
be seen as a type of discourse in that their judgements contain information and interpretations. Consequently, dynamically, when their
logic is understood, emotions can be used in conversation to shape a
person's perspective and provide an alternative view of reality.

Methodological Approach

For the following chapters, the above understanding of emotions is
foundational. Though the exegetical chapters will not make constant
reference to modern emotion theory, the reader should be aware that
the above theoretical understanding of emotions undergirds the
exegesis at every stage. This includes the fundamental assumptions
that emotions are not devoid of cognition but have a logical

communicative element that can be analysed, and that emotions are not universal but are culturally situated phenomena that arise commonly in social situations. Furthermore, the above theoretical discussion, by revealing the issues that are at stake surrounding emotions, will define the parameters of the investigation; it will shape the types of questions we can ask when we encounter an emotion term in the text. For example, key aspects of an emotion such as its object-directedness, its cognitive content in the form of an evaluative judgement, and its action-tendency will remain at the forefront of our discussion. Likewise, the dynamic relationship between emotions and values, goals, and worldview will be a recurrent theme. Important too will be the idea that emotions are interpretative; the author's use of emotion frames the audience's understanding of the object in relation to the subject in each given context. Moreover, the exegesis will also assume that the author's use of emotions functions at a social and formative level. Through his deployment of emotion, he is saying something to his audience about how they should perceive reality and in doing so is shaping the audience's sense of self and other. He is also making statements about appropriate and inappropriate courses of action. Thus, at a larger level, the exegesis, where it speaks of an individual's emotions, is not seeking to drive a wedge between the individual and the community. 1 Peter is written to a wide audience and therefore, necessarily, our talk of emotion, whether of 'believer' or 'believers', is examining emotional life as it is presented to the community as a whole and assumes that the individual is seen through this corporate lens. In fact, the corporate address is what helps to create an emotional regime for the whole community in which the individual is to locate herself.

So, having established the theoretical framework of our research, the following discussion will address how this investigation will seek to be culturally and historically sensitive, which is required by our theoretical understanding and is necessary for a responsible examination of emotion in the ancient world.

Since emotions are culturally constructed, before exploring individual emotions in the text it will be necessary to discover how these emotion terms were understood in their historical context. This will include recognising the range of emotional experiences that an emotion term can cover, and seeking to decipher, by outlining a definition, the basic characteristics of the emotion, especially what appraisal is encoded in the emotion term. In order to do this I will utilise Greco-Roman philosophical theories of emotion. I will primarily use Stoic theory, but will also refer to other philosophers such as Aristotle when necessary. Stoic theory is the most pertinent for my investigation because the Stoics, a highly influential school by the first century CE, offer the most developed understanding of emotions in the ancient world. Of course, we can appreciate that Stoic philosophers are among the most elite of society. So, one might question the appropriateness of using their material to open up our understanding of 1 Peter, a letter whose audience is certainly not elite. First, I must make it clear that in utilising Stoic material I am not claiming that 1 Peter is a Stoic, or directly influenced by Stoicism. Nor would I claim that its recipients were familiar with Stoic philosophy.[100] However, I would argue that Stoic material offers more than an elitist account of emotions. In order to under-score this, we need to appreciate the various levels at which one can speak about emotions. At some levels, talk of emotion is certainly shaped by Stoic philosophical assumptions and therefore is distinct to the outlook of the school. However, at another level the conver-sation is widely applicable to anyone who shares the same linguistic environment, like 1 Peter and the LXX. We must unpack this further in order to understand what I will and will not do with Stoic (and other Greco-Roman) philosophical theory.

The ancient theorists talk about emotions at three levels. The first level is the larger theoretical level. This level of discussion poses broader questions such as 'What are emotions?', 'What do they do?' The next level of discussion, which I consider the Stoics particularly helpful for, is the definitional level. Here each discrete emotion is investigated. At this level, Stoics, and other theorists, are seeking to understand emotion terms as they were *commonly used*. The philosophers, like the rhetoricians, in their definitions of emotion terms are not creating new terminology but are using terms widely understood in their Greco-Roman environment. Again, I must emphasise, certain ideas, specifically appraisals, are *already encapsulated* in the emotion term regardless of who uses them. The basic idea may not be the same across linguistic boundaries e.g. when we translate one Greek term into an English one. However, we must assume reasonably high consistency of meaning within a linguistic culture itself otherwise one could not be understood. For example, when people used χαρά there was a common understanding

---

[100] Having said this, since it could be argued that Stoicism was not only practiced by elites but also became a more popular philosophy, it is not outrageous to think that the author of 1 Peter and his audience may have encountered some Stoic ideas.

of what it meant (though this does not necessarily equate fully to our understanding of 'joy'). This common Greek linguistic usage is shared by 1 Peter by virtue of having a shared language.[101] Third, the Stoics, after defining an emotion, also have a particular evaluation of each emotion. For example, some emotions are considered suitable for the wise man, others are not and are contrary to virtuous living. Put differently, at this level the Stoics have their own categorisation (groupings) of emotions and stance on the ethical value of certain emotions. Thus, we can see that this third level is influenced by Stoicism's worldview, which includes notions of value and human flourishing. Hence, Stoic talk at this level is necessarily nuanced and distinctive to Stoicism. So, we can determine three levels of conversation: (1) general theory of emotion; (2) definition of each emotion; (3) contextualisation of and rationale given to each emotion. How will this investigation use each level?

Level 1 will be the focus of Chapters 3–4, which will reveal how emotions as a larger category were understood by Greco-Roman philosophy and rhetoric. For example, we will examine what they thought emotions were, how they arise, how they function within the ethical life of the human, and what role they play in persuasion. Such an exercise achieves two things. First, it endeavours to resist the dangers of anachronistic exegesis. We will discover that there is in fact a close historical and cultural fit between ancient conceptions and modern theory. Thus, the questions we are asking about emotions and the tools we are using are not just modern but were recognised and operative in the ancient world. Consequently, the comments we are making about the author's use of emotion are not arising from purely modern constructs but such ideas and connections exist in the ancient mind also, though modern terminology will aid our discussion. Second, we need to understand this larger conception of

---

[101] Teresa Morgan makes a parallel argument regarding the New Testament use of πίστις: '[T]here are strong reasons for supposing that the way the New Testament uses *pistis* language is not likely to be radically different from the way in which it is used in wider Graeco-Roman culture ... In the first place, it would be very unusual for a new cult to take a term in common use and immediately assign it a new meaning ... We should therefore assume, unless there is compelling evidence to the contrary, that early Christians used *pistis* language – and all other terms that were important to them – in a way that would have made sense to their audiences ... which means: with its normal range of meanings.' T. Morgan, 'Is *Pistis*/*Fides* Experienced as an Emotion in the Late Roman Republic, Early Principate, and Early Church?', in *Unveiling Emotions II: Emotions in Greece and Rome: Texts, Images, Material Culture*, ed. Angelos Chaniotis and Pierre Ducrey, Heidelberger Althistorische Beiträge und Epigraphische Studien 55 (Stuttgart: Franz Steiner Verlag, 2013), 191–214, at 212.

emotions if we are to use material relating to levels 2 and 3 well. This larger schema, within which Stoics locate emotion as a category and groups of emotions, helps us recognise loaded terminology. By this, I mean terminology that carries philosophical baggage and, through its use, nuances the conversation. We need to understand such nuancing if we are to determine what information about emotion in the Stoic material is more widely applicable and what is distinctively Stoic. If we can spot the Stoic nuancing, we will be able to better tease out the basic (or common) definitions of emotion terms.

In the exegetical chapters (5–8) levels 2 and 3 will be most important. First, when exploring each emotion, the Greco-Roman material will be used to outline a definition of each emotion. This will give us the key characteristics of the emotion in its most basic form. As such, the ideas contained in the emotion term itself can be appreciated. As Nussbaum comments, if we can access their definitions we can 'understand how they were individuating the kinds'.[102] These definitions are often very simple, and are shared by theorists of different schools, and I would argue, therefore, are common to the linguistic environment.[103] Subsequently, such definitions will give us the basic tools for assessing emotion terms in 1 Peter. Lastly, level 3 will be used as a point of comparison. This book will not import a Stoic contextualisation of emotions or its underlying rationale on to 1 Peter, since 1 Peter need not share Stoicism's worldview. Instead, 1 Peter should be allowed to speak for itself. For it may evidence a different stance towards certain emotions and use emotions in ways contrary to Stoicism, e.g. with different objects or in different contexts. However, the Stoic contextualisation of emotion and its embedding in a larger philosophical system will provide a useful discussion partner that will enable us to outline the contours of 1 Peter's use of emotion more clearly, particularly the interrelationship between 1 Peter's use of emotions and its theological outlook.

Lastly, we must turn to one further issue: 1 Peter's use of the LXX. Anyone familiar with the text of 1 Peter is confronted with 1 Peter's citations of, allusions to, and reliance on biblical material

---

[102] Nussbaum, *Upheavals*, 156.
[103] Cf. M. Patera, 'Reflections on the Discourse of Fear in Greek Sources', in *Unveiling Emotions II: Emotions in Greece and Rome: Texts, Images, Material Culture*, ed. Angelos Chaniotis and Pierre Ducrey, Heidelberger Althistorische Beiträge und Epigraphische Studien 55 (Stuttgart: Franz Steiner Verlag, 2013), 109–34, who argues, for example, that 'a certain usage of fear persists through several centuries of Greek thought' (109).

and themes. Thus, one might rightly ask, how will my exploration of emotions in 1 Peter take account of biblical influence? The outline above of the three levels of discussion is helpful for clarifying this. First, there is no unique Jewish philosophical discussion at the first theoretical level. In fact, where we do find philosophical discussion of emotions, for example in authors such as Philo or 4 Maccabees, the language, emotional categorisation, and definitions are borrowed from Stoicism. At the second level, the Septuagint, from which 1 Peter draws, shares the common understanding of basic emotion definitions detailed by philosophers. These basic ideas are encoded in the language terms that are used by the Septuagint and Greek theorist alike. Thus, what is most important is the third level. We need to discover how the Septuagint *uses* the emotion terms. In what contexts do they appear? Are there new or altered scenarios in which the emotion is used? If so, is there a rationale that allows it, given its definitional logic, to make sense in this context? It is at this level of contextualisation and rationale, which relies on worldview, that we discover the influence of the Septuagint on 1 Peter's use of emotion.

Therefore, the exegetical chapters will proceed in the following manner. They will first try to 'locate' and outline each emotion by recourse to Stoic philosophical material and the LXX. After doing so, they will proceed to an analysis of the use of that emotion in 1 Peter. Consequently, the exegetical work will focus on the parts of the text where specific emotion terms appear. Part III (Chapters 5–6) will look at joy and distress; Part IV (Chapters 7–8) will investigate fear, hope, and shame.[104] Regrettably, due to constraints, I cannot cover every emotion present in 1 Peter. So, even though this investigation will provide an in-depth analysis of the above emotions, it is still only a partial analysis of 1 Peter. After the separate exegetical chapters, the conclusion will provide a synthesis of the individual findings. In doing so, it will piece together from each emotion a combined view of the emotional reality presented by 1 Peter.

In pursuing the exegetical task, the analysis will be concerned with the rhetorical (persuasive) dimensions of the text, but its interest in rhetoric is consciously limited. Unlike Campbell, our interest is not in classifying the rhetorical species of the letter, identifying rhetorical units, nor locating and naming specific τόποι or stylistic features.[105]

---

[104] The reasoning for the grouping of these emotions will be presented in the chapters themselves.

[105] See Campbell, *Honor*. For more on classical rhetorical criticism of the New Testament see G. A. Kennedy, *New Testament Interpretation through Rhetorical*

By the same token, unlike Thurén, we are not seeking to provide an analysis of the whole argumentative framework of the text, nor to explore the phenomenon of argumentation itself with 1 Peter as a case study.[106] Our concern with argumentation will also draw rather little on modern theories of rhetoric,[107] because they have so far evinced limited interest in the role of the audience's emotion.[108] Instead, our engagement with emotion studies will provide richer and deeper tools for analysing the function of emotions than what may otherwise be gleaned from standard treatments of rhetoric in 1 Peter scholarship and modern rhetorical theory.

Our methodological base in emotion theory and in the ancient understandings of emotion will generate, however, a rich set of inter-pretative questions. For example, what is the object? What evaluation does the emotion communicate? Is the emotion being encouraged or discouraged? What does the emotion's contextualisation reveal about how the author is presenting reality? What does this indicate about the values and worldview of the text? How might this affirm or alter the audience's understanding of human flourishing? How does this use of emotion influence action? Lastly, what are the implications

---

Criticism (Chapel Hill: University of North Carolina Press, 1984); B. L. Mack, *Rhetoric and the New Testament*, Guides to Biblical Scholarship. New Testament Series (Philadelphia, PA: Fortress Press, 1990) and C. J. Classen, *Rhetorical Criticism of the New Testament*, WUNT 128 (Tübingen: Mohr Siebeck, 2000). The first major commentary to epitomise the early approach is H. D. Betz, *Galatians: A Commentary on Paul's Letter to the Churches in Galatia*, Hermeneia (Minneapolis, MN: Fortress Press, 1979). Of course, there has been progression in the use of classical rhetorical criticism since Betz with the focus now falling on elements of invention. For a general introduction to rhetorical criticism see M. J. MacDonald, ed., *The Oxford Handbook of Rhetorical Studies* (Oxford: Oxford University Press, 2017).

[106] See Thurén, *Argument*.

[107] E.g. C. Perelman and L. Olbrechts-Tyteca, *The New Rhetoric: A Treatise on Argumentation*, trans. John Wilkinson and Purcell Weaver (Notre Dame, IN: University of Notre Dame Press, 1969; originally published as *La Nouvelle Rhétorique: Traité de l'Argumentation* (Paris: Press Universitaires de France, 1958)) to name just one notable example. For the continuing influence of Perelman and Oblrechts-Tyteca's work, see the special issue of *Philosophy and Rhetoric* 43, no. 4 (2010) and J. T. Gage, ed., *The Promise of Reason: Studies in the New Rhetoric* (Carbondale and Edwardsville: Southern Illinois University Press, 2011).

[108] Thurén, a keen advocate of modern theories of argumentation, himself says that ἔθος and πάθος 'are to a great extent ignored by Perelman'; Thurén, *Argument*, 40. For an introduction to 'Modern and Contemporary Rhetoric' see part VI of MacDonald, *Rhetorical Studies*, 571–772 and R. P. Hart and S. Daughton, *Modern Rhetorical Criticism*, 3rd ed. (London and New York: Routledge, 2016). Hart and Daughton note the role of emotion in analysing argument, however, their comments remain focused on the speaker's own emotional integrity, authenticity, and register, which the audience judges. They do note that, when assessing argumentation, emotion and reason should not be artificially divided (82–3; cf. 221, 229).

of the author's use of emotion for the audience ethically, sociologically, and therapeutically? By this approach, this book will demonstrate how investigation of the emotions can open up new avenues for discussion and give crucial insights into the author's persuasive discourse, worldview, and ethics.

EXCURSUS: LOCATION OF THE LETTER

I have argued that it is important to be historically and culturally sensitive in our exegesis of emotion terms. I have also outlined, methodologically, how I intend to do this. However, the alert reader may have noticed that I have not yet addressed standard introductory questions such as the date of the letter, identity of the author, location of the audience, or its social make-up and situation. The reason I have not dealt with these in depth is because the fine details of these debates are not pivotal to my argument, and indeed, in some cases, the finer details are impossible to reasonably ascertain, such is the nature of a general letter and of the available evidence.

To avoid spending time rehearsing arguments easily accessible elsewhere, I will cover the areas of discussion only briefly. For the purposes of this enquiry, I understand the letter to be written in the latter stages of the first century (70–100 CE),[109] which suggests that the letter is pseudonymous, though, as Michaels argues, pseudonymity is hard to assert with great certainty.[110] Regardless, it matters little for the present investigation whether the author was Peter,[111] as the letter claims (1.1; cf. 5.1a, 12–13), or 1 Peter is a pseudonymous work.[112] The key point is that an authorial figure is using a form of

---

[109] Cf. N. Brox, *Der Erste Petrusbrief*, EKKNT 21 (Zürich: Benziger Verlag, 1979), 41; P. J. Achtemeier, *1 Peter: A Commentary on First Peter*, Hermeneia (Minneapolis, MN: Fortress Press, 1996), 43–50; R. Feldmeier, *The First Letter of Peter: A Commentary on the Greek Text*, trans. Peter H. Davids (Waco, TX: Baylor University Press, 2008), 39–40.

[110] Pseudonymity assumes the Apostle Peter's martyrdom occurred in 64–65 CE under Nero, though Michaels highlights uncertainties with this traditional understanding; see J. R. Michaels, *1 Peter*, WBC 49 (Nashville, TN: Thomas Nelson, 1988), lvii–lxi; see also lxii–lxvii for his discussion on authorship.

[111] Whether writing himself or communicating through an amanuensis, e.g. Silvanus (5.12); see E. G. Selwyn, *The First Epistle of St. Peter: The Greek Text with Introduction, Notes and Essays* (London: Macmillan, 1946), 7–36, esp. 9–10. Early Christian writers such as Eusebius, Irenaeus, and Tertullian took the letter to be Petrine; see Michaels, *1 Peter*, xxxii–xxxvi.

[112] For detailed argument on authorship see Achtemeier, *1 Peter*, 1–43. For discussion on whether the letter is the product of a Petrine circle see D. G. Horrell,

communication – the aural/oral delivery of a letter – to shape an audience's perspective and behaviour.[113] I have noted that in 1 Peter the audience's emotional life is itself presented in an idealised form; we do not have access to the original audience's actual emotional experience. The same could be said of the authority of the author. The very fact that the letter exhorts its audience assumes that, as far as the letter is concerned, the author is in a position to ask something of his audience and expects them to follow his leading.[114] We do not know whether specific members of the audience ever heeded his requests. In a sense, my approach requires dealing with the argument of the text as it presents itself. It is not trying to pin down the exact historical situation, but to understand the theological outlook its presentation of emotions reveals.

In terms of the location of the audience, the letter itself details its recipients in 1.1: 'ἐκλεκτοῖς παρεπιδήμοις διασπορᾶς Πόντου, Γαλατίας, Καππαδοκίας, Ἀσίας καὶ Βιθυνίας'. The geographical terms cover a large area in north Asia Minor (approx. 129,000 square miles).[115] Unlike 1 Corinthians, for example, we cannot pinpoint one distinct location of the audience. Neither does the letter address 'specific local issues'.[116] This has two implications: first, we cannot be overly specific about the audience with regard to location (e.g. rural or urban), culture, social customs, etc.;[117] and consequently, second, we can assume that the author could not be overly specific either. He would need to have argued in more general terms in order to construct an argument that could be comprehensible to all.[118] This idea

'The Product of a Petrine Circle? Challenging an Emerging Consensus', in *Becoming Christian: Essays on 1 Peter and the Making of Christian Identity*, ed. David G. Horrell, LNTS 394 (London: T&T Clark, 2013), 7–44. For arguments in favour of pseudonymity see Feldmeier, *Peter*, 33–9.

[113] In fact, Michaels argues 'the author consistently keeps his personality out of the letter. He is content to let his arguments stand on their own merits'; Michaels, *1 Peter*, lv.

[114] For discussion on why, if the letter is pseudonymous, Peter might have been named as this authorial figure see Horrell, 'Petrine Circle', 39–42.

[115] See J. H. Elliott, *1 Peter: A New Translation with Commentary*, AB 37B (New York: Doubleday, 2000), 84–5; cf. Michaels, *1 Peter*, 9; Achtemeier, *1 Peter*, 50.

[116] Selwyn, *St. Peter*, 1.

[117] Cf. Elliott, *1 Peter*, 90. Though some such as Selwyn have argued that we can assume Asia Minor remained strongly influenced by Hellenism at the time of the letter; Selwyn, *St. Peter*, 48; cf. Achtemeier, *1 Peter*, 26.

[118] See also Achtemeier, *1 Peter*, 50 who makes a similar point: 'readers will be addressed in as broad terms as possible, so that at least some parts of the letter will be relevant to each of the different groups of its readers'. This is particularly the case if the audiences were 'largely unknown to the author'; Michaels, *1 Peter*, xxxix (cf. xlv).

of a general audience helps us when it comes to looking at the rhetoric of the letter.[119] We can expect that the author would have to have used τόποι he anticipated could be widely understood. We can also expect that the same is true for his use of emotion terms. Because he cannot be overly specific, we can appreciate that he will tend towards using, like other rhetoricians did, the linguistically encoded and generally understood basic scenario of an emotion term, though of course, the author can deploy this general understanding to say something new. Thus, our aim in locating emotions in their cultural framework is not to be highly specific and overly atomistic. My challenge is to call the exegete to step out of his/her *modern* Western Anglo-American linguistic and cultural understanding of emotions, to try to seek to understand more about how these terms were used in the Greco-Roman linguistic and cultural world – recognising that there were variances in the Greco-Roman world too, but expecting that there must have been enough shared understanding for a letter to communicate meaningfully to such a wide area.

On the last two areas – the social make-up of the audience and its situation – we can make some substantive comment but also have to recognise that the letter does not give us all the information we might desire. There are few details that would pinpoint certain individuals or communities. The naming of specific individual Christians – διὰ Σιλουανοῦ[120] and Μᾶρκος ὁ υἱός μου (5.12–13) – and a coded reference to the author's own community – ἐν Βαβυλῶνι (5.13) – occur only briefly at the very end of the letter. The first two names are well-known early Christian missionary figures, like Πέτρος (1.1), and therefore do not help us in locating a specific community; conducting anything like a prosopographical investigation is impossible.[121] The name Βαβυλών has frequently and from an early time been interpreted as referring to Rome.[122] If this is the case, then this, along with the naming of places in 1.1, is the only other specific information we have, and it does not tell us about the audience, only potentially the location of the author. Furthermore, the author gives no hints of how he perceives the social status of

---

[119] It must be noted at the outset that I agree with Michaels that '1 Peter … appears to be tightly structured, a single letter composed all at one time and actually sent'; Michaels, *1 Peter*, xxxvii; cf. Feldmeier, *Peter*, 28–9.

[120] Cf. 1 Thess 1.1; 2 Thess 1.1; Selwyn, *St. Peter*, 9–10.

[121] This is even more the case if these names are fictionally added to support the pseudonymity of the letter. For discussion on the naming of Silvanus and Mark and its implication for the authorship of the letter see Horrell, 'Petrine Circle', 33–7.

[122] See Eusebius *Hist. eccl.* 2.15.2; Michaels, *1 Peter*, xxxii, xlvii, 310–11; Elliott, *1 Peter*, 91.

the wider community beyond naming certain demographics: slaves (οἰκέται), wives (γυναῖκες) and husbands (ἄνδρες) in the household codes (2.18–3.7), and elders (πρεσβύτεροι) and young people (νεώτεροι) towards the end of the letter (5.1–5).[123] Consequently, with little specific information, we would be amiss to say too much. The best we can do is guess that the audience looked like other Christian communities at the time: likely encompassing a range of individuals, but probably containing very few, if any, of the upper echelons of society and with the majority likely in a more precarious economic position.[124] The majority of scholars have rejected Elliott's assertion that the terms παρεπίδημος and πάροικος refer to a concrete political and legal situation of the audience.[125] Like the majority, I see παρεπίδημος and πάροικος as metaphorical terms. They do have a social aspect in that they indicate that the audience is part of a new Christian community that now finds itself no longer at home in its previous society/social networks.[126] But, such terms have an eschatological orientation rather than designating a specific legal status. As Feldmeier highlights, the believers' alienation is the 'flip side' of their election.[127] Thus, again, such terms do not help us with defining the social status of the audience. Scholars have argued

[123] It is true that the author does not address masters, only slaves. However, given other elements of the letter such as the types of activities mentioned in 4.2–4, we should not take this conclusion too far and assume the audience was predominantly servile; Selwyn, *St. Peter*, 49; cf. Elliott, *1 Peter*, 88–9, for the range of people groups that likely lived in the areas of Asia Minor covered by the letter. For a detailed discussion of the likely socio-economic status of the groups listed in 1 Peter see T. B. Williams, *Persecution in 1 Peter: Differentiating and Contextualizing Early Christian Suffering*, NovTSup 145 (Leiden: Brill, 2012), 117–27. Given the lack of information in 1 Peter itself, Williams' arguments are based on a general understanding of the socio-economic landscape of Roman Anatolia (see 104–17). Williams also highlights that it is incorrect to assume that a rural setting for the addressees would necessarily indicate poverty (102–3); cf. David G. Horrell, 'Aliens and Strangers? The Socio-Economic Location of the Addressees of 1 Peter', in *Becoming Christian*, 100–32, at 105–14, 122–9.

[124] See Selwyn, *St. Peter*, 49; Achtemeier, *1 Peter*, 55–7; Horrell, 'Aliens', 130; Williams, *Persecution*, 128; cf. S. J. Friesen, 'Poverty in Pauline Studies: Beyond the So-Called New Consensus', *JSNT* 26 (2004): 323–61; B. W. Longenecker, 'Exposing the Economic Middle: A Revised Economy of Scale for the Study of Early Urban Christianity', *JSNT* 31 (2009): 243–78. See Horrell, 'Petrine Circle', 37–9, 42–4, who argues that the letter itself represents a synthesis of proto-orthodox early Christian ideas, rather than any specific community or tradition.

[125] See Elliott, *1 Peter*, 94, 101–2, and his fuller treatment in *A Home for the Homeless: A Sociological Exegesis of 1 Peter, Its Situation and Strategy* (Philadelphia, PA: Fortress Press, 1981), 24–49. For a criticism of Elliott's position see Williams, *Persecution*, 97–103; Horrell, 'Aliens', 114–20.

[126] See Michaels, *1 Peter*, xxxv, 6–8.

[127] Feldmeier, *Peter*, 13–17.

over whether the letter is addressed to a predominantly Jewish[128] or gentile Christian audience.[129] As with most modern exegetes, this investigation will assume a mostly gentile Christian audience.[130]

Finally, we can turn to the situation of the audience. The letter is clear that the audience is experiencing hostility, depicted as trials (πειρασμοί), on account of their Christian identity and behaviour.[131] There is widespread agreement that the situation of hostility provides the occasion for 1 Peter. Thus, the letter seeks to address the audience's perception of these circumstances and consequently its behaviour.[132] Such trials include verbal reproach/accusations, intimidation, and physical abuse. We will address these more fully in the proceeding chapters as far as they relate to our investigation of emotion terms. A more substantial move of late has been to argue for the possibility that persecution may have come via third party legal conflict, i.e. in a law court setting (cf. 3.15; 5.9).[133] Travis Williams has argued rather persuasively in this regard.[134] However, as far as this

---

[128] Cf. 1.1's phrase παρεπιδήμοις διασπορᾶς, and the terminology of 2.9 (cf. Gal 2.7); see also Eusebius, *Hist. eccl.* 3.4.2–3; Michaels, *1 Peter*, xlvi. See Elliott, *1 Peter*, 89, for historical evidence for Diaspora Israelites in the area (cf. also 95–6).

[129] In fact, the letter makes no reference to the Jew–Gentile problem, which suggests it was not a concern for the author. For further discussion on this see Michaels, *1 Peter*, xlix–lv.

[130] Cf. 1.14, 18, 21; 2.10; 4.2–4. This assertion does not deny the clear influence of Jewish literature on 1 Peter, but, as Selwyn asserts, though the letter may 'have been *written* from a Jewish background', it does not 'prove that the same background can be postulated of those who were to receive it'; Selwyn, *St. Peter*, 43 (emphasis original). For arguments in favour of a gentile Christian audience see Michaels, *1 Peter*, xlv–xlvi; Achtemeier, *1 Peter*, 50–1; Feldmeier, *Peter*, 42; Horrell, 'Aliens', 120–2; Williams, *Persecution*, 91–5; cf. Elliott, *1 Peter*, 89–90, 96–7.

[131] Achtemeier, *1 Peter*, 28–9; Feldmeier, *Peter*, 4–5.

[132] I do not think it is necessary to decide on whether the letter is deliberative (so Campbell) or epideictic (so Thurén) in genre (see pp. 11, 13). In order to alter the audience's perception and behaviour, the author uses a range of persuasive means that could be grouped under different rhetorical genres. Troy Martin has forcefully argued that Petrine studies should take note of the developments in Pauline studies, which have moved beyond attempts to identify rhetorical species or arrangement in Pauline epistles. He comments that, after successive attempts have highlighted the weaknesses of such approaches, any attempts to conduct such an analysis are outdated. Martin, 'Rhetorical Step-Child', 44–54; cf. esp. 46–9 for aspects of 1 Peter that relate to the three rhetorical genres: judicial, deliberative, and epideictic.

[133] Commentators before the 1970s linked the persecution in 1 Peter with the reign of either Nero, Domitian, or Trajan; see Elliott, *1 Peter*, 98–100; cf. Achtemeier, *1 Peter*, 23–36. Williams' position is in opposition to those who see the persecution in 1 Peter as more local and 'spasmodic' without any official or judicial element. See Selwyn, *St. Peter*, 55; cf. Achtemeier, *1 Peter*, 33–6; Elliott, *1 Peter*, 90, 98; Feldmeier, *Peter*, 2; Brox, *Petrusbrief*, 27–32.

[134] Williams, *Persecution*, 138–78, 303–16. Though I agree with Williams that there may indeed have been the *possibility* of legal charges being brought against Christians,

investigation is concerned, what is of importance is that there is, or is perceived to be, a hostile other. It does not matter greatly whether the hostile other is a governing official or a family member. In either case, the audience will have an emotional response to opposition and abuse. Fear is no less real if it is fear of a husband rather than fear of a governor. Thus, it is not necessary for my argument to decide decisively on this matter. We can also say, rather uncontroversially, that the hostile other is outside of the Christian community. At some points the non-Christian other is specified, such as being named the master (2.18) or husband (3.1), at other times it is not (e.g. 3.15–16). Therefore, when the letter is not explicit, I will speak of a non-Christian hostile other[135] without defining this term any further. We will discover that the emotional orientation presented by the letter can provide resources for believers facing persecution at both a local and an official level.

Having dealt briefly with these introductory questions, we can return to our present investigation, starting with revealing how emotions were understood in the ancient world.

I find more convincing, to follow Elliott, the notion that the terminology in the letter indicates the majority of the addressees were facing a situation of 'persistent slander and verbal abuse from nonbelieving outsiders aimed at demeaning, shaming and discrediting the Christians in the court of public opinion'; Elliott, *1 Peter*, 100.

[135] Others such as Elliott have also used this terminology; see e.g. Elliott, *1 Peter*, 97–8.

PART II

EMOTIONS IN ANTIQUITY

3

STOIC PHILOSOPHY OF EMOTION

The previous chapter has established a theoretical framework by which we can investigate the role of emotions in 1 Peter. However, it was noted that, in order not to impose anachronistically modern theory on to an ancient text, we need to discover whether our main premises and heuristic tools are compatible with ancient views on emotions. This chapter and the next will demonstrate that there is a substantial fit between the modern theory outlined and certain ancient views. Our exploration will centre on ideas about emotions found in the disciplines of both philosophy and rhetoric. Stoicism will be the focus of this philosophical chapter. However, for reasons explained in the next chapter, a broader approach will be taken when looking at the rhetoricians.

Why choose the Stoics? As Sandbach notes, by 'the end of the first century BC Stoicism was without doubt the predominant philosophy among the Romans'. He goes on to say 'in the Greek world of the first two centuries of our era Stoicism clearly remained a lively influence'.[1] Long agrees, that, particularly with regard to ethics (a category under which the emotions fall), by 100 BCE the philosophical landscape was dominated by Stoicism and Epicureanism.[2] However, it is Stoicism that provides the most comprehensive and developed discussion of emotions in the ancient world. Therefore, the Stoic understanding of emotions will be central and other philosophical schools will be used comparatively.[3] As discussed above (pp. 41–3), this chapter will work at the general level of the theory of

---

[1] F. H. Sandbach, *The Stoics*, 2nd ed. (Bristol: Bristol Press, 1989), 16.

[2] A. A. Long, 'The Socratic Legacy', in *The Cambridge History of Hellenistic Philosophy*, ed. Keimpe Algra et al. (Cambridge: Cambridge University Press, 2005), 617–41, at 617.

[3] This is done with an awareness that Stoicism was not a uniform entity. Where there are apparent differences within the school, these will be noted. It is also worth recognising that sources for early Stoicism are fragmentary. We are often dependent on later authors, which makes piecing together Stoic thought difficult. Thus, the following will sketch the orthodox Stoic view as it is generally agreed upon. For the names and dates of the leading Stoics see the Appendix.

emotion. It will not discuss specific emotions in detail. For now, it is the larger questions that are of interest, such as, what is an emotion and how does it work? This will lead on to an examination of the importance of emotions for the individual and society, particularly with regard to ethics and agency. As we look at the Stoic theory of emotion, we will discover the 'spin' that the Stoics give the emotions through their positioning of emotions within the larger philosophical landscape and their categorisation of emotions. Appreciating this Stoic evaluation and nuancing of emotions will help us to be careful when using their definitions in our exegesis, enabling us to notice which elements are Stoic and which are more general.

EXCURSUS: A NOTE ON TERMINOLOGY

Before outlining the Stoic philosophical theory of emotions, it is worth noting some points about terminology. In the introduction I explained why I have chosen to use the English term emotion instead of other possible terms such as sentiment or affect. However, when approaching the ancient authors it is important to be sensitive with terminology. For example, the Greek term πάθος is used by Stoicism as a loaded, negative term. Because πάθος does not cover all emotions (the Stoics do have other 'good' emotions – εὐπαθεῖαι) it would be amiss to translate it simply as 'emotion'. Therefore, in the following discussion, I will follow convention by translating πάθος as 'passion', which means a negative mental disturbance.[4] However, ordinary usage and other Greek schools do not necessarily follow Stoicism's nuanced understanding of πάθος. For example, in general usage it covers the idea of something happening to you, of being affected in some way. Aristotle's usage seems to carry this general sense. In Epicurean usage πάθος can be akin to sensation.[5] Additionally, in Rhetorical discussion πάθος becomes a technical term for a mode of argumentation. Consequently, on each occasion I will allow the context and the standpoint of the philosophers to guide the translation of their technical terms in order to represent them faithfully. 'Emotion', in this chapter, will remain a broad term that does not infer any positive or negative assessment.

---

[4] Sandbach, *The Stoics*, 59–60. Cf. A. A. Long and D. N. Sedley, *The Hellenistic Philosophers. Volume 1: Translations of the Principal Sources with Philosophical Commentary* (Cambridge: Cambridge University Press, 1987), 420.
[5] See 'πάθος' in LSJ (1285).

Stoic Theory of Emotion

The Stoic discussion of emotions is not isolated, but occurs within wider debates about the nature, capacities, and functions of the soul (ψυχή). Consequently, in order to understand their arguments about the emotions we first need to investigate briefly Stoic conceptions of the soul.[6]

The Anthropology of Emotion

For Stoicism, according to Diogenes Laertius, the soul is an 'off-shoot' of the world-soul (7.143 = SVF 2.633).[7] The world-soul is completely rational (cf. Cicero, *Nat. d.* 2.29–30).[8] Therefore, on account of the soul's relationship to the world-soul, it is necessary that one acts according to nature by perfecting the soul's rationality.[9] For Stoicism, the soul is 'the seat of all mental states, including emotion' and is therefore the 'centre of consciousness' (sometimes referred to as νοῦς), and is located in the heart.[10] It is unified and

---

[6] The following is an outline of the salient ideas. It cannot be comprehensive due to the constraints of space. For more thorough treatments see T. Brennan, *The Stoic Life: Emotions, Duties, and Fate* (Oxford: Oxford University Press, 2005); M. R. Graver, *Stoicism and Emotion* (Chicago: University of Chicago Press, 2007); M. C. Nussbaum, *The Therapy of Desire: Theory and Practice in Hellenistic Ethics*, Martin Classical Lectures, New Series 2 (Princeton, NJ: Princeton University Press, 1994); J. Sihvola and T. Engberg-Pedersen, eds, *The Emotions in Hellenistic Philosophy*, The New Synthese Historical Library 46 (Dordrecht: Kluwer Academic, 1998).

[7] Diogenes Laertius' work is thought to be early third century CE. Book 7 focuses on Stoicism. The idea of a 'world-soul' seems to have its forerunner in Plato. See, Long and Sedley, *HP1*, 319, 494. All English translations of the *Stoicorum Veterum Fragmenta* (SVF) in this chapter are from Long and Sedley, *HP1*, unless otherwise stated.

[8] For Cicero, this perfect rationality indicates the world-soul's divinity.

[9] See Long and Sedley, *HP1*, 319. The idea of acting according to nature is a fundamental Stoic doctrine. In advocating living in agreement with nature the Stoics were following Cynic philosophy. For a list of other Stoic fundamentals found in Cynicism see Long, 'Socratic Legacy', 624. Stoicism is not alone in highlighting the rationality of the soul. Both Plato and Aristotle are keen to see at least some part of the soul as rational. Plato has a tripartite view of the soul, distinguishing reason from the spirited and appetitive parts (*Resp.* 9.436a–441c). Even Aristotle, who holds a bipartite position, still sees both the irrational and rational parts of the soul as having a share in reason: the rational by issuing commands, the irrational by obeying them (*Eth. eud.* 2.1.15–16, 1219b25–35; cf. *Eth. nic.* 1.13, 1102a25–30).

[10] Long and Sedley, *HP1*, 320. Cf. Lucretius who sees the mind as governing, but via the emotions displays itself to be in the chest (*Lucr.* 3.136–44 = *HP1*4B). (Where the ancient source has been accessed via its citation in Long and Sedley's *The Hellenistic Philosophers* it will be indicated by '=' followed by HP, the section number and passage letter e.g. = *HP1*4B). See also S. Everson, 'Epicurean Psychology', in *The Cambridge History of Hellenistic Philosophy*, ed. Keimpe Algra et al. (Cambridge: Cambridge University Press, 2005), 542–59, at 544.

rational. However, though seen as a unified whole, the soul has parts: sight, smell, hearing, taste, touch, seed, and utterance. The parts of the soul are not distinct and divisible as in Platonic theory but stretch out from the soul's commanding-faculty (τὸ ἡγεμονικόν), which is the command centre, equivalent to our conception of mind (Aetius 4.21.1–4[11]= SVF 2.836).[12] The Stoics also delineate the soul's powers: 'nutrition, growth, locomotion, sensation, impulse to action' (Calcidius[13] 220 = SVF 2.879).[14] Whereas some philosophers, like Aristotle, separate the intellect (νόος) and contemplative faculty (θεωρητικός) from other non-intellective abilities (*De an.* 2.2, 413b20–5; cf. 429a25–b5), the Stoics, because they have a unified soul, allow impulse to action along with impression, cognitive assent, and reason to be the commanding-faculty's capabilities (Stobaeus, *Ecl.* = SVF 2.826).[15] The question remains, where do the emotions fit into the soul's capacities? For Aristotle, the affections (πάθη) are one of the three things that take place within the soul, the other two being capabilities (δυνάμεις) and character (ἕξεις) (*Eth. nic.* 2.5, 1105b19–21; cf. *Eth. eud.* 2.2.4–5).[16] Yet, in Stoic theory the emotions (either passions or good emotions) are not a separate capacity of the soul, but occur through its other cognitive capabilities: impression, impulse, assent, and reason. It is through these capabilities that the

---

[11] Aetius was a 'Greek doxographer' who lived around 100 CE. The numbering of his work follows Long and Sedley in citing the chapter and sections of H. Diels' *Doxographi Graeci* (Berlin: 1879); see Long and Sedley, *HP1*, 492.

[12] Graver, *Stoicism*, 21–2; T. Brennan, 'The Old Stoic Theory of Emotions', in *The Emotions in Hellenistic Philosophy*, ed. Juha Sihvola and Troels Engberg-Pedersen (Dordrecht: Kluwer Academic, 1998), 21–70, at 23. Having said this, some have argued that within Stoicism there is disagreement: Chrysippus, who is taken to hold the orthodox view, sees the soul as a unified whole; Posidonius, according to Galen, returned to a Platonic tripartite view; and Panaetius was closer to an Aristotelian bipartite understanding; Long and Sedley, *HP1*, 321. Aristotle also questions the ability to separate parts of the soul, and likewise places faculties of the soul in a hierarchy (see *De an.* 2.2–3). Like the Stoics, Epicurus considers the soul responsible for sensation, but only as far as it is combined with the body (*Ep. Hdt.* 63–7 = *HP14A*).

[13] Calcidius was a 'Christian translator and commentator', fourth century CE; Long and Sedley, *HP1*, 493.

[14] In *Eudemian Ethics*, Aristotle also distinguishes the soul's different capacities (δυνάμεις) (*Eth. eud.* 2.1.15–16, 1219b25–35; cf. *De an.* 2.2–4).

[15] Long and Sedley, *HP1*, 321. For Aristotle, intellect is defined as the action of the soul that 'thinks and supposes' (*De an.* 3.4, 429a20, trans. Lawson-Tancred). Plato divides the functions of the soul into their parts: by the appetite we desire, will, and wish, with the rational we learn and calculate, and with the spirited we get angry. Each part also has its own particular pleasure: money, learning, and honour respectively (*Resp.* 4.436a–441c; 9.580e–581b).

[16] δυνάμεις and ἕξεις are defined in relation to the affections; cf. Plato (*Tim.* 42a–b) who sees 'love [ἔρως], mingled with pleasure and pain' as humanity's second capacity, followed by fear and spiritedness (φόβος and θυμός).

commanding-faculty passes judgement on information provided by the senses (Calcidius 220 = SVF 2.879). Consequently, as we will see, the Stoic view of the emotions is essentially cognitive, and emotions become a type of interpretive judgement. In preparation for later discussion, it is also necessary to note that for Stoicism, 'the mind [psyche] is necessarily a material thing, and that mental states and events are also physical facts or changes in the world'.[17] The soul is πνεῦμα, a 'highly energized gaseous material' that possesses 'remarkable properties which enable it to endow bodies with all the capacities needed for life, perception, and voluntary movement'.[18] This πνεῦμα consists of heat and air, which are hot and cold respectively and also cause opposite movements outwards and inwards. The dynamic between the two produces the soul's tension.[19] As a physical material, the soul's breath is capable of movement throughout the body, and it can be described as stretching towards or contracting from external objects. Further, the qualities of an individual, including moral qualities, can be explained by differences in the physical tension and structure of the soul.[20] Thus, the movement of the soul involved in emotion is considered to be a physical movement and the person is thought to be self-consciously aware of this alteration.[21] However, because the Stoics take a highly cognitive view of the emotions they are less concerned with outward physical aspects of emotions. Stoicism does note that the passions have bodily manifestations but their analysis of the emotions from their constitution to their therapy remains centred on the mental.[22]

Cognition and Emotion

We can now turn to the Stoic understanding of emotions, starting with the passions. It is necessary for our wider argument to establish that Stoicism took a cognitive view of the emotions.

---

[17] Graver, *Stoicism*, 18.
[18] Graver, *Stoicism*, 19.
[19] Graver, *Stoicism*, 19–20.
[20] Graver, *Stoicism*, 64–5; Long and Sedley, *HP1*, 320.
[21] Graver, *Stoicism*, 23, 28.
[22] Not all Greco-Roman philosophers ignored the physical aspects of emotions. Plato is particularly keen to associate the emotional disturbances with the irrational, mortal, physical parts of a human (see *Tim.* 69d). The Epicureans took a physiological view of the soul, with soul and body being interdependent. They locate both thought and emotion in the mind, but because the body and soul are interdependent, any sensations of the soul, including the affections, cannot occur without the body (*Ep. Hdt.* 63–7 = *HP14*A; *Lucr.* 3.136–76 = *HP14*B). Hence, the Epicurean descriptions

Definition of a Passion

Stoicism has four primary passions: fear (φόβος), desire (ἐπιθυμία), mental pain/distress (λύπη) and mental pleasure (ἡδονή) (Stobaeus, *Ecl.* = SVF 3.378).[23] Other emotions are categorised under these. As Stobaeus details:

> Ὑπὸ μὲν οὖν τὴν ἐπιθυμίαν ὑπάγεται τὰ τοιαῦτα· ὀργὴ καὶ τὰ εἴδη αὐτῆς, ... ἔρωτες σφοδροὶ καὶ πόθοι καὶ ἵμεροι καὶ φιληδονίαι καὶ φιλοπλουτίαι καὶ φιλοδοξίαι καὶ τὰ ὅμοια· ὑπὸ δὲ τὴν ἡδονὴν ἐπιχαιρεκακίαι καὶ ἀσμενισμοὶ καὶ γοητεῖαι καὶ τὰ ὅμοια· ὑπὸ δὲ τὸν φόβον ὄκνοι καὶ ἀγωνίαι καὶ ἔκπληξις καὶ αἰσχύναι καὶ θόρυβοι καὶ δεισιδαιμονίαι καὶ δέος καὶ δείματα· ὑπὸ δὲ τὴν λύπην φθόνος, ζῆλος, ζηλοτυπία, ἔλεος, πένθος, ἄχθος, ἄχος, ἀνία, ὀδύνη, ἄση.

The following are classified under appetite [desire]: anger and its species ... intense sexual desires, cravings and yearnings, love of pleasures and riches and honours, and the like. Under pleasure: rejoicing at another's misfortunes, self-gratification, trickery, and the like. Under fear: hesitancy, anguish, astonishment, shame, confusion, superstition, dread, and terror. Under distress: malice, envy, jealousy, pity, grief, worry, sorrow, annoyance, mental pain, vexation. (*Ecl.* = SVF 3.394)[24]

As Long and Sedley note, this shows that the term πάθος for the Stoic includes both the agitating emotions like sexual desire, as we might expect, but also states of mind like hesitancy.[25] Some of these

of the emotions are predominantly physical (*Lucr.* 3.262–322 = *HP*14D); Long and Sedley, *HP1*, 70–1; Everson, 'Epicurean Psychology', 553. For a fuller discussion on the Epicurean view of the soul see Everson, 'Epicurean Psychology', 543–6. Aristotle takes an intermediate view. He recognises that the affections contain some cognitive elements but notes that they cannot occur without the body and that by them the body is affected in some way. He describes the affections as reason in matter (δῆλον ὅτι τὰ πάθη λόγοι ἔνυλοί εἰσιν). They contain both a dialogical element ('because of one thing for the sake of another') and natural physical symptoms (*De an.* 1.1, 403a1–30, trans. Lawson-Tancred).

[23] Sandbach, *The Stoics*, 60–1. Plato had previously listed pleasure and pain as the first παθήματα, after this he also includes fear (φόβος), boldness (θάρρος), anger (θυμός), and expectation (ἐλπίς) (*Tim.* 69d).

[24] This is a fuller list than had previously been given in Aristotle's *Nicomachean Ethics* 2.5, 1105b21–3: λέγω δὲ πάθη μὲν ἐπιθυμίαν ὀργὴν φόβον θάρσος φθόνον χαρὰν φιλίαν μῖσος πόθον ζῆλον ἔλεον, ὅλως οἷς ἕπεται ἡδονὴ ἢ λύπη· (By the emotions, I mean desire, anger, fear, confidence, envy, joy, friendship, hatred, longing, jealousy, pity; and generally those states of consciousness which are accompanied by pleasure or pain [Rackham, LCL]).

[25] Long and Sedley, *HP1*, 419–20.

groupings, particularly those under ἡδονή appear strange to the English vocabulary. However, this again demonstrates that emotions and our understanding of them are deeply cultural.

According to Stobaeus:

Πάθος δ᾽ εἶναί φασιν ὁρμὴν πλεονάζουσαν καὶ ἀπειθῆ τῷ αἱροῦντι λόγῳ ἢ κίνησιν ψυχῆς <ἄλογον> παρὰ φύσιν (εἶναι δὲ πάθη πάντα τοῦ ἡγεμονικοῦ τῆς ψυχῆς),

They [the Stoics] say that passion is impulse which is excessive and disobedient to the dictates of reason, or a movement of the soul which is irrational and contrary to nature; and that all passions belong to the soul's commanding-faculty. (Stobaeus, *Ecl.* = SVF 3.378)

We noted that the commanding-faculty refers to the mental centre of consciousness. Therefore, from the above definition we can determine that Stoicism views *all* passions as cognitive. Terms such as irrational (ἄλογος) may seem to argue against this. However, we need to understand what Stoicism itself understands by irrational, and we will discover that it does not mean non-cognitive. Yet, designating the passions as 'contrary to nature' and 'irrational' does reveal that the passions are viewed negatively by Stoicism. Consequently, the wise man, who is the ideal person with perfected rationality, would not be susceptible to the passions.[26]

The Stoic definition is highly nuanced and more complex than previous definitions like Aristotle's, which simply states that the affections (πάθη) are 'such things as anger [θυμός], fear [φόβος], shame [αἰδώς], desire [ἐπιθυμία], and generally those experiences that are in themselves usually accompanied by sensory pleasure [ἡδονή] or pain [λύπη]' (*Eth. eud.* 2.2.4, 1220b10–15 [Rackham, LCL]). Thus, the Stoic definition must be unpacked. To do this we will investigate three of the four capabilities of the soul: impression, impulse, and assent. Concurrently, their relationship to the fourth capability, reason, will be highlighted.

Impression and Impulse

A passion starts with an impression (φαντασία). According to Chrysippus:

---

[26] The term 'wise man' in its Hellenistic usage had become 'a technical term for the paradigm of ethical understanding *and* every other positive attribute of a specific philosophy'; Long, 'Socratic Legacy', 621.

φαντασία μὲν οὖν ἐστι πάθος ἐν τῇ ψυχῇ γιγνόμενον, ἐνδεικνύμενον
ἐν αὑτῷ τε καὶ τὸ πεποιηκός·

An impression is an affection occurring in the soul, which
reveals itself and its cause. (Aetius 4.12.2 = SVF 2.54)

Here πάθος refers to an alteration of the soul, rather than the negative
emotion which is designated a passion. Philo, following Stoic thought,
reveals how an impression occurs:

ἡ μὲν οὖν φαντασία συνίσταται κατὰ τὴν τοῦ ἐκτὸς πρόσοδον
τυποῦντος νοῦν δι᾽ αἰσθήσεως·

The impression is produced by the drawing nigh of the external
object, as it stamps the mind through sense-perception. (*Leg.*
1.11.30 [Colson and Whitaker, LCL])[27]

Thus, an external object is needed for an impression.[28] This external
object, via sensation, is able to imprint itself on the internal soul
and in doing so physically changes the soul (cf. Plutarch, *Comm.
not.* 1084f–1085a = SVF 2.847; Diogenes Laertius 7.49 = SVF 2.52;
Aetius 4.12.1–5 = SVF 2.54).[29] Further, through the impression, a
human should have a self-conscious awareness not only that she is
being affected but also about *how* she is being altered by the object.[30]
It is the form of the impression that supplies information about
the external object.[31] Even if the object comes to a person through
vision, it is the impression on the soul that allows us to really

---

[27] The mind (νοός/νοῦς), as discussed above, is equivalent to the commanding-
faculty of the soul.
[28] Graver has argued that the object can also be a state of affairs that is registered
by the mind [read soul]; Graver, *Stoicism*, 24, 26.
[29] Plato had previously spoken of sense perception occurring through the soul's
disturbance. This disturbance would happen when the body moves through the environment. As it does so, the environment strikes the soul through the senses (*Tim.* 43c).
Cf. Aristotle, *De an.* 2.2, 413b20. For the Epicureans, the fact that a soul could be
acted upon was evidence for the soul's materiality; Everson, 'Epicurean Psychology',
550; see Epicurus, *Ep. Hdt.* 63–7 = *HP14A*.
[30] Long and Sedley, *HP1*, 321. Aristotle had also recognised the need of an
external object for sense-perception, and that the awareness of perception came from
the animal being moved or affected, i.e. altered (*De an.* 2.5, 416b30–417a5, 417b20–
30). Epicureans thought that sensation was an 'affection that was common to the
mind and the body', that is, something that caused a change; Everson, 'Epicurean
Psychology', 546.
[31] Aristotle in his discussion on perception had previously raised the idea that in
the process of perception the external object has affected the perceiving faculty and
altered it to be like itself (*De an.* 2.5, 418a1–5); cf. Epicurus, *Ep. Hdt.* 46–53 = *HP15A*.

perceive the object (Aetius 4.12.1–5 = SVF 2.54; cf. Aristotle, *De an.* 1.1, 403a5).[32] Therefore, for the Stoic, impressions are vital for perceiving the world around us. In some Stoic writers, an impression can also arise through non-sensory thought such as contemplation of abstract things or other objects presented to the soul by reason. According to Aetius, an impression can be caused by anything that can activate the soul (Aetius 4.12.1–5 = SVF 2.54; cf. Aristotle, *De an.* 3.3, 427b15–20). For the Stoics, an impression is the first step for all subsequent thought (cf. Cicero, *Acad.* 2.21). It is only after the impression that a person can have an opinion about the state of affairs.[33] In fact, Diogenes Laertius, goes on to assert that rational impressions, which occur in rational animals, are thought processes (7.49–51 = SVF 2.52, 55, 61).

The form of the impression can be understood as propositional: what they reveal about the object behaves like a statement e.g. 'this is white' or 'this is large'. In such a way, impressions have intentional objects.[34] For the Epicureans, the impression is always true. It is when we add our own opinion that falsehood and error occur (*Ep. Hdt.* 46–53 = *HP15A*). However, for the Stoic, an impression 'is not a belief'. 'To have an impression is simply to entertain an idea, without any implication of commitment to it.'[35] Belief *in* the impression *of* something requires the positive acceptance of the impression.[36] Thus, impressions can be convincing or unconvincing due to the proposition they present versus experience, and can contain varying degrees of truth (see Sextus Empiricus, *Math.* 7.242–6 = SVF 2.65).[37] Aristotle too noted the distinction between impression and belief. According to Aristotle, belief requires a conviction of the content of

---

[32] An impression can then become a memory, and a number of like impressions become experience. This can occur without the design of the person or can be as a result of a person's particular action (Aetius 4.11.1–4 = SVF 2.83). The latter from design are conceptions (ἔννοια) and can become stored thoughts by which further impressions are interpreted (Plutarch, *Comm. not.* 1084f–1085a = SVF 2.847). This means that an expert can interpret impressions differently to the layman; Long and Sedley, *HP1*, 240.

[33] Graver, *Stoicism*, 24.

[34] Long and Sedley, *HP1*, 240; Graver, *Stoicism*, 24. Cf. Brennan, 'Old Stoic', 22–3, who argues that humans are considered 'rational' by Stoicism in virtue of the fact that the 'thoughts, perceptions, beliefs, preferences, memories, dreams', in fact 'all mental contents' of the mature human are propositional. For more on impressions and their propositional content see Brennan, *Stoic Life*, 52–8.

[35] Long and Sedley, *HP1*, 239.

[36] Long and Sedley, *HP1*, 239–40.

[37] True impressions for Stoicism can be of two types: 'kataleptic' or 'merely true'. Kataleptic means that its truth is guaranteed. For more see Brennan, 'Old Stoic', 26–7; cf. Aristotle, *De an.* 3.3, 428a–b who notes that φαντασία can be true or false.

belief, therefore, an act of reason beyond the impression (*De an.* 3.3, 428a15–25). According to Diogenes Laertius, in Stoic theory, the impression will arise first and then assent, cognition, and thinking will not occur without it (7.49 = SVF 2.52). The priority of the impression is both a temporal and a logical priority.[38] So, impression is primarily perception; it occurs within the soul; and it is a necessary first step for further cognitive activities.

Having outlined an impression, we can move to discuss 'impulse', which, according to the above definition, is central to understanding a passion. Philo explains that impression and impulse are related:

> Thus the mind and the object of sense are always practising a reciprocity of giving, the one lying ready for sense-perception as its material, the other, like a craftsman, moving sense-perception [αἴσθησις] in the direction of the external object, to produce an impulse [ὁρμή] towards it ... The impression [φαντασία] is produced by the drawing nigh of the external object, as it stamps the mind through sense-perception; while the active impulse ... comes about by way of the mind's power of self-extension, which it exercises through sense-perception, and so comes into touch with the object presented to it, and goes towards it, striving to reach and seize it. (*Leg.* 1.11.29–30 [Colson and Whitaker, LCL])

An impulse (ὁρμή) is possible because of the breath-like nature of the soul. For humans the 'psychic breath' 'makes animals capable of sensation and of moving in every way' (Galen, *Intr.* 14.726.7–11 = SVF 2.716). After the impression has occurred, the soul that has been affected seeks to reach out towards it. Though Philo does not state this, one can also be repelled from the object. What is moved towards is, strictly speaking, not the object but the action contained in the proposition the impression provides (cf. Stobaeus, *Ecl.* = SVF 3.169).[39] The impulse therefore becomes a movement of the soul described in physical terms of expansions and contractions.[40] Consequently, impulse is understood as the impetus for action.[41] In

---

[38] Long and Sedley, *HP1*, 240.

[39] Graver, *Stoicism*, 27; Brennan, *Stoic Life*, 87.

[40] Other terms used for the movement of the soul are elation and deflation. The Stoic 'impulse' is akin to what other philosophers term appetite or desire. Cf. Plato, *Resp.* 4.437b–c, 439d; for Plato, non-rational desires are the result of the παθήματα.

[41] Epicureans also see images as the producers of volition and then movement occurs through the spirit entwined with the body. These images, however, appear to be projected images of what one wants to do, such as envisioning walking, rather than impressions of external objects to which one responds; see *Lucr.* 4.877–91= *HP1*4E.

fact, 'every intentional action stems from an impulse'.[42] The Stoics were not the first to link the idea of the movements of the soul to physical movement. Aristotle sees movement as coming from φαντασία and ὄρεξις (desire). Furthermore, seeking/desiring (ὀρέγω, and pursuing διώκω) is contrasted with avoiding (φεύγω). It is in virtue of this desire or avoidance that the being moves itself (*De an.* 3.9, 432b15–30; cf. 3.10, 433a15).[43] However, for Plato, it is simply pleasure or pain themselves that cause someone to be lured towards or flee something (*Tim.* 69d).[44] From this we can see that desires or impulses set goals for action. The Stoics equated the purposeful nature of the movement with an opinion that the action is appropriate in a given situation. Thus, Brennan provides the following definition of impulse: 'An impulse is an assent to an impression of a certain kind, i.e. an impression that attributes a certain kind of value to the agent's own potential action.'[45] Or, more succinctly: 'Impulse is an assent to an evaluative impression.'[46] Therefore, as an impulse, an emotion is 'a motion of the psyche towards some predicate' and the belief that this motion is the right thing to do.[47]

Even though for the Stoic a passion is described as contrary to nature and irrational, certain impulses can be according to nature, and, as an activity of the commanding-faculty, can be rational.[48] These are natural impulses because they drive one toward what nature deems fitting and necessary, but, they occur within boundaries of 'appropriateness'.[49] Stobaeus tries to define the difference

---

[42] Brennan, *Stoic Life*, 86. Cf. Cicero, who differentiates two movements of the rational soul: thought (*cogitatio*) and impulse (*appetitus*). It is specifically impulse that stimulates action (*appetitus impellit ad agendum*), whereas thought is to investigate truth (*cogitatio in vero exquirendo*), therefore impulse should be obedient to reason (*Off.* 1.132).

[43] Aristotle, in describing the locomotion of the soul, talks about it being a push or pull from the central point of the soul. This seems like an alternative way of expressing the same ideas of tension, expansion, and contraction (*De an.* 3.10, 433b20–5).

[44] Cf. Aristotle, *De an.* 3.7, 431a5.

[45] Brennan, *Stoic Life*, 87.

[46] Brennan, *Stoic Life*, 87.

[47] Graver, *Stoicism*, 28.

[48] Long and Sedley, *HP1*, 420.

[49] Cf. Plato, *Resp.* 8.558d–559b. Similarly, Epicurus thought that some desires are natural, and, of those that are natural, only some are necessary either for happiness, for life, or to keep the body free from stress. According to Epicurus, nature has shown which are the necessary desires and which are not by differentiating those that are easy to attain from those that are not (cf. *Ep. Men.* 127–32 = *HP*21B; *Stob. Flor.* XVII.23 cited in M. Erler and M. Schofield, 'Epicurean Ethics', in *The Cambridge History of Hellenistic Philosophy*, ed. Keimpe Algra et al. (Cambridge: Cambridge University Press, 2005), 642–74, at 659).

between an impulse that occurs in non-rational animals and the impulse that occurs in rational humans. The rational impulse is specifically a 'movement of thought towards something in the sphere of action', whereas irrational impulse is desire (ὄρεξις) (*Ecl.* = SVF 3.169).[50] Desire means desire to act, and, because there is no rationality to hold this desire in check, it will inevitably result in action. This is what one sees in children and animals.[51] Despite the Stoics allowing for natural impulses, the impulses involved in passions are not of the natural or rational variety but excessive and out of control. Aristotle before the Stoics noted that natural drives and emotions can be wrongly taken to excess e.g. fearing what one should not in a way one should not (*Eth. nic.* 3.7, 1115b30–35; 3.11, 1118b15).[52] For the Stoic, in a rational adult, an impulse, whether excessive or natural, can only exist if a person gives assent to the impression (see Plutarch, *Stoic. rep.* 1057a = SVF 3.177).[53]

Assent

Assent (συγκατάθεσις) means agreeing with and committing to the validity of the content of an impression, *and* the ability not to do so.[54] Thus, assent 'mediates between impressions and impulses'.[55] This goes beyond Aristotle, who sees simply the pursuit or the avoidance as analogous to assent and denial (*De an.* 3.7, 431a5–15; cf. *Eth. nic.* 6.2, 1139a20). The ability to choose whether to assent to something reveals that, for the Stoic, humans have the capacity to analyse the legitimacy of the impression. One does not have to go along with impressions but can judge what is being reported, including any inference about the value of the object. According to Long and Sedley, this is a Stoic innovation which 'is of cardinal importance to their epistemology and ethics'.[56] This capacity is founded on the assumption that nature has provided the rational person with the faculty of judgement so that she can live in accordance with

[50] Long and Sedley, *HP1*, 317.

[51] Sandbach, *The Stoics*, 64.

[52] For Aristotle, this excess in one emotion also shows a deficiency in its opposite emotion.

[53] Sandbach, *The Stoics*, 60.

[54] As Graver points out, assent is also described physically in terms of the tension of the soul with the wise person's assent having a strong tension and those with less assured assents having weak tension. Weakness therefore indicates submitting to impressions that the person with perfect understanding would reject; Graver, *Stoicism*, 26. For more on strong and weak assent and their relationship to the truth of an impression see Brennan, 'Old Stoic', 26–9.

[55] Long and Sedley, *HP1*, 322.

[56] Long and Sedley, *HP1*, 322.

nature.[57] This mental process – impression on the soul; assent to the impression's proposition; psychic impulse to action – is why passions can be deemed as cognitive and as a product of the commanding-faculty (see Aetius 4.21.1–4 = SVF 2.836; cf. Stobaeus, *Ecl.* = SVF 2.826). Furthermore, the commanding-faculty is the reasoning faculty. So, we can understand that for Stoicism, the whole process of a passion is bound up with cognition and rationality. This allows the possibility that one does not need to have a passion, for, if no cognitive assent is given, there will be no impulse and consequently no passion. For the Stoic, this halting of the impulse via assent happens within the one entity that is the commanding-faculty. Other philosophers like Plato did agree that one could resist impulses (appetites) through reason. The difference is that, for Plato, there are two antagonistic powers working – the rational part can decide whether or not to follow the appetitive part (*Resp.* 4.439c–d) – whereas, for the Stoic, the process happens within the unified soul. It is worth noting, in order to understand the relationship between a passion and ethical behaviour, that, in Stoic theory, there appears an implicit assumption that assent to the impression will necessarily end in action: the judgement (assent) and decision to act are equated.[58]

It has previously been stated that impression, assent, and impulse constitute the process of a passion (and good emotion). However, according to Galen there was disagreement within Stoicism on what constituted the passion, was it the impulse, or the judgement and the impulse? According to Galen, Zeno considered the passions to be the 'irrational contractions, lowering abasements and pangs, the rising elations and relaxed diffusions' that follow on (ἐπιγίγνομαι) the judgement, but not the judgement itself (Posidonius fr. 34A, trans. Kidd). Conversely, Chrysippus thought that the passion is the judgement, including both the ὁρμή and the λόγος that tells a person to act.[59] Graver has argued

---

[57] The Epicureans regarded all impressions as true and thought that reason did not have the power to contradict impressions because reason itself 'is in its entirety the product of the senses' (*Lucr.* 4.469–521 = *HP*16A). This does not mean that the sensations themselves were rational; they were still classified as irrational.

[58] Brennan, 'Old Stoic', 28. For Aristotle, the judgement relates to value and therefore sets the ends. Deliberation questions how to obtain those ends and so is accompanied by reasoning and thought. After this comes decision, which is the choice of how to act (*Eth. nic.* 3.2, 1111b25–1112a15; 6.2, 1139a20; cf. *Eth. eud.* 2.10.1–11, 1225b20–1226a25). This means that an affection of the soul that drives one towards a goal could result in numerous actions even though the end might remain the same.

[59] Sandbach, *The Stoics*, 64; Long and Sedley, *HP1*, 422. Posidonius, says Galen, disagreed with both Zeno and Chrysippus and saw the passions as 'neither

that Galen is wrong in presenting Zeno and Chrysippus as having different views, as she explains:

> Both clearly hold that having an emotion involves both the psychophysical change and the judgement, and both describe the relation between the two in very much the same way. For Zeno, the change supervenes on the judgement and would not be an emotion if it did not supervene on a judgement of this sort (i.e. an irrational judgement). For Chrysippus, the change is reliably produced by the judgement, which would not be an emotion if it did not produce a movement of this sort ... In reformulating the definition, Chrysippus seeks to bring out more clearly what was already implied in Zeno's version: that it is the nature of the judgement that defines what sort of impulse has occurred.[60]

Cicero seems to uphold that a passion includes both a judgement and impulse (*Tusc.* 4.6.11–7.15).[61] Furthermore, if we look in detail at the definitions of particular passions, reported by Adronicus (first century BCE), we see that both the movement of the soul (the impulse) and the accompanying opinion (the judgement or reasoning) form part of the definition (cf. *Tusc.* 4.7.14–15). For example:

> ἡδονὴ δὲ ἄλογος ἔπαρσις· ἢ δόξα πρόσφατος ἀγαθοῦ παρουσίας, ἐφ' ᾧ οἴονται δεῖν ἐπαίρεσθαι.

> Pleasure is an irrational swelling, or a fresh opinion that something good is present, at which people think it right to be swollen. (Andronicus, [*Pass.*] 1 = SVF 3.391)

So, it appears that it is difficult when describing a passion to separate the judgement and the impulse.[62] It is not necessary for us to go into this further, only to note that in Stoicism an emotion clearly contains

---

judgements nor what supervened on judgements, but were caused by the spirited and desiring powers or faculties' (Posidonius fr. 34A, trans. Kidd). For Galen, this moves back to earlier Platonic doctrine. However, John M. Cooper has argued that Galen is incorrect and that Posidonius accepted the main premises of the Chrysippian view of emotions but sought to refine the relationship between the bodily feeling and the passion in order to bolster the orthodox view against common lines of attack. See J. M. Cooper, 'Posidonius on Emotions', in *The Emotions in Hellenistic Philosophy*, ed. Juha Sihvola and Troels Engberg-Pedersen (Dordrecht: Kluwer Academic, 1998), 71–111.

[60] Graver, *Stoicism*, 33.
[61] Graver, *Stoicism*, 29–30.
[62] Cf. Brennan, 'Old Stoic', 30.

a judgement about an object and as a consequence has an action-tendency. Thus, it is not anachronistic to use such ideas, which are also present in modern theory, to investigate emotions in 1 Peter.

We have been able to determine what an impulse is, and how it relates to impression and assent. What we have not yet uncovered is how, for Stoicism, a passion's impulse is contrary to nature and irrational.

Contrary to Nature and Irrational

Before exploring the irrationality of the passions, which appears to argue against their coherent cognitive content, we need to investigate the view that the passions were excessive impulses and contrary to nature. According to Chrysippus, a rational animal is naturally guided by reason. However, a rational animal can be caused to move towards and away from objects in an alternative manner, 'pushed to excess in disobedience to reason' (Galen, *PHP*, 4.2.10–18 = SVF 3.462). As noted above, impulses are natural and should encourage a person to go in search of what is appropriate to her natural constitution (Diogenes Laertius 7.85–6 = SVF 3.178). But the natural impulse should be what 'accords with reason and goes only so far as reason itself thinks right' (Galen, *PHP*, 4.2.10–18 = SVF 3.462; cf. Stobaeus, *Ecl.* = SVF 3.389; Diogenes Laertius 7.85–6 = SVF 3.178).[63] Aristotle likewise thought that desire should act 'in accordance with what reason prescribes', resulting in desire being in harmony with reason and leading to appropriateness (*Eth. nic.* 3.12, 1119b5–15, trans. Rowe).[64] In describing an excessive impulse Chrysippus uses a now well-known example of a person's action of walking in contrast to running. In walking, one is moved by impulse but is in complete control and can stop or change direction whenever one wants. However, when a person runs, the movement exceeds the impulse and she can no longer immediately stop or change direction when she wills. The inability of the person to be in control of her action when running parallels the person in a passionate state who is carried away and is no longer following reason.[65] The passion, which is an excessive impulse that is going beyond the limits of reason, is therefore 'irrational'.[66]

---

[63] Long and Sedley, *HP1*, 420.

[64] In Aristotelian thought, this leads to proposing the 'mean' as the best state, i.e. not in excess, nor in deficiency (*Eth. eud.* 2.3.2–4, 1220b25–1221a10).

[65] Aristotle too notes that desire can be so strong and vigorous that it removes the ability to think rationally (*Eth. nic.* 3.12, 1119b5–10).

[66] Cf. Stobaeus, *Ecl.* = SVF 3.389; Stobaeus' uses a parallel description of a person on a disobedient horse, who, despite thinking that a course of action is incorrect,

So, does this description of passions as 'irrational' mean that the Stoics are in contradiction with themselves? Are the passions without reason and therefore not a cognitive judgement after all? For Chrysippus, the passions are 'irrational' because they do not carry *correct* reasoning, rather than because they are devoid of any cognitive reasoning element.[67] Because the passions are not based on true reasoning, they distort a person's ability to judge correctly.[68] This judgement is an assessment of value, i.e. whether it is right to pursue something or avoid something, or whether one should be elated or deflated. The person who is in a passionate state wrongly judges what is good and bad, and therefore what should be pursued or avoided. This faulty judgement takes reason to excess because it causes one to perceive things to be of greater worth than reason would determine them to be, and therefore to pursue or avoid them excessively.[69]

Appearances, Indifferents, and Opinion

As discussed above, the judgement involved in a passion relates to what is seen as valuable, in other words, what is evaluated as good (ἀγαθός) and bad (κακός).[70] Epictetus reveals how the soul's movement is affected by the good and the bad:

οὕτως πρὸς μὲν τὸ ἀγαθὸν ὀρεκτικῶς κινεῖσθαι, πρὸς δὲ τὸ κακὸν ἐκκλιτικῶς, πρὸς δὲ τὸ μήτε κακὸν μήτ' ἀγαθὸν οὐδετέρως.

[I]t is its [the soul's] nature to be moved with desire toward the good, with aversion toward the evil, and feel neutral toward what is neither evil nor good. (*Diatr.* 3.3.2–3 [Oldfather, LCL])

This is natural, but the problem occurs if one has a warped perception of what is good and bad. Other philosophers had previously noted how the affections could distort and pervert reason (Aristotle, *Eth. eud.* 8.1.5, 1246b15), but this was a symptom of the

---

is carried away by the passion to do something contrary to her reason; Long and Sedley, *HP1*, 420. Aristotle likewise had noted that someone could go to excess in the affections, but, he also thought people could be deficient in them too by not showing the appropriate strength of feeling in a given situation (*Eth. eud.* 2.3.5, 1221a10–15).
67 Cf. Graver, *Stoicism*, 37–8.
68 Sandbach, *The Stoics*, 62, 65.
69 Long and Sedley, *HP1*, 420–1.
70 The Stoic viewpoint sits in a vast ancient philosophical discussion about what the good is; there is not space to discuss this here.

power struggle between appetite and reason.[71] The Stoic viewpoint, instead, makes the person's entire faculty of judgement corrupted (cf. Plutarch, *Virt. mor.* 446f–447a = SVF 3.459). A warped capacity to judge will result in faulty assent, wrong impulses, and ultimately wrong actions. This is the situation of the inferior man, who cannot evaluate correctly.[72] The Stoics introduce the term 'opinion' (δόξα) to label judgements arising from faulty perception.[73] As Plutarch, in discussing the Stoics, summarises: 'desire and anger and fear and all such things are but perverse opinions and judgements [δόξας εἶναι καὶ κρίσεις πονηράς]' (*Virt. mor.* 447a [Helmbold, LCL]). Such opinions are therefore described as weak and based on misguided assent (Sextus Empiricus, *Math* 7.151–7 = HP41C).[74] For example, fear contains the belief that something bad is about to happen such as death or pain and therefore results in the opinion that it is right to avoid it. Yet, for the Stoic, death and pain are really indifferents (not morally good or bad). Therefore, any belief that they can bring real harm is false; subsequently, so is the opinion concerning appropriate action.[75] Thus, the problem with the passions is that they are mistaken opinions about what is truly valuable, and result in excessive behaviour. Therefore, 'as false beliefs ... they are all imperfections of our reason, and so directly deleterious to our end as the Stoics conceive it'.[76] Contrastingly, the wise man would not have 'opinions' because he would not give assent to incognitive impressions (impression that are not certainly true) and therefore he is incapable of

---

[71] Because Plato locates the passions in the body, he sees all information that is provided by the body, including the senses, as not productive of true knowledge. Only reason can provide the soul with true knowledge. For Plato, bodily feelings cause the person to believe what their sensations are telling them, this only appears to be truth but it is not. Plato comments that the diseased soul, i.e. the soul affected by desires and passions, is full of 'wants, desires, fears, all sorts of illusions' (*Phaed.* 65b–c, 66b–c, 79c–d, 82d–83c, trans. Grube).

[72] The Cynics before the Stoics had highlighted how false judgements of value would hinder one from attaining happiness and that these false judgements would produce 'emotional disturbances and weakness of character'; Long, 'Socratic Legacy', 624.

[73] As noted above, the Epicureans thought that our judgement of impressions could result in false opinions. Epicurus also talks of opinions as mistaken beliefs about how to achieve absence of pain and calmness, and that through these mistaken opinions tumultuous confusion takes hold of our souls; see *Ep. Men.* 132 cited in Erler and Schofield, 'Epicurean Ethics', 651–2.

[74] Opinion becomes a technical term relating to wrong perception. An inferior man will opine, a wise man will not (cf. Cicero, *Acad.* 2.145); Long and Sedley, *HP1*, 250, 420–1.

[75] Sandbach, *The Stoics*, 61.

[76] Brennan, 'Old Stoic', 31.

'being deceived and of erring'. He would, subsequently, 'live wor-
thily and do everything well' (Anonymous Stoic Treatise = SVF
2.131; cf. Stobaeus, *Ecl.* = SVF 3.548).[77]

Because a person is incapable of making a correct judgement, the
Stoics define the passions in terms of 'appearances': something that
seems to be so, but in reality is not. As Stobaeus comments regarding
Stoic thought:

> Ἐπιθυμίαν μὲν οὖν καὶ φόβον προηγεῖσθαι, τὴν μὲν πρὸς τὸ
> φαινόμενον ἀγαθόν, τὸν δὲ πρὸς τὸ φαινόμενον κακόν.

Appetite and fear come first, the former in relation to what
appears good, and the latter in relation to what *appears* bad.
(*Ecl.* = SVF 3.378, emphasis added)

However, the wise man knows that:

> Ἀγαθὰ μὲν οὖν τάς τ' ἀρετάς, φρόνησιν, δικαιοσύνην, ἀνδρείαν,
> σωφροσύνην καὶ τὰ λοιπά· κακὰ δὲ τὰ ἐναντία, ἀφροσύνην,
> ἀδικίαν καὶ τὰ λοιπά. οὐδέτερα δὲ ὅσα μήτ' ὠφελεῖ μήτε
> βλάπτει, οἷον ζωή, ὑγίεια, ἡδονή, κάλλος, ἰσχύς, πλοῦτος,
> εὐδοξία, εὐγένεια· καὶ τὰ τούτοις ἐναντία ... μὴ γὰρ εἶναι ταῦτ'
> ἀγαθά, ἀλλ' ἀδιάφορα κατ' εἶδος προηγμένα.

Goods comprise the virtues of prudence, justice, courage,
temperance, and the rest; while the opposites of these are
evils, namely folly, injustice, and the rest. Neutral (neither good nor evil, that is) are all those things which neither benefit nor harm a man: such as life, health, pleasure,
beauty, strength, wealth, fair fame and noble birth, and
their opposites ... such things [life, health, pleasure] ... are
not in themselves goods, but are morally indifferent, though
falling under the species or subdivision 'things preferred'.
(Diogenes Laertius 7.102 [Hicks, LCL])[78]

[77] The Stoics also spoke of the wise man suspending judgement if the impression
was not clear enough to be judged correctly, therefore again avoiding false opinion
(Plutarch, *Stoic. rep.* 1056e–f = SVF 2.993); Long and Sedley, *HP1*, 258. Aristotle
too allows that there can be 'apparent' goods, which are perceived as good by an individual, yet are not truly good and so they result in the person being deceived. But the
'good person discriminates correctly in every set of circumstances, and in every set of
circumstances what is true is apparent to him' (*Eth. nic.* 3.4, 1113a30, trans. Rowe).

[78] Cleanthes gives a slightly different listing of the good, which includes being
fearless (ἄφοβος) and 'un-distressed' (ἄλυπος) (SVF 1.557).

Thus, only the virtues are really good, and these virtues are integral to the person.[79] Even what might normally be considered good (e.g. health) are in fact indifferents (ἀδιάφορα).[80] Hence, the Stoics have a normative schema of what should and should not be valued.[81] The Epicureans also thought that correct perspective is fundamental, noting that to achieve happiness required the removal of illusions about the divine and a correct understanding of death which would subsequently eliminate misguided anxieties and fears.[82] However, the Stoic perception of the good sits in opposition to the Epicurean viewpoint, which saw pleasure as the ultimate good and pain as the ultimate evil (Cicero, *Fin.* 1.29–32).[83] For the Stoic, pleasure and pain are merely indifferents.[84] Consequently, the passions are problematic because they cause the person to seek wrongly what *appears* to be good and avoid what *appears* to be bad, whereas these objects are really indifferents.[85] However, to pursue virtue is always correct, as is to be repelled by vice. In addition to this, as Graver helpfully delineates, the opinions of value evident in emotions are not formed in the moment, but are based on already held beliefs about value. It is on account of this framework of belief that appropriateness to act is judged (cf. Cicero, *Tusc.* 3.11.24–5, 3.26.62).[86] Therefore, we can understand that for Stoicism, passions are not a momentary issue, but arise because of a problem with a person's entire belief system.

[79] The four listed virtues are similar to Plato's four virtues of wisdom, courage, moderation, and justice (*Resp.* 4.427e) and are likewise endorsed by Aristotle as excellences, though Aristotle includes more than the Platonic four (see *Eth. nic.* 3.6–12, 4.5, 5.1). Epicurus linked the virtues, particularly prudence and justice, to living pleasurably (*Ep. Men.* 132 = *HP*21B). For discussion on how the Epicurean views of virtue relate to ἀταραξία see Erler and Schofield, 'Epicurean Ethics', 666–9.

[80] Cf. Aristotle, *Eth. nic.* 1.4, 1095a15–20 and 7.13, 1153b1 for comments on what ordinary people normally pursue and avoid.

[81] Graver, *Stoicism*, 37.

[82] Erler and Schofield, 'Epicurean Ethics', 645–6

[83] Erler and Schofield, 'Epicurean Ethics', 647–8

[84] Having said this, pain here is πόνος, which refers to physical pain especially. Cf. Aristotle who seems to represent the common view that one's desire is always for the pleasant and the painful is contrary to desire (*Eth. eud.* 2.7.4–5, 1223a25–35; cf. 7.2.2, 1235b20).

[85] Indifferent can be used in two ways: first, to mean things that lead neither to happiness nor unhappiness; second, to refer to things that activate neither impulse nor repulsion (Diogenes Laertius 7.104). Even though things such as health and wealth can be indifferent, there are some that are according to nature, and therefore some that have value and should be selected as 'preferred', e.g. reason in certain circumstances would select health over disease. A good would not be 'preferred' as it inherently possesses the greatest value (see Stobaeus, *Ecl.* 2.79.18–80.13 and 82.20–1 = HP58C; cf. SVF 3.124, 128).

[86] Graver, *Stoicism*, 39–43.

Before moving on it is worth noting one last thing regarding the attribution of value present in emotions. Stobaeus (cited above), goes on to say:

Ἐπιγίγνεσθαι δὲ τούτοις ἡδονὴν καὶ λύπην, ἡδονὴν μὲν ὅταν τυγχάνωμεν ὧν ἐπεθυμοῦμεν ἢ ἐκφύγωμεν ἃ ἐφοβούμεθα· λύπην δέ, ὅταν ἀποτυγχάνωμεν ὧν ἐπεθυμοῦμεν ἢ περιπέσωμεν οἷς ἐφοβούμεθα.

Pleasure and distress result from these [appetite and fear]: pleasure, whenever we get the objects of our appetite or avoid the objects of our fear; distress, whenever we fail to get the objects of our appetite or experience the objects of our fear. (*Ecl.* = SVF 3.378)

From this we can see a clear link between the perception of the good and bad, and the attainment or non-attainment of a goal. One's perception of the good and the bad places a value on the object and determines whether it is something to be attained or avoided. Put differently, a goal based on these values is established. The person, because of her perception, is then driven to act in line with that goal, either toward or away from the object, and, consequently, experiences pleasure or distress at the realisation/non-realisation of the goal.[87] In general, this idea of the establishment of value is important because it means that someone may choose to act against what might be seen as the normal state of affairs because of working from a different value system e.g. a person is willing to suffer pain for a particular virtuous end (Aristotle, *Eth. nic.* 3.9, 1117b1; cf. Epicurus, *Ep. Men.* 129–30 = *HP*21B).

Now we have a better understanding of impression, assent, impulse, and their relationship to evaluation of the good and bad, we will be in a position to appreciate the Stoic nuances that are present in their definition of emotions generally (passions and εὐπαθεῖαι) and individually, which we will need in the coming exegetical chapters.

---

[87] Epicurus recognised this, noting that, if pleasure was the ultimate good and goal, then pleasure would determine choice and avoidance, and, in complete contrast to the Stoics, feelings (πάθος) become the way to judge the good (*Ep. Men.* 128–9). Sensation and feeling are made the primary criterion of truth, meaning that an understanding of good and evil is readily accessible to all; *Ep. Men.* 128–9 cited in Erler and Schofield, 'Epicurean Ethics', 649–50; cf. Cicero, *Fin.* 1.29–32, 37–9. It must be noted that λύπη and ἡδονή for Stoicism refers to mental pain and pleasure rather than a bodily sensation; see Sandbach, *The Stoics*, 62–3; Long and Sedley, *HP1*, 421; cf. Diogenes Laertius 7.85–6; Aristotle, *Eth. nic.* 6.1, 1120a25–30.

The above discussion has also been able to demonstrate that a number of elements present in modern theory can also be found among the ancients. First, emotions were thought to be cognitive and object-directed in that they contain a propositional judgement about the object. The judgement is an evaluative judgement based on one's understanding of good and bad. Acceptance of (assent to) this proposition (judgement) leads to an impulse, which is a drive towards action (i.e. an action-tendency), generally to pursue or avoid something. Further, we have seen that the ancients recognised that the evaluations of emotions are based on beliefs, and therefore that emotional life is not deterministically universal but can be changed by what one holds to be true.

The εὐπαθεῖαι

Before discussing how the Stoic view of the passions influences Stoic ethics, we must first complete the picture. It would be wrong to say that Stoicism saw all emotions as problematic. They did allow certain emotions, seeing them as 'natural and proper', e.g. the love of a parent for her child. Further, particular dispositions were appropriate in given relational contexts. For example, the 'appropriate disposition to oneself is benevolence [εὐνοητικός]' and to one's kindred and children is affection (στερτικός, i.e. disposed towards love) (Hierocles 9.3–10 = HP57B).[88] These are proper dispositions because they are innate and natural, being exhibited in the social behaviour of animals (Plutarch, *Stoic. rep.* 1038b = SVF 3.179, 2.724). For a Stoic such as Marcus Aurelius, it is possible to be 'entirely passionless yet full of affection'.[89] Consequently, in conjunction with the passions, the Stoics developed the idea of the εὐπαθεῖαι, the good emotions, which were stable and well-reasoned. The Roman Stoics termed the εὐπαθεῖαι *constantiae* on account of their stability.[90] There were three εὐπαθεῖαι: βούλησις (volition/wish/correct appetite), εὐλάβεια (caution/watchfulness/correct avoidance), and χαρά (joy/correct elation). These εὐπαθεῖαι were the good counterparts of the passions: βούλησις instead of ἐπιθυμία, χαρά for ἡδονή, and εὐλάβεια rather than φόβος. There was no equivalent to λύπη because this

---

[88] Hierocles was a Stoic philosopher, who flourished approximately 100–120 CE; Long and Sedley, *HP1*, 496.
[89] Sandbach, *The Stoics*, 59–60.
[90] Graver has argued that stability in εὐπαθεῖαι indicates lack of internal inconsistency in the state of mind underpinning the emotion, not absence of depth of feeling; Graver, *Stoicism*, 51.

would simply be the natural healthy state.[91] If it were to occur it would indicate the presence of evil, which for the wise man is only vice, and because the perfect wise man does not have internal vice he cannot be distressed.[92] The εὐπαθεῖαι were acceptable because they arose from assent to correct reasoning. For example, according to Diogenes Laertius:

> καὶ τὴν μὲν χαρὰν ἐναντίαν [φασὶν] εἶναι τῇ ἡδονῇ, οὖσαν εὔλογον ἔπαρσιν·
>
> Joy, the counterpart of pleasure, is rational [well-reasoned] elation [swelling]. (7.116 [Hicks, LCL])

We can see in this definition that some of the same elements detailed in the passions are present, such as a form of belief, indicated by the term εὔλογος (well-reasoned) and also an impulse, here seen as swelling. Furthermore, εὔλογος means that the evaluation of a εὐπάθεια is true and the objects are necessarily appropriate (cf. Seneca, *Ep.* 59.2–4).[93] Yet, this puts the εὐπαθεῖαι beyond the grasp of most people because only the wise man can consistently reason correctly. Like the passions, other emotions fall under these primary categories, as Diogenes Laertius details:

> καθάπερ οὖν ὑπὸ τὰ πρῶτα πάθη πίπτει τινά, τὸν αὐτὸν τρόπον καὶ ὑπὸ τὰς πρώτας εὐπαθείας· καὶ ὑπὸ μὲν τὴν βούλησιν εὔνοιαν, εὐμένειαν, ἀσπασμόν, ἀγάπησιν· ὑπὸ δὲ τὴν εὐλάβειαν αἰδῶ, ἀγνείαν· ὑπὸ δὲ τὴν χαρὰν τέρψιν, εὐφροσύνην, εὐθυμίαν.
>
> And accordingly, as under the primary passions are classed certain others subordinate to them, so too is it with the … good emotional states. Thus under wishing they bring well-wishing [goodwill] … friendliness, respect, affection; under caution, reverence and modesty; under joy, delight, mirth, cheerfulness. (7.116 [Hicks, LCL])

Therefore, we can see that the Stoics had a definite systemisation of the emotions, labelling some as problematic and others as good.

---

[91] This is different to the Epicurean viewpoint that one's ability to acknowledge the complete absence of pain was in fact to experience the greatest pleasure (see Cicero, *Fin.* 1.29–32, 37–9). Further, for the Stoic, a wise man would never experience mental pain because he would willingly accept all that happened to him, knowing that it was divinely ordained; Sandbach, *The Stoics*, 67.

[92] Graver, *Stoicism*, 54–5.

[93] Graver, *Stoicism*, 51–2.

As Graver highlights, the εὐπαθεῖαι become 'normative affect'.[94] We might say that, within the school, they have an established emotional regime. This regime is rooted in their whole philosophical system of thought, but also, as we might expect, given that emotions drive actions, feeds into their ethics.

Emotions and Stoic Ethics

The passions are important for Stoic ethics because a passion 'is not an idle and innocuous false belief, but a false belief taking effect in the agent's behavior' and this false belief 'is the only and sole cause of wrong action'.[95] It is this attribution of agency to the person that is central.

Assent and Agency

The passions result in action through assent and impulse. Therefore, because the human has the capacity to assent or disagree with the impression, the human is given complete agency over her emotions and is consequently responsible for her own actions (cf. Seneca, *Ira* 2.3.1–2.4 = HP65X; Plutarch, *Stoic. rep.* 1057a = SVF 3.177).[96] This differentiates an adult from an animal and a child who have no cognitive ability to assent but inevitably follow the impulse stimulated by the impression.[97] Having said this, the human is not born fully rational; one's rationality grows over time.[98] Being able to master the self through assent sits in contrast to the inability to have control over external circumstances. For the Stoic, one cannot control what happens to you, i.e. what nature dictates, but one can control the inner attitude toward the circumstances.[99]

The Stoic philosophers, like others, had to wrestle over questions about which movements and actions are voluntary, and which are

---

[94] Graver, *Stoicism*, 51.

[95] Brennan, 'Old Stoic', 32.

[96] The ultimate display of the person's control over action is the Stoic support for the wise man's appropriate suicide; see Cicero, *Fin.* 3.60; Long and Sedley, *HP1*, 428–9.

[97] Sandbach, *The Stoics*, 60; cf. Aristotle, *Eth. nic.* 3.2, 1111b5–25; *Eth. eud.* 2.7.4–8.3, 1223a25–1224a10.

[98] Long and Sedley, *HP1*, 321; Epicureans also thought that the person's ability to judge increased as they grew older. However, because this ability was linked to the body it also had the ability to degenerate in old age (*Lucr.* 3.417–62 = *HP14F*).

[99] The Epicureans took a similar view that we should only concern ourselves with what was in our power, which is our inner attitude; Erler and Schofield, 'Epicurean Ethics', 644.

involuntary. Are the passions ever instinctual, automatic reactions? For the Stoic, the answer is no. Every thought and movement should be under the power of the person's rational commanding-faculty (τὸ ἡγεμονικόν). Therefore, the person remains, at least theoretically, capable of having complete agency at all times. Consequently, all movements and actions are voluntary, including the passionate impulses.[100] Thus, despite the person once in a passionate state being out of control, it *is* in her power whether she has a passion in the first place due to the necessity of assent.[101] Subsequently, we must go one step backwards. As Graver states, 'the real cause or reason for the assent is to be found in the agent's own mental character, where by "mental character" is meant simply the structure and content of one's own belief set'. Those with a weak tension, i.e. incoherent internal belief, will easily assent to false impressions and therefore experience the passions.[102] Furthermore, because the passions result in actions and have bodily manifestations, from viewing one's actions, the quality of a person's soul can be seen.[103] For example, to display fear that results in cowardice shows that the person has a weak soul that has been carried along by the passion to the point of disobedience to reason, leading to vice. It is the commanding-faculty that is responsible for the judgement, assent, and ultimately actions. Thus, a soul (the whole person) can be categorised as noble/ good (καλός) or shameful (αἰσχρός) depending on the quality of her ἡγεμονικόν (Galen, *PHP* 5.2.49 = SVF 2.841). Aristotle agrees that 'we judge a man's character from his actions' (*Eth. eud.* 2.1.11, 1219b10 [Rackham, LCL]). However, Aristotle also adds the further dimension that someone's actions reveal what they see as the right goal. So, when we judge someone's character from an action, we are really judging the rationale behind their action and whether this is

[100] Aristotle had various categories of agency (see *Eth. nic.* 3.1, 1110b15–30; 1111a20–1111b1). Similar to the Stoics, voluntary action is based on thought (*Eth. eud.* 2.8.2, 1224a5). Therefore, for Aristotle it is only those actions that are under a person's control, the one's 'decided-for', that we praise or blame or can categorise as virtue and vice (*Eth. eud.* 2.6.10, 1223a10). See Aristotle, *Nichomachean Ethics. Translation (with Historical Introduction) by Christopher Rowe, Philosophical Introduction and Commentary by Sarah Broadie* (Oxford: Oxford University Press, 2002), 43.
[101] Graver, *Stoicism*, 62–3.
[102] Graver, *Stoicism*, 63–5; cf. Seneca, *Ep.* 102.8–10; Epictetus, *Diatr.* 3.3.2–4 = HP60F.
[103] Cf. Aristotle, who is clear that 'virtue belongs to the soul' (*Eth. eud.* 2.1.15, 1219b25, trans. Rowe), and asserts that by seeing someone's responses to pleasure and pain their disposition and character can be seen (*Eth. nic.* 2.3, 1104b1–5; cf. Plato, *Resp.* 4.441d–e, 442e–444; 9.581c; *Phaed.* 83d; *Tim.* 42b).

virtuous; because excellence of character necessarily makes the goal correct and stops one being deceived as to what the right course of action is (*Eth. eud.* 2.11.7–9, 1227b35–1228a1; *Eth. nic.* 6.12, 1144a5, 30). In Stoic terms, this would mean assessing from a person's actions whether she has really understood virtue or vice, or has allowed the passions to make her wrongly pursue indifferents to excess.

Conversely, the wise man, because he perceives virtue and vice correctly, has the ability to judge impressions correctly, and will have well-reasoned assent leading to appropriate impulses. Thus, he will always behave appropriately, i.e. according to nature. It could be argued that the wise man's quality of soul gives him an emotional disposition. As Stobaeus comments:

> They [the Stoics] say that a good man experiences nothing contrary to his desire or impulse or purpose on account of the fact that in all such cases he acts with reserve and encounters no obstacles which are unanticipated. He is also gentle, his gentleness being a tenor by which he is gently disposed in acting always appropriately and in not being moved to anger against anyone. He is also calm and orderly, this orderliness being knowledge of fitting activities, and his calm the proper regulation of his soul and body's natural activities and rests. The opposites of these occur in all inferior men. (*Ecl.* = SVF 3.564, 632)

The result, indicated by this excerpt, is that the wise man will always undertake fitting and natural activities, which the Stoics called 'proper functions'.

Proper Functions, Nature, and Virtue

The idea of a proper function (τὸ καθῆκον) is fundamental to Stoic ethics.[104] Seneca comments that no one 'will be able to perform what he should do unless he has acquired the system of being able to execute all the measure of proper functions in every matter' (*Ep.* 95.12 = HP66J).[105] This includes in emotional matters also. As Diogenes Laertius comments:

---

[104] 'Proper function' describes an action that is appropriate to nature (therefore to perfect reason). Examples include acting justly or prudently (Stobaeus, *Ecl.* = SVF 3.494; cf. Diogenes Laertius 7.108).

[105] Seneca uses the Latin *officium* here as the equivalent of the Greek τὸ καθῆκον for 'proper function'; cf. Cicero, *Fin.* 3.20–2.

τῶν γὰρ καθ᾽ ὁρμὴν ἐνεργουμένων τὰ μὲν καθήκοντα εἶναι,
τὰ δὲ παρὰ τὸ καθῆκον, τὰ δ᾽ οὔτε καθήκοντα οὔτε παρὰ τὸ
καθῆκον. καθήκοντα μὲν οὖν εἶναι ὅσα λόγος αἱρεῖ ποιεῖν.

Of activities in accordance with impulse, some are proper
functions, others are contrary to proper function, and
others belong to neither type. Proper functions are ones
which reason dictates our doing. (7.108 = SVF 3.495)

Thus, if emotions are judgements leading to impulse, then it is
important that one's emotional life is oriented aright if one is to perform proper functions.[106] Consequently, Seneca reveals that part of
virtue is reigning in desires and suppressing fear along with doing the
correct thing (*Ep.* 120.11). Proper functions involve both the selection
of things (the good) according to nature and continuous appropriate
selection (Cicero, *Fin.* 3.20–2). The task of the moral agent is to choose
which action is appropriate in each situation in order to live virtuously. This may mean choosing something such as death or disease –
indifferents that one would not naturally prefer, but that, in certain
situations, judgement and reason dictate are to be selected.[107] These
indifferents thus become 'preferred' in the given situation.[108] For the
Stoic, some proper functions are always correct – those clearly linked
to virtue – others can depend on circumstances (Diogenes Laertius
7.109). It is obvious that being under the sway of the passions would
be detrimental to selecting the right action because, as discussed
above, they drive one to pursue the wrong things because of a warped
judgement about value. Consequently, passions are necessarily contrary to proper functions.[109] Given that the passions prevent one from
living as nature intended, it is not surprising that the topic of how to
avoid the passions becomes vital for Stoic ethics.

[106] Aristotle likewise links virtue with the best movements of the soul which produce
the best functions and affections (*Eth. eud.* 2.1.24, 1220a30; cf. *Eth. nic.* 1.7, 1098a5).
[107] Long and Sedley, *HP1*, 358.
[108] The selection of the preferred equates to Aristotle's 'decision', which is a
calculated choice of one thing over another (*Eth. eud.* 2.10.15, 1226b5). Cf. Epicurus'
comments about whether to choose pleasure and avoid pain depending on judgement
of advantages or disadvantages in *Ep. Men.* 127–32 = *HP21*B.
[109] Cf. Stobaeus, *Ecl.* = SVF 3.501. Panaetius linked proper functions to emotions
via his conception of roles (*persona*). Two of the roles a person has to be aware of are
their mental nature and temperament. Given the above discussion one would assume
the passions would need to be controlled with regard to both mental state and temperament. Panaetius' doctrine allowed for individuals to discover how to act in line
with their personality but brought this within boundaries of avoiding excess. These
boundaries included feeling boundaries; see, Long and Sedley, *HP1*, 428.

It is also worth noting at this point that to select a seemingly negative thing such as death or disease as 'preferred' and according to nature is only comprehensible when we recall the deterministic Stoic perspective that the divine will may allot to the human what it wills. Virtuous action therefore has to be in line not just with human nature but the whole of nature's cosmic reason.[110] What constitutes good or bad, virtue or happiness is determined by the nature of the universe and its administration in the world (Plutarch, *Stoic. rep.* 1035c–d = SVF 3.68). This means that one should not partake in an activity that would contravene nature's laws, and in such a way one can live in line with the gods (Diogenes Laertius 7.87–8). What this reveals is that the control of the passions has to be understood in relation to the ordering of the universe. To be disturbed inwardly by passions means that one is living outside of the created order as nature intended. Instead, it is the ability to live virtuously according to nature that produces happiness. Consequently, one's emotional life affects one's ability to achieve this end.[111] Here we can see, once again, how the Stoics' positioning of emotions is influenced by their larger worldview.

The Therapy of Emotions

We have just discussed how the passions because of being excessive, contrary to nature, and irrational, were seen as the root of unhappiness, vice, and problems of character that result in wrongdoing.[112] Consequently, the passions were undesirable and the aim was to be entirely without them. This was termed ἀπάθεια. The Stoics were not the only school who discussed the place of the emotions. Aristotle, not seeing the emotions as inherently negative, advocated the intermediate way of moderation (*Eth. nic.* 2.6, 1106a25–1106b25; cf. *Eth. eud.* 3.7.1–10, 1233b15–1234a25).[113] For Aristotle, excellence with regard to the affections was 'to be affected when one should, at the things one should, in relation to the people one should, for the

---

[110] Long and Sedley, *HP1*, 351.

[111] Again, there is a large philosophical discourse on what leads to happiness. For Aristotle, it is activity that accords with excellence, which is an accordance with the highest aspect of a person – their intelligence (rationality) – which he also links with what is natural and divine (*Eth. nic.* 10.6–7, 1177a10–15).

[112] Long and Sedley, *HP1*, 419; The idea of happiness (εὐδαιμονία) as the goal of life was a significant topic of conversation for many philosophical schools; see Erler and Schofield, 'Epicurean Ethics', 648–9.

[113] Sandbach, *The Stoics*, 63.

reasons one should, and in the way one should' (*Eth. nic.* 2.6, 1106b20, trans. Rowe). However, Aristotle does think that some affections such as rejoicing over someone's misfortune (ἐπιχαιρεκακία), shamelessness (ἀναισχυντία), and grudging ill-will (φθόνος) do not allow the intermediate way but are necessarily connected with evil (*Eth. nic.* 2.6, 1107a5–10). Plato, on the other hand, despite thinking that it is impossible to destroy the passions, does think that reason should rule the body and its affections, in this way, one can 'achieve calm from such emotions' (*Phaed.* 84a, 94b–c, trans. Grube).[114] The general acceptance of self-control as a virtue suggests that many schools recognised the need to master the affections (Aristotle, *Eth. nic.* 7.1, 1145b10; Plato, *Resp.* 4.430a, 442c). Even the Epicureans, for whom pleasure was the goal of life, thought that the pursuit of pleasure should be limited by the dictates of reason and that the greatest good was prudence (*Ep. Men.* 132). Pleasure was defined as 'quiet of mind' and the 'absence of bodily pain'.[115] Quiet of mind here is ἀταραξία (absence of mental disturbance), suggesting a lack of disturbing passions. In fact, the Epicureans thought that philosophy was empty if it did not offer a therapy for the passions.[116] Due to their differing assessments of the nature and quality of emotions, the various philosophical schools advocated diverse therapies for the emotions. We will focus on the Stoic therapy.

A Simple Therapy?

If we start with the Stoic view that the passions are a faulty judgement, then the therapy is simple: correct the judgement. At its root, this means altering the perception of the good and the bad. For the Stoic, nature has deposited the seeds of the knowledge of good by what naturally accords to man (i.e. the good that is appropriate to him), but to perceive the truly good requires learning and experience.[117] Thus, being able to recognise the truly good advances

---

[114] Calm is the goal for Plato because the affections are seen as physical disturbances.

[115] Erler and Schofield, 'Epicurean Ethics', 644.

[116] Erler and Schofield, 'Epicurean Ethics', 646, 649.

[117] Plato, in an analogous way, thought that the soul, before being implanted into the human, had been instructed in how to behave by the great soul. After this point, any correct or incorrect action is the responsibility of the human (*Tim.* 42d–e). Cf. Aristotle, *Eth. nic.* 3.5, 1114a30–1115a1 for discussion on whether a person is responsible for their perceptions of good and bad, or whether nature has determined it in some way. The Stoics sit in contrast to Epicurus, who thought that by nature from birth we recognised pleasure as the good and pain as the bad (Cicero, *Fin.* 1.29–32); education in recognising the good or bad is not required. This also means that our view of pain or pleasure is not the consequence of upbringing or society; Erler and Schofield, 'Epicurean Ethics', 650.

alongside the perfection of rationality.[118] With this understanding, the eradication of the passions is at least theoretically possible, because if one can always follow reason in one's judgements then the passion will not exist.[119] As noted above, whether an impression ever ends up in a fully-fledged passion is under the power of the person. But what about instances where a person seems to cry for no reason, or reacts to a snake in the grass? The Stoics would argue that, in the latter case, the impression necessarily produces certain sensations, but this reaction is not based on an opinion (i.e. a faulty judgement) and thus occurs before mind and reason can act. The wise man, when he has had time to recognise the impression, will not assent to it, so stops fear before it develops (Gellius[120] 19.1.17–18 = HP65Y).[121] Hence, he is never really in a passionate state.[122] In terms of the former case, according to Graver, the 'category of inconsequential feelings not dependent on assent was identified quite early in the Hellenistic school, perhaps under the term "pre-emotions"' (προπάθεια), and this is how feelings that occur without judgement, such as inexplicable tears, could be labelled.[123] Seneca develops this concept most comprehensively (see *Ira* 2.1.3–5; 2.2.1–2.3.5).[124] The 'first movements' exist before the act of assent, so cannot be classed as a full passion, but may exhibit some of the bodily manifestations commonly associated with the passion.[125]

Even though the extirpation of the passions is theoretically possible, for Stoicism, the perfection of rationality can only be attained by the wise man. Subsequently, the normal man will not achieve ἀπάθεια, but could make steps towards it.[126] The Stoics thought, like other philosophical schools, that the way of progression was good

---

[118] Long and Sedley, *HP1*, 375.

[119] In a similar but less extreme way, Plato also thought that wrong desires could be limited by 'calculation', 'understanding', and 'correct belief' but this is found in only a few people who 'are born with the best natures and receive the best education' (*Resp.* 4.431c, trans. Grube and Reeve).

[120] Approximately 130–80 CE; Long and Sedley, *HP1*, 496. Gellius is outlining Epictetus' perspective; see Graver, *Stoicism*, 85–6.

[121] Graver, *Stoicism*, 86.

[122] Long and Sedley, *HP1*, 421.

[123] Graver, *Stoicism*, 78. For more on 'feelings without assent' see Graver, *Stoicism*, 85–108.

[124] Graver, *Stoicism*, 93–8.

[125] See R. Sorabji, 'Chrysippus – Posidonius – Seneca: A High Level Debate on Emotion', in *The Emotions in Hellenistic Philosophy*, ed. Juha Sihvola and Troels Engberg-Pedersen (Dordrecht: Kluwer Academic, 1998), 149–69, at 156–7, 160–2.

[126] In later Stoics such as Panaetius and others following him like Cicero this led to a valuing of moral education that could be relevant to training anyone who showed at least some mark of virtue; Long and Sedley, *HP1*, 427.

upbringing, education, and entering the path of philosophy.[127] In the ancient world, this type of education was only available to a few male elite. Groups of the population such as women, children, and slaves were bound to remain as inferior people who exhibited all kinds of 'diverse desires, pleasures and pains' (Plato, *Resp.* 4.431b–c, trans. Grube and Reeve).[128] In the promotion of education, particularly for the young, we can see an awareness that emotional life required social conditioning if the individual was to be formed correctly.[129] Emotions are particularly important in this moral training, because emotions are object-directed. For the ancient mind, the object is more often than not another human. So, control of the emotions affects how one acts towards another and will have consequences for society as a whole.

Conclusion

The above discussion has shown that the emotions are a significant topic for Greco-Roman philosophy: from where they sit within the person, to what they are, and how they occur. By the time we reach the later Stoics, highly developed and sophisticated descriptions of the passions have been produced. It is evident that the philosophers recognised, as do modern theorists, that the emotions are cognitive processes that include recognising an object, judging value, evaluating goal congruence, and providing impetus for action. Despite this, the ancients were cautious of the passions and their drives. The Stoics also recognised the fundamental link between perception of the good and bad and the emotion's judgement. Correct judgement, based on a truthful perspective, would lead to a εὐπάθεια, an appropriate impulse resulting in virtuous behaviour. The misguided passions would produce the opposite. In general the ancients warn against excess and promote the limitation of emotions by reason.

---

[127] Perhaps rather unsurprisingly, Plato and Aristotle also advocated education in philosophy as the main way to achieve happiness or to strengthen the rational over the passions and thus become virtuous (Plato, *Phaed.* 82c, 114e–115a; *Tim.* 90c; Aristotle, *Eth. nic.* 2.3, 1104b10–15).

[128] In contrast to this, Epicurus thought that the goal of the happy life was possible without particular education, thus allowing the average person to attain the Epicurean happy life. Having said this, *the Letter to Menoeceus* does suggest that if someone will learn Epicurus' doctrines by heart they will achieve ἀταραξία; Erler and Schofield, 'Epicurean Ethics', 644, 670.

[129] Plato himself notes that this education seems to be already happening through 'unwritten customs' and 'ancestral law', and recognises that such concerns are 'the bonds of the entire social framework' (*Laws* 7.793b, trans. Saunders).

The Stoics sought to eradicate the passions. The main therapy was cognitive: simply change the judgement. Others, such as Aristotle did not think that the emotions were inherently bad but advocated the intermediate way, avoiding excess and deficiency. The general acceptance that reason was to be preeminent over the affections led to a valuing of philosophical education as a means of correcting false judgements about the good and bad and therefore changing opinions about what should be pursued or avoided; this would then lead to right actions. If one was able to have self-mastery over the passions via assent and, consequently, live in line with nature, then one would have consistently appropriate ethical behaviour and achieve a virtuous happy life.

Thus, we can conclude, given these findings, that it is not anachronistic to investigate emotions in 1 Peter in terms of object-directedness, evaluative judgements, and action-tendencies. We can also see that the ancients themselves recognised that this opened up wider discussion about worldview, most notably systems of value, and attainment or non-attainment of personal goals. Thus, these are also legitimate areas of discussion for our investigation of 1 Peter. Further, the ancients knew that a person's emotional life directly influences her ethical life, which in turn influences her ability to achieve happiness, and has implications for society as a whole. Likewise, we can explore the influence of 1 Peter's emotional strategy on his ethics and the therapeutic and social consequences of this for the audience. Before we turn to 1 Peter, for the sake of completeness, and because the aim of this study is to investigate the role of emotions in 1 Peter's persuasive discourse, we must briefly outline how the emotions are understood within the rhetorical handbooks.

4

THE RHETORICAL USE OF EMOTION

Having looked at the philosophy of emotion, we now turn to rhetorical theory. In doing so we are changing gears: where philosophy is interested in virtue and the ideal, rhetorical theory is concerned with pragmatics. Rhetorical theorists are less worried about the proper bounds of emotion and more attentive to how emotions, both the speaker's and the audience's, are used in persuasion.[1] Hence, they may choose to arouse emotions that the philosopher would caution against (see Cicero, *De or.* 1.51.220–2). This does not preclude a philosophy of emotion lying beneath their use.[2] In fact, in Aristotle's *On Rhetoric* we encounter one of the most thought-through psychologies of emotions in the ancient world.[3] However, more commonly, the rhetoricians' discussion of emotions starts from what they observe in society. Put differently, they produced a formalised system based on what people ordinarily knew and used (Aristotle, *Rhet.* 1.1.1–2, 1354a1–11; cf. Cicero, *De or.* 1.32.146; Quintilian, *Inst.* 3.2). Despite the rhetorical handbooks being less philosophical, we can still glean insights into how emotions were conceptualised. Yet, as we will see, what the rhetoricians illuminate more than the philosophers is the cultural contextualisation and social reasoning present in emotions.

---

[1] D. Konstan, *The Emotions of the Ancient Greeks: Studies in Aristotle and Classical Literature* (Toronto: University of Toronto Press, 2006), 36.

[2] From Cicero's perspective, a good orator would be trained in philosophy (*Or. Brut.* 14).

[3] Kennedy suggests that Aristotle's comments on emotion in *On Rhetoric* could have been written initially for another context because the examples given are not from rhetorical situations but are more general; Aristotle, *On Rhetoric. A Theory of Civic Discourse. Translation with Introduction, Notes and Appendices by George A. Kennedy*, 2nd ed. (New York and Oxford: Oxford University Press, 2007), 113.

EXCURSUS: THE FAILURE OF STOIC RHETORIC

Whereas Stoic sources were the focus for our philosophical enquiry, they cannot be when it comes to rhetoric simply because there are none we have access to. Stoics such as Chrysippus did write on rhetoric, but no full works have survived, and, where we do have limited evidence, it is under the genre of dialectic, not rhetoric.[4] Catherine Atherton argues that Stoic rhetorical theory would have resembled other professional rhetorical theories. However, they would have been unorthodox within the area of style because the Stoics thought that good rhetorical style was no different to good dialectical discourse. This is due to the fact that the most important thing for Stoic discourse was correctness.[5] Consequently, rhetoricians like Cicero considered Stoic rhetorical theory a failure because it produced 'bald, unfamiliar, jarring' oratory that was 'devoid of clarity, fullness and spirit' (*De or.* 3.18.66 [Rackham, LCL]).[6] Appropriate style was important to all theorists and this included varying the style depending on the goal of persuasion. It was this ability to alter style appropriately, particularly with regard to the emotions, that brought success in persuasion.[7] Subsequently, this meant that applying the Stoic philosophical tenets to rhetoric was bound to fail. Fundamentally, if emotions such as passions are a vice, then it is not appropriate to use them in persuasion or induce them in an audience. Consequently, one of the main weapons of the orator is removed. Second, the Stoics' understanding of virtues and indifferents meant that many of the standard topics used by most orators in persuasion were not compatible with Stoicism because their underlying value system of good and bad did not correlate (Cicero, *De or.* 3.18.66).[8] Having said this, Quintilian states in *Institutio Oratoria* during a section speaking about those who do not advocate emotional appeal:

> I am less surprised by the philosophers, in whose minds emotion is a vice, and it seems immoral for a judge to be

---

[4] Dialectic here is 'the science of correct discussion by means of question and answer'; C. Atherton, 'Hand Over Fist: The Failure of Stoic Rhetoric', *The Classical Quarterly, New Series* 38 (1988): 392–427, at 396–7.

[5] Atherton, 'Hand', 398–9.

[6] Where a Stoic orator was considered to have good style, it was because he had absorbed influences from outside of Stoicism; Atherton, 'Hand', 393, 398, 401–2.

[7] Atherton, 'Hand', 394–5.

[8] Atherton, 'Hand', 401.

distracted from the truth, and inappropriate for a good man to take advantage of vices. None the less, they will admit that emotional appeals are necessary if truth, justice, and the common good cannot be secured by other means (*Inst.* 6.1.7 [Russell, LCL]).[9]

Here a small window is left, which allows the Stoic orator to use emotion in his speeches if the end goal of truth and virtue, which *is* acceptable, requires it. Despite this, the range of appropriate emotions available to the Stoic orator would be limited.[10] Furthermore, for the Stoic orator, the content of the discourse should not be determined by the audience or occasion, but by the subject matter. They thought that if the subject matter is presented with clarity then the impression it linguistically creates may also cause the audience to respond emotionally to the object. This is permissible because it is based on a correct representation of the object. Thus, emotional responses to natural preferences may also be allowed within this scheme.[11] However, in general, the Stoic position on emotion was not practicable for orators as Atherton explains:

> It seems he cannot appeal to what Stoicism regarded as the bad emotions, the πάθη, grief, fear, pleasure, and desire, or to the intricate moral pathology of anger, pity, hatred, jealousy, *Schadenfreude*, and so on (cf. e.g. Diogenes 7.110ff.), which are his unphilosophical rival's bread and butter … The only good emotions (varieties of εὐπάθεια) are those which the sage feels (Diogenes 7.116), joy, watchfulness, and wishing, with an understandably limited appeal to the ordinary public: a far cry indeed from Quintilian's remark that the defendant will make his hearers weep with pity, and the prosecutor make them shed tears of indignation (6.1.9).[12]

Atherton goes on to assert, it 'is impossible to pretend that what is known of Stoic stylistics looks satisfactory, even by ancient standards. It appears rigid at best and unworkable at worst'.[13] Yet, Stoic philosophy of the passions could have had some influence over rhetoric as a whole. Wisse, following Solmsen, though not certain,

---

9 'Philosophers' here is most likely referring to the Stoics; Atherton, 'Hand', 404–5.
10 Atherton, 'Hand', 405–7, 410.
11 Atherton, 'Hand', 411.
12 Atherton, 'Hand', 414.
13 Atherton, 'Hand', 415.

does comment that the lack of discussion about πάθος in the post-Aristotelian rhetorical handbooks until Cicero could be because of the influence of Stoic philosophy and their system of rhetoric.[14]

So, despite the Stoics being dominant philosophically, when it comes to rhetoric, we have to turn to specific rhetoricians. From the Greek side this is Aristotle[15] and Dionysius of Halicarnassus (f. 20 BCE); from the Roman it is Cicero (106–43 BCE) and Quintilian (*c*.35 – died after 96 CE).[16] There are differences between the Greek and Roman schools particularly with the Romans exhibiting more willingness to use overt, often ethically questionable, emotion to persuade.

Having established which sources we will be referring to and why, it is time to explore what they say, starting with πάθος as a type of persuasion. We will then go on to determine how the rhetoricians speak about the relationship between pathetic persuasion and audience judgement, rhetorical style, and speech content. Finally, we will look at the rhetorician's approach to understanding emotions.

Πάθος as Πίστις

In his *On Rhetoric* Aristotle introduces the three modes of persuasion (πίστεις): ἦθος, λόγος, and πάθος (cf. Dionysius of Halicarnassus, *Lys.* 19.2–4).[17] The first, ἦθος, is persuasion through the character

---

[14] See, J. Wisse, *Ethos and Pathos from Aristotle to Cicero* (Amsterdam: Adolf M. Hakkert, 1989), 80–3.

[15] Aristotle's work, though early for our investigation, influenced later rhetoricians more contemporaneous to 1 Peter. Much of Aristotle's innovation in *On Rhetoric* was still used in discussion by later authors. It is unlikely that in the early periods after its composition Aristotle's *On Rhetoric* was widely available, but it appears that later authors such as Cicero and Dionysius of Halicarnassus were familiar with the work and its premises. Quintilian also shows familiarity, but perhaps more on account of Cicero. Aristotle's three major types of rhetoric (forensic, deliberative, and epideictic); the parts of a speech (prologue, narration, proof, interrogation, and epilogue); selection of topics and arrangement; the three modes of persuasion (the character of the speaker, emotions, and logical argument), along with tropes and figures were still the major topics that occupied later rhetorical handbooks. Cf. Wisse, *Ethos*, 14, 56–9. For fuller discussion on the availability of *On Rhetoric* by the first century BCE see Wisse, *Ethos*, 152–63. Furthermore, it is difficult to discount *On Rhetoric* simply due to dating when it comprises one of the most detailed examinations of the πάθη.

[16] Though the *Rhetorica ad Herennium* (first century BCE Latin work of an unknown author, previously ascribed to Cicero) is often turned to as a source book for rhetorical theory, it is of limited value when discussing the emotions as it does not address emotion as a distinct topic, though emotions do appear in Book 4's examples; cf. Wisse, *Ethos*, 80.

[17] These modes of persuasion were later listed under invention (εὕρησις/εὕρεσις, *inventio*); Wisse, *Ethos*, 14.

of the speaker: we are persuaded because we believe the speaker to be trustworthy and have confidence in what he says (*Rhet.* 1.2.4, 1356a4–6; cf. Cicero, *De or.* 2.43.182–3; Quintilian, *Inst.* 6.2.13–19). The second, λόγος, is persuasion through the argument itself and its apparent truth (*Rhet.* 1.2.6, 1356a19–20). The last, πάθος, is described as persuasion:

> διὰ ... τῶν ἀκροατῶν, ὅταν εἰς πάθος ὑπὸ τοῦ λόγου προαχθῶσιν·

> by means of his hearers, when they are roused to emotion by his speech. (*Rhet.* 1.2.5, 1356a14–15 [Freese, LCL]; cf. Cicero, *De or.* 2.44.185)

Quintilian, however, lists both ἦθος and πάθος as species of emotional persuasion while still maintaining that ἦθος relates to the character of the speaker. He translates πάθος as *adfectus*, but does not think there is a good translation for ἦθος. For Quintilian, following Cicero, πάθος relates to more violent emotions, strong passions that command the person through disturbance; ἦθος on the other hand can cover a variety of mental states and relates to gentler and steady emotions that persuade through good will (*Inst.* 6.2.9–10). Wisse comments concerning Cicero's distinction between ἦθος and πάθος, which Quintillian likely follows, that 'there is no overlap between the two concepts: though they are similar in that both are aimed at influencing the audience's minds, their effect on these minds is different', πάθος specifically moves by 'impulse and perturbation of mind'.[18]

For the rhetoricians, the πάθη were so vital for persuasion that being able to move the audience emotionally became one of the three main aims of the orator (the others being to instruct and delight). However, Quintilian notes that persuasion through the emotions is not suitable for every topic. There are certain parts of a speech for which it is more apposite such as the introduction or epilogue. Yet, when emotional persuasion is appropriate, it is very powerful (*Inst.* 3.5.2–3; 6.1.1, 13–14, 51–3). Quintilian was not alone in recognising the strength of emotions. For Cicero, one's success in persuasion rests in one's ability to move the audience (*Or. Brut.* 69).[19] Dionysius, though noting the value of ἦθος, comments that the orator's strongest weapon is to lead the audience into an 'emotional state of mind'

---

[18] Wisse, *Ethos*, 236–7.
[19] Wisse, *Ethos*, 251.

(*Dem.* 18.25–30 [Usher, LCL]; cf. 58.18–24).[20] This suggests that persuading via the emotions was not about irrational manipulation, but
was thought to engage the person's cognitive faculties. For Cicero, persuasion via the emotions is 'aimed at moving the minds of our audience in the direction we want to' (*De or.* 2.27.114, trans. Wisse; cf.
Quintilian, *Inst.* 6.2.1).[21] Further, for Cicero, to be able to use pathetic persuasion requires that one has intimate knowledge of 'all the
mental emotions [*animorum motus*], with which nature has endowed
the human race'. It is in calming or exciting the *mens* of the hearer that
the power of oratory lies (*De or.* 1.5.17 [Sutton and Rackham, LCL];
cf. Quintilian, *Inst.* 6.2.7).[22] Quintilian reveals that the movement of
a person via the emotions (*affectus/adfectus*) is a movement of the
animus, which as noted, can refer to the mind specifically, or at the very
least the rational soul. Therefore, persuasion through the emotions is
another way that a person's reasoning can be altered. Lastly, we must
note Aristotle's recognition that this mode of persuasion is through
the hearer. It requires being able to affect the audience internally.
Thus, it is personal to the audience, not just asking them to agree with
logic but requiring that they be internally shaped.

We have noted that πάθος is a means of persuasion, and that it
was considered to be extremely effective. So, it remains to outline
why the rhetoricians had this stance towards the emotions.

Πάθος and Affected Judgement

Why did the orators put such a premium on persuasion through the
emotions? Aristotle gives his reasoning as follows:

---

[20] Though Usher has given the translation 'emotional state of mind' the Greek
simply says ἐπὶ τὰ πάθη (towards the emotions). Aristotle, in the above quote
says similarly εἰς πάθος (into an emotion). Aristotle goes on to link emotions and
judgement (discussed below), and in his discussion allows that emotions contain
reasoning. Therefore, it seems appropriate to see being led εἰς πάθος as being brought
into a particular mental state, thus, supporting the plausibility of Usher's translation.

[21] Wisse, *Ethos*, 236. Quintilian indicates that changing the judge's mind does not
necessarily mean he is led to the truth, but may indeed be distracted from it (*Inst.*
6.2.3–4).

[22] *Animus* here can refer generally to the 'rational soul in man', but also 'in a
more restricted sense, the mind as thinking', and the 'general power of perception
and thought, the reason, intellect, mind'; see 'ănĭmus' in C. T. Lewis and C. Short,
*A Latin Dictionary. Founded on Andrews' Edition of Freund's Latin Dictionary.
Revised, Enlarged, and in Great Part Rewritten by Charlton T. Lewis and Charles
Short* (Oxford: Clarendon Press, 1879). Accessed 16 April 2014. www.perseus.
tufts.edu/hopper/morph?l=animorum&la=la#Perseus:text:1999.04.0059:entry=
animus-contents.

οὐ γὰρ ὁμοίως ἀποδίδομεν τὰς κρίσεις λυπούμενοι καὶ χαίροντες
ἢ φιλοῦντες καὶ μισοῦντες·

[W]e do not give the same judgement when grieved and
rejoicing or when being friendly and hostile. (*Rhet.* 1.2.5,
1356a15–16, trans. Kennedy)

What Aristotle highlights is the link between πάθος and
judgement: one's emotional state changes one's judgement.[23] He
does not give a description of why this is the case. He simply states
that it is so. Aristotle adds later, when defining the πάθη:

Ἔστι δὲ τὰ πάθη, δι᾽ ὅσα μεταβάλλοντες διαφέρουσι πρὸς τὰς
κρίσεις, οἷς ἕπεται λύπη καὶ ἡδονή, οἷον ὀργὴ ἔλεος φόβος καὶ
ὅσα ἄλλα τοιαῦτα, καὶ τὰ τούτοις ἐναντία.

The emotions are all those affections which cause men to
change their opinion in regard to their judgements, and are
accompanied by pleasure and pain; such are anger, pity,
fear, and all similar emotions and their contraries. (*Rhet.*
2.1.8, 1378a19–21 [Freese, LCL])[24]

Thus, for Aristotle, if your end goal is to change the opinion and
subsequent judgement of the audience, you need to engage and
influence the audience's emotions.[25] Yet, still, the specific explanation
as to why emotions operate in this manner is not given. Perhaps,
slightly earlier in Book 2, we get an insight into Aristotle's reasoning.
Aristotle is aware that emotions cause the person to be disposed
(διάκειμαι) to a particular stance, specifically to hold a particular
opinion (*Rhet.* 2.1.4, 1377b30–1378a5). Though Aristotle does not
state it, his comments suggest that this is so because each emotion
contains an inherent judgement about the object; thus, to have a particular emotion necessarily means to carry a particular opinion. For
example, if a person has friendly feelings towards another then she
will judge her wrongdoing as of a lesser offence than if she feels hostile towards her. Consequently, emotions do not change judgement

---

[23] Konstan, *Emotions*, 27.
[24] Konstan argues, against Fortenbaugh, that Aristotle's definition of emotion here
constitutes his understanding of emotion generally not just in a rhetorical context
and that, as such, it evidences how Aristotle thought emotions were 'exploited in
social life generally' particularly in 'the daily negotiation of social roles'; Konstan,
Emotions, 34.
[25] Cicero likewise notes that people make decisions from their emotional state more
often than by a precept or statute (*De or.* 2.42.178–9).

in just any way, but particular emotions push the judgement in a particular direction.[26] It becomes clear that different emotional states cause the same facts to be interpreted differently, and, as such, can affect beliefs. As Konstan notes, this makes the role of evaluation in emotion dynamic: 'a belief enters into the formation of an emotion that in turn contributes to modifying some other belief or, perhaps, intensifying the original one'.[27]

Dionysius of Halicarnassus gives an example of how emotion can sway judgement from his own experience of reading Demosthenes:

> ὅταν δὲ τῶν Δημοσθένους τινὰ λάβω λόγων, ἐνθουσιῶ τε καὶ δεῦρο κἀκεῖσε ἄγομαι, πάθος ἕτερον ἐξ ἑτέρου μεταλαμβάνων, ἀπιστῶν, ἀγωνιῶν, δεδιώς, καταφρονῶν, μισῶν, ἐλεῶν, εὐνοῶν, ὀργιζόμενος, φθονῶν, ἅπαντα τὰ πάθη μεταλαμβάνων, ὅσα κρατεῖν πέφυκεν ἀνθρωπίνης γνώμης·

> But when I pick up one of Demosthenes's speeches, I am transported: I am led hither and thither, feeling one emotion and another – disbelief, anguish, terror, contempt, hatred, pity, goodwill, anger, envy – every emotion in turn that can sway the human mind. (*Dem.* 22.5–10 [Usher, LCL]; cf. Cicero, *Or. Brut.* 97)

The word γνώμη, translated 'mind', can mean the 'organ by which one perceives or knows' but it can also cover the idea of judgement and opinion.[28] For Quintilian, emotions allow the orator to move beyond bare logical arguments. An argument may cause the audience to think something to be true, but an emotion will cause them to want it to be so, therefore believe it to be, and consequently they will judge it to be (*Inst.* 6.2.5–6). Therefore, it appears that there is a consensus among the rhetoricians that if you want to alter someone's judgement and consequently her evaluation of the world then the most effective way to do this is by utilising her emotions. This is of course tremendously useful if you are trying to persuade someone to see an object from a given perspective and subsequently to act towards the object in line with this perspective. Furthermore, if we follow this logic, it also allows the relationship between object and emotion to be dynamic, working in either direction, so that you could utilise an already present emotion to create a new judgement

---

[26] Wisse, *Ethos*, 67.
[27] Konstan, *Emotions*, 37.
[28] See 'γνώμη' in LSJ (354).

about an object. As we will discover, this is important to 1 Peter's communicative strategy.

Argument from Πάθος: Style Over Content?

The ability to move the audience emotionally is also approached in the rhetoricians' discussion of style and delivery. Emotional appeal was linked to amplification, ornamentation, and the grand style (Cicero, *Or. Brut.* 20; 69).[29] Yet, it is within the area of delivery that much of the Roman examination of emotions occurs. Delivery is defined as 'the graceful regulation of voice, countenance, and gesture' ([Cicero], *Rhet. Her.* 1.2.3 [Caplan, LCL]).[30] Delivery is critical for the emotions, because 'nature has assigned to every emotion a particular look and tone of voice and bearing of its own' (Cicero, *De or.* 3.57.216 [Rackham, LCL]; cf. 3.57.217–59.223; *Or. Brut.* 55, 60).[31] Evidently, perhaps more than the philosophers, the orator was aware of the physical manifestations and bodily communication of emotions. For in delivery the orator had to display the emotions that he wanted the audience to have (Cicero, *De or.* 2.45.189–90; cf. *Or. Brut.* 132; Dionysius, *Dem.* 22.15–40; *Isocr.* 13.17–24); this could be his own emotions or voicing another's (Quintilian, *Inst.* 6.1.26; cf. [Cicero], *Rhet. Her.* 4.43.55–6). The latter is akin to acting, but still has to be believable to be effective. In fact, any display of emotion has to be apt otherwise it appears ridiculous and is ineffective (cf. Quintilian, *Inst.* 6.1.44–5; Dionysius, *Dem.* 53.6–21). What this reveals is that the orator must be aware of the commonly accepted 'scripts' or 'scenarios' of an emotion. Emotions have to be used in a contextually aware manner. However, for maximum impact, the speaker must be really moved by the emotion himself not just feign it (Cicero, *De or.* 2.45.189–90, 46.194–47.195; Quintilian, *Inst.* 6.2.26–8).[32] In fact, from Cicero's and Quintilian's perspectives it is impossible to incite an emotion in your audience if you are not displaying the emotion yourself.[33]

---

[29] Wisse, *Ethos*, 216–17.

[30] Delivery was a major aspect of rhetoric that required an awareness of the circumstances of the speech and the type of audience (Cicero, *De or.* 3.55.210–12).

[31] The author of *Rhetorica ad Herennium* agrees, commenting that movement, countenance, and tone of voice should all match the emotion that is suitable to the sentiments of the subject matter (3.15.26).

[32] For more discussion on the use of the orator's own emotions in persuasion see Wisse, *Ethos*, 257–68.

[33] However, the rhetoricians were aware that such exhibiting of emotion should not appear contrived because an audience is continuously judging you as the speaker and any hint of falsity would incline the hearer to be unfavourably disposed and would work against your cause; cf. Dionysius, *Lys.* 9.15–16; 13.17–24; 19.23–31.

So, does all this suggest that the use of πάθος in persuasion is simply emotional manipulation as some such as Wisse come close to suggesting?[34] Here we find an old argument enters the picture: that of whether rhetoricians were more concerned with style and delivery over content. In a sense, the modern dismissal of emotions in favour of reason could be seen to be analogous. Argument from πάθος, then, is simply whipping up the audience into a particular state in order to cloud judgement. Yet, this view does disservice to the complexity of emotions and to the astuteness of an audience. As Cicero comments, 'eloquence of orators has always been controlled by the good sense of the audience' (*Or. Brut.* 24 [Hubbell, LCL]). He goes on to say about someone that uses the grand emotive style without thought to content: 'For a man who can say nothing mildly, who pays no attention to arrangement, precision, clarity or pleasantry ... if without first preparing the ears of his audience he begins trying to work them up to a fiery passion, he seem to be a raving madman among the sane, like a drunken reveller in the midst of sober men' (*Or. Brut.* 99 [Hubbell, LCL]). This excerpt shows that it is clear to an audience when emotions appear out of place. As noted above, this suggests that the audience requires emotions to make sense contextually. They cannot just appear, but need to be appropriate to the situation and subject matter.[35] In fact, we find in Cicero an assertion that style is of no account if the underlying subject matter has not been mastered by the speaker (*De or.* 1.12.50–1; cf. 3.5.19–6.24; *Or. Brut.* 20, 119; [Cicero], *Rhet. Her.* 3.11.19).[36] This is particularly the case when it comes to the emotions, as Cicero states:

> Who indeed does not know that the orator's virtue is preeminently manifested either in rousing men's hearts to anger, hatred, or indignation, or in recalling them from the same passions to mildness and mercy? Wherefore the speaker will not be able to achieve what he wants by his words, unless

---

[34] Wisse does not want to see emotions as elevated to the '"level of rationality"'. Instead, he understands them as manipulated reactions that, though not rational, from the outside perspective can be explained rationally; Wisse, *Ethos*, 72–4.

[35] Elsewhere, Cicero describes this as propriety in delivery (*Or. Brut.* 69–74).

[36] Having said this, Quintilian is more concerned with sweeping the audience along with the tide of emotion rather than the link between the emotion and the subject matter (*Inst.* 6.2.7). As Wisse highlights, Aristotle's comments in *Rhet.* 3.7.5, 1408a23–4 could be said to downplay the importance of subject matter and look to an 'emotional' not a reasoned reaction, but the discussion leading to this comment links emotions to the mind and inference of truth, so the content of emotion is still important even if that content is not strictly truthful; Wisse, *Ethos*, 71–2.

he has gained profound insight into the characters of men, and the whole range of human nature, and those motives whereby our souls are spurred on or turned back. (*De or.* 1.12.53; cf. Dionysius, *Lys.* 7.10–12)

So, for the rhetorician, the ability to move a person is more than getting the audience to mirror emotion; it is a matter of intricate psychology and sociology.[37] If an emotion is to be fittingly accepted by an audience, then the whole cognitive content and contextual position of the emotion presented has to be appropriate. There is clearly some cognitive processing taking place in the reception of the orator's emotional delivery, whether the audience is aware of it or not.

Consequently, the propositional content of emotions is of interest to the philosopher and orator alike. For, the orator needs to be able to distinguish between how different emotions, because of their individual specificities, can impact his cause (cf. Quintilian, *Inst.* 6.2.15–16). He has to be able to 'track down the thoughts, feelings, beliefs and hopes of his fellow-citizens' and 'scent out' his audience's 'thoughts, judgements, anticipations and wishes' (Cicero, *De or.* 1.51.223; 2.44.186 [Sutton and Rackham, LCL]) if he is to win them over. This requires an in-depth awareness of the link between emotions, psychological state, evaluations, and goals. It is this entwining of emotions and motive that the orator must master if he is to move an audience towards a particular action. He has to know which emotion to arouse if persuasion towards a particular goal in a particular circumstance is to be effective (cf. Cicero, *De or.* 1.46.202; 2.9.35; Quintilian, *Inst.* 6.1.9). From Cicero's comments we can appreciate how complex emotional interaction is between author and audience, or between any humans for that matter. Therefore, it is not surprising that the rhetoricians, like the philosophers, took steps to understand and master the emotions.

Understanding the Emotions

Like Cicero (see above), Aristotle is clear that in order to use emotions in persuasion one needs to understand what each πάθος is, 'the nature and character of each, its origin, and the manner

---

[37] To understand this psychology, which is more theoretical than just working from experience, may require an acquaintance with philosophical views of emotion; Wisse, *Ethos*, 251.

in which it is produced' (*Rhet.* 1.2.7, 1356a23–5 [Freese, LCL]; cf. Cicero, *De or.* 1.51.220).[38] Similarly, Quintilian warns that trying to understand emotion is complex and should not be treated superficially (*Inst.* 6.2.2). However, unlike the philosophers, Aristotle in his *On Rhetoric* does not detail the internal processes of the πάθη such as impressions or impulses. Instead, he is more interested in the common external objects of distinct emotions and the rationale that an emotion displays.[39] As Wisse asserts, Aristotle is not interested in either the *causa materialis* or the *causa formalis* but is interested in the *causa finalis* and the *causa efficiens*.[40] In Book 2 of his *On Rhetoric* Aristotle elaborates on what areas should be discussed, these are: the state of mind of the emotionally affected person (or how the person is disposed – διάκειμαι); towards whom the emotion is customarily directed; and for what reasons the emotion is directed at them (*Rhet.* 2.1.9, 1378a22–3; cf. Cicero, *De or.* 2.51.206–52.211). Unless one can understand these elements one cannot create or dispel a πάθος in someone (*Rhet.* 2.1.9, 1378a25–6). Quintilian adds that one must know the natural duration of certain emotions, and therefore be careful not to try to get the audience to be affected by an emotion beyond its normal limits (*Inst.* 6.1.27–9; cf. [Cicero], *Rhet. Her.* 2.31.50).

There are a few things that these comments highlight. Again, emotion is linked with reasoning by the assumption that it has a rationale that can be articulated. Second, an emotion is object-directed. In the majority of Aristotle's examples the object is another person. Hence, if the object is a person, the rationale behind the emotion will typically require, often complex, social evaluations including judgements about the person's motives and intentions.[41] This therefore means that one has to appreciate detailed dynamics of human social relations such as a person's norms and values. Third, Aristotle seems to assume a shared cultural understanding of emotions by the fact that they can have customary or 'usual' objects. Fourth, pulling the last three points together, as Konstan highlights, Aristotle's view of emotion requires a narrative understanding of emotion.[42] One has to know the context, that is, the story, to make

---

[38] Quintilian even comments that, when emotion is the basis for an argument, the audience may need the elements of the emotion explained to them (*Inst.* 5.12.6–7).

[39] Cf. Quintilian, *Inst.* 6.1.15–20 for examples of the type of objects and situations an orator might think through when seeking to arouse a particular emotion.

[40] Wisse, *Ethos*, 71.

[41] Konstan, *Emotions*, 38–9.

[42] Konstan, *Emotions*, 28.

sense of the emotion and why it is apposite in a given situation.[43] Therefore, if an emotion occurs in a particular context it causes one to ask certain questions in order to understand why it is appropriate. Lastly, and perhaps most importantly for persuasion, it is taken for granted that it is possible to create an emotion in another, or remove it, even change it, most likely by altering the narrative so that a new interpretation is possible, which in turn can give rise to an a new emotion.

The combination of the Aristotelian elements discussed shows that ultimately emotions reveal a perceived ordering of experience. If one is to arouse a certain emotion then the object has to be evaluated correctly within the audience's own ordering (cf. [Cicero], *Rhet. Her.* 1.5.8; 2.31.50). If the object is wrongly positioned socially, and in terms of cultural norms and values, then the emotion will not be aroused because it will not correspond to the hearer's cultural emotional repertoire and will not produce the correct interpretation to warrant the emotion. Conversely, this leaves open the possibility that if the hearers are encouraged to ascribe certain emotions to particular objects, then the speaker is seeking to position objects within their cosmic reality and is perhaps addressing their valuing of the object.

For Quintilian, like Cicero, oratory is only really concerned with a limited sphere of strong emotions such as anger (*ira*), hatred (*odium*), fear (*metus*), envy (*invidia*), and pity (*miseratio*) (*Inst.* 6.2.20).[44] This is most likely because his focus is on a judicial setting. Aristotle's range of emotions addressed is broader and encompasses milder emotions that the later Roman rhetoricians would put under ἦθος.[45] Aristotle approaches a number of specific emotions in certain pairings: anger (ὀργή) and mildness (πραότης) (2.2–3, 1378a29–1380b33); friendliness (φιλία) and enmity (ἔχθρα) (2.4, 1380b34–1382a19); fear (φόβος) and courage (θάρσος) (2.5, 1382a20–1383b10); shame (αἰσχύνη) and shamelessness (ἀναισχυντία) (2.6, 1383b11–1385a15); kindliness (χάρις) and unkindliness (ἀχαριστία)[46] (2.7, 1385a16–1385b11);

[43] Of course, this is the context as it is being interpreted by the emotion bearer.
[44] The emotions treated in Cicero's *De or.* 2.51.205–52.211 include '*amor, odium, iracundia, timor, spes, laetitia, molestis, invidia, misericordia*' translated, following Wisse, as 'fervent partiality', 'hatred, anger, fear, hope, joy, grief, envy, pity' (cf. *De or.* 2.42.178, 44.185); Wisse, *Ethos*, 236–7.
[45] See Wisse, *Ethos*, 241–8 for a more detailed exposition of the differences between Aristotle and the Roman rhetoricians concerning the positioning of emotions under ἦθος and πάθος.
[46] As Kennedy notes the 'noun *akharistia*, "unkindliness," does not actually occur in the chapter, but Aristotle does use the related negative adjective and verb'; Aristotle, *Rhetoric*, 137.

pity (ἔλεος) (2.8, 1385b11–1386b7) and indignation (νέμεσις) (2.9, 1386b7–1387b21); envy (φθόνος) (2.10, 1387b22–1388a29) and emulation (ζῆλος) (2.11, 1388a30–1388b30).[47] The first five pairings are obvious opposites. The last two, though not opposites, are related to each other, perhaps showing the difference in quality between seemingly similar emotions.[48] Lists like these from rhetorical handbooks are useful in our investigation because they start to build a map of the emotional terrain. They also demonstrate that a particular culture can have a defined categorisation of emotions, which may not be the same as our English understanding.[49] It is not necessary to work through these groupings now as, where relevant, they will be highlighted in our analysis of 1 Peter.

Rhetorical Theory and 1 Peter

Before closing this chapter, it seems necessary to delineate the areas of rhetorical theory that are useful to the present investigation and those that are not. Despite the orators needing to have an intricate awareness of delivery and emotional performance, when it comes to 1 Peter, this is an aspect of theory that is irrelevant because we are forced to work with a written text, which, though it would have been originally performed, has no oral or visual performative aspect that we can access. It would be pure conjecture to try and describe what physical movements, facial expressions, or tones of voice would be accompanying the content of the letter. Instead, it is with the content of the letter that we have to stay. Furthermore, as highlighted in the introduction, we will not be looking to see which emotions the author is arousing in his audience. We are concerned with the emotions as they appear in the text and, therefore, the emotions of the audience as idealised by the author. However, what the above discussion of rhetoric has highlighted is that there are a number of areas of discussion that are still available to us. For example, all of what Aristotle highlights about how to understand an emotion – its typical objects, the rationale of an emotion, and the disposition it creates – can be utilised in our discussion. We can also take into our exploration the idea that if an emotion is to be persuasive it has to be fitting to the narrative context and, therefore, from a

---

[47] Thus, not only do we find in philosophical treatise an indication of which states are considered emotions, we also find them in rhetorical works.

[48] Wisse, *Ethos*, 68.

[49] Cf. Cicero, *De or.* 2.51.206–52.211.

particular cultural perspective, comprehensible. Furthermore, this leads us towards the recognition that emotions are cultural and occur in complex social situations. If we are to grasp fully emotions in 1 Peter, we have to be aware of this and seek to understand the cultural and social elements revealed by the use of emotions, which help explain why they are fitting. Lastly, rhetorical theory has also highlighted that it is possible to influence a person's perspective, values, judgements, and actions by using her emotions. We can take this knowledge and see that dynamically, by presenting particular emotional stances as correct, the author is addressing the audience's perspective, values, judgements, and actions. Thus, ancient conversation about πάθος as a rhetorical proof is more complex than New Testament scholars have often recognised, and, therefore, there is much present in ancient rhetorical theory that can aid us in our exploration of emotions in 1 Peter.

Lastly, it is also worth noting that the rhetoricians are trying to arouse an immediate emotional response for an instant specific end, e.g. indignation at a crime and a consequent guilty verdict. This, however, is not what a letter such as 1 Peter is aiming at. Instead, it wants to shape the audience to effect more long-lasting change: changes of perspective and ethical behaviour, perhaps we could say, a change of disposition. This does not mean that the insights from rhetorical theory cannot be applied as what they reveal about the content of and use of emotions is relevant to both emotions in a moment and longer lasting emotional states. However, what it may suggest is that the author of 1 Peter would have to work harder to bring about this lasting change by utilising and reshaping the foundational values of the audience's worldview, rather than simply whipping the audience into a fleeting emotion.

Conclusion

The above discussion has explained how the emotions were an important topic of discussion for ancient rhetoricians. It has established that engaging the audience's emotions was seen as vital for persuading the audience towards a particular course of action. This is because the rhetoricians understood that a person's emotional state predisposes her towards a particular judgement about an object. They also recognised the complexity of using emotions in communication and that this required an in-depth awareness of the qualities of each emotion, its customary objects, rationale, and narrative setting. In their discussion, the ancients evidence the social situating of emotions and the necessity of a shared cultural understanding of the content of emotions for effective communication. Furthermore, they show how emotions can be used to shape perception and, reflexively, how a new perspective can influence emotion. Thus, the information gleaned from the rhetoricians reveals that it is important, as the modern theorists outlined, to understand emotions in their cultural context. Therefore, in our approach to 1 Peter we need to endeavour to appreciate the positioning of certain emotions within the cultural repertoire, and, consequently, use this to help us appreciate the locating of objects of emotion within the audience's perspective. This will also require recognising the narrative context of an emotion, which means having an awareness of worldview, norms, and values.

Now, with an assurance that we are not being unduly anachronistic in our approach, we can move to the exegetical task.

PART III

THE PRESENT EXPERIENCE

5

JOY DESPITE DISTRESS
1 Peter 1.6–8

As noted above (pp. 39–40), our theoretical position on emotions outlined in Chapter 2 will undergird the following exegetical chapters. The key elements of an emotion – its object-directedness, its cognitive content in the form of an evaluative judgement, and its action-tendency – and the function of emotions in the life of the individual and society explored in that chapter – especially the dynamic relationship between emotion, values, goals, and worldview – will give parameters to and provide heuristic tools for the following discussion.

This chapter is the first in a two-part analysis of joy/rejoicing (χαρά, χαίρω, ἀγαλλιάω) and distress/being distressed (λύπη, λυπέω) in 1 Peter. First, we will focus on 1 Peter 1.6–8, leaving 4.12–13 for the next chapter's analysis. These two emotions, joy and distress, have been isolated for concurrent investigation for two reasons: (1) because of their temporal aspect – both are deemed present emotions; and (2) more importantly, because they appear side by side in the text itself. Thus, in this chapter we will explore the author's depiction of the audience's ability to rejoice despite distress (1.6) and its glory infused joy (1.8). We will outline which objects each emotion relates to, the judgement the emotions make, and the action-tendency they carry. We will then be ready to appreciate how the author is asking the audience members to see their world, and what implications this has for their own understanding of their position within it, which will lead on to discussion about their social relationships, ethical responsibilities, and own emotional life. In the next chapter we will investigate the paradox of joy in suffering.

However, the first task, in order to be sensitive to the historical and cultural shaping of emotions, is to locate χαρά and λύπη within the emotional repertoire of the time. We will do this by utilising Stoic discussion. We will move from the general understanding of emotions outlined in Part II to the definitions of individual emotions. At this definitional level, the Stoics are seeking to understand emotion terms as they were commonly used, and, therefore, it is this second level that will give us insights into the key characteristics that mark each emotion as distinct and nameable. However, throughout this process we will need to be aware of the third level of discussion – the contextualisation and rationale given to emotions. At the third level, Stoicism will provide a point of comparison but will not be allowed to be prescriptive for 1 Peter. Additionally, at this level, the LXX's use of emotions will be utilised to help us explicate the nuances of 1 Peter's own use of joy and distress.

The emotion terms for joy/rejoicing and being distressed that appear in 1 Peter 1.6–8 are: χαρά, ἀγαλλιάω, and λυπέω. For the sake of our examination of the Greco-Roman and LXX literature the search terms will be broadened to include the noun λύπη and the verb χαίρω (see 4.13). The following attempt to locate these terms will inform both this and the following chapter.

Locating Joy and Distress

As noted, we will start with Stoic definitions to outline the key characteristics of each emotion.

χαρά and λύπη in Stoicism[1]

Stoicism highlighted both χαρά and λύπη as primary emotions under which others were located.[2] Their relationship is depicted in Table 5.1.

The first point to note is that λύπη is one of the passions and is therefore categorised negatively by Stoicism, whereas χαρά is a εὐπάθεια and thus is appropriate even for the wise man (Seneca, *Ep.* 59.2).[3]

Andronicus and Diogenes Laertius provide the following definitions:

---

[1] For the use of χαρά before Epicureanism and Stoicism see I. L. E. Ramelli and D. Konstan, 'The Use of Χαρα in the New Testament and Its Background in Hellenistic Moral Philosophy', *Exemplaria Classica* 14 (2010): 185–204, at 185–7.

[2] Aristotle does list χαρά as a πάθος in *Eth. nic.* 2.5, 1105b21–3 and *De an.* 403a16–18 but does not discuss it in his lengthy treatment of emotions in *On Rhetoric*. For possible reasons for this see Ramelli and Konstan, 'Use of Χαρα', 186–7. For Aristotle λύπη is not a distinct emotion but is an attendant aspect of emotional experience generally (see *Eth. eud.* 2.2.4, 1220b10–15).

[3] In fact χαρά, or more properly χαίρω, is so acceptable that Marcus Aurelius can say that Universal Nature itself rejoices (*Med.* 9.35).

Table 5.1 *Stoic Primary Emotions*

	Object	Present	Future
Πάθος	Perceived good	ἡδονή (Pleasure)	ἐπιθυμία (Desire)
	Perceived bad	λύπη (Distress)	φόβος (Fear)
Εὐπάθεια	Well-reasoned good	χαρά (Joy)	βούλησις (Will)
	Well-reasoned bad		εὐλάβεια (Caution)

λύπη μὲν οὖν ἐστιν ἄλογος συστολή. ἢ δόξα πρόσφατος κακοῦ παρουσίας, ἐφ᾽ ᾧ οἴονται δεῖν συστέλλεσθαι.

Distress is an irrational contraction, or a fresh opinion that something bad is present, at which people think it right to be contracted [i.e. depressed]. (Andronicus [*Pass.*] 1= SVF 3.391, trans. Long and Sedley)

καὶ τὴν μὲν χαρὰν ἐναντίαν φασὶν εἶναι τῇ ἡδονῇ, οὖσαν εὔλογον ἔπαρσιν·

Joy, they say, is the opposite to pleasure, consisting in well-reasoned swelling [elation]. (Diogenes Laertius 7.116 = SVF 3.431, trans. Long and Sedley)

Given that joy is defined by its relationship to ἡδονή, it is worth detailing its definition also:

ἡδονὴ δὲ ἄλογος ἔπαρσις· ἢ δόξα πρόσφατος ἀγαθοῦ παρουσίας, ἐφ᾽ ᾧ οἴονται δεῖν ἐπαίρεσθαι.

Pleasure is an irrational swelling, or a fresh opinion that something good is present, at which people think it right to be swollen [i.e. elated]. (Andronicus [*Pass.*] 1 = SVF 3.391, trans. Long and Sedley; cf. Cicero, *Tusc.* 4.6.13)

So, we can determine the following characteristics of λύπη and χαρά:

1. λύπη has as its object the bad. Significantly, for this object to occasion distress the evil has to be considered present.[4] For Stoicism, because λύπη is a passion,

---

[4] Cf. Epictetus, *Diatr.* 4.1.84 where Epictetus comments that φόβος turns to λύπη

this viewpoint is described as a fresh opinion (δόξα πρόσφατος) which indicates that it is a misguided interpretation of the object. However, if we put to one side this Stoic colouring of λύπη we are still left with a workable definition. We can also appreciate that λύπη evaluates the object as an evil (κακός) and therefore, within the person's understanding of reality, as detrimental to her. This leads to the action-tendency associated with λύπη which is contraction (συστολή), that is, a movement away from the object.

2. χαρά has as its object the good, and, as with distress, the object has to be thought to be present to inspire joy. This is not stated in the definition of joy, but we can piece this together from looking at its counterpart passion, ἡδονή, which is the same as χαρά in all respects except for the foundation on which it is based – opinion rather than reason. Thus, according to Stoic categorisation, joy is marked by being well-reasoned (cf. Seneca, *Ep.* 23.6; 59.3–4).[5] It is differentiated from pleasure by the surety of the goodness of its object. We can also recognise that joy, by evaluating the object as good (ἀγαθός) deems the object to be beneficial to, or at least in accordance with, human flourishing. Consequently, we arrive at the action-tendency of χαρά, which is swelling (ἔπαρσις), that is, a movement towards the object.[6]

It is worth reminding ourselves that the movements of the soul were considered to result in outward behaviour. Thus, the evaluation of the object as good or bad directly impacts one's response to it, not just emotionally, but practically. To agree with the proposition present in each of these emotions is to position oneself to act accordingly.

---

when the anticipated object becomes present; cf. Cicero, *Tusc.* 4.7.14 and Marcus Aurelius, *Med.* 10.25.

[5] Here Stoicism is following Epicureanism in allowing χαρά to contain reasoning. Epicureanism was the first school to see χαρά as involving reason. They did not consider it an irrational πάθος but a sentiment. However, they did think that χαρά could involve false reasoning; see Ramelli and Konstan, 'Use of Χαρα', 188–91.

[6] The movements of the soul that could equally be translated as deflation for distress and elation for joy are probably a way of describing the physical feeling one has that makes one aware that the emotion is taking place. As such, they are similar to the modern notion of an emotion's positive or negative valence. Cf. Graver, *Stoicism*, 28–30.

As noted above, λύπη and χαρά are primary emotions under which other emotions are grouped. By looking at the range of affective experiences placed under λύπη and χαρά we can gain a better understanding of what emotion concepts they can cover. According to Diogenes Laertius on λύπη:

> εἴδη δ' αὐτῆς ἔλεον, φθόνον, ζῆλον, ζηλοτυπίαν, ἄχθος, ἐνόχλησιν, ἀνίαν, ὀδύνην, σύγχυσιν.

> Its kinds are pity, envy, jealousy, rivalry, heaviness [or vexation], annoyance, sorrow, anguish, confusion. (7.111; cf. Andronicus [*Pass.*] 2 = SVF 3.414)

Cicero follows Diogenes Laertius, giving a slightly modified list:

> ut aegritudini invidentia   ... aemulatio, obtrectatio, misericordia, angor, luctus, maeror, aerumna, dolor, lamentatio, sollicitudo, molestia, adflictatio, desperatio et si quae sunt de genere eodem.

> [U]nder the head of distress come ... 'envy' ... rivalry, jealousy, compassion, anxiety, mourning, sadness, troubling, grief, lamenting, depression, vexation, pining, despondency and anything of the same kind. (*Tusc.* 4.7.16 [King, LCL])[7]

What this shows is that λύπη does not narrowly cover grief or pain as it is often translated but can include more complex mental states like vexation, despondency, depression, even confusion (cf. *Tusc.* 4.8.17–19).

According to Diogenes Laertius, the Stoics categorised three concepts under χαρά:

> ὑπὸ δὲ τὴν χαρὰν τέρψιν, εὐφροσύνην, εὐθυμίαν.

> Under joy are enjoyment, merriment [or sociability], contentment. (7.116)[8]

---

[7] For how each of these is further defined see Cicero, *Tusc.* 4.8.17–19; cf. Stobaeus, *Ecl.* = SVF 3.413; Andronicus, [*Pass.*] 2 = SVF 3.414.

[8] I have translated τέρψις as enjoyment, but it could also mean delight; εὐφροσύνη as merriment, though Long and Sedley would prefer sociability; and εὐθυμία as contentment, though it also carries the idea of cheerfulness more generally; see Long and Sedley, *HP1*, 412.

Andronicus gives a description of each one:

> Τέρψις μὲν οὖν ἐστι χαρὰ πρέπουσα ταῖς περὶ αὐτὸν ὠφελείαις.
> Εὐφροσύνη δὲ χαρὰ ἐπὶ τοῖς τοῦ σώφρονος ἔργοις.
> Εὐθυμία δὲ χαρὰ ἐπὶ διαγωγῇ ἢ ἀνεπιζητησίᾳ παντός.

Enjoyment therefore is joy that is appropriately fitting to
surrounding advantages.
Merriment is joy at the deeds of the sound mind [self-control].
Contentment is joy at course of life or at the absence of
enquiry of all. (*[Pass.]* 6 = SVF 3.432)[9]

There is a distinct lack of exuberance in these further subcategories
of joy. Though joy is positive, it is not an excessive transport. Even
merriment is restrained by self-control (cf. Seneca, *Ep.* 59.15). It feels
alien to our modern idea of joy to list contentment (a stable state
that lacks questioning) as one of its species.[10] Again, this highlights
the cultural understanding of emotions. For the Stoics, the joy of
the wise man is stable, tranquil, and exhibits constancy. Constancy
by Seneca's time is such a constituent part of joy that he can speak
of joy as a sober matter (*res severa*) being able to endure poverty
and pain (*Ep.* 23.4).[11] This is because the good to which joy relates
is virtue (*Ep.* 27.3), which is always approved by reason and as a
consequence is solid and eternal (*Ep.* 66.31). Thus, joy is enduring.[12]
In the manoeuvre of associating joy with one's possession of virtue
(*Ep.* 59.17), the object of joy is made integral to the person and joy
becomes no longer dependent on externals, that is, things outside of
one's control.[13]

The above has outlined the basic characteristics of χαρά and λύπη
and the range of emotional experiences that these primary emotions

---

[9] Cf. Graver, *Stoicism*, 58.

[10] The *Oxford Dictionary* online defines joy as 'a feeling of great pleasure and
happiness' and lists 'delight, great pleasure, joyfulness, jubilation, triumph, exultation, rejoicing, happiness, gladness, glee, exhilaration, ebullience, exuberance,
elation, euphoria, bliss, ecstasy, transports of delight, rapture, radiance' as synonyms.
Accessed 26 November 2015. www.oxforddictionaries.com/definition/english/joy.

[11] Elsewhere Seneca does describe joy as 'relaxed and cheerful' (*Ep.* 66.12–13
[Gummere, LCL]) and also links the adjectives *hilaris* (cheerful) and *laetus* (glad) with
joy (*Ep.* 66.15), which shows that it can still carry a positive elative connotation.

[12] Seneca comments: 'it is a characteristic of real joy that it never ceases, and never
changes into its opposite' (*Ep.* 59.2 [Gummere, LCL]). He notes that in common language joy is often attributed to things such as the birth of a child or a marriage, but
that these things are not matters for joy because the same things often end up causing
sorrow (cf. *Ep.* 23.6).

[13] Cf. *Ep.* 56.7–9; 59.2; 92.12; see Graver, *Stoicism*, 46–50.

can cover. We will discover that some of these groupings are also present in the LXX, however, each emotion is not necessarily nuanced in the same way as in Stoicism.

Joy and Distress in the LXX[14]

There is one text in the LXX that seeks to address the emotions philosophically, this is 4 Maccabees. It does so only briefly in chapter 1. It states:

παθῶν δὲ φύσεις εἰσὶν αἱ περιεκτικώταται δύο ἡδονή τε καὶ πόνος· ... πολλαὶ δὲ καὶ περὶ τὴν ἡδονὴν καὶ τὸν πόνον παθῶν εἰσιν ἀκολουθίαι. πρὸ μὲν οὖν τῆς ἡδονῆς ἐστιν ἐπιθυμία, μετὰ δὲ τὴν ἡδονὴν χαρά. πρὸ δὲ τοῦ πόνου ἐστὶν φόβος, μετὰ δὲ τὸν πόνον λύπη.

The two most comprehensive sources of emotions are pleasure and pain ... The pleasure and pain of emotions have many sequences. Therefore, before pleasure is desire, and after pleasure is joy; before pain is fear, and after pain is distress. (1.20–3)

The basic understanding of emotions involving pleasure (ἡδονή) and pain (πόνος) is reminiscent of Aristotle's definition. Yet, we can also see a very similar mapping to Stoicism: three of the passions are listed (ἐπιθυμία, φόβος, λύπη) but instead of ἡδονή there is χαρά, probably because ἡδονή is already being used within each definition. Apart from the different use of ἡδονή, the same temporal aspect of the emotions is evident, as too is their relationship to the good and the bad (if we take ἡδονή to indicate the feeling of the presence of good, and πόνος the feeling of something bad).[15] However, there is little said beyond this, other than to accord with ancient philosophy in asserting that rational judgement via reason can rule the emotions (1.19). Thus, we need to turn to how the emotion terms are being used within the LXX.

We have been investigating χαρά and λύπη as emotion terms specifically. However, in 1 Peter the related verb forms χαίρω and λυπέω

---

[14] The following references follow LXX nomenclature and numbering.

[15] 4 Maccabees does not solely discuss emotions in terms of cognition, but includes bodily feeling also; cf. Philo, *Det.* 32.119–21 who mentions that there are four passions, lists λύπη and φόβος as among them, and then proceeds to define them in agreement with Stoicism. According to Philo, to possess virtue is what produces χαρά. Cf. QG 2.57 where the passions and εὐπάθεῖαι are listed as counterparts following Stoic categorisations.

are used, along with another verb for rejoicing: ἀγαλλιάω. Thus, as we proceed, we will broaden our investigation to include these.[16] We have also seen that in the Stoic mapping τέρψις, εὐφροσύνη, and εὐθυμία are types of χαρά. What we quickly discover in the LXX is that χαρά, ἀγαλλίασις/ἀγαλλίαμα, εὐφροσύνη, and their verbal forms (χαίρω, ἀγαλλιάω, εὐφραίνω) – along with τέρψις, though much less frequently – are close synonyms and at points are interchangeable.[17] This is particularly the case with εὐφραίνω and ἀγαλλιάω, but is also mirrored by χαρά and εὐφροσύνη which are often used in conjunction to convey the idea of 'rejoice and be glad/joy and gladness'.[18] A good example of the close connection of these terms is Ps 95.11–12:

> εὐφραινέσθωσαν οἱ οὐρανοί, καὶ ἀγαλλιάσθω ἡ γῆ,
> σαλευθήτω ἡ θάλασσα καὶ τὸ πλήρωμα αὐτῆς·
> χαρήσεται τὰ πεδία καὶ πάντα τὰ ἐν αὐτοῖς,
> τότε ἀγαλλιάσονται πάντα τὰ ξύλα τοῦ δρυμοῦ. (cf. Tob 13.15–16)

Let the heavens be glad, and let the earth rejoice;
let the sea roar, and all that fills it;
let the field [plain] exult, and everything in it.
Then shall all the trees of the forest sing for joy. (NRSVA)

Sirach 1.11–12 adds further support for the closeness of these terms:

> Φόβος κυρίου δόξα καὶ καύχημα
> καὶ εὐφροσύνη καὶ στέφανος ἀγαλλιάματος.

---

[16] We could not have investigated ἀγαλλιάω earlier as it does not occur in any Greco-Roman classical or early Hellenistic literature, except for one occurrence in Aeilus Herodianus' (or Pseudo-Herodianus; second century CE) Περὶ ὀρθογραφίας (part 3.2 p. 462) in which it is simply listed alongside other words that carry similar syllabic qualities. The verb ἀγαλλιάω appears in the LXX over 80 times, primarily in the Psalms. In the majority of occurrences it carries a sense of exultant rejoicing, often vocalised rejoicing (e.g. Pss 15.9; 94.1). It has an exuberant, effervescent tone, vibrant in emotional colour; cf. Morrice, *Joy*, 20.

[17] εὐθυμία does not appear in the LXX. The noun ἀγαλλίασις, like ἀγαλλιάω, can express vocalised rejoicing (Pss 41.5; 44.8; 46.2; 106.22; 117.15; Tob 13.1; *Pss. Sol.* 5.1), whereas ἀγαλλίαμα is used more for joy as an abstract concept and in this is closer to χαρά (Jdt 12.14; Sir 30.22; Ps 118.111; Isa 61.11).

[18] For εὐφραίνω and ἀγαλλιάω see 2 Kgdms 1.20; 1 Chr 16.31; Pss 9.3; 15.9; 31.11; 47.12; 66.5; 69.5; 89.14; 117.24; Isa 12.6; 25.9, etc.; cf. Morrice, *Joy*, 27. Additionally, (ἐν) εὐφροσύνῃ appears with ἀγαλλιάω to depict the mode of rejoicing (Pss 67.4; 104.43; Isa 29.19; 41.16; 61.10; 65.14). This creates a redundant repetition like 1 Peter 1.8's ἀγαλλιᾶσθε χαρᾷ. For use of χαρά/χαίρω with synonymous terms see Esth 8.15–17; 9.17–19; Tob 13.11–13; 1 Macc 4.59; 5.54; 2 Macc 3.30; Ps 125; Wis 8.16; Sir 30.16–22; Hab 3.18; Zeph 3.14; Zech 8.19; Isa 55.12; Jer 15.16; 16.9; 25.10; Bar 4.33.

φόβος κυρίου <u>τέρψει</u> καρδίαν
καὶ δώσει <u>εὐφροσύνην</u> καὶ <u>χαρὰν</u> καὶ μακροημέρευσιν.[19]

The fear of the Lord is glory and exultation,
and gladness and a crown of rejoicing.
The fear of the Lord delights the heart,
and gives gladness and joy and long life. (NRSVCE)

So, we can see that like with Stoic mapping these terms are closely bound. This would suggest that the LXX and the Stoic philosophers, because of their shared language, demonstrate the general grouping of these ideas together in their emotional repertoire. So, what about the emotion terms that joy/rejoicing is contrasted with?

In 2 Maccabees 3.30 χαρά and εὐφροσύνη are directly contrasted with ταραχή (disturbance) and δέος (fear/alarm): the former are depicted as the opposite and antidote to the latter (cf. 3 Macc 6.32). Likewise, in Isaiah 35.10 we find that ἀγαλλίαμα and εὐφροσύνη are present when ὀδύνη (pain/distress), λύπη, and στεναγμός (sighing/groaning) have departed (cf. Prov 10.1; 14.13; Wis 8.16; Sir 30.5, 21–2; Isa 51.11; 65.13–14; Bar 4.33–4).[20] These verses give the impression that joy is seen as a good, tranquil state and that distress (ὀδύνη, λύπη, πένθος) is negative and troubling. The two states are incompatible: where there is one there is absence of the other.

This leads us on to examine distress briefly. As these verses have highlighted, like with χαρά, λύπη is grouped with or used synonymously with other words that transmit similar emotional content such as ὀδύνη and πένθος (cf. Tob 3.1; Lam 1.22; *Pss. Sol.* 4.14–15). It can refer to grief, in the sense of mourning, as it is often translated (e.g. Tob 2.5; Sir 38.17–20 cf. Tob 13.16). However, it can also be linked with θλῖψις, indicating affliction (Sir 30.21–2; cf. Dan 3.50); συγχέω, which can be used of the mind to mean to trouble/confound (Jonah 4.1; cf. Tob 4.3); πόνος, which indicates physical distress or toil (Isa 1.5; cf. Gen 3.16–17; Jer 15.18), and the more general ταράσσω (Ps 54.3). It can also cover other troubling mental states such worry (Tob 10.3–6; Dan 6.19), despair (Isa 19.10; Tob 3.10) or even indicate angry disturbance (1 Kgdms 29.4; Esth 1.12; Ezek 16.43). Thus, we see, as the Stoic grouping revealed, that λύπη has a broad application and can cover both mental and physical distress.

---

[19] Here φόβος carries a different nuance to the Stoic passion. We will return to this in Chapter 7.
[20] ὀδύνη can mean pain of the body or also of the mind in terms of grief or distress, so is synonymous with λύπη; see 'ὀδύνη' in BDAG (692).

It is also worth noting, though rather obvious, that in the above examples joy and distress relate to the good and bad respectively. However, what we are yet to do is look at the specific contextualisation of these emotions and the rationale they reveal. In this way, we can see what types of events and objects are seen as appropriate occasions for these emotions.

For the Stoic, joy is the domain of the wise man, but in the LXX joy is predominantly the possession of God's people (Pss 47.12; 52.7; 88.13; 96.8; Isa 12.6). Here, the people of God are understood as those who are in a right covenant relationship with him; at the eschatological dimension this can include people of all nations. It is the righteous, faithful, or upright in heart, and those seeking God who rejoice (Pss 31.11; 69.5; 96.12; 117.15; 131.9, 16). This is specifically in contrast to the wicked who experience calamity (Pss 5.11–13; 34.1–10, 26–8; 67.1–5; 74.7–11; Isa 16.10; 65.13–14). Furthermore, creation can rejoice (1 Chr 16.31; Pss 18.5–6; 64.13; 95.11–12; 97.4, 8; Isa 35.1–2). Even God himself rejoices (Ps 59.8; Isa 65.19). From this, we can see that joy is presented positively, we might even say as the emotional goal. It not only signifies human flourishing but the thriving of creation, suggesting, like with Stoicism, that joy is part of aligning oneself with a larger cosmic enterprise.

Largely, God is the object of rejoicing. One can rejoice in the Lord/God (Pss 9.2; 31.11; 34.9; 62.12; 69.5; 96.12; Isa 25.19; 41.16; 61.10), in his name (Ps 89.13–17), or in his presence (Ps 67.4–5). Where the action infers shouting for joy, this is to the Lord/God (Pss 83.3; 94.1; 97.4). At other times the reason for rejoicing is God's action in the world: his salvation (Pss 9.15; 12.6; 20.2; 50.14; 94.1; 117.15; Isa 12.4; 25.9; 61.10; Hab 3.18), judgements (Pss 47.12; 95.10–13; 96.8; 97.8–9), mercy (Pss 30.8; 58.7; Isa 49.13), and greatness (Tob 13.9).[21] Sometimes it is God's attributes that make him the object of rejoicing: as maker and king (Ps 149.2), or inherently righteous (Pss 50.16; 144.7). Thus, we can see that, whereas for the Greco-Roman sage virtue is the highest good that occasions joy, for the LXX it is God himself and his action. God is rejoiced in because of his goodness towards his covenant people: he has revealed himself to be upright, eternally merciful, and true (i.e. faithful) to every generation (Pss 32.4–5; 99.5; cf. Pss 31.10–11; 131; *Pss. Sol.* 5). The covenant relationship is even a cause for God to rejoice (Isa 65.19). Subsequently, in this relational dynamic there is a coexisting

---

[21] Cf. 1 Chr 16.8–27; Pss 9; 44.7–8; 47.10–12; 88.1–19; God's judgement is particularly celebrated as impartial.

expectation that the person will have joy because God's goodness is assured to them (see Ps 32.18–22), which in turn brings stability (Pss 15.8–9; 20.7–8; 62.8; Isa 12.6).[22] Therefore, it is important to recognise that the subject experiences joy through their relationship with God, either as his people or as a created being correctly responding to its creator (1 Chr 16.31; Pss 94.1–7; 96.1–4; 149.2). In fact, joy becomes so fitting that one is commanded to serve God in joy (Pss 32.1; 80.2; 99.2). Consequently, the people can rejoice in God's law (Ps 118.14–16). The ability to choose to act in joy shows that joy is not simply an emotional reaction but a life orientation. As Barton comments, 'joy expresses a deep sense of *alignment*, both individual and corporate, with the will and ways of God'.[23] Thus, to rejoice in God becomes an identity marker of his people.[24] Conversely, if one acts against God then there is no joy or gladness (Isa 16.10; cf. Jer 16.4–9; 25.10; Joel 1.13–16) but inevitably turbulence, fear, shame, and distress (see above).

To rejoice in God is not always contingent on the present experience of the speaker. For example in Psalm 67 (LXX), alongside the writer's cry for deliverance, he calls those seeking God to rejoice in him. He does not yet have a tangibly present 'good' to rejoice about but, instead, looking to God is occasion enough for joy. This is based on a belief in God's justice and mercy that assure that he will ultimately bring good to the righteous (see Hab 3.18).[25] The deliberate choice of object combined with belief about this object allows the psalmist to shape his own emotions (cf. Pss 12.5–6; 30.1–9; 58.15–18). In doing so, this causes the person perspective on reality to be altered, with God being the dominant object whose presence provides the person with their evaluative schema and self-understanding.

The subjects and objects of distress are more varied. As noted above, distress can be mourning occasioned by the death of someone (Gen 42.38; Tob 2.5; Sir 38.17–20) but it can also be because of the thwarting of plans or desires (1 Kgdms 29.4; 1 Macc 6.4–13; Jonah 4.1). Distress can occur as part of God's judgement (Isa 50.10–11; Bar 4.30–4; cf. Deut 28.58–60; Wis 11.9–13; Amos 8.9–10; Isa 32.11); as a consequence of sin (Gen 3.16–17; 5.29; Tob 2.1–6; Sir

[22] Cf. Isa 35.10; 51.11; Pss 5.12; 74.10.
[23] Barton, 'Spirituality', 176–7.
[24] In some places joy because of right standing with God becomes a prophetic expectation; see Isa 35.1; 51.3; 65.17–19; cf. Pss 52.7; 125.5–6; Bar 4.36–7.
[25] Perhaps this is why the poor and downtrodden are able to rejoice in God (Isa 25.17–21).

14.1; 36.20; Isa 1.4–5; Lam 1.22); because of another's shameful behaviour (Prov 10.1; Sir 22.4; 26.28); or as a result of seeking false gods (Isa 8.16–23). Yet, the righteous, though very infrequently, can also find themselves in distress (Pss 30.10–12; 54.2–4). However, for the righteous, it is more common for God to be depicted as alleviating their distress (Tob 7.17; Ps 93.19; Isa 51.11 cf. Esth 9.22; Isa 14.3; 35.10; 40.29). It is evident that distress is seen as a negative emotion. At points distress is spoken of as having destructive qualities (Sir 30.21–3 cf. 38.20–1; Prov 25.20). Therefore, as with the Stoic definitions, distress is an indicator that something bad or harmful is present.

We can see from our survey that joy and distress in the LXX exhibit similar qualities to those acknowledged by Stoic philosophers. However, the occasions in which these emotions are appropriate are different. This is because they are based on a different assessment of what is good and bad, detrimental and beneficial to the human, that is, a different worldview. Joy comes from right relationship with God that recognises his goodness and distress is a consequence of evil, whether your own or another's. Where the righteous are experiencing distress because of others, there is a promise that God, who is ever faithful, is able to turn their sorrow into joy. Here, there is a difference with Stoicism. For the righteous person, her emotions are not shaped by an integral object (one's own virtue), but by God, who is external to the person.

So, having examined joy and distress in the LXX and Stoic philosophy we can now turn to their use in 1 Peter, utilising the above insights to give us greater precision in our analysis.

Joy Despite Distress: 1 Peter 1.6–8

The first mention of rejoicing and being distressed sit side by side in 1.6, which says:

ἐν ᾧ ἀγαλλιᾶσθε ὀλίγον ἄρτι, εἰ δέον ἐστίν, λυπηθέντας ἐν ποικίλοις πειρασμοῖς

in whom you rejoice, even if it is necessary now for a little while for you to be distressed by various trials.[26]

---

[26] I follow Mark Dubis here in seeing λυπέω as 'an emotional state of grief or distress' rather than simply physical suffering; M. Dubis, *1 Peter: A Handbook on the Greek Text*, BHGNT (Waco, TX: Baylor University Press, 2010), 11.

The second occurrence of rejoicing comes in 1.8:

ὃν οὐκ ἰδόντες ἀγαπᾶτε, εἰς ὃν ἄρτι μὴ ὁρῶντες, πιστεύοντες δὲ
ἀγαλλιᾶσθε χαρᾷ ἀνεκλαλήτῳ καὶ δεδοξασμένῃ

whom, though you have not seen, you love; in whom, though now not seeing, you believe and rejoice with joy that is inexpressible and filled with glory.

These verses will be the focus of this chapter. We will deal with each emotion term sequentially, starting with ἀγαλλιάω in 1.6.

The Context of ἀγαλλιάω

Verses 1.3–12 form the opening of the main body of 1 Peter and serve to introduce key themes and lay foundations for what follows.[27] A number of commentators see 1.6 as the beginning of a new sub-unit (1.6–9) indicated by the preposition and relative pronoun construction ἐν ᾧ (cf.1.10).[28] There is a shift at 1.6, but, if the sentence is artificially divided here, we are in danger of missing the flow of ideas. As will be demonstrated, ἀγαλλιάω is dependent on the preceding material. The above discussion has revealed that ἀγαλλιάω can express exuberant, even vocalised, joy. If this is the case, what makes this emotion fitting at this point, especially for an audience undergoing persecution? This contextualisation of and rationale for joy needs to be unpacked. We will do this through exploring the wider context of 1.3–9.

The first thing to establish is who the subject of rejoicing is. The 2nd person plural ἀγαλλιᾶσθε (1.6) reveals that the recipients are collectively the subject. This, along with the broad recipient list in 1.1, indicates that the author views such rejoicing as appropriate for all believers. 1 Peter is replete with LXX quotations and allusions. Therefore, it is not surprising that we find ἀγαλλιάω in 1 Peter ascribed to a defined group, the believers, and in a similar contextual setting. In the LXX rejoicing was oriented towards God (we

[27] Achtemeier, *1 Peter*, 90; Elliott, *1 Peter*, 329. For more on the literary relationship between 1.3–12 and 1.13–5.11 see D. W. Kendall, 'The Literary and Theological Function of 1 Peter 1:3–12', in *Perspectives on First Peter*, ed. Charles H. Talbert, NABPR Special Studies Series 9 (Macon, GA: Mercer University Press, 1986), 103–20.
[28] Michaels, *1 Peter*, 25–7; Achtemeier, *1 Peter*, 90; J. Schlosser, *La Première Épître de Pierre*, CBNT 21 (Paris: Les Éditions du Cerf, 2011), 59, 67–8; Elliott, *1 Peter*, 338, etc.

will return to this below), but was specifically occasioned by his just judgements, mercy, and salvation. We find two of these highlighted in 1.3–9: mercy and salvation.

Verses 1.3–5 open with praise of God (εὐλογητὸς ὁ θεός) that focuses on his actions towards believers. All of these actions are specifically said to be according to his great mercy (κατὰ τὸ πολὺ αὐτοῦ ἔλεος).[29] Thus, at the outset of the letter, the author identifies the believers as those who have experienced God's mercy. In the LXX the term ἔλεος is the word used to convey God's covenant faithfulness and 'goodness towards his people'.[30] Consequently, the use of ἔλεος is intended to mark this special relationship in 1 Peter too, but this time for the Christian. This will be affirmed in 2.10 where receiving God's mercy is shown to be the definitive marker of his people.[31] Thus, the letter opens with a tone of intimacy between God and the believer, and the presence of the idea of covenant relationship is glimpsed.[32] That rejoicing is ascribed to the believers, who have received God's ἔλεος, suggests that, like in the LXX, the author sees rejoicing as the possession of God's people. The second theme of salvation is tied to the first, being one of the actions arising from God's mercy: the believer is delivered to salvation (1.5). At this point the covenant relationship reveals itself again for it is through the believers' faith (or faithfulness) that they are in this favourable position.[33] Faith here means belief but also trust and 'exclusive commitment to God'.[34] Consequently, in 1.3–5 we have two sides of a special relationship

---

[29] Elliott, *1 Peter*, 329. It is worth noting that for God to have, and be led, by an emotion was not a Hellenistic way of thinking but is distinctly biblical; see Feldmeier, *Peter*, 64–5.

[30] Elliott, *1 Peter*, 331. Cf. Exod 34.6; Num 14.18; Ps 85.5; Joel 2.13; Michaels, *1 Peter*, 18. Contra Bigg, it is not God's pity on our misery or Christ's sympathy; C. Bigg, *A Critical and Exegetical Commentary on the First Epistles of St. Peter and St. Jude* (Edinburgh: T&T Clark, 1901), 99.

[31] Elliott, *1 Peter*, 441–2; D. W. Kendall, '1 Peter 1:3–9', *Interpretation* 41 (1987): 66–71, at 67–8.

[32] Achtemeier supports the relational aspect of 1.3–5 being primary when he comments that the opening blesses God for what he has done, which is chiefly to create a new people; Achtemeier, *1 Peter*, 92. If Elliott is correct that the eulogy of verses 1.3–5, which publicly declare God's honour, was the type of public praise expected from the client in a patron–client relationship, then it could be that even the form of these opening words encourages the hearers to remember their relational standing with God; Elliott, *1 Peter*, 331.

[33] The fact that 1.9 says that they are obtaining salvation that is the goal of their faith (τὸ τέλος τῆς πίστεως ὑμῶν) suggests it is the believers' faith not God's faithfulness that it emphasised in 1.5.

[34] Elliott, *1 Peter*, 337; cf. Michaels, *1 Peter*, 23.

established. It is in this context that the believers' joy is deemed fitting.[35]

There are, however, some Christian aspects to these familiar themes. First, God is the Father of our Lord Jesus Christ (1.3). Therefore, God's relationship with the believer is shaped by reference to Christ and Christ is made central to the special relationship (cf. 1.21).[36] It is those under Christ's lordship that have God as father.[37] Thus, the relationship between God and the believer is described in familial terms.[38] Added to this is the believers' new begetting, which comes through the resurrection of Jesus Christ and 'implies God as progenitor'. So, we can appreciate that the relationship is understood not only as covenant obligation but as one between newly begotten believers and their heavenly Father.[39] God's role as father implies his 'authority over them … his paternal affection, protection, and care for them'.[40] Second, God's merciful action of salvation is through Christ's death and resurrection. It is this one act that displays God's mercy and becomes the essential basis of the Christian's faith in God (1.21). Thus, the believers' relationship to God, and therefore their understanding of their own identity and existence, cannot be understood apart from Christ or separately from his death and resurrection.[41]

So, we can see that ἀγαλλιάω is being used in a context that follows the LXX but is also different because of the place given to Christ. Thus, in 1 Peter the believers' rejoicing occurs within the context of God's relationship with his people and *his* deeds *for* the believer. Consequently, in the following discussion of joy this relational focus that the author has deliberately established must be kept in mind.

---

[35] Cf. 1 Peter 2.7–9. An added indication that ἀγαλλιάω is occurring where a covenant relationship is in view is the mention of inheritance (1.4). Inheritance of the land of Israel was a significant aspect of the covenant relationship and was often lost or gained depending on fidelity to the covenant. Here, however, the inheritance is not territorial but is a 'transcendent reality'. Cf. Dan 12.13; *Pss. Sol.* 14; Mark 10.17; Titus 3.7; Elliott, *1 Peter*, 335–6; Feldmeier, *Peter*, 71. In fact in *Pss. Sol.* 14.10 the faithful, in contrast to sinners, κληρονομήσουσιν ζωὴν ἐν εὐφροσύνῃ (in/with gladness will inherit life). See also Achtemeier, *1 Peter*, 96 who comments that in post-exilic literature the inheritance is God himself, which supports my argument that relationship with God is the focus here.

[36] L. Goppelt, *A Commentary on I Peter*, ed. Ferdinand Hahn, trans. John E. Alsup (Grand Rapids, MI: William B. Eerdmans, 1993), 80–1; Michaels, *1 Peter*, 17.

[37] Feldmeier, *Peter*, 63.

[38] Familial and household language is used throughout the letter; see 1.14, 2.2, 5, 17; 4.17; 5.9, 12.

[39] Elliott, *1 Peter*, 331.

[40] Elliott, *1 Peter*, 364.

[41] Cf. Feldmeier, *Peter*, 78.

EXCURSUS: THE FORCE OF ἀγαλλιᾶσθε

Before discussing the object of rejoicing we need to determine the time component and force of ἀγαλλιᾶσθε. There are three options: (1) present indicative – 'you are rejoicing'; (2) present imperative – 'rejoice'; (3) a present indicative with future meaning – 'you will rejoice'. Martin prefers the third option.[42] For Martin the aorist participle λυπηθέντες indicates that distress occurs before rejoicing.[43] Furthermore, the application of ἄρτι to λυπηθέντες suggests that persecution is happening now in the present. Therefore, ἀγαλλιᾶσθε, which comes second sequentially, must be understood as future.[44] In this reading, not only are joy and distress contrasted but they are differentiated by the time periods in which they exist, with the present being marked only by distress.[45] However, the close repetition of ἀγαλλιᾶσθε in 1.8, which is also combined with ἄρτι and other present verbs causes problems for reading ἀγαλλιᾶσθε in 1.6 as future. Thus, in order for ἀγαλλιᾶσθε to be symmetrically future in 1.8, Martin has to force the present participles ὁρῶντες and πιστεύοντες to be 'participles of the imperfect'.[46] However, such squeezing of ὁρῶντες and πιστεύοντες into an antecedent time frame both ignores the presence of ἄρτι and is completely unnecessary if ἀγαλλιᾶσθε is allowed to retain its typical present force. So, how should we understand the aorist participle λυπηθέντας? It is not a problem to see distress as occurring before ἀγαλλιᾶσθε if we take a more expansive view of what can be classed as 'present'. Present could refer to the whole time frame in which the believer currently sits – the current epoch before the eschaton. Present does not have to refer to a specific punctiliar moment. Within this specific epoch, which is 'now', they have experienced trials (and are likely to continue experiencing them); but, also now in the same time frame, and perhaps more presently, they rejoice. Both occur in the present epoch, but suffering can have occurred prior to this current reference to rejoicing.[47]

---

[42] T. Martin, 'The Present Indicative in the Eschatological Statements of 1 Peter 1:6, 8', *JBL* 111 (1992): 307–12, at 307. Cf. Goppelt, *I Peter*, 88–9; Michaels, *1 Peter*, 26–8; Millauer, *Leiden*, 183–4, though Millauer does not rule out option 1.

[43] Martin is working with the *NA27* rendering of 1.6 and therefore discusses λυπηθέντες rather than λυπηθέντας.

[44] Martin, 'Present Indicative', 309; However, Schlosser argues against this, saying that one cannot in every case rely on the aorist participle having to refer to a previous event; Schlosser, *Pierre*, 73.

[45] But if 1 Peter is following a tradition that allows joy in suffering (cf. 4.13), putting joy and suffering into different time periods is unnecessary; Brox, *Petrusbrief*, 64.

[46] Martin, 'Present Indicative', 309.

[47] This does not stop current rejoicing being affected by the future. Elliott and Feldmeier note the difficulty of separating time periods in the letter. However, they

Moreover, if joy is a more stable state indicating permanent orientation, then it is closer to a disposition, and, as such, it could have an overarching quality. To keep rejoicing remains the present ongoing disposition despite changing circumstances that at points may be distressing. Given the potential benefits of asking the audience to see rejoicing now as fitting despite distress (discussed below), it seems that option 1 is preferable to option 3 and so ἀγαλλιᾶσθε should be read as retaining its present force.[48] The majority of scholars dismiss option 2 because it is generally agreed that the exhortative content of the letter begins at 1.13. At 1.6 we are still firmly within the initial blessing material in which declarations rather than imperatives are more appropriate.[49] Therefore, the following discussion will read ἀγαλλιᾶσθε in 1.6 and 1.8 as present indicatives with present force.

Deciphering the Object

Having explored the general context of rejoicing and that rejoicing is part of the audience's present experience, we now need to answer another question: what or who is the object of the believers' joy? Syntactically, the answer is simple: the relative pronoun ᾧ that precedes ἀγαλλιάω indicates the object of the emotion. The problem is that the antecedent of the relative pronoun is uncertain.[50] The phrase ἐν ᾧ ἀγαλλιᾶσθε (1.6) is commonly rendered with the demonstrative: 'in (all) this you (greatly) rejoice' (see ESVUK; NIV; NKJV; NRSVA).[51] Thus ᾧ refers to something from the previous material, though it is not clear what. It could be any of the clauses introduced by εἰς which detail the benefits of the believers' new begetting: their salvation that will be revealed in the last time (1.5); their protection by God's power (1.4–5); their inheritance that is being kept for them (1.4); their living hope (1.3); or perhaps, as many commentators think, all of these.[52]

---

emphasise that the future impinges on the present. Feldmeier, therefore, sees present joy as possible because of the anticipation of eschatological joy. Elliott likewise accepts a present reading because 'present and future realities … intersect and overlap'; Feldmeier, *Peter*, 80; Elliott, *1 Peter*, 339.

   [48] For further support for a present reading see J. N. D. Kelly, *A Commentary on the Epistles of Peter and of Jude* (London: Adam & Charles Black, 1969), 53; K. H. Schelkle, *Die Petrusbriefe: Der Judasbrief*, HThKNT 13 Fasz. 2, 3rd ed. (Freiburg: Herder, 1970), 34; Brox, *Petrusbrief*, 63–4.

   [49] Martin, 'Present Indicative', 307–8; cf. Selwyn, *St. Peter*, 126; Michaels, *1 Peter*, 27–8; Achtemeier, *1 Peter*, 100; Elliott, *1 Peter*, 329; de Villiers, 'Joy', 72.

   [50] P⁷² omits ἐν ᾧ altogether; Achtemeier, *1 Peter*, 99.

   [51] All versions: Accessed 27 November 2015. www.biblegateway.com.

   [52] Achtemeier, *1 Peter*, 92, 100; Elliott, *1 Peter*, 333; cf. Kelly, *Epistles of Peter*, 53; Brox, *Petrusbrief*, 63; Schlosser, *Pierre*, 73; Thurén, *Argument*, 71; de Villiers, 'Joy', 71–2.

Elliott translates ἐν ᾧ ἀγαλλιᾶσθε as 'Consequently you exult with joy' and thus sees the entire thought expressed in 1.3–5 as the antecedent. Elliott reads ἐν ᾧ as a 'temporal or circumstantial conjunction', which he argues is used elsewhere in the letter (2.12; 3.16, 19; 4.4) to mean '"in this connection," "in which case or circumstance when"'. Hence, he thinks it is used similarly here.[53] Achtemeier likewise cites 4.4 as evidence to support his view that ἐν ᾧ refers to the material in the preceding verses. For Achtemeier the ἐν ᾧ in 4.4 proleptically anticipates 'the cause for offence on the part of the unbelievers' and so means 'therefore' or 'for that reason', which favours the same meaning here in 1.6.[54] The result of Achtemeier and Elliott's reading is that joy is a response to God's *action*. In view of the LXX usage, this is certainly a plausible option.

However, the other instances of ἐν ᾧ cited by Elliott and Achtemeier are not exactly the same as in 1.6. In 2.12 and 3.16 ἐν ᾧ is introduced by ἵνα so that the whole phrase operates as a consequence clause. This does not occur in 1.6 where ἐν ᾧ stands alone. This suggests that when the author wants to speak about the consequence of something he does not do this by ἐν ᾧ alone but adds to it the conjunction ἵνα. Further, as Martin comments, in these verses and in 4.4 'it is impossible to relate the relative pronoun to a preceding noun'. In 1.6 it is possible to do this, even if we are not sure which noun it should be! Martin also rightly notices that in 3.19 we find the construction ἐν ᾧ but, because an obvious antecedent noun (πνεῦμα) is present, few argue for a consequential reading. Instead, 'in which' or 'in whom' is preferred.[55] Thus, 3.19 and the variances in other uses of ἐν ᾧ provide evidence that ἐν ᾧ in 1.6 does not have to carry a consequential or circumstantial meaning. Rather, ἐν ᾧ could refer to a specific object. In this context, this could be καιρός (1.5), θεός (1.3), or Ἰησοῦς Χριστός (1.3).[56] In the following, I want to argue that θεός is a plausible option and should not be dismissed too readily.

As far as I know only Hort argues for Χριστός or θεός.[57] Most scholars fail to mention Χριστός or disregard it with no real

[53] Elliott, *1 Peter*, 338–9.
[54] Achtemeier, *1 Peter*, 100.
[55] Martin, 'Present Indicative', 309.
[56] Achtemeier, *1 Peter*, 100.
[57] F. J. A. Hort, *The First Epistle of St Peter 1.1–2.17: The Greek Text with Introductory Lecture, Commentary and Additional Notes* (London: Macmillan, 1898; repr., Eugene, OR: Wipf & Stock, 2005), 39–40.

reasoning given. Achtemeier discounts Χριστός (like θεός) on the basis that Χριστός is too far away from the relative pronoun.[58] We will focus on θεός and καιρός as the stronger options, mentioning Χριστός only briefly. Troy Martin, in line with his future reading of ἀγαλλιᾶσθε, concludes that ἐν ᾧ refers to καιρῷ ἐσχάτῳ, which turns ἐν ᾧ into a temporal adverbial expression meaning 'at which time'.[59] So, the whole phrase becomes 'at that time you will rejoice'.[60] καιρῷ ἐσχάτῳ does immediately precede ἐν ᾧ and is itself introduced by ἐν. Such repetition could stylistically indicate that the two are to be linked. Luke 6.22–3 provides a parallel example and could be cited to support rejoicing at a future given time (χάρητε ἐν ἐκείνῃ τῇ ἡμέρᾳ). However, contextually, Luke 6.22–3 locates the rejoicing in the time of persecution. The future time of Luke's Gospel is the present experience of 1 Peter and so Luke 6.22–3 actually supports the idea that the author of 1 Peter can expect rejoicing despite present persecution. To agree with Achtemeier, it would be better to find an alternative that allows ἀγαλλιᾶσθε to retain its present force.[61] Moreover, as Jobes notes, the syntax of the LXX, which frequently has rejoicing in (ἐν) something, argues against the adverbial sense of the prepositional phrase because in the LXX the ἐν indicates the reason for rejoicing.[62]

An alternative option is to take θεός (1.3) as the antecedent. The resulting translation would be 'in whom'. Many scholars dismiss this option quickly, usually due to the distance between the relative pronoun and its antecedent which is thought to be θεός in 1.3, though θεός does in fact occur again in 1.5.[63] However, I find this alternative a strong possibility for a number of reasons. First, God is introduced as the subject in 1.3 and remains the focus throughout.

[58] Achtemeier, *1 Peter*, 100.

[59] Martin, 'Present Indicative', 309; cf. Bigg, *Epistles of St. Peter*, 103; Goppelt, *1 Peter*, 88–9; Michaels, *1 Peter*, 27.

[60] Bigg, who views καιρῷ ἐσχάτῳ as the antecedent, also places joy in the future but still comments that joy 'belongs to the Revelation of glory, and so living hope makes it present even in the midst of suffering'; Bigg, *Epistles of St. Peter*, 103; cf. H. Windisch, *Die katholischen Briefe*, HNT 15, 2nd rev. ed. (Tübingen: J. C. B. Mohr (Paul Siebeck), 1930), 53. De Waal Dryden tries to get around the problem of having a present ἀγαλλιᾶσθε happening in the last times by seeing καιρῷ ἐσχάτῳ as the whole of the messianic age, which is both future and present; J. De Waal Dryden, *Theology and Ethics in 1 Peter: Paraenetic Strategies for Christian Character Formation*, WUNT 2.209 (Tübingen: Mohr Siebeck, 2006), 73–5.

[61] Achtemeier, *1 Peter*, 100; cf. de Villiers, 'Joy', 70–1.

[62] K. H. Jobes, *1 Peter*, BECNT (Grand Rapids, MI: Baker Academic, 2005), 92.

[63] See Kelly, *Epistles of Peter*, 53; Achtemeier, *1 Peter*, 100; Schlosser, *Pierre*, 73.

All of 1.3–5 from ὁ κατὰ τὸ πολὺ αὐτοῦ ἔλεος onwards continues to refer to and expand the description of θεός.[64] Furthermore, every verb in 1.3–5 indicates the presence of another agent, which is clearly God: he has begotten the believers; keeps their inheritance; guards the believers; and will reveal Christ.[65] Thus, it is evident that God has been established as the focus and throughout 1.3–5 it is God who is intended to *remain* the focus.[66] This is not surprising if De Waal Dryden is correct that the purpose of 1.3–12 is to realign 'affective commitments by eliciting gratitude and strengthening allegiance' to God.[67] Given this intent and focus, it is not implausible that the author sees the object of, and basis for, rejoicing in 1.6 as θεός because it continues the line of thought from 1.3 to 5.[68] Furthermore, this centring on God and his action suggests that θεός is a more likely antecedent than Χριστός.

Second, ἀγαλλιάω is being used in a context of giving praise to God (εὐλογητὸς ὁ θεός).[69] This is in line with LXX usage in which, overwhelmingly, ἀγαλλιάω occurs in a context of praise. Within these biblical contexts the object of ἀγαλλιάω is predominantly God (see above). du Toit rightly recognises this when he comments that if ἐν ᾧ does refer to θεός then this is 'completely in the spirit of numerous analogous expressions in the Old Testament, especially in the Psalms, where we continually read that the faithful rejoice "in the Lord"'.[70] This common use and plausible background suggests that if ἐν ᾧ is

---

[64] Cf. A. B. du Toit, 'The Significance of Discourse Analysis for New Testament Interpretation and Translation: Introductory Remarks with Special Reference to 1 Peter 1.3–13', *Neotestamentica* 8 (1974): 54–79, at 60–1.

[65] I follow here Achtemeier's translation of ἀναγεννάω as 'begetting anew', which emphasises the role of the Father, rather than 'being born anew', a more feminine image. I also follow Achtemeier in seeing φρουρουμένους as passive rather than middle. Thus it should be read as another reverential passive denoting God's action, like the neighbouring passives of τετηρημένην and ἀποκαλυφθῆναι; Achtemeier, *1 Peter*, 92–7.

[66] Achtemeier himself recognises that the eulogy of 1.3–5 indicates the theocentric nature of the letter; Achtemeier, *1 Peter*, 94; cf. Elliott, *1 Peter*, 330.

[67] De Waal Dryden, *Theology*, 87; cf. Thurén who thinks that the motivating factor in 1.3–5 is thankfulness; Thurén, *Argument*, 95–6.

[68] Contra Elliott, who thinks that in verse 6 the letter shifts away from God's action to the believer's behaviour. I would argue that the fact that rejoicing requires an object actually keeps the focus on God through the believer's emotion. It is not until we reach the audience's distress that the attention moves to the believer; Elliott, *1 Peter*, 329.

[69] This could suggest a liturgical context for this emotion. However, a liturgical context does not detract from ἀγαλλιάω being an emotion term as emotional experience can be a significant part of individual and corporate worship as the Psalms attest.

[70] du Toit also agrees that this would fit with the doxological opening of 1.3; du Toit, 'Discourse Analysis', 68; cf. Hort, *Epistle of St Peter*, 40. We see God as the focus of rejoicing in other New Testament texts: Acts 2.25–6, 28, 46; Jude 1.24; Rev 19.6–7. The best example is Mary's song in Luke 1.46–7.

to refer to a specific object, it is more likely to be God than καιρῷ ἐσχάτῳ.

Third, the author's next use of ἀγαλλιάω in 1.8 seems to have as its occasion another object, Jesus Christ. We find ἀγαλλιάω appears again in a clause introduced by a preposition plus pronoun construction (εἰς ὃν) whose antecedent is clearly Ἰησοῦ Χριστοῦ (1.7). Achtemeier argues that εἰς ὃν should be directly linked to ἀγαλλιᾶσθε making the phrase between – ἄρτι μὴ ὁρῶντες πιστεύοντες δέ – an apposition. In this reading, δέ emphasises the contrast between not seeing *but* believing, rather than acting as a conjunction between believing and rejoicing (cf. οὐχ ἑαυτοῖς ὑμῖν δέ, 1.12). Thus, εἰς ὃν ... ἀγαλλιᾶσθε should be translated 'in whom you rejoice'.[71] Though Achtemeier's reading would be beneficial to my argument, it has a couple of problems. First, εἰς standardly governs πιστεύοντες, and, second, there are no examples in the LXX of ἀγαλλιάω preceding εἰς (ἐν or ἐπι are preferred). But, this does leave ἀγαλλιᾶσθε without an explicit object. However, since the preceding verbs in the clause (ἰδόντες, ἀγαπᾶτε, ὁρῶντες, πιστεύοντες) clearly relate to Jesus, it suggests that ἀγαλλιᾶσθε should be read this way too, and so infers rejoicing in Christ. Consequently, this would allow the author to be consistent in his usage: the first rejoicing is in God, the second in Christ. Therefore, for these three reasons, I think the strongest antecedent and therefore the object of the emotion is θεός. Thus, ἐν ᾧ can be translated as 'in whom'. Having said this, I do not want to discount the entirety of 1.3–5 as a viable option for being the cause of rejoicing, so long as we do not lose sight of the particular relationship the author has established. The benefits the believers have received are not to be rejoiced in as isolated items in themselves; they are their possession only because of God's mercy towards them and through Christ. Thus, it is this relationship that is central to joy.[72] Like in the LXX, 'joy expresses a *profound sense of connectedness*' that joins 'God and God's elect people'.[73] If such rejoicing is dependent on one's intimacy with God, then it becomes a distinctive

---

[71] Achtemeier, *1 Peter*, 103.

[72] See Selwyn who thinks both θεός and the entirety of 1.3–5 are viable options that in fact merge into one another; Selwyn, *St. Peter*, 126; cf. du Toit, 'Discourse Analysis', 68. Thurén rightly notes that to receive something valuable causes joy. However, he reduces the reason for rejoicing in 1.6 to the obtaining of salvation rather than acknowledging the relationship between the believers and God, which gives a larger dimension to the believers' rejoicing; Thurén, *Argument*, 96.

[73] Emphasis original; Barton, 'Spirituality', 178.

marker of the believers and is exclusive to them. The audience are those who rejoice in God.

Having established that the audience are being presented as those who presently rejoice in God, we are still to determine what this emotional presentation communicates to the audience and what the implications of this are.

Presenting What Should Be Valued

The first thing that we can say is that by presenting the believers as those that rejoice in God, the author creates a dividing line between believer and nonbeliever.[74] Consequently, this presentation brings with it an expectation about the accepted emotional orientation of the believer, which is different from his non-Christian neighbour. In order to understand more about this orientation, we need to investigate further the evaluative function of emotions.

We have established that each emotion makes a particular evaluative judgement about its object. For joy, the object is evaluated as good and beneficial to the flourishing of the person. Thus, the author declares that the only legitimate perspective for the believers is to recognise that God, and his actions, are good and beneficial for them.[75] This is a simple point, but it is important because it is the first step in creating a system of value, which will inevitably affect the believers' goals and actions. As the ancient rhetoricians recognised, if the author wants to be able to move people to act in a certain manner, he has to get them to *see* things a particular way, and the use of rejoicing reveals that the first task at hand is to persuade (or remind) the audience to value God. The later ethical commands will make sense only in relation to the system of value that is being established here.[76] To use joy to focus on God also has the additional effect of making God 'the central character of the meta-narrative'.[77]

---

[74] However, the lines between corporate and individual experience are blurred. By addressing a group's emotions the author also addresses the emotional life of any individual within the group that sees herself as part of the corporate experience. This is the case for every emotion addressed in 1 Peter. Thus, when I speak of emotional orientation in the letter, I am referring to the orientation expected of the group, an expectation to which the individual believer is also being asked to subscribe.

[75] Cf. 2.9; Jas 1.17.

[76] Kendall notes the foundational role of 1.3–12 in establishing the shape of the Christian life, which makes coherent the exhortations that follow; Kendall, 'Theological Function', 104.

[77] De Waal Dryden, *Theology*, 85. Barton, following philosopher David Kangas, recognises that emotions acquire significance from their 'metaphysical horizons'.

De Waal Dryden rightly highlights with this comment that the author's system of value sits within a larger worldview that has its own narrative in which God is indispensable.[78] The author has reminded his hearers that in this narrative God has acted favourably towards them in Christ and has bestowed on them numerous goods (1.3–5). These goods are now a present reality for the believers and so they can rightly rejoice in God.[79]

We saw in our introductory discussion that emotions evaluate a situation in relation to a person's goals. Thus, here, we can understand reflexively, that to provide an evaluation about God by utilising joy is to tell the believers what their goal should be. If joy presents God as good and beneficial to flourishing, then one should aim to be in favourable standing with God, which is what the believer because of Christ is currently experiencing.[80] This goal and the goods associated with it become the reference point by which all other objects and goods should be evaluated. We will discover that the author's use of other emotions such as fear, hope, and shame work from the reality that joy reveals. The evaluation of God as good and beneficial leads us finally to joy's action-tendency. Psychologically, joy puts one in a favourable state of mind towards the object, and, through its positive presentation, encourages behaviour that pursues the object. Thus, we can see that, if the audience take on this emotional stance, they are disposed towards behaviour that will maintain their good standing with God. Therefore, evoking the audience's joy is rhetorically powerful for the author. It is important that the author is able

---

However, here the emotion is working reflexively to direct the audience towards a metaphysical reality; Barton, 'Spirituality', 172.

[78] This requires that the audience accepts the narrative that the author is establishing. As De Waal Dryden notes, the narrative provides the framework for the lives of the audience through which they can interpret their experiences; De Waal Dryden, *Theology*, 39, 44.

[79] Given this reality, even exuberant rejoicing would be fitting here. Contra Michaels who does not think that the author would expect all believers to be rejoicing given their current situation; Michaels, *1 Peter*, 27.

[80] Here, and throughout, I use the term 'flourishing' not to indicate that the author of 1 Peter adheres to a particular philosophical concept of εὐδαιμονία, but more to refer to what the author, through what he presents as valuable, seems to understand as successful human living, i.e. the right and most beneficial course to pursue but not necessarily a τέλος in a strict philosophical sense. As we will see, the author's idea of successful human living is deeply influenced by his theological and eschatological outlook, and cannot be separated from God's action in Christ. The goals he establishes through his use of emotions have implications for the believer's life in the present, but these goals, though sometimes partially accessible in the present, have their ultimate consummation in the future. Thus, a Christian's concept of 'flourishing' may be at odds with her philosophical neighbour because it is rooted in a different worldview.

to help the audience see their Christianity positively, particularly as it is their Christianity that is currently the cause of their suffering. By presenting the Christian life as one of joy it colours it positively and reminds the audience of the good that as Christians they have accessed and can continue to know.

The author's use of joy here has sociological and therapeutic implications. Setting God as the object of joy means that the cause of rejoicing is external to the individual and therefore joy is dependent on another. The added implication is that one's ability to have joy is released from the relational dynamic of human with human. This is a similar outcome to Stoicism's stance where virtue, which is integral to the person, produces joy.[81] According to Seneca, self-sufficiency enables enduring joy because it is 'not borrowed from without'; if it were, it would cease. But, 'because it is not in the power of another to bestow, neither is it subject to another's whims' (*Ep.* 59.18 [Gummere, LCL]; cf. *Ep.* 23.6; 72.4–5; 98.1–2). Thus, in both systems of thought, one's positive emotional life can be achieved regardless of the present sociological and material circumstances. The result for both the Stoic and the Christian is that one will evaluate one's relationship to the other differently, with the other becoming less significant to one's goals. For neither Stoicism nor Christianity does this infer solitariness but it does suggest detachment.[82] One difference between Stoic and Christian joy is that, though both depend on a cosmic perspective, Christian joy is based on the concrete historical reality of what God has done in Christ. It is this historical event alone that has proved God's character, allows present access to goods, and frames future expectations, thus, enabling joy.

Furthermore, not only is the cause of joy outside of the person, but the goods to which it looks are beyond temporal constraints, being eternal in nature.[83] Consequently, the cause of rejoicing is moved both beyond the control of the recipients and outside of their temporal space.[84] Moreover, joy's evaluation is also mapped on to and highlights a much larger eternal cosmic reality. Thus, importantly for what is to follow, the goods that occasion joy are not contingent on the believer or her present temporal situation and therefore neither

---

[81] Stoicism still recognises the divine (reason) in this, as reason is both outside and inside the person, the inner reason being a fragment of the divine.

[82] Cf. Marcus Aurelius, *Med.* 5.16, 30.

[83] See the adjectives used of their inheritance: ἄφθαρτος (uncorrupted), ἀμίαντος (undefiled), ἀμάραντος (unfading) (1.4).

[84] Like Barton says of Paul's views in Philippians, joy despite distress reflects 'the vivid, felt horizon of participation in the life of heaven'; Barton, 'Spirituality', 185.

is her ability to rejoice. Perhaps terms like παρεπίδημος (1.1; 2.11) and πάροικος (2.11) indicate that the author desires the audience's primary values, from which the emotion of joy works, to come from outside of its present temporal and spatial location. This would support Achtemeier's inclination that the author is working from an apocalyptic framework in which a transcendent reality has been revealed.[85] Here, joy asks the believers to orient themselves around this reality.[86] The consequence of this is that the believer's joy can have a stable quality. Because the goods that occasion joy are stable, so is the believers' emotional state. The believers know the goodness of God in the present and can expect this to continue for eternity. Therefore, their joy in God can become a permanent emotional disposition.[87] The author's expectation of the perpetual joyous state of the believer is even more extraordinary when it is coupled with the next phrase – ὀλίγον ἄρτι, εἰ δέον ἐστίν, λυπηθέντας ἐν ποικίλοις πειρασμοῖς (even if it is necessary now for a little while for you to be distressed by various trials). Thus, it is to the audience's distress that we must now turn.

Concurrent Distress

Alongside joy we encounter the first reference to the audience's suffering, which will soon pervade the letter. Here, the suffering is inferred by reference to various trials (ποικίλοι πειρασμοί). These trials are described as distressing (λυπηθέντας) the believers.[88] As

---

[85] Achtemeier, *1 Peter*, 106–7; cf. M. Dubis, *Messianic Woes in First Peter: Suffering and Eschatology in 1 Peter 4:12–19*, Studies in Biblical Literature 33 (New York: Peter Lang, 2002), 39–42 for more on the apocalyptic spatial and temporal dimensions of 1 Peter.

[86] We might see this as in line with Holloway's demarcation of emotion-focused coping strategies, in which in order to make sense of the current situation one's self-concept is restructured by valuing certain domains above others. Here it would be eternal over temporal; Holloway, *Coping*, 122–7. Similarly, for Seneca, because the person's emotional life is moulded by being in line with nature, the mind of the wise man can be pervaded by eternal calm like the 'ultra-lunar firmament'. He goes on to emphasise the enduring quality of joy (*Ep.* 23.4–6 [Gummere, LCL]); cf. *Ep.* 59.16.

[87] For the emotional stability of the Stoic wise man see Epictetus, *Diatr.* 4.4.36–37; Seneca, *Ep.* 59.14; 71.27–9.

[88] There is a difference in manuscript evidence for whether the text should read λυπηθέντες or λυπηθέντας. Elliott asserts that λυπηθέντες, though perhaps more grammatically difficult, is the best reading (Elliott, *1 Peter*, 339). However, the *NA28* prefers λυπηθέντας. The accusative reading aims to ease the problem that one would expect to find εἰ δέον followed by an infinitive verb with an accusative noun as the subject. Either way, there is little difference in meaning between the two; λυπέω is clearly being applied to the audience; Achtemeier, *1 Peter*, 99, 101; cf. Michaels, *1 Peter*, 25.

demonstrated above, λύπη and λυπέω do not only pertain to physical suffering but cover mental distress including anxiety, despondency, and confusion. In addition to this, the fact that in 4.12 the audience are exhorted not to be surprised (μὴ ξενίζεσθε) by the trial (πειρασμός) suggests that these trials are particularly troubling mentally. Perhaps the audience are having difficulty with reconciling their present experience of persecution with their expectations.

Whereas the object of joy was a matter of debate, the cause of distress is clear: ποικίλοι πειρασμοί. Commentators agree that ποικίλοι πειρασμοί refers to the audience's persecution. Yet, this persecution does not happen without an agent. Therefore, though the trials are the cause of distress, the object of distress is the agent. There are three possible agents: (1) God, (2) hostile people, or (3) the devil (cf. 5.8). In support of option 1, some argue that εἰ δέον suggests divine will and thus God is the source of the trials.[89] However, the remaining presentation of the letter argues against God as agent and object. God is depicted as the one who is the just judge and saviour of those who suffer (1.5; 2.23; 3.12; 4.16–19; 5.5, 10–11) and cares for them (2.25; 5.7). He is also the one who is able to preserve them through the current time.[90] Furthermore, to have God as object would be difficult because it would make God simultaneously the object of joy and distress. In the LXX it is possible for God to be the object of two seemingly different emotions, e.g. joy and fear (Ps 2.11). However, the above historical discussion of λύπη, and by extension λυπέω, revealed that in both Greco-Roman sources and the LXX distress is opposed to joy. Thus it would be somewhat awkward to have both relating to God here. It is more plausible to see the hostile human other as the agent, given the rest of the letter which consistently depicts the other as the cause of suffering, whether this is masters (2.18–19), unbelieving husbands (3.1), or the generic other (2.12, 15; 3.9, 13–14, 16; 4.14).[91] The only other reference to λύπη (2.19), which occurs in the context of unjust

---

[89]   In the New Testament Jesus' suffering is particularly portrayed as a divine necessity: Matt 16.21; Mark 8.31; Luke 17.25; 24.7; John 3.14; Acts 17.3 etc.; Achtemeier, *1 Peter*, 101; Elliott, *1 Peter*, 339–40; cf. Brox, *Petrusbrief*, 64–5; Schlosser, *Pierre*, 69; de Villiers, 'Joy', 73. For Dubis, this phrase indicates the need for God's people to suffer in the period of the Messianic woes. The trials are an essential part of God's eschatological plan because through them he tests his people; Dubis, *Messianic Woes*, 69–70, 78.

[90]   Feldmeier, *Peter*, 81.

[91]   Feldmeier's comments that the believers' sorrow is based on alienation from the world around them would support my reading, though Feldmeier himself leaves the source of trials open; Feldmeier, *Peter*, 80–1.

suffering at the hands of a human master, supports option 2. Option 3, the devil (διάβολος) is made a possibility by 5.8. However, that the devil is only mentioned once reduces its prominence in the letter. It could be that the hostility of the other is understood by the author to be part of the cosmic battle of evil forces against God and his people.[92] But, despite this cosmic framework, the actual physical agent would still be the human other. Consequently, it is most plausible to see the hostile other as the agent of the trials and therefore the object of distress.

Having established the subject, object, and cause of the emotion, we can now outline the evaluation that distress would make of the situation. Distress occurs when one experiences in the present something judged as bad and detrimental to one's goals. Therefore, the believers are distressed because they see their trials as something bad that is having a negative impact on them. For the Stoic, this would be due to false opinion and therefore a misguided interpretation of events (cf. Cicero, *Tusc.* 4.6.14). But 1 Peter does not chastise the audience for this reaction or say that it is illegitimate.[93] By recognising this emotion the author demonstrates that he is able to appreciate the negative impact of persecution on the audience. He does not ask for it to be apathetically accepted. However, this presents the author with a problem not encountered by the impassive Stoic sage: the emotion's action-tendency. The action-tendency of distress is avoidance. Thus, it is likely that if this emotion dominates, then the audience would seek to avoid this negative scenario. This would involve either evading the harmful agents, or changing the dynamic of one's encounter with the agents so that their desire or ability to harm is altered. For the believers, the former would require becoming an isolated community away from contact with hostile individuals; the latter would require appeasement or gaining power. Since gaining power is improbable for the audience which is likely composed of the poor, slaves, and women, appeasement is the most feasible. Consequently, if persecution is on account of their Christian life, then, to appease the hostile other, the audience would have to behave more acceptably (as defined by the hostile party), which would require acculturation and, in the extreme case, defection from the faith.[94] Some have argued that acculturation is in fact

[92] Achtemeier, *1 Peter*, 106.
[93] Jobes, *1 Peter*, 93–4; Holloway, *Coping*, 148.
[94] These would be included under Holloway's 'problem-focused' strategies of dealing with prejudice; see Holloway, *Coping*, 117–22.

1 Peter's social strategy for dealing with persecution.[95] However, this
study does not take this stance for reasons that will become clear
throughout the course of discussion. Instead, I take the position that
the author desires none of the above outcomes. If this is the case,
then the author needs to rhetorically deal with the emotion of distress so that it is not the dominant emotional state that influences the
believers' actions.

Re-Evaluating the Present Situation

If emotions are a judgement, then to alter the emotion in order to
affect the action-tendency one needs to amend the audience's evaluation of events. In this context, this means altering the audience's
perspective about the harmful status of the πειρασμοί (trials). This is
precisely what the author does. First, he comments that they are only
for a short time (ὀλίγον), thus aiming to reduce their magnitude.[96]
Second, and more significantly, he goes on to declare that they have
a purpose:

> ἵνα τὸ δοκίμιον ὑμῶν τῆς πίστεως πολυτιμότερον χρυσίου τοῦ
> ἀπολλυμένου, διὰ πυρὸς δὲ δοκιμαζομένου εὑρεθῇ εἰς ἔπαινον
> καὶ δόξαν καὶ τιμὴν ἐν ἀποκαλύψει Ἰησοῦ Χριστοῦ

> so that the genuineness of your faith, which is of greater
> worth than gold (which though perishing is tested by fire),
> may be found to result in praise, glory, and honour at the
> revelation of Jesus Christ. (1.7)

These comments work at the level of evaluation. The author
demonstrates that, instead of being detrimental, a good can actually
come from the trials: the genuineness of their faith can be proved,
which will lead to more benefits – praise, glory, and honour.[97]

---

[95] This of course brings us into the famous Balch–Elliott debate. I will deal with
this debate in the conclusion once we have a fuller picture of the author's argument
from the investigation of all the emotions.

[96] As Achtemeier comments, ὀλίγον indicates a short time rather than the unim-
portance of the suffering; Achtemeier, *1 Peter*, 101; cf. Schlosser, *Pierre*, 69.

[97] Thurén notes this reading, but provides two other alternative interpretations
in which the motivation for suffering is to obtain glory. However, these are weak
alternatives. 1 Peter is not seeking to promote suffering as a route to the good, but
instead, as we will see, to promote the value of faithfulness; see Thurén, *Argument*,
97–100. Here I read praise, glory, and honour as the believers' (rather than God's),
which will be bestowed upon the believer at the point of judgement; Schlosser,
Pierre, 70.

In line with interpreting εἰ δέον as divine will, some scholars read 1.7 as indicating that God is testing the believer. Knowing that this testing comes from God should provide an encouragement for the believer. Added to this is the further consolation that they should not see themselves as victims but those who are being refined.[98] Thus, the comparison with gold is read as indicating the purification of the believers' faith.[99] In arguing for this, commentators draw on LXX background (e.g. Zech 13.9; Wis 3.5–6; Sir 2.1–6). This may be the case in the LXX where suffering often occurs due to disobedience, and purification generally works at a community level, but it is not the situation here.[100] The audience are those in right relationship with God who have already been purified (1.2; cf. 1.14). Instead, the author acknowledges that trials *test* faith.[101] For the author, it is faith (or faithfulness) that is important, as demonstrated by the value explicitly given to its genuineness (πολυτιμότερον χρυσίου).[102] To agree with Michaels, it seems that the author's point 'is not so much to assert directly that the reader's faith is proved genuine by a process of testing … as to extol the value, in God's sight, of this "genuine

[98] For more on parallels to the concept of refining fire see Achtemeier, *1 Peter*, 101–2.
[99] Brox, *Petrusbrief*, 64–5; Feldmeier, *Peter*, 83–4; Schlosser, *Pierre*, 69–70; de Villiers, 'Joy', 64, 73.
[100] The texts quoted by Dubis to support the purification motif actually work at a community level and thus indicate the need to purge the wicked from the community not refine the person; see Dubis, *Messianic Woes*, 16, 61; cf. also Elliott, *1 Peter*, 341. For Brox, the idea of purification through suffering is not problematic as it sits in a commonly accepted Jewish tradition of describing persecution as purifying fire; Brox, *Petrusbrief*, 65. See K. D. Liebengood, *The Eschatology of 1 Peter: Considering the Influence of Zechariah 9–14*, SNTSMS 157 (Cambridge: Cambridge University Press, 2014), 107–16, who rightly points out that texts like Wisdom and Sirach are concerned with the training of wayward community members. This is not the case with 1 Peter. The believers do not suffer because they have strayed and need correction but because they are faithful to God. For Liebengood, instead, it is a marker of the eschatological period in which the believer lives. Liebengood prefers Zech 13.8–9 as the background to the fiery trials imagery.
[101] To agree with Elliott, the author is not saying here that trials are necessity to prove faith but a possibility; Elliott, *1 Peter*, 339–40. Contra Brox, *Petrusbrief*, 65. This is not to say that one should not realistically expect persecution because of one's allegiance to Christ (see Jobes, *1 Peter*, 95). But it does argue against those who see suffering as an obligatory part of the Christian life. See Kendall, 'Theological Function', 108; Michaels, *1 Peter*, 28–9.
[102] Cf. S. R. Bechtler, *Following in His Steps: Suffering, Community, and Christology in 1 Peter*, SBLDS 162 (Atlanta, GA: Scholars Press, 1998), 181–2. Achtemeier comments that highlighting gold as perishable 'implies an argument from the lesser to the greater: if perishable, and hence less valuable, gold must be tested, how much more must faith, which is imperishable and hence of greater value'; Achtemeier, *1 Peter*, 102. I agree with Achtemeier that it is an argument from lesser to greater, but it is the eternal value of faith that is being emphasised over the temporal quality of gold, not the greater need for faith to be tested.

faith" and to affirm its ultimate (i.e., eschatological) significance'.[103] Therefore, to return to the matter of distress, instead of being problematic, the trials can be seen as having a positive outcome because they show the quality of the believer's much valued faith.[104]

We can see in this argumentation that the author is trying to reconfigure what the audience sees as important. By introducing faith into the picture we find that the believers' relationship with God, which was so important in 1.3–5, is again highlighted. In this instance, πίστις does not simply mean belief but carries a sense of 'faithfulness' and 'reliability'. It infers a commitment to stay loyal to a party, demonstrated by external behaviour.[105] Thus, if the audience are to accept the argument that trials prove faithfulness and that this is positive, they first have to agree that faithfulness is valuable. 1.3–5 has established why this is so, but just in case the audience have forgotten the benefits of their relationship with God, the author gives them an added affirmation: their genuine faith will result in praise, glory, and honour.[106] Like with 1.3–5, this aims to help the audience reassess their goals. According to 1.7, worthwhile praise, glory, and honour come only via faithfulness to God not from other social relationships. Whereas distress would cause one to focus on the hostile other, the author's rhetorical manoeuvre has reinterpreted the trials so that the audience's focus has been moved to their standing with God. Again, God becomes the primary object in their outlook, and, in presenting how to achieve praise, glory, and honour, the author has made remaining faithful to God the highest goal. Other goals such as physical well-being, public honour, or social acceptance become less important and therefore the loss of them is less distressing. Consequently, if faith is valuable and trials prove

---

[103] Michaels, *1 Peter*, 30. This makes sense of the comparison with gold, which when it goes through fire proves its nature. See Selwyn, *St. Peter*, 129, who agrees that this reading gives a straightforward analogy between metal refining and character proving; cf. Bigg, *Epistles of St. Peter*, 104; Kelly, *Epistles of Peter*, 54; Liebengood, *Eschatology*, 134.

[104] Contra Goppelt, who thinks that faith needs to be purified; Goppelt, *1 Peter*, 90–1. Cf. Sir 2.1–9, which shares the motif of testing in fire alongside an exhortation towards trust in God and faithfulness.

[105] Elliott argues that belief here is not primarily cognitive assent. However, I do not think this is a helpful distinction; one has to have a belief about the truth of a situation in order to act in line with it faithfully. As Achtemeier comments, Christian faith is 'the visible evidence of the unseen reality evoking that trust'; Elliott, *1 Peter*, 340; Achtemeier, *1 Peter*, 97; see also Feldmeier, *Peter*, 78; Schlosser, *Pierre*, 69.

[106] Cf. Jas 1.12. These terms are used throughout the letter of God and Christ (1.11, 21; 2.6–7, 12; 4.11; 5.1), thus demonstrating here the positive position of the audience; Elliott, *1 Peter*, 342; cf. Achtemeier, *1 Peter*, 102.

faith, then trials can be re-evaluated because at the very least they cannot inhibit one from obtaining the highest goal, and at best they highlight that one possesses the valued faithfulness. The fact that the phrase ends with 'at the revelation of Christ' reminds the audience of the larger cosmic narrative in which the interpretation of this situation sits. It is not a matter of temporary personal comfort but of aligning oneself with an overarching cosmic reality and with an eschatological expectation.

So, we can see that by changing the evaluation of the trials the author can reduce the appropriateness of distress by bringing in the good. Consequently, he can achieve his primary aim, which is to show that persecution is not something that has on all accounts to be avoided. Furthermore, the displacement of the object of distress by the insertion of the theme of faith/faithfulness means that the audience's relational dynamic with the hostile human agent is made less significant. The re-evaluation of trials declares that the hostile other's actions cannot really do lasting damage to the believer's primary goals. Thus, one does not need to be distressed by them. In this case, one's behaviour should not be a response to the hostile individual but instead should be shaped by one's desire to remain faithful to God because only he secures the good. Subsequently, the author leads the audience towards the desired end of having a dispositional outlook that will promote maintaining their Christian conduct in the face of hostility. The likely added effect of this is that, through the re-evaluation of the significance of the hostile other, the author is able also to reconfigure the believers' emotional ties, asking them to prefer their new life in God over their old social bonds.[107]

One added benefit of the above reading is that it prevents one from falling into the trap of seeing trials as the thing to be rejoiced in, as some have argued.[108] It is clear from the above argument that trials are not the focus but faith. As Feldmeier rightly notes, at this point in the letter the emphasis is on joy *despite* suffering.[109] The author does not depict his audience as rejoicing in trials. The trials

[107] This, as De Waal Dryden notes, is important in the conversion and re-socialisation process; De Waal Dryden, *Theology*, 24–5.

[108] Elliott argues 1 Peter is following 'Israelite and Christian tradition in which adversity is portrayed as an occasion of testing of trust in God and a reason for joy'; Elliott, *1 Peter*, 341; likewise Achtemeier concludes 'the thrust of these two verses [1.6–7] is therefore that present trials may be greeted with joy, since they are necessary if faith is to have the kind of proved character that God finds acceptable at the final judgement'; Achtemeier, *1 Peter*, 102; cf. Selwyn, *St. Peter*, 127–9.

[109] Feldmeier, *Peter*, 85.

are not the object of joy, only the cause of distress, which is precisely what necessitates the need for them to be reinterpreted. Joy, however, is distinctly focused on God and the benefits he has bestowed. The believers are not encouraged to be elated and shout for joy because they are being afflicted. It is faithfulness and commitment to God that is commendable and important, not the suffering itself.

With the author's emphasis on the eschatological value of faith he returns to more naturally positive themes. It is with his transition that we can turn to the final subject of this chapter: rejoicing in Christ.

Unspeakable and Glorified Joy

The author uses the mention of Christ's eschatological revelation to transform the tenor and focus swiftly away from distress and trials. Instead, Christ becomes the primary object. Because the object has changed so does the emotional tone to love and joy (1.7–8). Christ as object is introduced in both clauses of 1.8 by the relative pronoun (εἰς) ὅν. It is agreed that the antecedent in both instances is Ἰησοῦς Χριστός (1.7).[110] Thus, we can understand that the cause, and most likely object, of rejoicing is Christ.[111] The author is clearly drawing on the audience's perspective of their relationship with Christ since he evokes alongside their joy their love for Christ. Both of these emotion terms (ἀγαπᾶτε and ἀγαλλιᾶσθε) should be read as present indicatives: 'their joy is present just as are their love and their faith'.[112] Amazingly, the believers can rejoice in Christ even though they have not seen him.[113] This is important for the second generation of believers who did not have direct physical access to Christ. Yet, through these positive emotions, the author depicts the believer in a close relationship with Christ. As Feldmeier comments, 'In faith and love, the (yet) absent one is (already) present to them – and therefore their present is filled with joy.'[114] Again there is juxtaposition between present states. In the previous verses the contrast is between present suffering and the ability to rejoice in God. In 1.8, not being

---

[110] Achtemeier, *1 Peter*, 102; Elliott, *1 Peter*, 342, etc.

[111] See p. 125 for discussion on why ἀγαλλιᾶσθε most likely has Christ as its inferred object.

[112] Achtemeier, *1 Peter*, 103; cf. Elliott, *1 Peter*, 343; Schlosser, *Pierre*, 71.

[113] Faith versus sight is a common trope in early Christianity see Mark 15.32; John 4.48; 6.30; 20.29; 2 Cor 5.7; Achtemeier, *1 Peter*, 102. For Brox, the problem of not seeing Christ was more of an obstacle to joy than the trials; Brox, *Petrusbrief*, 66.

[114] Feldmeier, *Peter*, 86.

able to see Christ, which could be disheartening, is contrasted with the ability to still love and rejoice in him.

If we work from the evaluation present in the emotion of joy, we discover that Christ, like the Father, is being presented as good and beneficial to the believers' flourishing. This is not surprising, given that all the benefits given to the believer in 1.3–5 were only available through the resurrection of Christ.[115] Here in 1.8–9 the relationship between Christ and the believers' salvation is made more prominent: by their faith in Christ they are obtaining the salvation of their souls.[116] Thus, according to the author, the believers can rejoice because of their relationship to Christ and their coming salvation.[117] Pertinent to our discussion on emotions is that the salvation of their souls is named as their goal (τὸ τέλος). We established at the outset that emotions are evaluations of a situation in view of a person's goals. Here the author makes explicit what the audience's ultimate goal is (or should be): salvation. We also noted that joy is appropriate when one has a good in the present. Thus, the author spells out for the audience why, in view of Christ, an emotion of joy is most fitting: through their faith in Christ there are receiving their desired goal.[118] The present participle κομιζόμενοι (obtaining) suggest that they should see their salvation as present, occurring concurrently with their belief and rejoicing.[119] Perhaps this reveals that the audience has already set a high priority on salvation, or that the author is encouraging it to do so.[120] We can also see that through joy the author is asking the believers to value Christ, but, once again, he

---

[115] Elliott, *1 Peter*, 334–5.

[116] Souls here is not an entity within a human being but, following biblical tradition, it means the whole human being; Kelly, *Epistles of Peter*, 58; Achtemeier, *1 Peter*, 104; Elliott, *1 Peter*, 344; contra, Feldmeier, *Peter*, 87–92.

[117] Elliott, *1 Peter*, 343; cf. Kendall, '1 Peter 1:3–9', 69; Thurén, *Argument*, 100–1; Schlosser, *Pierre*, 71.

[118] The verb κομίζω carries a sense of acquiring, or coming into possession of something (see BDAG, 557). In the New Testament it often relates to eschatological reward (cf. 5.4). What is obtained is not always positive and can depend on one's deeds; see 2 Cor 5.10; Eph 6.8; Col 3.25; Heb 11.39; Elliott, *1 Peter*, 344. We find in other New Testament texts that joy, like here in 1 Peter, is linked to the possession of an eternal good; cf. Matt 5.11–12; Heb 10.32–6.

[119] Achtemeier, *1 Peter*, 104, 107; Feldmeier, *Peter*, 87; Contra Elliott who sees rejoicing in 1.8 as looking towards future salvation; Elliott, *1 Peter*, 339. Even though they are already obtaining their salvation, the rest of the letter does suggest that they await the fullness of their salvation when Christ is revealed. Therefore, the full realisation of their goal will not occur until Christ's final glorious revelation (1.6–7, 13; 4.13; 5.1, 4, 6, 10).

[120] The author does not specify here what salvation is from, but we must take it, in view of general Christian tradition, to mean eternal salvation. In line with OT

is also promoting the value of their faith(fulness). For it is through their faith in and fidelity to Christ that their salvation is accessed. Consequently, their emotional outlook and their priorities should be shaped by the 'future goal that has already broken into present reality'.[121] Subsequently, the believers can justifiably rejoice despite distressing trials.[122] Moreover, the implication is that the audience's behaviour will be ordered around these values and goals.[123] If the believers take on the author's presentation of reality as displayed by his use of emotions then he can successfully motivate them towards particular behaviour, which, in this instance as with 1.6, is to pursue fidelity.

The description of rejoicing in 1.8 is more heightened than in 1.6. In 1.8 the phrase ἀγαλλιᾶσθε χαρᾷ produces a redundant repetition: 'rejoicing with joy'. χαρά is further described as ἀνεκλάλητος (unspeakable) and δεδοξασμένη (glorified). If ἀγαλλιάω does have a vocalised element then this creates an interesting paradox: they are shouting for joy because they have a joy that is beyond words. This implies that the joy the believer has in Christ is somehow beyond human capacity to explain but is present and real enough for the person to rejoice. Not only is the joy unspeakable but it has been glorified. Against Selwyn, this is more than feelings of happiness that come after conversion.[124] Glory suggests divine and heavenly attributes. Thus, this description indicates the relationship between their joy and the divine. First, joy in both 1.6 and 1.8 has heavenly beings, God and Christ, as its object. Subsequently, it points the believer towards this realm. Second, all the goods that the believer obtains through their relationship to God through Christ, which enforce their reason to rejoice, are present though also eternal. In this way, the good to which joy points is unchanging. Hence, their rejoicing, which is a response to these goods, can be stable and continue into eternity. Consequently, by this emotion, the audience are firmly incorporated into the divine realm. In a sense, they are

---

and Jewish sources this salvation probably infers escape from divine judgement and involves new creation rather than escape from the body; Achtemeier, *1 Peter*, 97, 104.

[121] Kendall, 'Theological Function', 108; cf. Kelly, *Epistles of Peter*, 57–8; Feldmeier, *Peter*, 87.

[122] Contra Michaels who moves rejoicing here to the future and so concludes that the audience will only be able to rejoice after suffering; Michaels, *1 Peter*, 29, 33–4.

[123] Cf. De Waal Dryden, who comments that within the larger cosmic narrative the τέλος 'of that world subsequently becomes a reference point for all action'; De Waal Dryden, *Theology*, 31. Selwyn also notes that τέλος can indicate the chief good of a process or action; Selwyn, *St. Peter*, 132–3.

[124] Selwyn, *St. Peter*, 132.

already participating in the glorious joy they will experience in full when Christ is revealed.[125] Thus, their joy can be seen as presently glorified.[126] The emotion is lifted beyond any temporal or situational constraints and as such resembles the divine on which it focuses. As Kendall rightly asserts, 'neither affliction nor insecurity can quench it'.[127] The therapeutic upshot of this is emotional stability for the believer and the potential to have a permanently positive outlook, resulting in confidence.[128]

Conclusion

In the above exploration of joy and distress in 1 Peter 1.6–8 we have seen how the emotion terms have been used to highlight particular objects and thus also to promote an evaluation of that object. We discovered that the emotion of distress occurs briefly in a paragraph whose overwhelming tone is one of rejoicing. Clearly, the author wants to emphasise the reality that joy points towards and to minimise the impact of the judgement given by distress. The use of joy in these verses directs the audience towards their relationship with God and Christ. Its promotion asks the audience to see God and Christ as good and beneficial to their flourishing. Further, it asks the audience to internalise the value system on which this judgement is based, with fidelity to God and Christ becoming the highest goal. Therefore, joy empowers the believers through '*the felt knowledge of what really matters*'.[129] Addressing the audience's emotions in this way is immensely powerful because it does not ask them merely to accept statements about God, but to be internally shaped by them. This outlook, with its values and goals, will have ethical implications because it affects the believers' drive towards action.

Whereas joy highlighted the good, distress focused on the negative impact of the audience's persecution. The judgement of distress is that trials are only negative and therefore should be avoided, consequently encouraging behaviour that could effect this avoidance. However, the author does not desire this behavioural outcome so works hard to help the audience re-evaluate the situation in order to

---

[125] Achtemeier, *1 Peter*, 103–4; see also Bigg, *Epistles of St. Peter*, 107; Feldmeier, *Peter*, 86–7.

[126] Cf. Kendall, 'Theological Function', 108.

[127] Kendall, 'Theological Function', 108.

[128] Achtemeier, *1 Peter*, 104.

[129] Barton, 'Spirituality', 191 (emphasis original).

alter the judgement and thus reduce the desire for avoidance. In his argumentation he turns the cause of distress into another occasion to promote the value of faith and faithfulness. Elliott comments regarding the reality of distress that it tempers the believer's joy.[130] However, I would argue the exact opposite. The above has shown that the reality that joy points towards actually tempers the distress.[131] Through promoting joy and minimising distress the author is using the emotions to direct the audience towards a particular cosmic reality. By presenting this emotional stance as the norm for the believer, he is asking the audience members to accept this cosmic reality, which inevitably impinges on their present, gives meaning to it, and directs their evaluation of events.

We noted some sociological implications of the author's use of these emotions, most notably the reduction in significance of the hostile other for attaining necessary goals. Instead, the primary relationship that is espoused is that of the faithful believer with their merciful God through Christ. It is faithfulness to this relationship that is held up as the path to joy and therefore flourishing. For the believer, all other objects and events are to be evaluated in relation to this primary relationship and chief goal. Establishing this framework sets the foundation for later ethical commands and will also be beneficial for helping us to understand the author's presentation of the believer's relationship to the nonbeliever as we progress through our investigation.

It is apparent that the author opens the letter on an intensely positive note. His use of joy reminds the audience of their present favourable position. Furthermore, his positioning of joy in relation to eternal goods suggests that this positive emotional stance has the potential to become a stable and enduring outlook. Consequently, at the outset of the letter, the author is able to establish the tenor of the audience's perspective, which will be carried through into the more difficult areas of discussion tackled in the letter. From this overwhelmingly positive tone, we see that the author wants to inspire the audience to have confidence and encourage the believers that their choice to align themselves with Christ, which is currently bringing affliction, is indeed the best decision they could make. Thus, finally,

---

[130] Though Elliott does note that grief and suffering are cast in a positive light; Elliott, *1 Peter*, 339.

[131] Cf. Holloway, *Coping*, 148.

we can affirm, as a number of scholars note, that the author of 1 Peter does indeed present the possibility that the Christian can rejoice *despite* suffering.[132] With this, we must now turn to the next use of joy in 1 Peter and to the more troubling paradox of rejoicing *in* suffering.

---

[132] Elliott, *1 Peter*, 339. It must be noted that rejoicing despite suffering is not unique to 1 Peter, it can be found in other New Testament texts (Heb 10.32–6) and particularly in the sayings of Jesus (Matt 5.11–12; Luke 6.22–3), which seem to foretell the type of persecution that the audience are undergoing. There are also some Jewish parallels in Wis 3.4–6, 2 Bar 52.6–7, and Sibylline Oracles 5.269–70. Achtemeier notes Romans 5.3–5 and James 1.2 as parallels. However, Romans 5.3–5 does not form an exact parallel because it shows boasting in suffering, which is not the same as rejoicing despite suffering. Likewise, James asks his audience to consider their trials pure joy, thus equating trials with joy. Again, this is different to what we find here in 1 Peter 1.6–8; Achtemeier, *1 Peter*, 99–100.

6

JOY IN SUFFERING

1 Peter 4.12–13

In the previous chapter we investigated the author's presentation of joy despite distress. In this chapter our attention will turn to 4.12–13 in which we discover that the author goes one stage further and asks his audience to rejoice in suffering.[1] This chapter will work from the same understanding of joy presented at the outset of the previous chapter. The progress of our discussion will follow a simple trajectory: it will first outline what the author is asking the audience to rejoice in; then it will seek to decipher the rationale for this; and, in doing so, it will highlight the implications for the audience. In order to understand the rationale behind the author's depiction of joy, we will spend the majority of the discussion unpacking the author's presentation of suffering. This will involve significant engagement with the *imitatio Christi* sections of the letter (2.18–25; 3.17–18; 4.1–2).

Despite joy being pivotal at the outset of the letter for setting the audience's orientation and establishing values, there is no further reference to rejoicing until 4.13, in which the author says:

> ἀλλὰ καθὸ κοινωνεῖτε τοῖς τοῦ Χριστοῦ παθήμασιν, χαίρετε, ἵνα καὶ ἐν τῇ ἀποκαλύψει τῆς δόξης αὐτοῦ χαρῆτε ἀγαλλιώμενοι.

> But as far as you participate in the sufferings of Christ, rejoice, so that also at the revelation of his glory you may rejoice exceedingly.

From 4.12's repetition of fire imagery (πύρωσις) and testing (πειρασμός) we can understand that the situation of persecution

---

[1] Various terms are used throughout the letter to indicate both the believers' and Christ's suffering. One term is παθήματα (1.11; cf. 4.13; 5.9) from πάθημα, which can mean 'emotion or condition, affection'. However, I do not think it carries this sense in 1 Peter, it has more of the general sense of 'that which befalls one', i.e. to suffer; see 'πάθημα' in LSJ (1285).

present in 1.6 is the context for 4.13 also.[2] Consequently, this new section of the letter (4.12–19) returns to the issue of the audience's relationship with their hostile community.[3] However, in the new call to rejoice, the emotional challenge for the audience reaches new levels.

The Occasion for Joy

In 4.13 there are two occasions for joy: participating in Christ's suffering and at the revelation of his glory. Thus, rejoicing exists in two different time frames and with different actualities. The first is in the present. The mood of χαίρετε could be either indicative or imperative. Given that χαίρετε is being compared with μὴ ξενίζεσθε (do not be surprised), the best reading is imperative (rejoice).[4] Therefore, the author is exhorting the audience to have a particular emotional response to their situation, indicating that rejoicing should be a present reality for the believer. The second occasion for joy is less definite; it exists in the future but is dependent on the previous clause as a prerequisite.[5] The consequence of rejoicing in the present is that they will also be able to rejoice in the future.[6] The occurrence of ξενίζω and ξένος reveals that the believers are astonished by what they are experiencing and suggests inner distress and turmoil, even cognitive confusion about events that feel incongruous to their new Christian status.[7] As Schlosser comments, '*[o]n souffre plus quand les événements pénibles sont inattendus et incompréhensibles*'.[8] Yet,

---

[2] Some scholars have argued that 1.6–7 and 4.12–13 refer to different situations, the first potential, the second actual; Windisch, *katholischen Briefe*, 76; see Goppelt, *I Peter*, 310. However, I agree with those who see both 1.6–7 and 4.12–13 as referring to the same historical situation; Kelly, *Epistles of Peter*, 183–5; Goppelt, *I Peter*, 311; Brox, *Petrusbrief*, 211–12; Michaels, *1 Peter*, 258.

[3] Elliott, *1 Peter*, 768. Most scholars see 4.12–19 as a sub-unit of the letter within a major section that runs form 4.12–5.11; Selwyn, *St. Peter*, 6; Kelly, *Epistles of Peter*, 183; Goppelt, *I Peter*, 311; Michaels, *1 Peter*, xxxvii, 257; Achtemeier, *1 Peter*, 304, etc. This is against the older perspective that 4.12 may indicate the start of a new letter or sermon; see Windisch, *katholischen Briefe*, 76–7.

[4] Michaels, *1 Peter*, 262; Schlosser, *Pierre*, 259.

[5] I read χαρῆτε ἀγαλλιώμενοι with a future sense as indicated by the context of Christ's coming revelation; Michaels, *1 Peter*, 262–3; Elliott, *1 Peter*, 777.

[6] Brox, *Petrusbrief*, 215; Achtemeier, *1 Peter*, 307; Schlosser, *Pierre*, 260.

[7] Feldmeier, *Peter*, 224; cf. Kelly, *Epistles of Peter*, 184; Schelkle, *Petrusbriefe*, 122; Goppelt, *I Peter*, 313; Brox, *Petrusbrief*, 212–13. To agree with Achtemeier, this is unlikely to be 'paralysing shock', but perplexity; Achtemeier, *1 Peter*, 305; cf. de Villiers, 'Joy', 80.

[8] Schlosser, *Pierre*, 258. ('We suffer more when the painful events are unexpected and incomprehensible.')

in the face of this understandable reaction, the author declares that, instead, joy is the right response to persecution.[9]

In the previous chapter we determined that joy is appropriate when something evaluated as good and beneficial is present. We must, therefore, conclude that the author is asking the audience to see their present suffering as a good to be rejoiced in and evaluated positively.[10] Relying on the Jewish tradition that suffering can be welcomed as a test of faithfulness, or a disciplining of the righteous,[11] some commentators misread the text and conclude, similar to 1.6–7, that the reason for rejoicing is the testing mentioned in 4.12.[12] Others, like Bechtler, argue that suffering in 1 Peter sits in a framework of God's final judgement. Persecution indicates that judgement has started and therefore is a reason to rejoice because it marks the beginning of the end and reveals the believers' election.[13] But the clear reason for rejoicing is given in 4.13 not 4.12. Thus, as other

---

[9] In the New Testament, outside of 1 Peter, χαίρω is linked with suffering only in Col 1.24, Matt 5.11–12, and Luke 6.22–3. In Colossians the author rejoices ἐν τοῖς παθήμασιν, which refers to his own suffering and is associated with the θλίψεων τοῦ Χριστοῦ. Thus it could present a similar idea to 1 Peter 4.13. In Matt 5.11–12 and Luke 6.22–3 the context is that of reproach, persecution, and ostracising. But the rejoicing is occasioned by the knowledge of the eternal reward they will receive for suffering for Christ, not the suffering itself.

[10] Cf. Elliott, *1 Peter*, 768; Holloway, *Coping*, 223.

[11] See Elliott n. 577 for a list of Jewish texts that exhibit this tradition and New Testament echoes; Elliott, *1 Peter*, 776.

[12] Selwyn, *St. Peter*, 127, 222; Nauck has argued that a joy in *persecution* tradition underlies 1 Peter here and in 1.6–7. The Jewish texts of 2 and 4 Maccabees, 2 Baruch, Judith, and Tobit are offered in support of this. James 1.2, 12 are also considered to contain this tradition. The focus of these texts is joy's relation to πειρασμός and in them Nauck sees the topos of thanking God for the trials. But in 1 Peter 1.6 and 4.13 joy, though it sits next to trials, is not *in* the trials, i.e. the persecution. Read carefully, joy has a different object; see Nauck, *Freude im Leiden*. Estrada, who surveys the texts presented by Nauck and later Millauer concludes: 'The idea of tribulation as a cause of joy is rarely considered in Judaism.' He later says, 'One does not find, however, any explicit text in Jewish writings which talks about joy in suffering.' Thus he goes on to posit: 'It is likely that 1 Pet reflects a saying of Jesus, which had become part of the ethical tradition of early Christianity to search for meaning in suffering' and 'Peter is a full adaptation of Christian thought characterized by an affirmation of present experience as divine blessing and of its Christological basis'; B. Estrada, 'The Last Beatitude: Joy in Suffering', *Biblica* 91 (2010): 187–209, at 197–208. However, Millauer himself would agree that the specific idea of rejoicing in Christ's suffering flows from the Synoptic speech of Jesus, and identifies sharing in Christ's suffering as the reason for joy in 4.13; Millauer, *Leiden*, 88, 184–5.

[13] Bechtler, *Following*, 145–6, 200. Likewise, Millauer's investigation of suffering in 1 Peter operates from the idea that 1 Peter has absorbed the Jewish tradition that the elect are purified through suffering, so at numerous points in his exposition God's judgement and purification provide the meaning for suffering; Millauer, *Leiden*, 127–9, 33.

scholars rightly conclude, it is sharing in Christ's suffering that is the reason for joy, not the trials.[14] The basis for joy is fundamentally Christological because the phrase καθὸ κοινωνεῖτε τοῖς τοῦ Χριστοῦ παθήμασιν reveals that it is not any suffering that should produce joy, only suffering that can be deemed to be sharing in Christ's.[15] Therefore, in order to understand the rationale for how suffering can be seen as an occasion for rejoicing, first we need to qualify what the author means by τοῖς τοῦ Χριστοῦ παθήμασιν. Then, second, we must determine the significance of the participatory language used (καθὸ κοινωνεῖτε).

The Sufferings of Christ

A number of scholars note the use of the definite article before Χριστός, which is an unusual way for the author to refer to Christ.[16] Nevertheless, the majority translate τοῖς τοῦ Χριστοῦ παθήμασιν as 'the sufferings of Christ' or 'Christ's sufferings', making no real distinction between this reference to 'the' Christ and other uses of Χριστός in the letter.[17] Elliott does recognise the definite article in his translation 'the sufferings of the Christ' but for Elliott the definite article 'reflects an older stratum of tradition in which *the Christ* still functioned as a title for Jesus as *the Messiah*'. Consequently, he sees Χριστός and ὁ Χριστός as equivalent.[18] However, for Dubis, the definite article reveals a specific emphasis on Christ as the Messiah. In Dubis' interpretation the genitive is not subjective but descriptive. Consequently, '[t]hese sufferings are "messianic" because they are associated with the advent of the Messiah'.[19] So, τοῖς τοῦ Χριστοῦ παθήμασιν indicates a specific period of suffering called the 'messianic woes'.[20] According to Dubis, the cross inaugurated these woes.

[14] Kelly, *Epistles of Peter*, 185; Goppelt, *I Peter*, 312, 315; Brox, *Petrusbrief*, 214–5.
[15] Feldmeier, *Peter*, 224. The καθὸ does not refer to the 'degree of suffering' but instead to the 'commonality of suffering'; Elliott, *1 Peter*, 774; cf. Michaels, *1 Peter*, 262.
[16] Χριστός is used with the definite article only in 3.15 and 5.1. Cf. 1.3, 7, 11, 13, 19; 2.5, 21; 3.16, 18, 21; 4.1, 11, 14; 5.10, 14 where Χριστός is used alone or with Ἰησοῦς; Elliott, *1 Peter*, 775; Schlosser, *Pierre*, 259, 270.
[17] Kelly, *Epistles of Peter*, 183; Goppelt, *I Peter*, 309; Michaels, *1 Peter*, 256; Achtemeier, *1 Peter*, 303; Feldmeier, *Peter*, 222.
[18] Elliott, *1 Peter*, 767, 775.
[19] Dubis, *Messianic Woes*, 99–100.
[20] Martin likewise argues for the Messianic woes interpretation; see Martin, *Metaphor*, 244–52. Elliott and Achtemeier also acknowledge the underlying tradition of the messianic woes here; Elliott, *1 Peter*, 775; Achtemeier, *1 Peter*, 306; cf. Schlosser, *Pierre*, 258–9.

Therefore, here the author 'views the readers as undergoing that period of eschatological distress that early Judaism anticipated as occurring immediately prior to the Messiah's advent [parousia]'.[21] In such a reading, the stress is placed on the current experience of the believer and the apparent reference to the Christ-event is reduced. Dubis argues that this does not have to be so because the messiah 'also underwent the messianic woes at the cross'. He prefers the ambiguity of the genitive because it can refer to both Christ's historical suffering and the messianic woes.[22] However, it is possible to maintain an understanding that the Christian is likely to suffer before the parousia from 4.12's claim that they should not be surprised at their trials, without making τοῖς τοῦ Χριστοῦ παθήμασιν a technical reference to 'the messianic woes'.[23] Dubis' reading loses the significance of the Christ-event and gives the audience's suffering too much weight. The audience's suffering is the topic of 4.12–16, but in 4.13 it is being specifically interpreted through its relation to the Christ-event. I therefore prefer the translation 'the suffering of Christ'.[24]

So, having established that τοῖς τοῦ Χριστοῦ παθήμασιν refers to Jesus' sufferings on the cross, we need to outline the characteristics of Christ's suffering as depicted by the author. According to 1 Peter, Christ in his suffering was blameless/sinless (1.19; 2.22), righteous (3.18), did not unduly retaliate (2.22–3), but trusted God, who foreknew his suffering (1.3, 11, 18–21; 2.4), to judge (2.23; cf. 2.4, 7).[25] Thus, his suffering was unjust. Christ's suffering was also vicarious, it happened *for* them (1.18–19; 2.21, 24–5; 3.18). Moreover, Christ's suffering and his subsequent glorification by God are bound together (1.11, 21; 3.22; 4.13; 5.1).[26] We must keep all these elements in mind when we come to interpreting what sharing in Christ's suffering means in 4.13.

---

[21] Dubis, *Messianic Woes*, 100–1.

[22] Dubis, *Messianic Woes*, 101–2.

[23] Cf. Liebengood, *Eschatology*, 116–27 who maintains that 1 Peter has a definite eschatological outlook but denies that the messianic woes from Jewish apocalypticism are a strong basis for 1 Peter's suffering theology.

[24] This is supported by the use of πάθημα and the cognate verb πάσχω throughout the rest of the letter, which clearly refer to the death of Jesus on the cross. See 1.11; 2.21–4; 3.18; 4.1; and most likely 5.1. A wider understanding of Jesus' suffering as encompassing his entire earthly experience is potentially possible. However, the pattern throughout 1 Peter of Jesus' suffering being followed by his glorification suggests that suffering is being conceptualised as Jesus' crucifixion followed by his resurrection (cf. 3.18).

[25] Cf. 2 Cor 5.21; Heb 4.15; 7.26; 1 John 3.5 for the idea of Christ as sinless in his suffering; Elliott, *1 Peter*, 529.

[26] Schlosser, *Pierre*, 259.

This trope of innocent, righteous, non-violent suffering becomes the benchmark for the believers' suffering. However, unlike Christ, when the author speaks of the believers' suffering he is not referring to one historical event but an ongoing issue.[27] They experience various difficulties: accusation (2.12), threats (3.16), reproach (4.14), and reviling (3.9).[28] Verses 2.18–19 and 4.1 could indicate that they are suffering physically.[29] In conformity to Christ, the believers' suffering should be unjust/righteous and not due to wrongdoing (2.19; 3.14, 17; 4.15); and, like Christ, they should entrust themselves to their faithful creator by continuing to do good (4.19; cf. 2.23).[30] It appears that the principal cause for their suffering is their Christian identity and 'good' Christian behaviour (2.20; 3.13–14, 17; 4.14–16). Thus, Christian suffering has an added dimension: it is for Christ, on account of being a Christian.

However, in 4.12 is seems that, despite being aware of Christ's suffering, the audience are surprised at their own. Verse 4.12's negative command (μὴ ξενίζεσθε) tells the audience that they should expect their present difficulties, presumably as a logical consequence of their relationship to Christ and perhaps because of their eschatological understanding.[31] For the believers, the narrative of Christ's death and resurrection, which shapes their worldview, should also form their expectation of the present and the future.[32] This verse draws on wider tradition, evident elsewhere in the New Testament, that the followers of Christ will suffer as their Lord did (see Matt 5.11–12; 10.25; Mark 13.9–13; John 15.18–20; 16.1–4).[33] Some have seen behind this expectation a Jewish understanding that the righteous follower of God will suffer, particularly in the

---

[27] For Achtemeier, the use of the present participles γινομένῃ and συμβαίνοντος (4.12) indicate that the problem is ongoing; Achtemeier, *1 Peter*, 305.

[28] There is considerable debate, which I cannot enter into here, about the types, sources, and level of persecution depicted in 1 Peter. For a comprehensive discussion see Williams, *Persecution*.

[29] I would not want to go so far as Millauer to say that suffering in 4.13, because of its connection with Christ's death, includes the strong possibility of death; Millauer, *Leiden*, 89.

[30] In fact, they are encouraged to go one stage further and return blessing for abuse (3.9).

[31] Brox, *Petrusbrief*, 213–14.

[32] Holloway suggests that the consolation of 'it is to be expected' is similar to Cyrenaic consolatory techniques; see Holloway, *Coping*, 214–20.

[33] Cf. Acts 14.22; Phil 1.27–30; 1 Thess 3.3; 2 Tim 3.12; 1 John 3.13; Kelly, *Epistles of Peter*, 184; Michaels, *1 Peter*, 260; Achtemeier, *1 Peter*, 304–5. This does not mean that similarities between 1 Peter, 1 and 2 Thessalonians, and James were due to a common 'persecution source' as Selwyn hypothesises; Selwyn, *St. Peter*, 443, 450–2.

last days.[34] Brox, though he recognises the underlying Jewish tradition of persecution, rightly stresses that it is also distinctively Christian in finding its meaning and motivation in the passion of Christ.[35] The passion viewpoint and Christian expectation mean that a life of suffering becomes the Christian norm.[36] This does not mean, contra Dubis, that suffering is a necessity in 1 Peter, but, because of the pattern of Christ, it is a realistic expectation.[37] So, what does it mean for the suffering believer to participate in Christ's suffering?

Participation in 1 Peter

Having established what is meant by τοῖς τοῦ Χριστοῦ παθήμασιν in 4.13, we now need to examine κοινωνέω. Though there has been discussion recently that has challenged assumptions about the meaning of κοινωνέω, in line with Ogereau, I take it to have the sense of: ' "to have" or "to do something in common with someone," and, by implication, as "to share, to take part/participate in something in common with someone" '.[38] Therefore, the believer rejoices because they participate in suffering in common with Christ.[39] But how is the audience to understand its participation? Dubis has identified three ways of interpreting participating in Christ's suffering: '(1) imitation of Christ; (2) mystical union with Christ; or (3) messianic

[34] See 2 Esdr 13.16–19; 2 *Bar* 25; *Jub* 23.12–15; 1QH 2.21–2; Achtemeier, *1 Peter*, 306; cf. Elliott, *1 Peter*, 774.

[35] Brox, *Petrusbrief*, 214; cf. Millauer, *Leiden*, 76–7.

[36] Schlosser, *Pierre*, 258; cf. Selwyn, *St. Peter*, 450; Brox, *Petrusbrief*, 215.

[37] Dubis, *Messianic Woes*, 63–4.

[38] J. M. Ogereau, 'A Survey of Κοινωνία and Its Cognates in Documentary Sources', *NovT* 53 (2015): 275–94, at 277. Ogereau's article is in response to Norbert Baumert who has argued against assuming κοινωνεῖν and μετέχειν are synonyms and therefore that κοινωνέω necessarily means to 'participate in' or 'to have a share in'. He prefers the notion of commonality or association; see N. Baumert, *Koinonein und Metechein – synonym? Ein umfassende semantische Untersuchung*, SBB 51 (Stuttgart: Katholisches Bibelwerk GmbH, 2003). However, Ogereau's article has demonstrated, using other documentary sources not accessed by Baumert, that κοινωνέω and its cognates have to be taken contextually. To associate or partner with someone in the majority of cases also involves the activity of sharing or participating in something. Having said this, it is not detrimental to my proceeding argument if association or partnership is, as Baumert suggests, the overriding force of κοινωνέω. For a summary of Baumert's views and some implications for New Testament studies see A. T. Lincoln, 'Communion: Some Pauline Foundations', *Ecclesiology* 5 (2009): 135–60.

[39] Scholars note the parallels with Pauline ideas found in Rom 8.17; 2 Cor 1.5–7; Phil 3.10–11; cf. 2 Tim 2.11–12; Selwyn, *St. Peter*, 221; Feldmeier, *Peter*, 224. Schelkle sees direct influence of Pauline theology here; Schelkle, *Petrusbriefe*, 123.

woes'.⁴⁰ I will utilise these categories and add a fourth: union as solidarity with Christ.

Imitation of Christ

It is evident that the believers are to imitate Christ. There are three ways in which this happens: by their behaviour, thinking, and the reason for suffering.⁴¹ The behavioural aspect is clear in 2.21, where Christ leaves the believers a pattern (ὑπογραμμός) that they might follow in his footsteps. This is elucidated through listing Christ's behaviour (2.22–3): he did not sin, speak deceitfully, retaliate, or threaten, but trusted God. Imitating Christ's thinking occurs in 4.1, where the believers are asked to arm themselves with the same ἔννοια as Christ. Lastly, in 2.20–1 and 3.17–18 where the call to imitate Christ is present, suffering is qualified as suffering for doing good, which infers that the believers are only imitating Christ if they suffer for the right reasons. Some scholars interpret sharing in Christ's suffering as imitation only.⁴² However, I would agree with Dubis that, though imitation is present in the letter, the use of κοινωνέω suggests more than similarity, it speaks of sharing in something, and so there must be a further understanding of 4.13.⁴³

Mystical Union with Christ

Dubis explains mystical union with Christ as, 'to suffer in Christ rather than simply like Christ. Here the notion is that believers are incorporated into Christ so that they participate in Christ's historical sufferings. And Christ likewise participates in the sufferings of his body, the church'.⁴⁴ At points in 1 Peter the believers appear to be in union with Christ. One indication of spiritual union is 2.24. Here Christ bears the believers' sin on the cross (cf. 3.18) so that they can die to sins and live for righteousness.⁴⁵ Thus, if this depicts union, the believer is spiritually incorporated into Christ's death

---

⁴⁰ Dubis, *Messianic Woes*, 96.
⁴¹ Dubis, *Messianic Woes*, 97.
⁴² Selwyn, *St. Peter*, 221; Michaels, *1 Peter*, 262.
⁴³ Dubis, *Messianic Woes*, 97. Cf. Millauer, who also considers following in Christ's footsteps as more than imitation. Instead, it means walking in obedience to God's ways; Millauer, *Leiden*, 68–9, 84.
⁴⁴ Dubis, *Messianic Woes*, 98.
⁴⁵ Here I read ἀπογίνομαι metaphorically as to die because it is paralleled with ζάω. Cf. Windisch, *katholischen Briefe*, 66; Schelkle, *Petrusbriefe*, 85; Goppelt, *1 Peter*, 214; Feldmeier, *Peter*, 175–6. Others prefer the idea of separation from sin; see Selwyn, *St. Peter*, 181; Bigg, *Epistles of St. Peter*, 148–9; Michaels, *1 Peter*, 148; Achtemeier, *1 Peter*, 202–3; Elliott, *1 Peter*, 535.

and, given the notion of living to righteousness, also his resurrection.[46] However, there is no expansion here. Unlike in Romans 6.1–
11, union is not explicitly linked to baptism, though some read 2.24
this way.[47] Further, 1 Peter uses the phrase ἐν Χριστῷ (3.16; 5.10,
14) which in the Pauline corpus has been interpreted by some as spiritual union; but does it mean that here?[48] In order to discover this,
we will investigate 5.10 and 5.14 but leave 3.16 until later. In 5.10
the author says that God has called them 'in Christ' into his eternal
glory. This could be saying that their incorporation into Christ
enables their entry into eternal glory.[49] Feldmeier offers an alternative. He reads 'in Christ' in 5.10 as meaning the born anew people
who belong to God.[50] In this case, ἐν Χριστῷ in 5.10 refers more
to incorporation into a group of people than spiritual union. 5.14
supports Feldemeier's reading. It closes the letter by wishing Εἰρήνη
ὑμῖν πᾶσιν τοῖς ἐν Χριστῷ (lit. Peace to you, all the ones in Christ).
Here ἐν Χριστῷ functions in a similar way to λαὸς θεοῦ in 2.10 in
that it distinguishes the believers from others and so designates a
particular group of people.[51] Consequently, in 5.14, ἐν Χριστῷ does
not have to mean mystical union but could refer to a body of people.
But, equally this corporate usage could be a consequence of a union
idea: spiritual union with Christ is what brings one into a defined
body of people distinguished by their incorporation into Christ.[52]

[46] Selwyn argues that there is no mystical union here, but the thought is ethical
and psychological indicating abandonment of sin; Selwyn, *St. Peter*, 181. I agree
with Selwyn (cf. Goppelt, *1 Peter*, 214; Feldmeier, *Peter*, 176) that sins here are practical deeds rather than a particular power but this does not necessarily discount some
idea of union with Christ. The believer can live separated from sin because of the
empowerment that identifying with Christ's death brings; see Schelkle, *Petrusbriefe*,
85–6; Brox, *Petrusbrief*, 138.
[47] See Windisch, *katholischen Briefe*, 66; Schelkle, *Petrusbriefe*, 86; Elliott, *1
Peter*, 536.
[48] The phrase ἐν Χριστῷ is found in the New Testament only in 1 Peter outside of
Paul; Feldmeier, *Peter*, 196. For Kelly, this is evidence of Pauline influence; Kelly,
Epistles of Peter, 145.
[49] Elliott, *1 Peter*, 865; Here I read ἐν Χριστῷ as referring to the whole phrase, both
καλέσας and δόξαν. Thus the whole Christian life is in Christ rather than Christ being
the instrument of calling, contra Achtemeier, *1 Peter*, 345; cf. Michaels, *1 Peter*, 302.
[50] Feldmeier, *Peter*, 251.
[51] Cf. Michaels, *1 Peter*, 313.
[52] Brox, *Petrusbrief*, 248. Cf. Elliott, *1 Peter*, 892 for whom 'in Christ' expresses 'the
union of all those enjoying personal fellowship with Christ'. Kelly reads ἐν Χριστῷ as
implying the baptismal regeneration of the believer that has moved him 'into a new
sphere of existence: he is united with Christ and shares his risen life'; Kelly, *Epistles
of Peter*, 221. Bigg follows von Soden in seeing no reference to mystical union here,
instead 'in Christ' is simply another name for Christian; Bigg, *Epistles of St. Peter*,
198; cf. Schelkle, *Petrusbriefe*, 136; Achtemeier, *1 Peter*, 356.

Other examples in 1 Peter that could infer spiritual union are the stone imagery of 2.4–6; the offering of sacrifices to God διὰ Ἰησοῦ Χριστοῦ (through Jesus Christ, 2.5); and the adaptation of Isa 11.2 in 4.14. For Dubis, 4.14 is 'suggestive of an incorporation theology' because the Spirit that rests on the Messiah in Isaiah now rests upon the believers.[53] From this survey, it does appear that the idea of spiritual union with Christ is potentially present in the letter, but the examples are not explicit and some could imply simply being part of a body of people. Regardless, I do not think that mystical union is what is being referred to by κοινωνέω in 4.13, though it is potentially related to it.

Messianic Woes

Having discussed above that I do not consider τοῖς τοῦ Χριστοῦ παθήμασιν to be a technical designation for the 'messianic woes', subsequently, I do not think participation here is primarily participation in the messianic woes, as Dubis argues.[54] I do not deny that an idea of a period of eschatological suffering preceding the eschaton could have influenced the eschatological perspective of the letter, but it is not in the foreground here. The focus in 4.13 is the believer's relationship with Christ and the nature and significance of Christ's suffering, which has wider implications than just the messianic woes. I therefore want to argue for κοινωνέω as indicating union with Christ, but not spiritual union, rather union as a chosen social identification with Christ, that is, as solidarity.

Union as Solidarity with Christ

By focusing on Christ's suffering, the author is really asking the audience to evaluate their own suffering. In 4.12 the audience's persecution is in view, but then, immediately, Christ's suffering enters the frame. The adverb καθό (in so far as) links the two verses and directs the audience towards this comparison.[55] Thus, the picture of Christ's suffering previously established in the letter becomes the reference point by which the believers can evaluate their own.[56] Christ's

---

[53] Dubis, *Messianic Woes*, 103.
[54] Dubis, *Messianic Woes*, 99–104.
[55] See Michaels, *1 Peter*, 262.
[56] As Bechtler rightly notes, the Christ who suffered and was glorified is used to 'legitimate the symbolic universe of its addressees … The letter in effect superimposes Christ's experience onto that of his followers so that Christ's experience becomes the interpretive lens thought [sic] which Christian experience is viewed'; Bechtler, *Following*, 180.

suffering exhibited a number of qualities: it was innocent, unjusti-
fied, non-retaliatory; it was followed by glorification; it was based
on a particular mindset; and it revealed trust in God. Therefore, the
believers in 4.13 are asked to consider whether their suffering is like
this. They only participate in Christ's suffering if their suffering is
unjust (is a consequence of doing good) and if they continue to do
good even under conditions of suffering.[57]

If we were to stop here then κοινωνέω would be imitation.
However, 3.16 is illuminative for 4.13. In 3.16 the author speaks
about the recipients' good conduct 'in Christ' (τὴν ἀγαθὴν ἐν Χριστῷ
ἀναστροφήν). Thus, doing good comes from their relationship to
Christ *and* demonstrates that they are in Christ. Put differently, their
outward behaviour exhibits both their identity and allegiance, that
is, their solidarity. The comparison between suffering as a thief or
murderer and as Christian (4.14–16) indicates that good behaviour
is a fundamental aspect of Christian identity.[58] If doing good is
so important, we are led to ask, what does doing good mean, and
who determines it? What constitutes 'good' is determined by three
things: God's character and will – they are to be holy as God is holy
(1.14–15); God's action in Christ; and the model of Christ's life.[59]
This awareness of God and his action in Christ provides a framework for their behaviour (cf. 2.19; 4.19).[60] If the audience do good in
line with this framework they align themselves with God and Christ,
i.e. choose to live out of their union with Christ. At a secondary
level, this worldview determines the believers' norms and values. In
solidarity with Christ they live these values. As Bechtler comments,
the letter 'contrasts two competing realities': (1) the believers' – one

---

[57] Feldmeier, *Peter*, 226. The need for suffering to be on account of doing good is
emphasised throughout the letter (2.20; 3.13–14, 17; 4.14–16).

[58] Cf. Brox, *Petrusbrief*, 161.

[59] Thus, to agree with Williams, contra Winter, I cannot see that 'good works'
implies euergetism here or elsewhere in 1 Peter; Williams, *Persecution*, 258–69; see also
fuller discussion in T. B. Williams, *Good Works in 1 Peter: Negotiating Social Conflict
and Christian Identity in the Greco-Roman World*, WUNT 337 (Tübingen: Mohr
Siebeck, 2014), 68–104, 249–50.

[60] Achtemeier supports this when he comments that 'ἐν Χριστῷ makes clear that
"good" is here defined not by cultural norms but by the Christian faith'; Achtemeier,
1 Peter, 236. Williams has argued that Jews in the Second Temple period departed
from the Hellenistic understanding of good works as having a social focus and instead
gave them theological meaning. New Testament writers mirrored this theological
shift. Good deeds for both Judaism and Christianity were important for one's relationship with God (we will return to this in our discussion on fear in Chapter 7).
However, for the Christian, 'good works' moved beyond Torah observance to virtue
patterned after Christ; Williams, *Good Works*, 107–62.

of truth, and (2) non-Christians' – one of ignorance.[61] To which reality the believers subscribe is shown by their behaviour. It is this acceptance of the reality of, and subsequent allegiance to, Christ, demonstrated in doing good, that brings them into conflict with their surrounding society through a clash of enacted values, and results in suffering (cf. 4.2–4).[62] Thus, at the meta-level their suffering occurs because of, and highlights, a clash of worldviews. 4.14 and 4.16 reinforce that the cause of suffering is identifying with Christ when they declare that the audience suffers ἐν ὀνόματι Χριστοῦ and ὡς χριστιανός.[63] Furthermore, this makes sense of why suffering can be expected, because choosing solidarity with Christ necessarily puts you in opposition to outside society that does not recognise Christ and is opposed to God's ways.[64] Thus, the descriptions of Christ's and the believers' suffering throughout the letter, along with 3.16, point towards understanding participation as solidarity with Christ.[65] Furthermore, the believers' solidarity with Christ is rooted in and reveals an agreement with the cosmic reality manifested in Christ's life, death, resurrection, and glorification.[66] As Jobes comments, 'The Christian who stands fast and suffers for the gospel is responding to an eternal reality that will outlast death and even history itself.'[67]

I want to clarify the difference between participation as solidarity, mystical union, and imitation. Over against mystical union, participation as solidarity emphasises that participation in 1 Peter is

---

[61] Bechtler, *Following*, 110.

[62] Brox, *Petrusbrief*, 161–2, 214; Feldmeier, *Peter*, 224. Cf. 2 Tim 3.12 for another example of 'in Christ' conduct resulting in persecution.

[63] Elliott's position that ἐν ὀνόματι Χριστοῦ means not 'in the name of' but 'because of Christ', inferring 'because you belong to, are affiliated with, Christ' supports my union as solidarity with Christ reading; Elliott, *1 Peter*, 779–81; cf. Goppelt, *1 Peter*, 314.

[64] Cf. Jobes, *1 Peter*, 286–7.

[65] Elliott supports this solidarity reading when he says that in the New Testament κοινωνέω is used to show the 'solidarity that believers have with God, Christ and one another'. Later, Elliot asserts that their innocent suffering unites them with Christ, but the above reveals the opposite: it is their union with Christ that brings suffering; Elliott, *1 Peter*, 774–6. Cf. Feldmeier's comments that the believers participate in Christ by having a way of life that 'accords with Christ'; Feldmeier, *Peter*, 257; Goppelt likewise says, 'Participation in Christ's sufferings … is not just a sign but also the realization of a solidarity with Christ that comes from him and is then brought to realization by us'; Goppelt, *1 Peter*, 315.

[66] As Dryden comments: 'Their new status originates in the πρόγνωσις θεοῦ πατρός. The source of their election and their current status as strangers is the choice of their father God … Thus, their personal and corporate stories are caught up into the larger story of God's work of salvation'; De Waal Dryden, *Theology*, 67.

[67] Jobes, *1 Peter*, 287.

socio-religious rather than an inner ontological alteration of the individual.[68] It relates to social commitments and allegiances. It is about to whom one belongs and to what truth and values one subscribes.[69] Solidarity is distinguished from imitation because in the solidarity reading Christ is not just a prescriptive model but instead allegiance to Christ is the whole basis of behaviour. It does not require the believers to imitate Christ's suffering but instead to adopt and align themselves with the cosmic truth that Christ reveals. Therefore, to participate in Christ's sufferings is to suffer because of solidarity with Christ, which results in experiencing innocent suffering on account of unbending good behaviour arising from allegiance to God.

Now we have outlined what participating in Christ's sufferings means we can return to our main theme, which is to identify why such participation is an occasion for rejoicing.

Christian Suffering and the Good

The result of the participatory language in 4.13 is that the interpretation of their experiences and their subsequent emotion becomes bound up with the person of Christ and his story. By seeing suffering as the result of being united with Christ it means that suffering no longer needs to be evaluated negatively, because being united with Christ and God is good and secures the good (cf. 1.3–9).[70] This aligning of oneself with God means, as Mary Douglas says of Jewish religion, that the believer can 'rejoice in living the sacred order'. Barton rightly adds that this is especially evident 'when the existential stakes for the individual or the community are highest, as in matters considered worth living and dying for'.[71] Therefore, suffering for solidarity with Christ can be an occasion for joy.[72] Furthermore, being united with Christ now also promises that, like Christ, one's unjust suffering will ultimately be vindicated. Additionally, to

---

[68] Liebengood agrees, describing τοῖς τοῦ Χριστοῦ παθήμασιν as 'sufferings which come from associating oneself with those who demonstrate faithful allegiance to Christ', and that κοινωνέω 'is best understood in terms of being partners of or associating with a particular group'; Liebengood, *Eschatology*, 142.

[69] Cf. Goppelt, *I Peter*, 245–6; Elliott, *1 Peter*, 632.

[70] See argument of Chapter 5. For de Villiers, the author's desire to give the audience a 'proper perspective on Christian suffering' is the main purpose of the letter; de Villiers, 'Joy', 64.

[71] Douglas cited by Barton; Barton, 'Spirituality', 174.

[72] Thus, contra Thurén, joy is not primarily teleological and concessive, aimed at encouraging the audience with their final eschatological salvation. There are present reasons why joy is fitting; Thurén, *Argument*, 172–4.

see suffering as unjust and on account of doing good means that suffering can be seen as a positive legitimisation of Christian behaviour. These evaluations allow joy to be an appropriate emotion.

There are some obvious consequences of this understanding for the audience's sense of identity and their role in society. The self is understood in relation to Christ, and as such suffering is a marker that positively affirms identity rather than causing shame.[73] The primary concern becomes one's position with Christ not one's standing in the community. One's relationship with Christ may result in being shunned by society, but this does not have to affect self-esteem because the root of one's identity is not one's association with the outside community but one's solidarity with Christ and God's people.[74] Thus, joy, like in 1.6–8, is reminding the audience to focus on the significance of its relationship with Christ. Rhetorically, using joy here is seeking to reinforce internally a worldview and sense of Christian self that could otherwise be deconstructed by the experience of reproach. If Berger and Luckmann are right that one's understanding of the world is mediated by our relationship with a significant other, then here, joy is asserting the significance of Christ as the primary reference point through whom all other meaning is made meaningful.[75] This is likely to change how the believers value the hostile others and, consequently, will shape their emotional interactions with them. Again, a therapeutic consequence of seeing suffering as occurring because of identification with Christ is stability. One's relationship with Christ, which is a cause for rejoicing, cannot be negatively affected by suffering. Suffering for doing good can only reveal that you are 'in Christ' and therefore reaffirm that relationship. Consequently, one does not need to be distressed

---

[73] We will return to the discussion of shame in Chapter 8. See Bechtler, who acknowledges that God's action of creating a new community in Christ has given this new community a symbolic universe in which Christ is central and 'within which threats to honor coming from outside the community can be reinterpreted, by means of this symbolic universe, as honor-enhancing participation in the experience of Christ'; Bechtler, *Following*, 180–1.

[74] In terms of a coping strategy, Holloway might describe this as 'disidentification' where the previous negative domain has been replaced by a new one, that is, in this instance value is established from their spiritual reality rather than their earthly social existence, thus allowing emotional distancing from the negative domain. See Holloway, *Coping*, 139–40, 156. Dryden also recognises the importance of the strategy of dissociation from one's previous life, including affective commitments, which 1 Peter promotes by presenting the old and new life with their perspectives in stark antithesis; De Waal Dryden, *Theology*, 33–4.

[75] In fact, Berger and Luckmann argue that 'no radical transformation of subjective reality (including of course identity) is possible without such [affective] identification'; Berger and Luckmann, *Social*, 157.

but can have a positive outlook, and, more importantly, Christian behaviour and witness are maintained.

We mentioned at the outset that for joy to be appropriate, sharing in Christ's suffering has to be evaluated as good. The above discussion has laid out a rationale for why this is possible. However, there are wider implications of both aligning oneself with Christ and therefore continuing to do good in the face of opposition. We will now investigate these, which will include recognising the witnessing (or transformational) possibility of suffering for doing good; that suffering reveals sin-free living; and that it results in blessing and glory.

The Witness of Strange Suffering

One significant good of Christian suffering is its witnessing potential. Despite some like Bechtler and Holloway declaring that 1 Peter has virtually no evangelistic emphasis, I would argue that it is actually full of the potential of Christian witness.[76] 2.9 makes it clear that the primary purpose of God's new people is to proclaim (ἐξαγγέλλω) the virtues (ἀρεταί) of God who has called them out of darkness into his light. The language of darkness to light signifies conversion,[77] and the word ἀρετή does not mean moral virtue but the 'manifestations of his power', which 'in a Jewish-Christian setting must be God's saving acts'.[78] Thus, 2.9 is a call to Christian witness.[79] It is highly likely that those who had themselves been converted through the proclaiming (εὐαγγελίζομαι)[80] of the gospel (1.12) would recognise the relevance of proclamation for others.[81]

---

[76] Bechtler, *Following*, 114; Holloway, *Coping*, 176.

[77] Cf. Eph 5.8–11; 1 Thess 5.4–9; Elliott, *1 Peter*, 441.

[78] Kelly, *Epistles of Peter*, 99; cf. Schelkle, *Petrusbriefe*, 65; Goppelt, *I Peter*, 149–50; Achtemeier, *1 Peter*, 166.

[79] Feldmeier, *Peter*, 141; cf. Schelkle, *Petrusbriefe*, 65; Elliott, *1 Peter*, 439–40. Some argue that ἐξαγγέλλω should be read, due to the priestly function of the community, as worship rather than missionary proclamation. See Kelly, *Epistles of Peter*, 100–1; Michaels, *1 Peter*, 110; Schlosser, *Pierre*, 131, 141 (Schlosser does allow that worship in voice and life may impact on mission). It seems strange to read ἐξαγγέλλω, which means to 'proclaim, report' (BDAG, 343), as not including some expression towards unbelievers. Elliott supports this when he asserts that ἐξαγγέλλω is used for 'public declarations of praise'; Elliott, *1 Peter*, 439–40; cf. Achtemeier, *1 Peter*, 166. Even Bechtler, who sees no witness in 1 Peter, concedes that the period of time in which the audience exists is specified as the period of the proclamation of the gospel; Bechtler, *Following*, 127; cf. 1.10–12.

[80] εὐαγγελίζομαι is used 54 times in the New Testament to speak about the Christian proclamation of salvation through Christ; Elliott, *1 Peter*, 349–50.

[81] See Goppelt, *I Peter*, 150; cf. Schelkle, *Petrusbriefe*, 65.

However, in 1 Peter the mode of proclamation is not preaching but good conduct. This is most strongly identified in 2.12 and 3.1–2. In 2.12 the believers are exhorted to have good conduct among their hostile neighbours so that those speaking against them might glorify (δοξάζω) God on the day of visitation (ἐν ἡμέρᾳ ἐπισκοπῆς).[82] There is disagreement as to whether this verse indicates conversion of nonbelievers, and, if it does, at what point this takes place. The majority interpret ἐν ἡμέρᾳ ἐπισκοπῆς, I think rightly, as referring to the final judgement.[83] Therefore, for Achtemeier, this verse says that, at the final judgement, the nonbeliever will recognise that Christians were acting in line with God and so will be led to glorify God at this point.[84] But others, like Bigg, prefer the idea of conversion because 'the heathen could not be said to glorify God in the Revelation, unless they had already been converted'.[85] I agree with Bigg's logic, and therefore side with those who read δοξάζω as indicating that good conduct is aiming at present conversion of the nonbeliever.[86] As Feldmeier comments:

> [T]he author directs the interest of his addressees to the winning of others. To some degree boldly, but absolutely not without an instinct for its effect on the general public, the offence is interpreted as an opportunity for recruitment and thereby the possibility is open to transform the destructive pressure of suffering into an opportunity to actively take advantage of.[87]

Thus, doing good presents an evangelistic possibility.[88] 1 Peter is not alone in this, as Elliott comments, 'Such sensitivity concerning

---

[82] For possible background to the unique Petrine phrase ἐν ἡμέρᾳ ἐπισκοπῆς see Elliott, *1 Peter*, 470–1.

[83] The other alternative is the present confronting of the nonbeliever. For Schückler, this means God's gracious visitation that brings his salvation and enlightening; see Elliott, *1 Peter*, 471; cf. Selwyn, *St. Peter*, 171; Kelly, *Epistles of Peter*, 106; G. Schückler, 'Wandel im Glauben als missionarisches Zeugnis', *ZMR* 51 (1967): 289–99, at 293.

[84] Achtemeier does not state whether judgement will end positively or negatively for the nonbeliever; Achtemeier, *1 Peter*, 178; cf. Holloway, *Coping*, 176–7.

[85] Bigg, *Epistles of St. Peter*, 138–9.

[86] Selwyn, *St. Peter*, 170; Brox, *Petrusbrief*, 113; Michaels, *1 Peter*, 118; Elliott, *1 Peter*, 465, 470.

[87] Feldmeier, *Peter*, 150.

[88] Matthew 5.11–16 provides a useful parallel to 1 Peter. The same context of being persecuted for Christ is evident. The Christian is described as the light of the world (5.14) intended to shine before men by their good works (τὰ καλὰ ἔργα) so that the people who see will glorify (δοξάζω) their father in heaven (5.15–16). The close parallels suggest that 1 Peter is aware of Jesus traditions here.

the positive impact of behaviour on outsiders is typical of the early Christian movement.'[89] This reading of 1 Peter 2.12 is strengthened by 3.1–2 in which it is categorically stated that the non-believing husband might be gained (κερδαίνω) without a word by the wife's pure conduct (ἁγνὴ ἀναστροφή), that is, the husband is won to the faith.[90]

But how does this good conduct bear witness? Achtemeier argues that good behaviour is conduct that 'will also be recognized as appropriate by nonbelievers'. The aim of having such conduct is 'to blunt harassment and persecution but also to win over some of those who oppose them'.[91] Why should the nonbeliever be won over by this good conduct? For those who see witness in 2.12, Michaels summarises the majority view well:

> The scenario was not that Christians would proclaim to them [nonbelievers] the gospel of Christ, like those who first brought the Christian message to the provinces of Asia … but that simply by observing the 'good conduct' or 'good works' of those who believed in Christ, the accusers would see that their charges were false. Acknowledging the faith of the Christians as true and the God of the Christians as worthy of their worship, they would 'glorify God on the day of visitation'.[92]

Yet, this argument does not seem particularly convincing. It is based on the idea that all humans can recognise good. But Achtemeier himself notes that not all people have the same idea of 'good'.[93] 'Good' is not a universal concept; it is determined by society and culture. Thus, if good conduct is recognised as such by the hostile neighbour, it is unlikely to win someone over to another view of reality, i.e. to Christ or the Christian God, because such 'good' would be in-line with the other's current worldview. It would not cause them to recognise

---

[89] Cf. 1 Cor 10.31–3; Phil 2.15; Col 4.5–6; 1 Thess 4.11–12; Elliott, *1 Peter*, 469.

[90] Many agree that κερδαίνω is a distinctly missionary term. See Matt 18.15; 1 Cor 9.22; Michaels, *1 Peter*, 157; Achtemeier, *1 Peter*, 210; Elliott, *1 Peter*, 558, etc. See also D. Daube, 'κερδαίνω as a Missionary Term', *HTR* 40 (1947): 109–20.

[91] Achtemeier, *1 Peter*, 172. A number of other scholars also recognise this as 1 Peter's strategy against abuse. See Selwyn, *St. Peter*, 170; Michaels, *1 Peter*, 118; Elliott, *1 Peter*, 466–70; Jobes, *1 Peter*, 170–2. If this were the case, this would be an example of a 'problem focused' coping strategy, which seeks to change the attitude of the other by altering the opinion about the prejudiced person through disconfirming stereotypes. See Holloway, *Coping*, 117–19, 174–5.

[92] Michaels, *1 Peter*, 118; cf. Goppelt, *I Peter*, 158–60.

[93] See Achtemeier, *1 Peter*, 176–7.

Christ but would reinforce the norms they already hold.[94] If this is the case, then perhaps good conduct is not intended to be a witness and is simply a way of minimising distress by acculturation.[95] The problem is that 1 Peter distinguishes sharply between the believers' 'in Christ' life and their previous cultural identity (1.14–15). The letter does not describe Greco-Roman society's behaviour or culture in positive terms (1.18; 4.3–4).[96] Instead, good conduct is linked to God's character and will (1.15–16).[97] Doing good within this framework is a fundamental part of their Christian identity (cf. 4.18–19). As Bechtler comments, the idea of 'doing good' may be a widely accepted value. But it is likely that the Christian and nonbeliever will disagree on what 'good' is due to their different norms.[98] In fact, it appears their doing good (ἀγαθοποιέω) is being labelled as doing evil (κακοποιέω; 2.12).[99] This is not just a mismatch, but an opposition of values. Furthermore, our discussion on joy has revealed that the author is working to establish a change of primary reference group in the mind of the audience (cf. 1.22–3; 2.9–10). Why would he seek to encourage them to be moulded to their previous society again? The designation πάροικος and παρεπίδημος in 2.11 suggests he is not doing so.

A better answer for how good conduct can bear witness is found in the idea of participating in Christ's suffering because of allegiance to God. The believers do good because of an awareness of God and live in accordance with his norms revealed in Christ.[100] Thus, their good conduct is interpreted as 'good' only within a defined scheme of

---

[94] Cf. Schückler, 'Wandel', 292–4. Schückler recognises the need for the non-believer to be opened to a new reality. However, I do not conclude with Schückler that the recognition of 'good' and of the true reality depends solely on God's gracious visitation, that is, only via God's agency in an elective sense.

[95] See Williams, *Good Works*, 167–84 for arguments against this misconception of the social function of good works in 1 Peter. Though I agree with the majority of Williams' argument, I would not want to remove all trace of optimism that good works might influence the audience's social situation, but I agree that it is not through accommodation and conformity. Again, I will return to the social strategy of 1 Peter in the conclusion.

[96] See De Waal Dryden, *Theology*, 91–5, 114–15 who argues that no middle ground is left by 1 Peter.

[97] Cf. Goppelt, *I Peter*, 158.

[98] Bechtler, *Following*, 93; contra Brox, *Petrusbrief*, 113, though Brox is aware of the paradox, which he thinks does not trouble the author, that on the one hand the Christian can be defamed for their Christian life, but on the other hand, their life can also be a witness.

[99] Goppelt, *I Peter*, 158; cf. Brox, *Petrusbrief*, 113; Williams, *Good Works*, 173–4.

[100] In this I agree with Schückler that their good behaviour is not primarily aimed at affecting the believer; it is orientated around God's will. It only has the ability to witness so long as it points to the faith and God; Schückler, 'Wandel', 294.

reality.[101] It is this meta-narrative that is the basis for their identity and subsequent conduct.[102] As Achtemeier rightly comments, within this schema they can aim to cause as little offence to the other as possible but, 'where their Christian calling collides with social custom or political expectation, they must defy that custom and be ready to suffer, as was Christ, rather than abandon their calling to follow God'.[103] Thus, at points, the Christian will defy the norms and expectations of surrounding society. Consequently, Christian behaviour may seem odd to and conflict with the surrounding society (cf. ξενίζω, 4.4).[104] It is at the point of confusion and conflict that one questions meaning, trying to make sense of the other's behaviour. One usually does this by recourse to one's understanding of reality. However, when something does not fit with the established worldview, or challenges it, the worldview itself comes into question.[105] Therefore, the 'strangeness' of the believers' behaviour challenges the other's accepted worldview and points towards another reality. In this regard, it is the *basis* of the believer's different behaviour that is important for witness, not simply its degree.[106] This strange behaviour may leave the other in confusion or it may cause the bewildered to question the believer's conduct and therefore afford the believer the chance to profess God in both word and deed.[107] At this point of curiosity there is an opportunity for the other to encounter a new reality that centres on Christ and if accepted may lead to conversion.[108] As mentioned above, the

[101] Cf. Elliott, *1 Peter*, 466 who comments that καλός in both LXX and the New Testament 'designates behaviour that is honourable in the sight of God.' Cf. Deut 6.18; 12.28.

[102] De Waal Dryden, *Theology*, 118.

[103] Achtemeier, *1 Peter*, 194.

[104] As Schückler comments, 'Der Wandel im Glauben wird von den Nichtgläubigen als fremd, befremdlich und als beunruhigend empfunden. Sie haben keine plausible Erklärung für diesen christlichen Wandel, der sich exponiert, aussetzt und distanziert von dem "überlieferten" Wandel' ('The way of life of the believers is felt by the non-believers as alien, strange, and disturbing. They have no plausible explanation for this Christian manner of life, which exposes, presents, and distances itself from the "passed down" manner of life'); Schückler, 'Wandel', 291.

[105] Berger and Luckmann, *Social*, 104–8.

[106] De Waal Dryden, *Theology*, 135 (following Volf).

[107] As De Waal Dryden comments, 'difference and mission come together in *identity* … In maintaining their virtuous conduct "as aliens and strangers", the Christians reveal their distinction from outsiders; but inherent in this distinction is an invitation. Because their identity is constructed positively, it does not exclude outsiders'; De Waal Dryden, *Theology*, 137–8.

[108] Michaels notes that ἐποπτεύω (2.12) 'suggests an act of observing that leads to a change of mind or outlook, like having one's eyes opened to something not seen before'. For Michaels this indicates the *cause* of conversion, not necessarily the moment of conversion; Michaels, *1 Peter*, 118.

believers participate in Christ's suffering because they continue to do good in solidarity with God and Christ. Thus, doing good is what displays allegiance, causes suffering, and can be a witness. It is perhaps an even greater witness to another reality that someone would choose to suffer, maintaining loyalty to God, rather than change behaviour. Such strange behaviour and strange suffering has the potential to bear witness to God and therefore can be evaluated as good and a reason to rejoice.

If we allow that participating in the sufferings of Christ means aligning oneself to the truth demonstrated in the narrative of God's action in Christ, then we can see further implications for the believer in the *imitatio Christi* sections of 1 Peter. As we approach these sections of the letter, we need to retain what we have just established: that doing good, especially suffering for it, can be a witness to another reality.

Suffering for Others

The first significant comparison between the suffering believer and the suffering of Christ is in 2.18–25. This passage evidences the line of thought we have been working with; it shows the relationship between acting because of a consciousness of God (2.19), doing good (2.20), and suffering unjustly for it (2.19).[109] Such behaviour is commendable before God. More than this, suffering on account of doing good is what they are called to (2.21).[110] The reasoning is then given:

ὅτι καὶ Χριστὸς ἔπαθεν ὑπὲρ ὑμῶν,
ὑμῖν ὑπολιμπάνων ὑπογραμμόν,
ἵνα ἐπακολουθήσητε τοῖς ἴχνεσιν αὐτοῦ,

because Christ suffered on your behalf,
leaving a pattern for you,
so that you might follow in his steps. (2.21)

There are two things highlighted for the audience: that Christ suffered for them and that they should follow in his steps. Many

---

[109] Here συνείδησις θεοῦ is an awareness of God rather than conscience. It still contains a moral element through being conscious of God and his will. See Michaels, *1 Peter*, 140; cf. Goppelt, *1 Peter*, 197–8; Elliott, *1 Peter*, 519.

[110] This is not a call to suffering, but a call to a life that is 'in Christ' and demonstrates allegiance to God in doing good. Michaels supports this when he says that in 2.21–5 Christ is given as an 'example of doing good, not as an example of patient endurance'; Michaels, *1 Peter*, 141; contra Kelly, *Epistles of Peter*, 118.

scholars recognise the call to imitate Christ, and this is indeed present.[111] But what should be made of the first clause: that Christ suffered on behalf of them? Scholars take different approaches. Kelly does not think that it intended to emphasise the vicarious nature of Christ's suffering, but is simply 'an integral part of the creedal sentence quoted'.[112] Feldmeier reads it as another encouragement to imitate Christ's suffering.[113] Goppelt agrees, but emphasises the discipleship element of following Christ and as such Jesus' suffering for them becomes 'encounter and obligation'.[114] But encounter and obligation is already present in the idea of calling (2.21a). In Goppelt's reading nothing is added by the reminder that Christ suffered *for them*. So, what is the author doing here? Is he simply drawing lines of reciprocal allegiance? Achtemeier comes close to this: Christ suffered for them, therefore, because of their devotion, they are called to suffer for Christ.[115] Or is the motive supposed to be one of gratitude?[116] All these views miss a more obvious implication of this phrase, which is shown by the parallelism between the believers' innocent suffering and Christ's that runs through 2.21–5.

The majority of commentators acknowledge the correspondence between the believer and Christ here, but think this finishes at 2.23. Thus, 2.24–5 speak about the atoning work of Christ's death, which has consequences for the believer but exhibits no parallelism.[117] However, in terms of composition, as Michaels posits, there is 'no sharp distinction in vv. 21–5 between Christ as an example to Christian believers of nonretaliation … and Christ as redeemer

---

[111] It is no doubt right that the parallelism between the believers and Christ is based on the theme of innocent suffering and that the example of Christ is used to encourage a non-retaliatory response to persecution; Elliott, *1 Peter*, 523, 525–32; Feldmeier, *Peter*, 169–70, 174.

[112] Here Kelly, like others, notes the liturgical quality of 2.21–5; Kelly, *Epistles of Peter*, 119.

[113] Christ's death is read as leaving an ethical imperative for the believer; Feldmeier, *Peter*, 173–4.

[114] Goppelt, *1 Peter*, 202–6; Achtemeier, likewise, emphasises discipleship rather than imitation; Achtemeier, *1 Peter*, 199. Cf. Thurén who also sees obligation as a motivating factor here; Thurén, *Argument*, 144.

[115] Achtemeier, *1 Peter*, 198–9.

[116] See Selwyn, *St. Peter*, 92, 179.

[117] Kelly, *Epistles of Peter*, 147; who holds the same position concerning 3.18; cf. Elliott, *1 Peter*, 525–7; W. J. Dalton, *Christ's Proclamation to the Spirits: A Study of 1 Peter 3:18–4:6*, Analecta Biblica 23, 2nd ed. (Rome: Editrice Pontificio Istituto Biblico, 1989), 126. Thurén is an exception. He thinks that '22–24a explains what these footsteps are'; Thurén, *Argument*, 143. Jobes also lists 2.21–5 as example, but does not relate 24–5 to the believers specifically; Jobes, *1 Peter*, 196–200.

of Christian believers'.[118] Perhaps continuity between 2.23 and 24 indicates that the audience should see the pattern of Christ as relevant for them from verse 22 to verse 25. This is supported by the fact that each successive idea is introduced by a repeated relative pronoun. This pattern runs through 2.22–4 and suggests that following in Christ's steps goes beyond 2.22–3's nonviolent suffering. Moreover, the verses appear in a chiastic structure: Christ suffered for you (2.21); sinless example (2.22); non-retaliation example (2.23); Christ bore our sins (2.24). Therefore, framing verses 22–3, which are pulled out as imitation elements, are two reminders that Christ's death was *for them*. What this does is frame Christ's historical suffering in the larger narrative of God's work of salvation. In asking the audience to follow in Christ's footsteps and then bringing in this larger reality, the author also draws their everyday suffering into this larger framework.

The outcome for the believer of Christ's suffering is four things: being separated from sin, living for righteousness, being healed, and their returning to the shepherd and overseer of their souls. It could be that these verses (2.24–5) detail how the believer has been enabled by Christ to live a righteous life.[119] Yet, as mentioned, by listing these outcomes, the author is emphasising the larger narrative of God's redemptive work through Christ in which the believer participates.[120] This is particularly highlighted in the second *imitatio Christi* section (3.17–18). After associating suffering for doing good with the will of God, the author gives the reason:

ὅτι καὶ Χριστὸς ἅπαξ περὶ ἁμαρτιῶν ἔπαθεν,[121]
δίκαιος ὑπὲρ ἀδίκων,
ἵνα ὑμᾶς προσαγάγῃ τῷ θεῷ,

because, also, Christ once for sins suffered,
a righteous man on behalf of unrighteous people,
so that he might bring you to God. (3.18)[122]

---

[118] Michaels does not pull out the full implications of this, but again follows the majority in separating off 2.21–3 as example from 2.24 to 5 as significance; Michaels, *1 Peter*, 136, 143.

[119] Elliott, *1 Peter*, 523, 528; cf. Achtemeier, *1 Peter*, 203.

[120] If ἐπεστράφητε (2.25) is passive rather than middle, then it implies the activity of God in the redemptive process; cf. Elliott, *1 Peter*, 539.

[121] That the death of Jesus is expressed as suffering rather than dying for sins demonstrates a desire to bring the Christ event into direct comparison with the believer's suffering. Cf. 2.21; Feldmeier, *Peter*, 201; also Elliott, *1 Peter*, 525.

[122] Like with 2.22–5, some see traditional hymnic material underlying this passage; Kelly, *Epistles of Peter*, 146. However, this does not have to be so, as Feldmeier

In both 2.21–5 and 3.17–18 the end point is the reminder that through Christ's righteous suffering they have been brought to God.[123] Consequently, in both contexts the larger plan of salvation is accentuated.[124] Selwyn, who does ask how far the believer's suffering should be paralleled with the atoning death of Christ, comments that it is the *motive* and *principles* underlying Jesus' innocent suffering and atoning death that can be copied. He then clarifies: 'the motive on which St. Peter dwells is that of winning people for God', which is shown in both *imitatio Christi* passages.[125] Thus, for the above compositional reasons, I think it is perfectly plausible, given the audience have been asked to see their suffering as parallel to Christ's in every other respect, that the parallel with Christ's suffering can also encompass the place of the believers' suffering in the larger redemptive plan of God.[126] This is not to say that the believer's suffering is like Christ's in atoning for them or others, but it shares similarity in its motivation and potential outcome.[127]

We have argued that doing good has the ability to witness by signalling to the norms of another reality. If we draw this together with the concept of righteous suffering for the other, demonstrated by Christ, we can understand that the believers can, like Christ, see that their suffering might be used to bring people to God. In their *righteous* suffering the *unrighteous* other can be made aware

asserts, it simply recounts in a dense form common Christian confessional material; Feldmeier, *Peter*, 198; cf. Selwyn, *St. Peter*, 195. For arguments against underlying hymnic material in 2.21–5 see Michaels, *1 Peter*, 136–7.

[123] Thurén recognises the emphasis the author places on the consequences of Christ's suffering in 3.18. However, he simply concludes that the author wants to give value to unjust suffering by indicating that it can lead to a good result; Thurén, *Argument*, 160. Jobes also sees 3.18 as relevant to the believer only in as much as it demonstrates 'the way to follow Christ to victory'; Jobes, *1 Peter*, 237–8.

[124] Indeed, Elliott notes how 3.18–22 goes further than 2.21–5 in displaying the 'once-for-all nature of Christ's suffering' and in detailing the 'cosmic scope of Christ's action'; Elliott, *1 Peter*, 640; cf. Selwyn, *St. Peter*, 195; Goppelt, *1 Peter*, 254–5.

[125] Selwyn, *St. Peter*, 97–8, 195. Bigg argues similarly, though he allows more parallelism in atonement than I think 1 Peter allows: 'He [Christ] died as the innocent sin-offering, and our sufferings have in their degree a similar value; He bought us near to God, and we may bring others. But these lessons are allusively conveyed, and do not lie on the surface'; Bigg, *Epistles of St. Peter*, 161.

[126] De Waal Dryden does think that 'Christ's work on the "tree"' can be 'both vicarious and exemplary' because Christ's death is an 'active obedience to God's will' and demonstrates 'continuing to do good in the face of unjust suffering'. However, for De Waal Dryden, this parallel stops at the moral sphere; De Waal Dryden, *Theology*, 187–8.

[127] I agree with the majority of scholars who hold to the uniqueness of Christ's vicarious death; Michaels, *1 Peter*, 201–2; Achtemeier, *1 Peter*, 246–7; Elliott, *1 Peter*, 525.

of the consciousness of God that motivates them and be brought into a new reality. Thus, the believer can appreciate the value of their suffering not only for themselves but for the potential salvation of the other. By participating in Christ's suffering, their proclamatory suffering can play a part in God's redemptive plan.[128] If this is true, it is remarkable, because it means that in 2.18–25 not only are slaves given moral responsibility but they are also made key agents in ministering God's salvation to others.[129] I do not think the potential impact of Christian suffering on the non-Christian other would be lost on an audience who themselves have been converted to Christ. They could easily understand that God's redemptive plan stretches wider than them alone and that others too can be brought into God's community. As they participate in the sufferings of Christ they can share in this.[130] This makes sense of why the author consistently moves beyond the pattern of Christ's death to its larger significance.

Consequently, both 2.24–5 and 3.17–18, like 2.9, are reminders to the audience of their previous state and way of life: a way that was marked with ignorance and wrongdoing like that of their abusers (cf. 1.18; 4.3). As Michaels notes, in 3.18 '[f]or a moment, the readers of the epistle are themselves put in the position of the "unjust" who afflict them unjustly'; they were previously 'alienated from God and needing to be reconciled'.[131] They were unrighteous sinners who have been recipients of grace and mercy. All this is God's doing, not their own. Because of this, the believers can have confidence in their salvation and demonstrate moral strength in doing good, but they cannot have an arrogant or superior attitude toward their accusers. Such a perspective could help the sufferer to respond to their persecutors confidently, yet gently and with respect (2.17; 3.16). We noted earlier

---

[128] That 2.15 says that those speaking against the Christians will be shamed might seem to argue against any indication of witness in 2.19–25. However, shaming does not have to refer to eschatological judgement, which would condemn the persecutor (see Feldmeier, *Peter*, 197). If it refers to shaming in the present then that shaming, which would occur because of a realisation of the falseness of their accusations, would concurrently prove the validity of the Christian way of life and so could be a mode by which the persecutor comes to recognise the other reality that good conduct points to.

[129] Elliott, *1 Peter*, 513; cf. Feldmeier who links 2.20 with 2.12 and 3.1–2 to draw the conclusion that the 'slaves who are outwardly powerless can give a not insignificant contribution to the Christian mission'; Feldmeier, *Peter*, 172.

[130] Cf. Mark 13.9–10 where suffering for Christ is a witness to others and is linked to the need for the gospel to be preached to all nations. Moreover, the idea of personal suffering being for others as part of the extension of the gospel can be seen in Col 1.24–5.

[131] Michaels, *1 Peter*, 202.

that joy seeks to underline the importance of their solidarity with Christ and displace the significance of the hostile other. If taken to the extreme, this could result in the complete devaluing of the other. However, a reminder of the believers' place before conversion and the indication that they could be used to extend salvation to others could provide a corrective to this negative attitude so that the other remains valuable, just not the most significant. Thus, we can conclude that one good of suffering innocently, i.e. sharing in Christ's sufferings, is that it points to Christ and an alternate system of reality and therefore could draw others towards salvation. This participation in God's redemptive plan is a good worth rejoicing in.

This leads us to a second, interlinked good: the transformative value of righteous suffering. It logically follows that if nonbelievers are won to Christianity by the witness of the sufferer then the accusers' actions towards the believer are likely to be transformed and persecution will cease.[132] In 3.13 the author indicates that doing good has potential to change the situation when he asks: Καὶ τίς ὁ κακώσων ὑμᾶς ἐὰν τοῦ ἀγαθοῦ ζηλωταὶ γένησθε; (Now who will harm you if you are eager to do what is good?; NRSVA). This question begs the response, 'No one', and thus encourages a positive perspective on the impact of doing good.[133] However, the author concedes that this may not always be the outcome (3.14). The most overt allowance for transformation of the social situation is the winning conduct of the wife (3.2). Therefore, there is a positive expectation that doing good because of solidarity with Christ has the potential to alleviate persecution. Yet, the reality appears that doing good will, in most cases, lead to suffering. However, because they can rejoice in sharing in Christ's sufferings, even when doing good does not alter the social situation, they do not need to be despondent but can continue to do good regardless.

Suffering and Sin-Free Living

We can now turn to the last *imitatio Christi* portion of 1 Peter. At 4.1–3 the implication of sharing in Christ's suffering for the believer's

---

[132] Cf. 2.12, 15; 3.16. As argued above, humiliation of the abuser in these verses might lead to a change of attitude on the part of the accuser. Some of these verses do not necessarily indicate conversion but instead correction of the nonbeliever.

[133] Admittedly, this could be read eschatologically, meaning that the abuser cannot ultimately harm the believer (de Villiers, 'Joy', 77), so does not necessarily warrant an expectation of present change of circumstances.

ethical life is revealed.[134] After a brief diversion, the author returns
to the topic of Christ's suffering through the phrase Χριστοῦ οὖν
παθόντος σαρκί (Christ, therefore, having suffered in the flesh), which
recalls the θανατωθεὶς μὲν σαρκί (having been put to death in the
flesh) of 3.18.[135] The audience are then exhorted: καὶ ὑμεῖς τὴν αὐτὴν
ἔννοιαν ὁπλίσασθε (and you, arm yourselves with the same way of
thinking). Thus, the audience are asked to imitate Christ's perspective on suffering. The reason is given: ὅτι ὁ παθὼν σαρκὶ πέπαυται
ἁμαρτίας.[136] Here ὁ παθών refers to the suffering Christian not
Christ.[137] It speaks of the persecution they are undergoing, not fig-
urative suffering (or death) in baptism.[138] The perfect tense of παύω
means that the effect of having such an attitude is ongoing.[139] Here
the word ἁμαρτία refers to 'active wrongdoing contrary to the will of
God', rather than any particular power.[140] Thus, the resulting translation is 'because the one who suffers in the flesh has ceased from
sinning'. The direct link between having the same thinking as Christ
with regard to suffering and the ability to constantly live a morally
upright life is apparent. This is underscored by the author in 4.2
where the εἰς shows the goal of the new state: εἰς τὸ μηκέτι ἀνθρώπων
ἐπιθυμίαις ἀλλὰ θελήματι θεοῦ τὸν ἐπίλοιπον ἐν σαρκὶ βιῶσαι χρόνον (so
as to live for the rest of your earthly life no longer by human desires
but by the will of God; NRSVA).[141]

    There is a danger that, if we do not read these verses carefully,
we interpret 1 Peter as saying that suffering is necessary to overcome

---

[134] Elliott, *1 Peter*, 711.

[135] Michaels, *1 Peter*, 224–5; Achtemeier, *1 Peter*, 276; Feldmeier, *Peter*, 212. This
has the effect of making 3.19–22 seem like an excursus.

[136] Contra Achtemeier and Martin, I read ὅτι as explanatory rather than outlining
the content of ἔννοια; Achtemeier, *1 Peter*, 278; Martin, *Metaphor*, 227–9. For support
for reading ὅτι as explanatory see Michaels, *1 Peter*, 226; Elliott, *1 Peter*, 714; Dalton,
Christ's Proclamation, 221. The designation of 'in the flesh', like with Christ, means
the suffering the believer experiences while in their physical body, that is, in the present human existence. Thus, suffering can include psychological suffering also; cf.
Achtemeier, *1 Peter*, 280–1.

[137] Achtemeier, *1 Peter*, 278–9; Schlosser, *Pierre*, 235; Contra Michaels, *1 Peter*,
226–9.

[138] Contra Kelly, *Epistles of Peter*, 168–9; Schlosser, *Pierre*, 235. Schlekle affirms
the baptismal interpretation, though very tentatively; Schelkle, *Petrusbriefe*, 114.
A comparison with Romans 6 is usually the basis for this interpretation.

[139] Elliott, *1 Peter*, 714. I also read πέπαυται as middle, thus 'indicating the initia-
tive of the subject'; Dalton, *Christ's Proclamation*, 222.

[140] So, can be translated as the active 'sinning' as Elliott suggests; Elliott, *1 Peter*,
715; cf. Bigg, *Epistles of St. Peter*, 167; contra Kelly, *Epistles of Peter*, 166.

[141] Cf. Thurén who says that εἰς τό indicates the intended result: 4.1 gives the
means, 4.2 the purpose; Thurén, *Argument*, 82.

sin.[142] This has led some to the conclusion that suffering is purificatory, or even atoning.[143] Yet, 1 Peter is clear that only Christ's vicarious suffering is atoning (1.18–19; 2.24; 3.18) and that the believer has already been purified by obedience to the gospel (1.22). Goppelt offers an alternative, commenting that 'suffering leads to doing right' because suffering 'destroys and judges the flesh'.[144] Goppelt relies on an anthropological understanding of flesh that is opposed to spirit so that the battle becomes with one's own flesh.[145] Goppelt does not go so far as to say that suffering frees from sin, he reserves this for Christ, but that flesh is 'handed over to suffering unto death in discipleship'. Flesh and sin belong together. Therefore, one has to die to be free from sin.[146] Though 1 Peter does say that Christ was put to death in the flesh and made alive in the spirit (3.18), the Pauline opposition of flesh and spirit is not operational here. As Elliott comments, the audience is not released from the power of sin but ceases sinful behaviour.[147] Furthermore, Goppelt's reading makes awkward the following phrase in which the author says that the remaining time *in the flesh* (τὸν ἐπίλοιπον ἐν σαρκὶ βιῶσαι χρόνον) should be lived in the will of God. More problematically, Goppelt's reading infers that the audience is expected to emulate Christ's death, and thus positively encourages martyrdom. However, nowhere does 1 Peter say that suffering 'in itself is a good thing'. Suffering is always because of doing good.[148]

---

[142] See Windisch, *katholischen Briefe*, 73. I use the word 'danger' here not to import a modern conception of suffering and the Christian life into 1 Peter, but to warn that a misreading of the text can cause us to produce an image of the ideal Christian life that is not representative of what the author himself appears to be advocating.

[143] See Selwyn, *St. Peter*, 209. Texts cited in support of this are 2 Macc 4.12–16; *2 Bar* 13.9–10; *1 En* 67.9. But as Kelly rightly notes, these texts speak more of discipline than purification; Kelly, *Epistles of Peter*, 167. Cf. Millauer who rejects suffering as atoning, but stresses its purificatory function; Millauer, *Leiden*, 127–9. Many scholars note the comparison with the Israelite martyrological tradition in which the death of the righteous atoned for Israel. The majority rightly dismiss that such tradition is present in 1 Peter. Elliott correctly asserts that passages used to support the purification interpretation refer to suffering that is deserved because of sin, not innocent suffering; see Elliott, *1 Peter*, 715–16.

[144] Goppelt, *I Peter*, 278.

[145] Goppelt, *I Peter*, 276–8.

[146] Death here is primarily metaphorical like that applied to baptism, though Goppelt does not limit suffering to spiritual ideas, but includes physical suffering too; Goppelt, *I Peter*, 280–1; cf. Martin who follows Goppelt; Martin, *Metaphor*, 229–31. Millauer also speaks anthropologically and thinks that flesh is the problem. He does not see a Pauline baptismal tradition here, but instead believes these verses indicate that suffering strikes the flesh and thus effects judgement and purification; Millauer, *Leiden*, 128–33.

[147] Elliott, *1 Peter*, 716.

[148] Michaels, *1 Peter*, 225.

Additionally, there is no need to see suffering here as indicating death; it evokes instead the audience's present persecution. Elliott's position shares similarities with Goppelt's. For Elliott, this passage reveals the 'disciplining function' that suffering can have, in that it 'assists in the control of the flesh, which is prone to sinning'. Elliott uses Israelite wisdom tradition (e.g. Prov 3.11–12; 23.13–14; Sir 22.6; 30.1) and Hebrews 12.7–11 to argue that one learns obedience from suffering. He concludes that suffering 'disciplines the physical body (*sarx*) by which sinning is carried out and thereby trains one to cease from sinning'.[149] However, though Hebrews does depict the disciplining function of suffering, I do not think 1 Peter supports this. In 1 Peter, suffering is a consequence of their solidarity to Christ in doing good. Thus, suffering is a result of their obedience to God, not productive of it.[150]

In our interpretation we need to start where the author does. His primary point of departure is Christ's thinking. The word ἔννοια indicates 'understanding', 'thinking', even 'mindset', which leads to a particular resolve; it refers to the cognitive aspect of behaviour.[151] The point is one's perspective on suffering and its relation to ethical behaviour, not the necessity of physical suffering for moral purity.[152] Moreover, a certain kind of suffering is in view, which has already been established: innocent suffering that is a consequence of doing good because of a consciousness of God.[153] We must also understand 'sin' as disobedience to God. Thus, here the example of Christ is found in his *conviction* to continue to act righteously and endure unjust suffering in obedience to God's will.[154] Here, the

---

[149] Elliott, *1 Peter*, 716–17.

[150] As Holloway discusses, 1 Peter does follow the Jewish idea that a person may suffer because he is righteous, but he argues that '1 Peter moves beyond the broader consolatory theme of suffering as a form of testing that perfects the sufferer, to the related but much more narrowly focused theme of suffering because one is in some significant sense *already* righteous.' However, Holloway does go on to conclude that such 'suffering can still perfect the sufferer'; Holloway, *Coping*, 198.

[151] Elliott, *1 Peter*, 713; cf. Bigg, *Epistles of St. Peter*, 167. Contra Millauer, *Leiden*, 131.

[152] Achtemeier's comment that 'ἔννοια is also found in the LXX, primarily in Proverbs, and refers, to be sure, to mental activity, but primarily in the form of intention or disposition in the sphere of moral actions' supports this; Achtemeier, *1 Peter*, 277. Cf. Michaels who emphasises that it is not suffering that is important but the attitude of mind in a moment of crisis; Michaels, *1 Peter*, 225.

[153] What has already been said about Christ's attitude can be added to this picture: his refusal to do wrong or retaliate (2.22–3), and his entrusting of himself to God (2.23); Elliott, *1 Peter*, 713.

[154] De Waal Dryden, *Theology*, 183. Brox describes Christ's *Gesinnung* (attitude/disposition) as to rejoice in suffering. Joy may be the final outcome, but the

believer is asked to imitate Christ's resolve. Therefore, to be free from sin does not require suffering, but instead, those who have already suffered, because of unbending obedience to God, have proven that they have ceased from sin, i.e. disobedience.[155] Consequently, as De Waal Dryden highlights, Christ's example is in his *disposition* not his specific activity.[156] As such, the author is addressing the audience's perspective rather than prescribing suffering, because it is their perspective that governs how they act. This reading is supported by the following εἰς clause in which the author sets in contrast the desires of humans and the will of God. Thus, the purpose of having the same resolve as Christ is to be able to live continually in God's will. A life oriented in this manner represents the Christian ethical norm.[157] Consequently, again, the Christian worldview centred on Christ is to define their actions. Therefore, we can understand 4.1 as saying that those who have the same mindset as Christ, in that they have chosen unbending obedience to God in doing good and are suffering on account of it, have shown that they have ceased from sin, i.e. from active disobedience to God's will.

The above reading of 4.1 is strengthened when we take into account the wider matrix of thought present in 4.1–3. In 4.1–3 a number of ideas converge: attitude (cognition; ἔννοια), human desire (ἐπιθυμία), God's will (θέλημα), bodily suffering, and sinful action. If we compare these ideas with Greco-Roman philosophical understandings of the self and of the root of ethical behaviour we find that a better understanding of the rationale of this passage emerges.[158]

ἐπιθυμία is used in two ways in 1 Peter: as a specific type of wrongdoing (4.3) and more generally for desire as a wider concept.[159] The second usage is evident in 4.2 (cf. 2.11). These desires are categorised as of humanity (ἀνθρώπων, 4.2) and of the flesh (σαρκικῶν, 2.11).

disposition is surely unbending obedience; Brox, *Petrusbrief*, 191. Christ's 'insight' is not to renounce the flesh and thus be willing to submit the flesh to judgement, as Millauer argues; Millauer, *Leiden*, 133.

[155] See Achtemeier who follows the same logic; Achtemeier, *1 Peter*, 280. Cf. Bigg, *Epistles of St. Peter*, 167; Jobes, *1 Peter*, 262–6.

[156] De Waal Dryden, *Theology*, 189.

[157] Schlosser, *Pierre*, 236.

[158] Very few scholars utilise Greco-Roman philosophy here, with the exceptions of Feldmeier and Achtemeier. Achtemeier cursorily notes that ἐπιθυμία is an important Stoic term; Achtemeier, *1 Peter*, 280. Feldmeier develops a deeper discussion about desires (Feldmeier, *Peter*, 102–5), but does not apply his material to 4.1–2.

[159] Cf. Mark 4.19; Rom 1.24; Eph 2.3; 1 John 2.16; Achtemeier, *1 Peter*, 280; see also Selwyn, *St. Peter*, 210. ἐπιθυμία is one of the four primary πάθη (see Table 5.1). Though we will touch on some aspects of desire briefly here, there is not scope to detail it as fully as the other emotions we are investigating.

Such descriptions refer to general human motivations that are contrasted with the will of God. For the author these human desires are obvious in the surrounding Greco-Roman culture (cf. 4.3–4)[160] and they are a marker of the believers' previous, ignorant (ἄγνοια) way of life before Christ (1.14). Consequently, we can see the link between cognition and desires. The former desires are ones that come out of a mistaken perspective – ignorance.[161] This is why it is important that in the current situation they have the right way of thinking, because right perspective will bring the right desires.[162] These desires in turn influence goals and behaviour.

Human desires as a category could infer a number of things. In Greco-Roman philosophy ἐπιθυμίαι are often associated with basic bodily drives such as for food, drink, and sex. In all ancient philosophies these 'unfiltered animalistic impulses abolish the freedom of people for a self-determined life'.[163] Therefore, they must be controlled. Yet, desires as a category can also be extended to cover a want for more abstract items such as wealth, status, and honour. In philosophy, natural desires are not always negative as they encourage the person towards a state of well-being. However, the good life is generally perceived as one that has control over desires, particularly unhelpful ones. As we have seen with Stoicism, unhelpful desires are due to a wrong perspective, or a wrong system of value, and lead to misguided behaviour. It is perhaps when confronted with pain that these values are most tested. For many humans the desire for health, well-being, status, and acceptance are high on the agenda and so will motivate actions. However, if something is of higher value than these or other goods, then one will be motivated toward the higher good and will be willing to forgo other seeming goods (see Seneca, *Ep.* 71.2–5). Perspective influences what is seen as good, which in turn influences priorities. In fact in *Ep.* 71.24 Seneca clearly states '[i]t matters not only what you see, but with what eyes you see it'; in the context this is to do with what to value and what course to pursue (cf. *Ep.* 71.13–14, 18). For Stoicism, this ultimately ends in the acceptance of whatever befalls. The wise man has yielded up all things to god including his body and possessions and is focused

---

[160] Achtemeier, *1 Peter*, 280.

[161] Ignorance is specifically an ignorance of God. Feldmeier explains that this leads to 'a perverted orientation of being and behaving'; Feldmeier, *Peter*, 105.

[162] 1 Corinthians 15.34 provides a parallel where ignorance of God is linked to sinning, whereas righteousness is linked to soberness, i.e. clear thinking/perception. Cf. also Eph 4.17–24; Feldmeier, *Peter*, 105; Dalton, *Christ's Proclamation*, 219.

[163] Feldmeier, *Peter*, 102 3.

instead on his moral purpose.[164] Subsequently, one should not try to avoid suffering, if that is what nature wills (Marcus Aurelius, *Med.* 2.17; 4.25–7; cf. Seneca, *Ep.* 71.16; 107.12). In 1 Peter the higher system of value is bracketed under the label of God's will. It is this consciousness of God that sets perspective and prioritises goods.

Thus, in 4.2–3 we have two schemes at work. Feldmeier describes it as an 'antagonism between two spheres of power'.[165] However, it is really an antagonism between two perspectives on reality, two systems of value that carry different priorities reflected in differing behaviour.[166] The believers are to have end goals that are different to the desires of humans, that is, those of surrounding culture. These goals are beyond the present physical situation of the audience and are eschatological, eternal, and spiritual.[167] This orientation was established in 1.3–9 and throughout the letter it has been linked to solidarity with Christ. Consequently, their previous goals and behaviour are no longer compatible with their new understanding of being in allegiance with Christ.[168] The author desires the audience to have the right ἔννοια because if they do they will set the course of their life and action aright. If Christ's resolve is the pattern of this ἔννοια, then doing good in accordance with God's will will be evaluated as of more importance than other goods such as physical well-being or status, which explains why the believer will be willing to suffer for doing good.

We can now return to our original topic, that those who have suffered righteously have ceased from sin. From an appreciation of the wider matrix of thought, we can expand this to say that they have set God's will as a priority and learned continuously to do good in the face of other competing priorities. It is a priority on God's will that allows one to suffer in the flesh with the right attitude, not conversely (contra Elliott) suffering in the flesh, which gives one control over the flesh and consequently allows one to choose God's will.[169]

[164] See Epictetus, *Diatr.* 4.4.39–46; Marcus Aurelius, *Med.* 7.2; Seneca, *Ep.* 23.2.
[165] Feldmeier, *Peter*, 213.
[166] Bigg's comment that ἐπιθυμίαις and θελήματι 'express the rule by which the man shapes his life' supports my argument; Bigg, *Epistles of St. Peter*, 167. Elliott too sees a conflict between governing standards and norms here; Elliott, *1 Peter*, 719; cf. Schlosser, *Pierre*, 236.
[167] This does not mean that the audience's physical distress is not important. The letter does show that the audience's lives are of value as is indicated by παρατίθημι in 4.19, which is a verb used of entrusting something valuable into the care of another; Elliott, *1 Peter*, 805.
[168] Schlosser, *Pierre*, 238.
[169] Elliott himself even says that the will of God is 'the central criterion of Christian conduct'; Elliott, *1 Peter*, 719.

Perspective and priorities come first, action second. Hence, the author starts with the thinking of Christ. Therefore, 4.1 reveals that participating in Christ's suffering results in the good of a sin-free life. This ethical benefit is a good that can occasion joy.

So, having looked at the *imitatio Christi* sections of 1 Peter we have been able to discover four more goods that come from sharing in Christ's suffering: the witnessing potential of righteous suffering; that such proclamatory suffering can, potentially, bring others towards salvation; that it may through impacting the other lead to the transformation of their situation; and, lastly, that suffering for doing good demonstrates obedience to God, and, therefore, also reveals a sin-free life.

We can now turn to the last goods of participating in the suffering of Christ: blessing and glory.

Blessing and Glory

In 2.19–20 the author declares that to bear unjust suffering because of a consciousness of God is commendable before God (χάρις παρὰ θεῷ). χάρις here carries the sense of 'favourableness' rather than referring to God's graciousness (cf. parallel use of κλέος in 2.20).[170] Hence, it indicates honour and reward. Consequently, again, the author presents a re-evaluation of suffering. As Bechtler comments, 'The behaviors for which the readers are being reviled are precisely the behaviors that God enjoins and calls good, and the vilification such behaviors evoke in the larger society results not in loss of honour … but God's approval.' Moreover, Bechtler rightly notes that this approval is a present reality for the suffering believer.[171] Thus, by participating in Christ's suffering they are obtaining a present good which one could rejoice in – God's commendation. In fact, in 3.14, 1 Peter goes beyond commendation to say that if the audience should suffer for righteousness they are blessed (μακάριος).[172] It does not give the reason for this, or what blessing means, but we can infer from the preceding use of Psalm 34 that blessedness refers to one's standing with God. To be blessed means that the believer has God's favour: his eyes are towards the righteous and his ears attentive to

---

[170] Elliott, *1 Peter*, 518.

[171] Bechtler, *Following*, 191–2.

[172] Cf. parallels in Matt 5.11–12; Luke 6.22–3. See Martin for discussion on possible background to the idea of the 'blessedness of the righteous sufferer'; Martin, *Metaphor*, 216–18.

their prayers (3.12). The idea of blessing is repeated in 4.14 where
the audience are blessed when they are reproached for the name of
Christ. This iteration might indicate that suffering for righteousness
in 3.14 is equivalent to suffering on account of Christ. However, in
4.14, reasoning for counting oneself blessed is given: because the
spirit of glory and of God rests on them.[173] This is the divine Spirit
who raised Christ from the dead (3.18). Furthermore, the glory that
has previously been attributed to God and Christ in the letter is
now said to rest on them.[174] Consequently, they do not receive glory
because they suffer, but they suffer because God's glory is already
on them, and as such they can see themselves as blessed in their
suffering.[175] So, not only does continuing to do good in the face of
suffering reveal a consciousness of God, their suffering also affirms
their identity by demonstrating God's glorious presence in their lives.
These things are goods in which the believer can rejoice.

Now we have explored the range of goods that participating in
Christ suffering brings in the present, we can return to the final good
presented in 4.13. Here it reveals that sharing in Christ's suffering
now means that one will also be able to rejoice at the revelation of his
glory (4.13). Though it is not outrightly stated, there is an inference
that, as the believers participate in Christ's suffering, they will share
in his glory (cf. 1.7; 5.1, 10).[176] Christ's example, which they follow,
sets their expectation. Choosing allegiance to Christ now means that
they will share Christ's vindication and glorification in the future
(cf. 5.10).[177] Put differently, solidarity now equals the benefits of
solidarity later. With this future glorification of Christ in view, the
emotion of joy is intensified. They will not just rejoice, but χαρῆτε
ἀγαλλιώμενοι (rejoice exceedingly).[178] Whatever joy the believer can
have now in suffering is nothing in comparison to the joy that is
to come. Though the Christian may have to suffer for a short time,

---

[173] The phrase ὅτι τὸ τῆς δόξης καὶ τὸ τοῦ θεοῦ πνεῦμα ἐφ' ὑμᾶς ἀναπαύεται is unique
in the Bible, but is thought to be an expansion of Isa 11.2; Elliott, *1 Peter*, 782.

[174] The changes that have been made to the Isa 11.2 passage emphasise this,
ἀναπαύσεται has become ἀναπαύεται and the introduction of ἐφ' ὑμᾶς applies the messianic prophecy to the believers; Feldmeier, *Peter*, 225–6.

[175] It could be, as Jobes comments, that the presence of the Spirit is also meant to
be understood as an empowering presence; Jobes, *1 Peter*, 288.

[176] Cf. Michaels, *1 Peter*, 263; Achtemeier, *1 Peter*, 306; Martin, *Metaphor*, 243, etc.

[177] As Elliott points out, Christ's glorification involved his resurrection and
ascension to God's right hand, which subsequently infers his vindication; Elliott, *1
Peter*, 777.

[178] For Millauer, this expectation of future joy after suffering follows Jewish ideas
of *Freude nach dem Leiden*; see Millauer, *Leiden*, 167–9, 185.

God will eventually restore, support, strengthen, and establish them (5.10; NRSV).

Christ's narrative of suffering and then consequent glory (1.11) is the proof that secures their own future and gives the believers as his followers their self-understanding.[179] Furthermore, their cosmic understanding of God as the faithful creator and the one who has all dominion through the ages (5.11) enables them to believe that God has the desire and power to reward the faithful. The inseparable link between righteous suffering and glory provides a positive valence to suffering. Thus, to share in Christ's righteous suffering, along with all the above goods, means sharing in the enduring eternal good of his glory too. The incomparable nature of the good of sharing in Christ's glory is emphasised by the use of two rejoicing terms that are attached to it (4.13). As Elliott notes, the emphasis on the glory, salvation, and blessing that the believer anticipates, means that the letter ends with 'an intensified eschatological assurance that the innocent suffering of the faithful will ultimately be vindicated by a faithful Creator'.[180] Once again, joy is used to bring the eschatological dimension to bear on the present experience and reminds the audience of its place in the cosmic narrative.

Conclusion

To ask the believers to rejoice in suffering is to encourage them to re-evaluate suffering, or more specifically to evaluate participating in Christ's suffering as a good. From a comparison with Christ's suffering the believers can see that there are a number of goods that their suffering both reveals and may effect. First, because it arises due to solidarity with Christ on account of doing good, suffering can be seen as a positive identity marker; it confirms allegiance to God, which 1.3–9 has revealed is a good in itself and secures the good. Once again, joy is being used to reinforce the value of the believer's relationship with God and Christ. We have also discovered, through examining suffering for doing good in the rest of 1 Peter, that Christian suffering has the potential to bear witness to another reality, thus to impact the other, and perhaps to transform the believers' current situation. The author also affirms that such suffering will result in both blessing now and glory to come. All of these are goods in which the believer can rejoice.

---

[179] Feldmeier, *Peter*, 95; Bechtler, *Following*, 79–80.
[180] Elliott, *1 Peter*, 768.

Through his presentation of suffering, the author has worked hard to present what is valuable, which is continuing to do good as proof of allegiance to God. Consequently, fidelity to God is the highest goal. The setting of this as the primary goal changes the landscape in which suffering is evaluated. This goal, when raised above others, for example public honour or personal safety, means that, when faced with a situation in which suffering may be the outcome of doing good, the primary goal of obedience to God is what determines the believers' actions. To rejoice in sharing in Christ's suffering indicates that the believers have internalised this system of value, and consequently will not shrink back from situations in which suffering might occur on account of their faith. Instead, spurred on by the end goal, reinforced by the emotion, one will continue to do good and remain faithful to God despite difficulties. Thus, the suffering believers can understand that they are actively choosing to live in line with God's will and can look towards eternal reward.

The secondary effect is the disempowering of the abusers. This does not mean that in society they are not powerful but it does mean that, for the believer, the hostile other loses significance and power. Subsequently, their ability to affect the audience's emotions and behaviour is diminished. In this sense, with a particular perspective of reality, the recipients, who are mostly subordinates, are actually empowered to have control over the destiny of their lives. They can appreciate, as they align themselves with the narrative of Christ and choose fidelity to God, that they are setting themselves on the path to flourishing. As a result, the author's call to rejoice in suffering not only impacts identity and behaviour but, at the deepest level, challenges what it means to flourish as a human. Joy in participating in Christ's suffering envisages a new way of being in the world.[181] Successful human existence means to be in line with the Father's will and to show trust in him and fidelity to the covenant relationship by living a Christian life of doing good. This can, and may very well, include suffering on account of it. Thus, rejoicing *in* suffering is no longer paradoxical, but, within this scheme of reality, is a perfectly appropriate response to being persecuted on account of Christ.

Having looked at the present experience of the believer, which is one of joy despite distress and joy in suffering, we can turn to the future expectations of the audience. In the next two chapters we will explore fear, hope, and shame in 1 Peter.

---

[181] Cf. Barton, 'Spirituality', 191.

PART IV

FUTURE EXPECTATION

7

FEARFUL HOPE

This chapter will investigate fear and hope in 1 Peter. These emotions have been grouped together because of their shared future orientation, because of their associations with power, and because they are linked in biblical tradition and 1 Peter. Initially, we will investigate fear and hope separately. However, in examining the implications of the author's use of fear and hope, the two emotions will be brought together. As with the previous chapters, we will use Greco-Roman philosophy, notably Stoic theory, to outline the key components of each emotion. We will then explore the use of fear and hope in the LXX before turning to 1 Peter. The LXX will be particularly illuminative for understanding 1 Peter's emotional rationale. In our exegesis of 1 Peter, key questions will remain: What is the object of the emotion? What evaluation of the object does the emotion present? What does this have to say to the audience about its value system and goals? Lastly, how does all this impinge on behaviour and identity?

Locating Fear

First, it is necessary to outline the key components of fear (φόβος) and what emotional experiences it can encompass.

φόβος in Stoicism

Fear (φόβος) is one of Stoicism's four primary πάθη (Stobaeus, *Ecl.* = SVF 3.378).[1] As such, it is an irrational, excessive movement of the soul that is to be extirpated. This is not to say that Stoicism classed every inhibitory emotion negatively. They did have a

---

[1] See Table 5.1.

counterpart εὐπάθεια to φόβος: εὐλάβεια (well-reasoned caution/discretion) (see Diogenes Laertius 7.116).

The Stoics defined fear as follows:

> φόβος δὲ ἄλογος ἔκκλισις· ἢ φυγὴ ἀπὸ προσδοκωμένου δεινοῦ.

> Fear is an irrational shrinking [aversion], or avoidance of an expected danger. (Andronicus, [*Pass.*] 1 = SVF 3.391, trans. Long and Sedley; cf. Aristotle, *Rhet.* 2.5, 1382a)

In *Tusculan Disputations* 4.7.14–15, Cicero confirms this description of fear (*metus*) and adds that fear results 'in a kind of withdrawal and flight of the soul' (*metus recessum quendam animi et fugam* [King, LCL]; cf. *Tusc.* 3.11.25; 4.6.11). Thus, we can outline the key elements of fear: fear is irrational and future orientated. More specifically, it looks towards something threatening and so has in view the bad or harmful.[2] Therefore, it evaluates the object negatively as detrimental to one's goals. Words such as ἔκκλισις and φυγή along with *recessus* (retreat) and *fuga* (fleeing/flight) reveal that fear's action-tendency is avoidance.

Having outlined fear, we can now determine which emotional experiences φόβος covers. According to Andronicus Rhodius:

> Φόβου εἴδη ιγ´.
> Ὄκνος· αἰσχύνη· δεῖμα· δέος· ἔκπληξις· κατάπληξις· [δειλία·] ψοφοδέεια· ἀγωνία· μέλλησις· ὀρρωδία· θόρυβος· δεισιδαιμονία.

> There are 13 kinds of fear:

> Hesitation, shame, terror, alarm, consternation, amazement (timidity), fear at every noise, anguish of mind/anguish, unfulfilled intention, terror, clamour, fear of the gods/superstition. ([*Pass.*] 3 cf. Stobaeus, *Ecl.* = SVF 3.394)[3]

Andronicus' listing shows that φόβος can encompass numerous experiences such as fear of knowing what to do (μέλλησις); fear of noise or crowds (ψοφοδέεια; θόρυβος); alarm that paralyses (δέος); anguish over failure (ἀγωνία); excessive fear of the gods (δεισιδαιμονία); fear of ill repute (αἰσχύνη); and even shock at impressive objects (κατάπληξις).

---

[2] The future orientation of fear distinguishes it from distress (see Cicero, *Tusc.* 3.11.25).

[3] Andronicus goes on to define each of these kinds of fear (see [*Pass.*] 3 = SVF 3.409); cf. Diogenes Laertius 7.112–113; Stobaeus, *Ecl.* = SVF 3.408; Cicero, *Tusc.* 4.8.19.

However, for Stoicism, every variation of fear listed, regardless of its quality, is viewed negatively and is contrary to successful living. In comparison, the emotional experiences grouped under εὐλάβεια are two: αἰδώς (respect for the opinion of others/honour/self-respect) and ἁγνεία (purity) (see Andronicus, [*Pass.*] 6 = SVF 3.432; Diogenes Laertius 7.116). The former is caution about rightly considered faults; the latter is caution about sinful action before the gods. Thus, εὐλάβεια is primarily concerned with right actions and moves one towards virtue.[4]

From the above definition of φόβος we can conclude that the object of fear must be perceived to have the potential to harm the person. This requires an assessment of the object. Moreover, it involves a *relative* evaluation of the object in comparison with the person, particularly in relation to power. However, power in itself is not enough; there also has to be an indication that the powerful object is likely to harm.[5] Consequently, fear arises when one appraises the object as equally or more powerful than oneself and therefore able, and likely, to impinge on one's attainment of goals. For the clearest discussion of this in the ancient world we have to move from the Stoics to Aristotle.

In *On Rhetoric* 2.5 Aristotle says that people 'do not fear all evils … only such as involve pain or destruction' (*Rhet.* 2.5, 1382a22–4 [Freese, LCL]). Thus, Aristotle confirms that fear's chief concern is harm.[6] Aristotle reasons:

εἰ δὲ ὁ φόβος τοῦτ᾽ ἐστίν, ἀνάγκη τὰ τοιαῦτα φοβερὰ εἶναι ὅσα φαίνεται δύναμιν ἔχειν μεγάλην τοῦ φθείρειν ἢ βλάπτειν βλάβας εἰς λύπην μεγάλην συντεινούσας·

If then this is fear, all things must be fearful that appear to have great power of destroying or inflicting injuries that tend to produce great pain. (*Rhet.* 2.5, 1382a27–30 [Freese, LCL])

Here power (δύναμις) is highlighted as the essential content of the judgement. In *On Rhetoric* the objects of fear are generally *people* who are perceived to be stronger than the fearful person (*Rhet.* 2.5,

---

[4] Cf. Epictetus, *Diatr.* 2.1.1–7.

[5] In social situations this may involve an advanced social judgement such as assessing the enmity of the other; Konstan, *Emotions*, 132–3.

[6] For Cicero, fear can be on account of an individual's or universal perils (*De or.* 2.51.209). For Aristotle, harm has to appear near to inspire fear (*Rhet.* 2.5, 1382a24–6).

1328b14–18; cf. Epictetus, *Diatr.* 1.24.59–63).[7] However, one can also fear a rival because of competition for goods; the rival's acquisition of goods necessarily means one's lack (*Rhet.* 2.5, 1328b12–14; cf. Seneca, *Ep.* 13.12). These comments affirm that fear is concerned with the object's relationship to one's goods and goals. Epictetus comments:

> Why, look you, no one is afraid of Caesar himself, but he is afraid of death, exile, loss of property, prison, disfranchisement. Nor does anyone love Caesar himself, unless in some way Caesar is a person of great merit; but we love wealth, a tribuneship, a praetorship, a consulship. When we love and hate and fear these things, it needs must be that those who control them are masters over us. (*Diatr.* 4.1.60 [Oldfather, LCL])

Fear, by evaluating the object as having control over one's good, gives the object power (mastery) over the fearer (cf. *Diatr.* 2.2.25–6; 4.1.85). Conversely, one will not be afraid if one sees oneself as stronger or superior to the other (*Rhet.* 2.5, 1383a31–1383b1) on account of having wealth, strength, friends, and power, or if one has nothing left to lose (*Rhet.* 2.5, 1382b34–1383a5). These statements enforce the relationship between fear, power, and the attainment of goods. By repositioning these elements, the Stoics were able, theoretically, to extirpate fear. If the good is removed from the hands of the other, then the other's fearsome mastery is nullified. Thus, when the Stoic labels virtue the only true good and makes it integral to the person (see Seneca, *Ep.* 74.1, 5–6; cf. Epictetus, *Diatr.* 2.2.1–4) he severs the link between the other and the good (cf. Seneca, *Ep.* 74.23–6; Epictetus, *Diatr.* 4.7.8–10), which removes the other's power and destroys fear (cf. Epictetus, *Diatr.* 4.1.81–90; 4.7.1–5).

Therefore, we can summarise that fear is future orientated, evaluates the object as potentially harmful, and has an action-tendency of avoidance. φόβος can cover a range of emotional experiences from fear of personal failure to fear of the gods. Lastly, fear as an emotion highlights power dynamics: it reveals the perceived relative positioning of the subject and object in respect of the attainment or maintenance of goods. We can now turn to the use of φόβος in the LXX.

---

[7] Whereas, for Stoicism, fear of death is the chief fear to overcome; see Seneca, *Ep.* 4; 80.5–6; Epictetus, *Diatr.* 2.1.13–14; 3.26.38–9.

Fear in the LXX

As noted in Chapter 5 (p. 111), 4 Maccabees 1.23 echoes the Stoic mapping of the passions and thus φόβος is listed alongside λύπη and ἐπιθυμία (cf. Philo, *Abr.* 41.236; *Ios.* 14.79). 4 Maccabees does not define φόβος except to say: πρὸ δὲ τοῦ πόνου ἐστὶν φόβος, μετὰ δὲ τὸν πόνον λύπη (Before pain is fear, after pain is distress). 'Before' suggests anticipation and therefore that φόβος has a future orientation, and the use of πόνος (pain) infers anticipation of harm. Philo gives a fuller account:

> ἐπίλυπον μὲν γὰρ τὸ ἀνθρώπινον γένος καὶ περιδεές, ἢ παρόντων κακῶν ἢ προσδοκωμένων, ὡς ἢ ἐπὶ τοῖς ἐν χερσὶν ἀβουλήτοις ἀνιᾶσθαι ἢ ἐπὶ τοῖς μέλλουσι ταραχῇ καὶ φόβῳ κραδαίνεσθαι·

> For mankind is subject to grief and very fearful of evils either present or expected, so that men are either distressed by disagreeables close at hand or are agitated by troublous fear of those which are still to come. (*Abr.* 36.202 [Colson, LCL])

Thus, again, fear looks to future harm (cf. *Praem.* 12.71). Philo also blames fear for 'diverting and distorting the straight course to which his [one's] face was set' (*Mos.* 2.139 [Colson, LCL]; cf. *Leg.* 2.2.8; *Prob.* 22.159). These comments show an understanding that fear motivates avoidance.[8] For both 4 Maccabees and Philo fear is a passion and therefore negative (*Leg.* 2.4.11). Hence, for Philo, the virtuous man is not subject to fear (*Prob.* 21); he is independent (cf. *Ios.* 14.68–71) and takes no account of death, poverty, disrepute, or pain and so is free from slavery, including slavery to fear.[9] Thus, once again, the Jewish philosophical texts exhibit affinity with Stoic ideas.

We can now return to the LXX. Like with joy, we discover, on account of a different worldview, the LXX departs from Stoic ideas. Fear (φόβος/φοβέω) can be used, particularly in historical texts, in the above outlined way, occurring in situations where there is danger to life or the nation. The objects of fear can be leaders (Josh 4.14; 1 Kgdms 12.18), kings (3 Kgdms 3.28; 4 Kgdms 1.15; Isa 7.10), tyrants (Dan 5.17–19), other nations (Isa 10.24; Jer 49.11 (42.11

---

[8] Cf. Philo, *Fug.* 1.3 where fear is listed alongside hate and shame as one of the three reasons for flight.

[9] This is achieved through philosophical training (Philo, *Prob.* 3.18–4.23; 17.111; cf. *Prov.* 2.7–8); cf. 4 Macc 8.15.

MT)), one's enemies (Judges 7.3; 1 Kgdms 7.7; 17.11; 1 Macc 9.6), even the nation of Israel (Esth 9.2–3; Josh 10.1–2). However, the customary object of fear is God. Here we find the most striking difference with Stoicism: fear of God is actively encouraged. Moreover, it is commanded of Israel (Ps 21.24) and expected of all people (1 Chr 16.30; 2 Chr 6.33; Ps 101.16).

Fearing God can infer reverence or worship (Ps 5.8; Dan 4.37a), but it is a richer concept than this and sits within a network of ideas. One strong trope is that the fear of the Lord is the beginning of wisdom (Ps 110.10; Prov 1.7; Sir 1) – wisdom being not just knowledge but the practice of right actions and as such is the biblical equivalent of Greco-Roman virtue (see Sirach 1.11–13 below). It naturally follows that fearing God means obeying his commands. Ecclesiastes 12.13–14 states:

Τέλος λόγου τὸ πᾶν ἀκούεται
Τὸν θεὸν φοβοῦ καὶ τὰς ἐντολὰς αὐτοῦ φύλασσε,
ὅτι τοῦτο πᾶς ὁ ἄνθρωπος.
ὅτι σὺν πᾶν τὸ ποίημα ὁ θεὸς ἄξει ἐν κρίσει
ἐν παντὶ παρεωραμένῳ,
ἐὰν ἀγαθὸν καὶ ἐὰν πονηρόν.

The end of the matter; all has been heard.
Fear God, and keep his commandments;
for that is the whole duty of everyone.
For God will bring every deed into judgement,
including every secret thing,
whether good or evil. (NRSVA)[10]

Thus, fearing God must be demonstrated in behaviour.[11] To fear God is to conduct one's life aright (1 Kgdms 12.23–4). Consequently, one can be taught to fear the Lord through behavioural norms (Ps 33.12–15). The rationale for fearing God is multi-layered. It is because of his goodness, love, and mercy (Ps 117.4; Sir 2.8–9) but also his judgement and wrath (Ps 89.11–12; Isa 59.18–19). These dual aspects encourage the people towards good behaviour and guard the people from undertaking sinful actions (Ex 20.20; Jer 39.40).[12] As such,

[10] See also Ex 20.20; Deut 10.12–21; 17.19; 31.12; Lev 19.14, 32; 25.17, 36, 43.
[11] This is also because obedience reveals the attitude of the heart (Isa 63.17; Sir 2.15–17).
[12] Fear of punishment can also prove preventative in a community context (Deut 13.12; 19.20; 21.21).

fearing God leads to obedience and, subsequently, righteousness and reward (Ps 18.8–12; Prov 8.13; 15.27a; *Pss. Sol.* 18.7–9). Conversely, those with no fear of God deny his ways and behave badly (Ps 35.2; Isa 63.17). Thus, fear of God defines the dimensions within which one should live. Whether one fears God or not, demonstrated in behaviour, becomes a boundary marker between persons. Therefore, the righteous can be categorised as 'the fearing', that is, those who fear God. Isaiah 8.12–13 makes it clear that one's emotional orientation can provide a line of division:

τὸν δὲ φόβον αὐτοῦ οὐ μὴ φοβηθῆτε οὐδὲ μὴ ταραχθῆτε· κύριον αὐτὸν ἁγιάσατε, καὶ αὐτὸς ἔσται σου φόβος.

Do not fear what they fear nor be troubled; reverence the Lord himself, he is your fear.

The declaration that the Lord alone is their fear demands that the person orientate herself around this relationship (cf. 4 Macc 13.14–15). All other figures of power must be assessed in light of one's emotional perception of God.

As a result, fearing God nullifies other fears. His people are not to fear other gods (Judges 6.10; 4 Kgdms 17.35–9)[13] or other nations (Deut 1.29; 7.17–18; 31.6, 8; Num 14.9; 21.33–5; Josh 10.8, 25; 2 Chr 20.15–17). For Jeremiah 10.5, this is because the gods of the nations have no ability to do good or evil. So, again, we see that the link between fear, power, and the presence or absence of goods emerges. For the LXX, it is only fear of God that is beneficial. In fact, those who fear God will live in absence of turbulent fear (Pss 3.7; 90.1–6; 111; Isa 54.14; Jer 17.7–8), unlike the ungodly or disobedient (Deut 28.58–9, 66–7; Ps 52.6; Mic 7.17; Zech 9.1–5; Isa 19.16–17; 51.13). The righteous person's lack of fear is rooted in her relationship with God. As those who fear God and are therefore obedient, they position themselves within God's favour and subsequently his power is on their side. Consequently, they do not fear others because God, the supreme power, is with them (Deut 20.3–4; Josh 1.9; Pss 22.4; 26.1; Isa 12.2; 41.10, 13; Jer 26.28; Dan 3.17).[14] Thus, the psalmists' declaration that they will not fear is a statement of allegiance to and trust in God (Pss 26.3; 55.4–5, 12; 117.6–7).

[13] Here, fear can convey a sense of reverence and worship (cf. 4 Kgdms 17.7–8, 25), but also relates to active serving.
[14] This also seems to be linked to the people being God's possession (Isa 43.1–4).

The above reveals that fear of God is different to the Stoic negative delineation of fear in that it is depicted as having a positive
outcome, and therefore becomes important to the attainment of
one's goals (see Sir 1.11–13). Sirach 40.26 says: οὐκ ἔστιν ἐν φόβῳ
κυρίου ἐλάττωσις (there is no lack in the fear of the Lord; cf. Ps
33.10). Thus, fearing God is the route to the good. Put differently,
those who fear God are those that depend on him for the good
(see Prov 22.4; Sir 2.7–11; cf. *Pss. Sol.* 6.18; 17.34).[15] Therefore,
in the LXX, fear of and hope in God are two sides of the same
coin. Moreover, the causal link between fearing God and attaining
the good demonstrates the underlying belief in God's power to
provide.[16]

Having said that fear of God looks to the good, this is not to say
that for such a fear all the components of φόβος outlined above are
necessarily altered. God is still feared because of his power, and also
his potential to harm. If he has power over the good, he can bestow
it but he can also withhold it. There are plenty of instances where
God inspires dread in people (Ex 23.27; Deut 5.5; Isa 2.10; 19.16–17;
24.17–23). It is this very real fear of God's wrath and judgement that
causes people to assess their behaviour in light of his commands (cf.
Eccl 12.13–14). The recognition of judgement along with the future
orientation of fear pushes one's emotional life on to an eschatological stage. It is not just a present orientation but speaks of an
awareness of an eschatological reality.

From our discussion we have established that the use of fear
in Jewish philosophical texts has affinity with Stoic philosophy.
However, we have also seen that fearing God in the LXX departs
from Stoic ideas but that the use of φόβος is not altered beyond
recognition because God still remains the powerful object who is
able to impinge upon one's attainment of goals. Instead, φόβος is
reframed in relation to God so that it can be seen as a positive
emotion with positive outcomes. Fear, which is aware of God's capacity to harm but also his ability to provide the good, motivates
the person to keep God's commands. By linking fear via obedience to flourishing, fear of God demarcates the boundary lines
within which one should live. With our understanding of fear from
Stoicism and its modification in the LXX we can progress to our
exegesis of 1 Peter.

---

[15] Cf. Ps 60.6; Prov 10.27; Eccl 8.12–13; Tob 4.21.
[16] Thus, for the biblical authors, fear of God can be coexistent with other positive
emotions such as gladness (Ps 85.11).

Fear in 1 Peter

Terms that indicate fear occur in virtually every chapter of 1 Peter, which suggests that this emotion is particularly pertinent for the audience. The primary emotion terms of interest are φόβος (fear; 1.17; 2.18; 3.2, 14, 16) and φοβέω (to fear; 2.17; 3.6, 14), but πτόησις (intimidation;[17] 3.6); ταράσσω (to trouble/disturb; 3.14); and μέριμνα (anxiety/worry; 5.7) will also be commented upon when relevant. Fear terms appear in 1 Peter in a positive and negative manner. The first two sections of our exegesis will focus on where fear is encouraged; the third section will unpack the author's negation of fear. We will leave discussing some of the implications of the author's presentation of fear until after we have explored his use of hope.

Establishing the Boundaries: 1 Peter 1.17

The first use of φόβος is in 1.17, which says:

> καὶ εἰ πατέρα ἐπικαλεῖσθε τὸν ἀπροσωπολήμπτως κρίνοντα κατὰ τὸ ἑκάστου ἔργον, ἐν φόβῳ τὸν τῆς παροικίας ὑμῶν χρόνον ἀναστράφητε.

> And if you call on as father the one who impartially judges according to each person's work, conduct yourselves in fear during the time of your exile.

The prepositional phrase ἐν φόβῳ, or a slight modification, is used elsewhere in the letter (2.18 (ἐν παντὶ φόβῳ); 3.2).[18] However, it is this first use of ἐν φόβῳ that establishes the framework for the later uses.

Fear of the Eschatological Judge

The first task is to determine the object of φόβος. Even though the object is not explicit, commentators agree that the object is God. This is unsurprising, given the influence of the LXX evident in this section (cf. 1.16 and Lev 19.2). Thus, as in the LXX, fear of God is actively encouraged: the believers are to conduct their lives 'in fear'. So, why, for the author, is fear the appropriate emotional response to God in this context? To understand this contextualisation we must look at how God is portrayed.

---

[17] πτόησις can be either the 'act of causing someone to be intimidated, *terrifying, intimidation*' or the 'experience of being intimidated, *fear, terror*'; see BDAG (895).
[18] μετὰ … φόβου in 3.16 functions similarly.

God is presented as Father (πατήρ) and as the one who judges (ὁ κρινῶν).[19] However, scholars disagree about which of these characteristics inspires fear. For Selwyn, their 'in fear' holy conduct 'rests upon the revelation of God's Fatherhood revealed in Christ'.[20] According to Selwyn, the weight of the sentence falls on πατήρ, so that the clause should read 'if you invoke the impartial Judge as Father'. He argues that the 'ground of Christian piety is less that God is the impartial Judge than that He is known as Father'.[21] Thus, God's mercy and forgiveness provide the reason for the Christian's reverence.[22] Achtemeier similarly downplays the link between φόβος and judgement. He argues that ἐν φόβῳ indicates holy reverence toward God because of his actions in Christ for the believer.[23] Elliott combines God's two characteristics by suggesting that, 'Paternal authority includes the right and responsibility of judging and disciplining the behavior of family members.' However, Elliott later links φόβος with God's holiness rather than his judgements.[24] Evident in these readings is a tendency to render φόβος as 'reverence'.[25] Michaels, who also prefers 'reverence' for φόβος, thinks that φόβος is appropriate because God is the 'final Judge of every human being'.[26] However, for Michaels, the full argument is based on understanding God as both Father of the believers and judge of all, but in 1.17 his role as judge is primary.[27] As Thurén comments, the nuance of the two alternatives becomes either: 'God is an impartial judge *but* you can appeal to him as father', or 'You call him Father *but* he is

---

[19] For Michaels, to use ἐπικαλεῖσθε in conjunction with πατήρ suggests that the prayers of Jesus (Luke 11.2 cf. Rom 8.15; Gal 4.6) are the background to 1 Peter here. Therefore, 1 Peter is identifying the Christian community by the manner of their prayerful address; Michaels, *1 Peter*, 60–1. Cf. Achtemeier, *1 Peter*, 124; Elliott, *1 Peter*, 364–5.

[20] Selwyn, *St. Peter*, 142.

[21] For Selwyn, 'reverence for father and mother was one of the primary principles of the *tōrah*'. He adds, the father in Jewish society would have 'ranked higher' than a judge; Selwyn, *St. Peter*, 141–3. Others (Martin, Holloway) interpret the emphasis here as respect for the father. The background is the common idea of the *pater familias* who had absolute power over the household; Martin, *Metaphor*, 169–71; Holloway, *Coping*, 163–5.

[22] Selwyn cites Ps 130.4 in support of this view. However, the LXX (Ps 129) does not have the same emphasis, in fact φόβος is absent from the psalm; see Selwyn, *St. Peter*, 143.

[23] Achtemeier, *1 Peter*, 125.

[24] Elliott, *1 Peter*, 365–6.

[25] See also Martin, *Metaphor*, 171.

[26] Michaels, *1 Peter*, 60–2; cf. Windisch, *katholischen Briefe*, 56; Brox, *Petrusbrief*, 79–80.

[27] Michaels, *1 Peter*, 60.

an impartial judge.' The first sounds a note of assurance, the latter warning.[28] We noted above that fear arises in contexts where the power dynamic between subject and object becomes pertinent, particularly in relation to goods and goals. Both the presentation of God as Father and judge reveal God's superiority over the believer, so, in terms of power, both could be appropriate objects of φόβος. Furthermore, both a father and a judge have the capacity to affect a person's goals. However, it seems more readily fitting, if φόβος is to retain the sense of fear that anticipates harm, which I want to argue is rhetorically necessary, that a judge is more commonly associated with potentially detrimental consequences than a father. Thus, in what follows I will take God's status as judge to be the reason for the author's use of φόβος at this point.

God's status as judge is clear, but the time frame of his judgement is ambiguous. The present participle κρίνοντα with the present verb ἐπικαλεῖσθε could suggest that the act of judging is happening in the present. However, φόβος, which is future orientated and the eschatological tone set by 1.13 point towards a future time of judgement. However, both present and future could be relevant here: God is presently assessing their current deeds but his ultimate judgement will occur at a future date. That 1.13 mentions hope for grace at Christ's revelation suggests that an eschatological judgement is in view. At this time of judgement, God will judge everyone (ἕκαστος)[29] impartially (ἀπροσωπολήμπτως) according to their work (ἔργον).[30] Thus, the use of fear in 1.17 by its future orientation and association with God's judgement is seeking to orient the audience emotionally towards an eschatological reality. By using fear specifically, it colours this reality with a level of warning.[31] As Michaels comments, 'divine election (v1) and calling (v15) are not the same as favoritism. Christians are not exempt from judgement just because they address God as Father'. In fact, they will be judged first (4.17).[32]

---

[28] Thurén, *Argument*, 111; cf. Schelkle, *Petrusbriefe*, 47; Goppelt, *I Peter*, 111–12; Schlosser, *Pierre*, 96.

[29] Including the living and the dead (ζῶντας καὶ νεκρούς, 4.5). The idea of God as universal judge is present in both the LXX and other New Testament texts. Cf. Ps 61.13; Prov 24.12; Matt 16.27; Rom 2.6; 2 Tim 4.14; Michaels, *I Peter*, 61.

[30] New Testament parallels to 1.17's impartial judgement according to works include Rom 2.11; Eph 6.9; Col 3.25; cf. Selwyn, *St. Peter*, 143; Achtemeier, *I Peter*, 124–5.

[31] Though, as Thurén notes, the 'negative aspect of the Judgement always remains implicit'; Thurén, *Argument*, 206.

[32] Michaels, *I Peter*, 61.

Fear, Goals, and Action

We have seen that fear highlights the relationship between the powerful object and one's attainment of goals. Thus, to say that God is to be feared is not to say in theological terms that God is the source of evil, but instead that God has power over desired goods: he can bestow or withhold the good (the absence of good equalling harm). Our discussion on joy in Chapter 4 revealed that the author has presented God as the source of inheritance, protection, salvation, praise, glory, and honour (1.3–9) at the outset. Now, 1.18 adds redemption.[33] Furthermore, God alone is able to extend grace to the believer at Christ's revelation (1.13).[34] Thus, fear, by reminding the believers of God's power over their flourishing, encourages the recipients to give import to their standing with God.[35] The fact that fear adds an element of risk to this relationship allows a different emotional dynamic not brought by joy and hope. Fear, because the outcome of events is not settled, encourages one to deliberate about one's behaviour in light of the powerful object and the end goal.[36] Thus, fear puts the spotlight on one's current standing and behaviour. Interestingly, if there is no hope of deliverance then one will not even deliberate but will become resigned to one's fate.[37]

With this in mind, we can understand the link the author makes in 1.17 between fear of God, judgement, and conduct. The emphasis on obedience, holiness, and conduct runs throughout 1.14–17.[38] However, the believer's conduct (ἀναστρέφω, ἀναστροφή; 1.17, 18) is not only to be holy and good (cf. 3.16) but also ἐν φόβῳ.[39] The believers' emotional stance towards God is prescriptive for their mode of living. The LXX understanding of the fear of God helps us to see why φόβος in 1 Peter is related to conduct in this way. In the LXX fearing God is synonymous with obeying his commands. Those

---

[33] 'God is the decisive actor in all key redemptive events that run through 1 Peter'; Michaels, *1 Peter*, lxviii.
[34] The use of φέρω emphasises that God's agency is needed for the believers to experience grace; Michaels, *1 Peter*, 56.
[35] As Michaels comments, 'Although Christian existence centers on Jesus, God … is the ultimate source and its ultimate goal'; Michaels, *1 Peter*, 70.
[36] See Aristotle, *Rhet.* 2.5.14, 1383a5–10.
[37] See Aristotle, *Rhet.* 2.5.14, 1383a5–10.
[38] A number of scholars note that 1.16 relies on Lev 19.2 (LXX), which is part of the holiness code of Lev 17–26; Michaels, *1 Peter*, 59; Achtemeier, *1 Peter*, 122.
[39] ἀναστροφή means 'behaviour', 'conduct', but more broadly 'way of life'; see Elliott, *1 Peter*, 362–3.

who acknowledge God's authority demonstrate it by their emotional posture and their subsequent 'in fear' behaviour. Therefore, reflexively, their behaviour reveals their perspective and allegiance. Consequently, on these grounds, their works can be judged as representative of their life orientation.[40] Their 'in fear' behaviour, to be judged favourably, must accord with God's standard of holiness (1.15). As such, their emotional stance gives boundaries to their behaviour.[41] This works at an individual and community level.[42] That God impartially judges reminds the audience that other human categories of status are of no value; what matters is holy obedience.[43] Those who fear God recognise his role as judge and his power over the good, and moderate their behaviour accordingly.[44] Therefore, fear is rhetorically useful because it causes the audience to assess their *present* behaviour in view of these new standards (cf. 1.14, 18) and the future reality of judgement.[45] As a result, those who fear God and live obediently are expressing their faith in God and agreement with his norms.[46] Thus, using φόβος, because it forces deliberation about current behaviour in light of future expectation, is performing an important rhetorical function in upholding boundary markers and motivating certain behaviour.

This leads us to the delicate topic of whether, if the above is correct, 1 Peter presents the believers' behaviour as salvific, because it is their obedience in the present that will be judged. For Michaels, this is a Pauline question that 1 Peter is not concerned with.

---

[40] Scholars note the singular ἔργον (rather than ἔργα). As Michaels recognises, ἔργον signifies their ἀναστροφή. It is their mode of life as a whole that is the issue, not a list of deeds; Michaels, *1 Peter*, 61; cf. Goppelt, *1 Peter*, 113; Elliott, *1 Peter*, 365.

[41] Cf. Elliott, *1 Peter*, 360–2. This recognition leads scholars like Achtemeier to see ἐν φόβῳ as shorthand for 'in accordance with the will of … God'; Achtemeier, *1 Peter*, 125.

[42] Of course, their holiness and identity is rooted in God's holiness and his calling of them; cf. Michaels, *1 Peter*, 59; Achtemeier, *1 Peter*, 120–1.

[43] Cf. the designation τέκνα ὑπακοῆς (1.14). Though the genitive ὑπακοῆς may simply be a Semitism, it could be a genitive of quality and thus indicate that the children's primary characteristic is obedience; Achtemeier, *1 Peter*, 119; cf. Selwyn, *St. Peter*, 141; Elliott, *1 Peter*, 357.

[44] Such fear could be seen as similar to Stoic εὐλάβεια in that it arises from a correct assessment of the situation and recognises the potential of *real* harm.

[45] This is more than encouraging the believers to 'break … with former allegiances and alliances and the immorality that these associations entail'; Elliott, *1 Peter*, 359. It is not simply refraining from certain things, but about allowing the truth about God to transform one's whole way of *seeing*, which ultimately affects allegiances and behaviour.

[46] Cf. Achtemeier, who sees obedience as 'a virtual equivalent of "faith"'; Achtemeier, *1 Peter*, 119–20.

Michaels sees salvation in 1 Peter as following Jesus, which includes imitating his conduct.[47] But, perhaps this is an over simplification. 1.13, which opens the paragraph, has already established that the believer must hope solely in the grace that will be brought to them at Christ's revelation, that is, at the point of judgement. The letter also details that the precious blood of Christ has rescued them from their former vain, ignorant life (1.19). Consequently, it is evident that the believer's hope for salvation is their faith in what God has done in Christ (cf. 1.7–9, 21).[48] So, why is the author so concerned about their behaviour? First, for the author, the primary act of obedience is to accept Christ (see 1.22; 2.4–8).[49] But second, we can understand that, as with the LXX, fear of God and hope in God are co-existent stances. To fear God is to recognise his power over your good; to hope in him is to expect that his power will bring the good to you. We can now make sense of why God is presented as *both* Father and judge. The latter emphasises that all will be judged according to one definite standard and therefore fear is appropriate, but the former reminds the believers of the relationship they have with God through Christ and so encourages them that they can, as obedient children, hope on God's grace at the very same time of judgement.[50] But, to follow De Waal Dryden, '[H]ope [or fear] is not simply an attitude of heart, but a commitment to see the appropriation of salvation in the present through personal and corporate transformation in the moral sphere.'[51] Thus, both fearing God and hoping in him are visible outwardly by behaviour, because behaviour reveals not only the norms one lives by but also who one is looking to for the good. As such, one's behaviour demonstrates faith in God and can be judged.[52] It is only via depending thoroughly on God that one will secure the

---

[47] Michaels, *1 Peter*, lxxiii–iv.

[48] Thus, Thurén rightly recognises the tension in the letter between the apparent certainty of salvation and the indication that good behaviour is a condition for final salvation; Thurén, *Argument*, 202–3; cf. Schelkle, *Petrusbriefe*, 47.

[49] Cf. Michaels, *1 Peter*, 56–7.

[50] Thus, I agree with Selwyn that God's mercy provides motivation for the Christian. However, I would differ from him in that I see this as linked with hope, rather than fear; Selwyn, *St. Peter*, 143; cf. Elliott, *1 Peter*, 356.

[51] De Waal Dryden, *Theology*, 100.

[52] Cf. Michaels who affirms that 1 Peter sits next to James in affirming that 'faith validates itself in action, to the extent that faith and action are indistinguishable'; Michaels, *1 Peter*, lxxiv; cf. Achtemeier, who comments that though the Christian lives by God's grace she is not to 'presume on God's grace' and is to recognise that the same grace requires a transformed life of obedience to God; Achtemeier, *1 Peter*, 125.

good: salvation.[53] Verses 1.18–21 go on to emphasise this by retelling the grounding narrative, which enforces the value of Christ and God for the believer.[54] That this wider rationale starts with εἰδότες suggests that this is a view of reality the believers have already accepted.[55] Thus, in view of this understanding of their redemption through Christ's blood, it makes sense to the audience why, with this perspective, they should conduct their life in fear of (obedience to) God: because God is the sole instigator and only source of eternal good.[56] Therefore, we can also say that those who fear God are those that recognise his, and Christ's, value to them.[57] Again, we see that the author is trying to shape the audience's value system and, consequently, its goals.

With this in mind we can address the action-tendency of fear. Michaels comments:

---

[53] Williams has recently argued that good works as obedience 'plays an important role at the final judgement. This is because ultimate salvation still lies in the future (1.5; 2.2) when the genuineness of each person's faith will be discovered (1.7). At that time demonstrating that one has lived a life of good works will be crucial for avoiding the wrath of God and achieving eternal life. Consequently, in the soteriology of 1 Peter it would appear that the grace of God and the efforts of humans are held in tension – both are necessary requirements for eschatological salvation, but neither is sufficient to achieve final salvation by itself'; Williams, *Good Works*, 253–4. Though I find Williams' argument quite convincing, I think he has put too much soteriological weight on the believers' behaviour. Their behaviour shows their allegiance and their dependency, thus is a demonstration of faith. It does not in itself position the believer, but instead good works come out of their present relationship with God and their emotional orientation. As Jobes comments, 'the indicative of God's grace precedes the imperative of God's commands'; Jobes, *1 Peter*, 116.

[54] Michaels sees 1.18 and following as providing not just the reason for fear, but for the whole thrust of 1.13–17; Michaels, *1 Peter*, 63. We see a cluster of value terms at this point. The futility (μάταιος) of their former way of life handed down by their forefathers is compared to the great worth of Christ, whose blood is more precious (τιμίος) to their redemption than perishable (φθαρτός) silver or gold. φθαρτός and χρυσίον echo 1.4–7's depiction of what should be valued.

[55] Cf. Achtemeier, *1 Peter*, 123; Elliott, *1 Peter*, 369. Achtemeier comments that the passage as a whole (1.17–21) 'reflects much of the common Christian tradition found throughout the NT'. Others have seen hymnic or confessional material here. Cf. De Waal Dryden, *Theology*, 85 who reminds us that '[t]o give credence to a narrative is to adopt its system of values'.

[56] The passive participles in 1.20 (προεγνωσμένου, φανερωθέντος) indicate that everything that has occurred for the believer is because of God's action; Achtemeier, *1 Peter*, 131.

[57] My statement follows the logic of 2.3–8, that those who believe are those that see Christ as precious because they accept the word. This is assumed by the opposite, that those who do not accept the word are those that reject Christ (do not value him). Cf. 1 Clem 7.4; Michaels, *1 Peter*, 65. There is also the added dimension, which Jobes highlights, that the believers' conversion is the thing that 'has brought them into relationship with God', but also 'brings them knowledge of sin and God's wrath upon it'; Jobes, *1 Peter*, 116.

The imperatives of hope and of godly fear have more to do with eschatological expectations than with ethics, and more to do with the reader's relationship to God than with their relationships to each other or to their pagan neighbours. The only word that bears on their social relationships is 'conduct', and nothing specific is said about their conduct except that it is to be 'holy', a quality traditionally defined in religious or cultic rather than ethical terms.[58]

Though I agree with Michaels that fear causes the audience to have an eschatological orientation, I disagree that the use of fear has little bearing on ethics. A primary function of an emotion is that it motivates action, and therefore emotions cannot be separated from ethics. As noted above, the action-tendency of fear is avoidance, specifically, evasion of harm. How are we to understand this action-tendency with regard to fearing God? Fear of God does not mean that God as the object of fear is to be avoided. Instead, because φόβος, in the positive sense, values God as the source of good, paradoxically, though one fears God, what one wants to avoid is isolation from God. To be a recipient of God's negative judgement would bring separation; thus, the consequences of negative judgement are to be avoided. It is important to see that fear of God motivates action by a very real sense of potential harm. In the LXX this would be stated quite clearly as fearing the wrath/anger of God. We do not have a wrathful image of God in 1 Peter. But the highlighting of God's mercy in Christ (1.3); that the believers have to hope on grace (1.13); and that God is judge (1.17) infers that without Christ one is in a trepidatious position. Therefore, to align oneself with God through Christ is the way to avoid the feared negative outcome of judgement.[59] By emphasising the presence of potential harm, fear drives the recipients towards aligning themselves with God. Moreover, by indicating that works will be judged as evidence of allegiance, it motivates particular ethical conduct.[60]

---

[58] Michaels, *1 Peter*, 71.
[59] Cf. Thurén who rightly comments that, though the judgement serves as a warning, '[t]he addressees are not persuaded with a reward, since the point of departure in the motivation is that they already are on the right side'; Thurén, *Argument*, 206. Thus, the motivation is towards fidelity not new reward.
[60] Cf. Brox, *Petrusbrief*, 79 who notes that the image of judgement impels appropriate caution.

'Fear' or 'Reverence'?

Modern exegetes seem to be averse to seeing God as a terrible figure and downplay his fearsomeness by changing 'fear', which is aware of danger, to 'reverence'.[61] Whereas reverence does recognise the unique place of God, it reduces the sense of God's power over one's attainment of goals. Achtemeier is paradigmatic: 'Christians are to live in an attitude of holy reverence ... rather than to live in terror at the thought of divine judgement.'[62] But in 1.14–17 the author chooses to focus on God as holy judge. The ancients would not have had a problem with understanding the gods as fearsome (cf. Ps 2.11–12).[63] The divine is powerful, and therefore terrible. My problem with 'reverence' is that not only does it import our modern tendencies into the text, but it also diminishes the motivating function of φόβος, which is required in the context of addressing the audience's conduct. For the use of φόβος to be rhetorically successful, there has to be a real sense of potential harm.[64] Otherwise, as discussed above, one would not deliberate about one's conduct in light of the powerful object nor plot a course of action that would avoid the projected negative consequences. You may respect a person, but unless you think that she has some mastery over your good, you will not modify your conduct in respect of her. However, to allow φόβος to maintain a note of warning does not mean that the believers are in a state of paralysed terror, but it does allow it to have the motivating force required by bringing an eschatological reality before the believers' eyes.[65] Furthermore, it does not mean that the believers now live in fear when they did not before. They previously had values and goals, and therefore fears that motivated them and shaped their behaviour

---

[61] Cf. Selwyn, *St. Peter*, 142–3; Achtemeier, *1 Peter*, 123, 125. Though Selwyn does note if εἰ is to be taken concessively, then the first clause of 1.17 would be 'a warning against allowing God's fatherly love to obscure the truth of His awful majesty and righteousness', and that if the judge were the focus then fear rather than reverence would be apt; Selwyn, *St. Peter*, 142–3. Exceptions include Elliott and Goppelt. Elliott, though he prefers to translate φόβος as reverence in acknowledgement of its positive function, does allow that in the biblical tradition it denotes 'awe-dread-reverence', which is a 'motive for keeping his [God's] commandments'; Elliott, *1 Peter*, 365–6. Goppelt sees fear as 'trepidation in light of accountability before God'; Goppelt, *1 Peter*, 113.

[62] Achtemeier, *1 Peter*, 125.

[63] To say that God should be feared does not mean that God is temperamental and unpredictable as the Greco-Roman gods. His character is stable, and thus his judgement is sure and just.

[64] Cf. Thurén, *Argument*, 112–13.

[65] See Goppelt, *1 Peter*, 111–13.

(cf. 1.14).[66] The difference is that now these have been reoriented, with God becoming their primary fear.

For a Stoic, φόβος meant an irrational turbulent state. Perhaps as modern exegetes we have absorbed this conception and therefore dislike that a biblical author could encourage fear of any kind. However, even the Stoics, who promote ἀπάθεια, cannot envisage a wise life without some kind of fear; they simply rename it εὐλάβεια (caution). But 'caution' still recognises the potential for one's actions to lead to harm and asks the person to direct behaviour in light of this. The difference is that εὐλάβεια is well-reasoned, so that the harm to be avoided is a true evil. Consequently, the Stoics recognise that this type of emotion has value in helping the wise man lead a virtuous life. The underlying problem, which the Stoics were aware of, is that one constantly has to select right actions. Yet, how does one decide which to choose? Fear (or for the Stoics, caution) is one emotion that assists in navigating the decision-making process by providing information about what to avoid. As such, in light of one's goals, fear cuts off certain avenues of behaviour. Thus, fear, as the LXX also shows, is necessary for providing boundaries to action. Boundaries are an essential part of human existence that bring not only stability to a group but also help the individual to locate herself within reality. Given a particular worldview, they reassure the person about how they can attain the good. Fear of God in 1 Peter is performing this boundary-marking function. Therefore, instead of being turbulent and irrational, fear of God is stabilising because it deliberately positions the believers in their new Christian reality and gives them information about what are the appropriate actions to take. In this way, like in the LXX, fear of God becomes a life-directing dispositional outlook.[67] As such, fear of God in 1 Peter is inseparable from the letter's eschatological expectations.

Having examined the groundwork of 1.17, we can progress to investigating how fear of God impacts upon the audience's evaluation of the other and the self.

---

[66] Michaels reads ἐπιθυμίαι in 1.14 as a neutral term meaning 'impulses' rather than specifically 'evil desires'. Therefore, for Michaels, these desires represent a wide range of goals, such as for 'wealth, power, or pleasure'; Michaels, *1 Peter*, 57. The fact that they are categorised as ignorant, that is, based on not knowing God, means that these desires are presented negatively and characteristic of both their former life and the way of their previous society; see Achtemeier, *1 Peter*, 120.

[67] This dispositional reading is inadvertently recognised by scholars. For example, Michaels says that the Christians are asked 'to maintain an attitude of godly fear'; Michaels, *1 Peter*, 62.

Locating Other Figures of Power: 1 Peter 2.17–18; 3.1–2, 16

The next use of fear terminology (φοβέω) occurs in 2.17, which explains how the believers should relate to various groups:

πάντας τιμήσατε, τὴν ἀδελφότητα ἀγαπᾶτε, τὸν θεὸν φοβεῖσθε, τὸν βασιλέα τιμᾶτε.

Honour all people, love the brotherhood, fear God, honour the Emperor.

Again, God is the object of fear and fear is actively encouraged. Thus, we must expect that 1.17 undergirds 2.17's exhortation. Once more, fear reappears in a context where the believers' behaviour is addressed; though they are free, they are not to do evil because they are God's slaves (2.16).[68] This subordination brings back to the foreground via different imagery the relative power dynamic between the believers and God, highlighting the need for obedient service. It is of note that this relational dynamic directly precedes the horizontal and vertical relationships addressed in 2.17.

Creating an Emotional Regime

2.17 begins with the stance that the believers should have towards all people, which is one of honour. Next, the mutual relationship of the Christian believers to one another should exhibit the quality of love. Then, the author lists two relationships in which a powerful figure is mentioned: first God, then the Emperor. Only God is to be feared, whereas the Emperor, like all other people, is to be honoured.[69] Consequently, in 2.17 the author establishes an 'emotional regime' (see pp. 34–5, 37–8).[70] Such regimes shape 'the forms of social relationships and course of action that are open' to someone. As such, regimes 'play an important role in shaping and reproducing structures of power'.[71]

---

[68] 2.11–12 has spoken about their conduct more generally, whereas 2.13–3.7 gives specific exhortations.

[69] Scholars note the similarity between 2.17 and Prov 24.21. However, 1 Peter downgrades Proverbs command from fearing the king to honouring the Emperor; see Windisch, *katholischen Briefe*, 64; Schelkle, *Petrusbriefe*, 77; Michaels, *1 Peter*, 131–2. Contra Selwyn, this change of verb seems more deliberate than simply stylistic; Selwyn, *St. Peter*, 174–5.

[70] Riis and Woodhead, *Sociology*, 10. Cf. Holloway, *Coping*, 182, who acknowledges 'a clear prioritizing of commitments'. The prioritising of God over the Emperor is not altered by disagreements about how the four commands are structurally related to each other; see Jobes, *1 Peter*, 177; E. Bammel, 'The Commands in I Peter II.17', *NTS* 11 (1965): 279–81.

[71] Riis and Woodhead, *Sociology*, 10.

It is his application of φόβος to God alone that enables the author to present God as the highest authority. For fear indicates mastery. Even the command to submit to ruling bodies, e.g. the Emperor, is based on one's acknowledgment of God (διὰ τὸν κύριον)[72] not on account of the Emperor's own position (2.13).[73] Rhetorically, in view of the background of 1.17, by applying fear to God alone, the author reminds the recipients that God has ultimate power over their good and warns them that he is the object of primary importance in their worldview. It also brings to bear on the current situation the boundaries that 'fear of God' creates, therefore limiting the scope of submission required in 2.13.[74] Furthermore, the Emperor is to be honoured, like all other humans, which minimises his unique power and places him on the same plane as the rest of humanity.[75] Thus, to agree with Achtemeier, 2.17 'establishes a hierarchy of values and allegiances'.[76] But, we must acknowledge that this is effected through the use of emotion language due to the emotion's evaluative judgement and propositional content. The brief mention of fear carries into this new context the outlook and assumptions apparent in 1.17–21. This emotional structuring of reality continues into the household codes.

Acting 'in Fear'

Immediately, in 2.18, which is addressed to οἱ οἰκέται (the household slaves), the author commands:

> Οἱ οἰκέται ὑποτασσόμενοι ἐν παντὶ φόβῳ τοῖς δεσπόταις, οὐ μόνον τοῖς ἀγαθοῖς καὶ ἐπιεικέσιν ἀλλὰ καὶ τοῖς σκολιοῖς.

---

[72] Whether κύριος refers to God or Christ (cf. Michaels, *1 Peter*, 124) here makes little difference to our argument. Either way, the believers' response to ruling bodies comes from their Christian faith (cf. ἐν κυρίῳ, Eph 6.1; Col 3.18, 20 and ὡς τῷ κυρίῳ, Eph 5.22; Col 3.23). The whole phrase does not, as Selwyn suggests, refer to an inward loyalty to the State; Selwyn, *St. Peter*, 172.

[73] Cf. Michaels, *1 Peter*, 124; Achtemeier, *1 Peter*, 182–3.

[74] For Schlosser, this evidences both loyalty and resistance; Schlosser, *Pierre*, 159. The nature of the obligations towards powerful figures may be subtly indicated by the terminology used by the author. For (apart from 3.6) ὑπακοή is reserved for God and Christ (1.2, 14, 22) but ὑποτάσσω is used for human relationships. Thus, '"obedience" (ὑπακοή) is a primary and radical commitment while ὑποτάσσειν represents a secondary and more limited one'. Michaels suggests that the chiastic arrangement of 2.17 emphasises that obligations to wider society are secondary to those toward God and the brotherhood; Michaels, *1 Peter*, 123–4. Thus, we must disagree with Selwyn that 1 Peter's comments endorse moral allegiance to the State; Selwyn, *St. Peter*, 87.

[75] According to Achtemeier, this manoeuvre aims to combat the cult of the Emperor that was growing in Asia Minor; Achtemeier, *1 Peter*, 180.

[76] Further, it is adherence to this hierarchy that 'made negative social pressure inevitable'; Achtemeier, *1 Peter*, 188.

Slaves, be subordinate in all fear to your masters, not only to
the good and fair ones but also to the harsh ones.[77]

In this new relational scenario the author repeats the command to
act 'in fear' (ἐν (παντὶ) φόβῳ). There is disagreement about whether
the object(s) of fear are the masters or God. If the verse were read
on its own it would be plausible to conclude that the slaves are being
asked to act in fear of their masters.[78] However, given the emotional
regime of 2.17 and the use of ἐν φόβῳ in 1.17, God as the object is
preferable.[79] This is supported by the next phrase in which the slaves
are commended for bearing unjust suffering precisely because of a
consciousness of God (συνείδησις θεοῦ, 2.19).[80] Therefore, in 2.18 and
2.19 the slave's behaviour arises from an awareness of God rather
than because of fear of his/her master. Even in this new context, in
which another power dynamic is in view, fear of God is the driving
factor for behaviour.[81] If our reading is correct, the phrase ἐν φόβῳ
changes the tenor of the exhortation. It is not a negative fear of
another human (cf. 3.14) that colours the action of subordination,
but the positive fear of God in which the slaves actively choose to
align themselves with a certain reality in doing good.

We can infer the same for the use of ἐν φόβῳ in 3.1–2 where
the wives (αἱ γυναῖκες) are being asked to be subordinate to their
husbands (τοῖς ἰδίοις ἀνδράσιν, 3.1). The phrase ἐν φόβῳ is used to
refer to their (ἁγνὴ) ἀνατροφή, which has the potential to win over
an unbelieving husband. The fact that fear has no obvious referent
in 3.2, and that conduct driven by fear is named holy (ἁγνός) further
supports the argument that 1.14–17 is the framework for the use of

---

[77] Here I am following Achtemeier who notes that ὑποτάσσω 'is closer to "subordinate" than to "submit" or "obey", and advocates finding one's proper place and acting accordingly, rather than calling upon one to give unquestioning obedience to whatever anyone … may command'; Achtemeier, *1 Peter*, 182.

[78] It appears that Selwyn reads 2.18 this way, perhaps with the double sense that fearing the master is part of fearing God. However, his comment is so brief that it is hard to determine his position; Selwyn, *St. Peter*, 175–6. Martin, following Bammel, takes a different position, reading submission here and in 3.1–6 as a 'conferment of honour'; Martin, *Metaphor*, 204–5.

[79] Contra Brox, *Petrusbrief*, 131; Holloway, *Coping*, 183–5, in agreement with Schelkle, *Petrusbriefe*, 80; Goppelt, *1 Peter*, 194; Michaels, *1 Peter*, 138; Achtemeier, *1 Peter*, 193–5; Schlosser, *Pierre*, 166.

[80] The use of ἐνώπιον τοῦ θεοῦ (3.4) 'suggests a similar orientation' for the wives' conduct; D. G. Horrell, 'Fear, Hope, and Doing Good: Wives as a Paradigm of Mission in 1 Peter', *Estudios Bíblicos* 73 (2015): 409–29, at 413.

[81] Cf. Michaels, *1 Peter*, 138; Achtemeier, *1 Peter*, 193; De Waal Dryden, *Theology*, 157.

ἐν φόβῳ here and in 2.18. Consequently, ἐν φόβῳ is shorthand for fear of God. This is bolstered by 3.6, which discourages fear of the husband.[82] Again, the motivating factor is the wife's relationship toward God and not the husband's position. This is the same for μετὰ φόβου in 3.16. This time, the behaviour in question is the believers' response to their accusers. We can note that sandwiching the exhortation to respond 'with fear' is the appeal to set Christ as Lord in their heart (3.15), and that to respond in fear coexists with having a good conscience (συνείδησιν ἔχοντες ἀγαθήν, 3.16). Both of these elements indicate that an awareness of one's allegiance to God and the norms that partner this are to influence behaviour.

In each of these three cases of persecution, the reference to acting in (or with) fear brings God into the scenario and consequently gives the situation a new configuration. The believer–God relationship usurps the subordinate–master/husband or persecuted–abuser relationship with the consequence that the master, husband, and defamer are sidelined. Instead, God remains the emotional focus. Furthermore, because emotions highlight objects salient to personal goals, to make God the emotional focus in these scenarios is to present the believers' relationship with, and obligation toward, God as more significant to their flourishing than their relationship with the master/husband/hostile other.[83] By using the phrase ἐν φόβῳ to recall 1.17's fear of God, the author reminds the audience of their life orientation that is to direct their behaviour. This is not to say that the believers' relationships with their masters, husbands, or hostile other have no value, but their value is relativised. The other figures of power, though in human terms they may have dominance and influence the present well-being of the believer, from the Christian perspective have lessened importance because, in comparison to God, they do not have power over primary eternal goods. To use fear in this way widens the audience's perspective beyond the present toward seeing its present in light of a larger reality. By both 'sidelining' dominant figures and by recalling a larger reality over which the dominant figures have no power, we can see how through using

[82] Those who interpret ἐν φόβῳ in 2.18 as fear of God tend to apply the same interpretation to 3.2 for similar reasons; see Michaels, *1 Peter*, 158; Achtemeier, *1 Peter*, 210. Cf. Brox, *Petrusbrief*, 143–4.
[83] Perhaps this desire to recognise the difference in value between the believer's different relationships is shown by 1 Peter's terminology. The normal word for master κύριος is reserved for Christ and δεσπότης is used instead. Likewise, δοῦλος is only used of the Christian–God relationship and οἰκέτης is used for the slave–master paradigm; cf. Michaels, *1 Peter*, 138.

fear the author is able to reposition the powerful figures within the audience's worldview.

On the surface, it looks like fear of God is being used to bolster the norms of the surrounding society. Some scholars have read the household codes this way. For them, 1 Peter does not advocate a change in the stratification of society. Instead, the hierarchy and power structures are maintained. In fact, the Christians are being encouraged to win the favour of the powerful other by their good submissive behaviour within these structures. This, for some, adds weight to the assertion that the letter pushes people towards assimilation to surrounding culture.[84] However, what this line of reasoning fails to see is that there *is* a change to both ethical norms and social structure, even if at present it is only within the perspective of the Christian. The believers' behaviour towards those in authority over them is no longer driven by the mastery of that person but is motivated by their fear of God.[85] It is God's holiness and standards that drive their behaviour. This may, as previously stated, allow some crossover with the norms of society, but it is not driven by the norms of society to the extent that it seeks its approval. It is driven by duty toward God as συνείδησις θεοῦ (2.19) and ἁγνὴ ἀναστροφή (3.2) reveal.[86] In such a way, the believers' conduct is freed from being tied to their relationship with the master/husband because the believers' behaviour is fundamentally not a reaction to the human power.[87] This is why the author can logically ask the slaves to submit to their masters

[84] See Balch, who has argued that the household codes serve an apologetic function. Though he says that the wife would have been unwilling to conform as far as giving up her Christian faith, the Christian would have 'had to conform to the expectations of Hellenistic-Roman society' in order to remove accusations. Therefore, the slaves' and wives' submission is aiming to exhibit what the surrounding culture expected; D. L. Balch, *Let Wives Be Submissive: The Domestic Code in 1 Peter*, SBLMS 26 (Atlanta, GA: Scholars Press, 1981), 85–8, 92, 109. See also Brox, *Petrusbrief*, 126–7; Jobes, *1 Peter*, 183. For Bird, this upholding of kyriarchal structures is problematically abusive to the weaker party; J. G. Bird, *Abuse, Power and Fearful Obedience: Reconsidering 1 Peter's Commands to Wives*, LNTS 442 (London: T&T Clark, 2011). I will return to the author's social strategy in the conclusion.

[85] This is where Bird's reading is a misrepresentation of the author's intention. She reads 'fear' as fear of the masters, and therefore that it necessarily upholds kyriarchal structures and shows the author's collusion with such a system. Bird therefore misses the displacement of the fearsome other; Bird, *Abuse*, 91–6, 107.

[86] As Achtemeier discusses, this approach may seek to give the least offence possible to surrounding society, but not at the cost of their faith. Their obligation to God takes priority and therefore may cause offence to outsiders and lead to suffering; Achtemeier, *1 Peter*, 194–5.

[87] Cf. Achtemeier who offers a similar reading; Achtemeier, *1 Peter*, 196; also Schelkle, *Petrusbriefe*, 80. As Schlosser comments, the author preserves the internal liberty of his audience, who can refuse to be intimidated; Schlosser, *Pierre*, 185.

regardless of the masters' behaviour (2.18). It matters not how the master acts, because it is the slaves' internal orientation towards God that determines their behaviour.[88] In this way, the power structure for the believer has changed. If one is looking to the human for honour, security, protection, or any good, then they retain their mastery. But to fear God, and in doing so, to recognise him as the source of good, negates the mastery of the other. The human structures of society have not outwardly changed.[89] What *has* changed is the believer's perception of figures within those structures. This psychological and emotional stance paves the way for potential deviance rather than assimilation.[90] For, when the mastery of the other is negated, one is able to behave in ways considered deviant to the other because one is less concerned about one's relationship to the powerful figure for achieving one's own goals. The fact that they seem to be encountering difficulty for their Christian behaviour (cf. 2.19) would suggest that such 'deviance' is already occurring. As Michaels notes, that wives have adopted the Christian faith, most likely against the religion of their husband, is already a subversive act.[91] Thus, to fear God shows that the believer has internalised a different scheme of reality with its own norms, values, and structures.

We have examined the instances where fear is positively encouraged. What remains is to assess the occurrences where φόβος/ φοβέω are used negatively and therefore discouraged.

Positioning the Believer: 1 Peter 3.6, 14–15

For the author, fear of God is encouraged; however, other fears are inappropriate. The first negation of fear occurs in 3.6 where

---

[88] For the wife, living in fear of God would undoubtedly involve no longer worshipping the household gods, which would cause her problems within the household. Thus, the wife, like other believers, faces the problem of competing solidarities; see Achtemeier, *1 Peter*, 208, 211.

[89] Having said this, the author does hold out the hope that a wife's 'in fear' behaviour might win over the husband (3.1–2) and therefore affect the household. But, this is not the same as expecting a large-scale change of the entire structure of society.

[90] Michaels acknowledges the psychological element here, noting that the believers have a 'firm commitment of heart and mind to God' (128). This mental perspective is based on a spiritual reality: the audience are free people who have been liberated from subjugation to their ancestral ways (1.18) and have a new master (2.16). Michaels further asserts that by presenting the believers as 'free people' (2.16) the author indicates that they have a choice over their actions, whether to comply or not; Michaels, *1 Peter*, 124, 128–9; see also Achtemeier, *1 Peter*, 186–7. Horrell notes that refusing fear of the other shows that the author does not require wholesale assimilation and conformity; Horrell, 'Fear', 421–2.

[91] Michaels, *1 Peter*, 157.

the wives are exhorted to do good and not to fear any intimidation (ἀγαθοποιοῦσαι καὶ μὴ φοβούμεναι μηδεμίαν πτόησιν). Commentators disagree on whether the participles should be read as imperatival, conditional, or explanatory.[92] I take them to be conditional. However, their force makes little difference to my argument. What is clear is that the believing wives, who do (or are to do) good, are to be without negative fear. Put differently, fear is not fitting for this category of person.[93] There is no obvious object of fear. From the context it could be the unbelieving husband who is the source of intimidation and therefore the object of fear. Or, perhaps, the μηδείς gives the absence of fear a universal scope: they are not to fear intimidation from anyone. In this negative, and more standard, presentation of fear, φοβέω can be understood to carry the elements outlined in the Stoic definition: it focuses on a powerful (intimidating) object, expects harm, and most likely encourages avoidance. However, that fear is presented as inappropriate means that the wives are being discouraged from having the perspective that fear presents.[94]

The only other negative presentation of fear is in 3.14, which says: τὸν δὲ φόβον αὐτῶν μὴ φοβηθῆτε μηδὲ ταραχθῆτε (literally, 'the fear of them do not fear nor be troubled'). These verses (3.14–15) depend on Isaiah 8.12–13, with the above phrase being nearly an exact citation.[95] There is discussion around how this phrase should be translated: either as (1) 'do not be afraid of them or be troubled', or (2) 'do not be afraid of what they are afraid of nor be troubled'.[96] How this verse is read does make a difference to our investigation. In the first option, the objects of fear are the people that seek to harm the Christians on account of their righteous behaviour (cf. 3.13). With the second option, the whole worldview of the other is held in question: one should not fear what they hold to be fearsome. The first option is preferable due to the surrounding context (though the

---

[92] See Michaels, *1 Peter*, 166–7.

[93] Though, as Holloway notes, this indicates that, for some wives, living with their non-Christian husband was a terrifying prospect; Holloway, *Coping*, 190.

[94] The fact that the author discourages fear does not mean, contra Bird, that he is 'disregarding the various dynamics of the daily reality of those to whom he speaks' by 'offering universal directives'. Instead, it shows the opposite: he is acutely aware that the wives are experiencing intimidation on account of their Christian faith. Bird later comments that the author does not try to diminish the fear of his audience, and finds this problematic. This comment shows she has missed the intention of the author altogether, which is precisely to remove fear of the other; Bird, *Abuse*, 97, 112.

[95] The only difference is that 1 Peter has αὐτῶν, the LXX αὐτοῦ.

[96] The NIV takes the former, the NRSVA the latter.

second is not unhelpful).[97] The verse before mentions ὁ κακώσων ὑμᾶς (the ones who will harm you, 3.13) and then verses 3.15–16 highlight ὁ αἰτῶν ὑμᾶς (the one asking you, 3.15) and οἱ ἐπηρεάζοντες (those mistreating (you), 3.16). Therefore, at the forefront of this passage is the hostile other. Given that this other is the focus throughout 3.13–16, it seems most plausible that he/she is the intended object in 3.14. So, we can conclude that the author is exhorting his audience not to fear the potentially harmful other.[98] Consequently, as with 3.6, the author is asking the audience not to subscribe to the evaluation that fear grants.

Why No Fear Is Appropriate

But what is the author's rationale for why fear is inappropriate in either scenario? In 3.6 and 3.14 the immediate context is the believers' behaviour: 3.6's command follows the exhortation to do good (ἀγαθοποιέω); in 3.14 the believers are suffering on account of righteousness (διὰ δικαιοσύνην). Behaving righteously and 'doing good' are synonymous terms, both of which are parallel to the ἐν φόβῳ holy conduct previously stated (1.14–17; 3.2). The believer's good 'in Christ' conduct is further emphasised in 3.16–17. From this, we can understand that the believers' behaviour detailed in the context of the command not to fear is conduct that accords with God's holiness and demonstrates allegiance to him. Thus, it is only the obedient, holy, righteous believer who should not fear the intimidating other. Here, the LXX background is present in which, paradoxically, those who fear God will have no fear of the other. We need to unpack this negation of fear further.

We have become familiar with the idea that fear attributes to the object greater relative power, particularly power to harm. Consequently, to deny fear of something is to strip the object of these qualities. Thus, in 1 Peter, the audience is being asked no longer to see the abusive other as a powerful person with the capacity to harm. The secondary consequence is that the other's value is reinterpreted. To ask the audience to see the other as not harmful is to say that the other has no power over the person's good. Therefore, in terms of the believers' goals the other is devalued, even irrelevant.

---

[97] Cf. Jobes, *1 Peter*, 228–9.

[98] For Holloway, such a regulation of one's emotional involuntary response is the first step to 'readying oneself to cope with prejudice'. However, as we shall see, it is not about halting a response, but changing one's worldview so that such fear is no longer fitting to one's dispositional outlook; Holloway, *Coping*, 200.

However, we must recognise that the negation of fear is only logical when considered concurrently with fear of God. In both 3.6 and 3.14 fear of God is either explicitly or implicitly present. The wives ἐν φόβῳ ἁγνὴ ἀναστροφή (3.2) provides the umbrella term for 3.3–4's specific conduct and is prescriptive for ἀγαθοποιέω in 3.6. In 3.14 the author's use of Isaiah 8.13 leads on to the alternative to fearing the other: κύριον δὲ τὸν Χριστὸν ἁγιάσατε ἐν ταῖς καρδίαις ὑμῶν (but in your hearts sanctify Christ as Lord; 3.15). In the original context the κύριος would be understood to be the God of Israel. However, here it is Christ that is Lord. For those who knew the scriptural reference, they would understand that Isaiah 8.13 reads: κύριον αὐτὸν ἁγιάσατε, καὶ αὐτὸς ἔσται σου φόβος. Thus, in Isaiah, having God as their sole fear is the basis for not fearing the other. Though the latter part of the verse is not present in 1 Peter, it is not implausible that this is the foundation of the author's negation of fear. Consequently, two fears are being opposed to each other, one negative and one positive. The positive fear of God, like in the LXX, nullifies the negative fear of the other. To understand this abrogation of negative fear, we must recall what is within the concept of fearing God: that God has ultimate power over the good and is therefore the only one able truly to harm, and the only one of import to one's flourishing. With this perspective, the other's power to harm is negated and as a result they can no longer be an object of fear.

Secondary Implications of Negating Fear

The secondary implication is that, from the believers' perspective, the relative standing of the hostile other is altered. The believers now no longer necessarily view themselves as at the mercy of the other. Instead, because the power dynamic that matters is between humans and God, all humans are in the same position. In fact, the righteous believer is in a better position than the unbeliever because she has chosen allegiance to God. This is not to say that the believer is superior, rather the status of one human over another is irrelevant because no person holds power over eternal goods. Perhaps this is why it is possible for the audience to honour all people, without competitive concern for their own honour. It is also why they can give an account to their questioners with gentleness (3.16).

Lastly, we can also note that if the evaluation of the other has been altered so that the other is no longer fearsome, then fear's action-tendency will also be removed. It is this that the author is aiming at. The action-tendency of fear is avoidance of harm. As mentioned in the last chapter, this means either separating oneself from the harmful other or changing the nature of one's relationship with the other. For slaves and wives separation is not a realistic option.[99] The second option could be achieved by increasing one's power, which, again, is unlikely for the subordinate, *or* by making the powerful figure favourable towards you. This last option is the only one available to the believers. If they are being persecuted because of their Christian identity and conduct, then the easiest way to remove persecution is to change these aspects. Thus, fear of the other motivates the Christian to abandon her faith, or at least behave contrary to it via conforming to the accepted norms of the powerful. Such 'avoidance' would ease their social situation and remove the threat of harm. But, this conformity 'would mean in effect the dissolution of the Christian community as a distinct entity within Roman culture'.[100] Therefore, it is vital that the author presents a reality in which such fear is absent so that all tendency towards this behaviour is nullified.

Having surveyed the author's use of fear, and noted some of the implications of his usage, we can proceed to investigating hope in 1 Peter. We will leave plotting the sociological and therapeutic consequences of the above until we have explored the interrelated emotion of hope. I mentioned briefly above that fear and hope are two sides of the same coin. However, at that point, I left much of what could have been said about hope untouched. Therefore, it is now necessary to complete the picture by providing a detailed exegesis of the role of hope in 1 Peter. We will start, as is now our custom, by locating hope within the repertoire of emotions.

Locating Hope

The first thing that has to be established is whether hope is an emotion. Recent studies on emotion have categorised it as such. For Cavanaugh et al. hope is a positive emotion 'associated with common achievement scenarios'.[101] They then assign to hope a number of key features that we have come to recognise as constituent parts of an

---

[99] Further, as Achtemeier rightly comments, 'there is no idea here [in 2.11–4.11] of withdrawing from the hostile world, and forming a conventicle of the righteous in the midst of the *massa perditionis*. It is clear from the tone of this portion of the letter, as of the letter as a whole, that the author fully expects Christians to continue to participate in the life of their societies'; Achtemeier, *1 Peter*, 170.

[100] Achtemeier, *1 Peter*, 186.

[101] L. A. Cavanaugh et al., 'Hope, Pride, and Processing During Optimal and Nonoptimal Times of Day', *Emotion* 11, no. 1 (2011): 38–46, at 38; cf. E. M. W. Tong,

emotion such as an appraisal and behavioural tendencies.[102] Lazarus is particularly adamant that 'hope is a response to goal outcomes' like other emotions such as anger and shame, and therefore 'it should be treated as an emotion'.[103] Further, he adds that it exhibits other phenomena associated with emotions such as 'a change in the intensity of one's mental state', which is often present in subjective affect.[104] Thus, current theorists categorise hope as an emotion, but did the ancients?

Is Hope an Emotion for the Ancients?

The Greek emotion terms of interest to us are ἐλπίς and ἐλπίζω, which are generally considered to carry the sense of hope or expectation. Whereas φόβος, χαρά, and λύπη appear in the Stoic lists of the πάθη and εὐπαθεῖαι, ἐλπίς does not. This could suggest that ἐλπίς is not considered an emotion for the Stoics or the ancient world generally. However, this is not necessarily so. There is other evidence that reveals that hope was placed among the emotions and was not considered an altogether different psychological phenomenon. Hope appears in discussion as a point of comparison. For example, Andronicus, when defining ἀγωνία (anguish/trepidation) that is a type of φόβος, says:

> Ἀγωνία δὲ φόβος διαπτώσεως· ἢ φόβος ἥττης· ἢ φόβος ἐμποιητικὸς τῶν ἐναντίων ἐλπίδων, περὶ ὧν ὄρεξιν σφοδρὰν ἔχομεν.

> Anguish is fear of failure; or fear of defeat; or fear productive of the opposite of hope about that which we have great desire. ([*Pass.*] 3 = SVF 3.409)[105]

Thus, hope is placed as the opposite of fear. Moreover, it is done so in the context of attainment, indicating that hope is related to some sort of goal. His comments also infer that hope and fear both look

---

'Differentiation of 13 Positive Emotions by Appraisals', *Cognition and Emotion* 29 (2015): 484–503, at 485–6, which lists hope as one of thirteen positive emotions investigated.

[102] Cavanaugh et al., 'Hope', 38.

[103] R. Lazarus, 'Hope: An Emotion and a Vital Coping Resource Against Despair', *Social Research* 66 (1999): 653–78, at 663.

[104] Lazarus, 'Hope: An Emotion', 663.

[105] This is the only occurrence of ἐλπίς in Andronicus' Περὶ Παθῶν book 1 or 2.

to the desired goal but with opposite evaluations. Cicero is the most helpful. He lists fear and hope as opposites and provides a definition:

> *si spes est exspectatio boni, mali exspectationem esse necesse est metum.*

> if hope is expectation of good, fear must be expectation of evil. (*Tusc.* 4.37.80 [King, LCL])

Thus, hope looks towards a future good.[106] Such a brief excerpt is perhaps too scant evidence for arguing that hope was viewed as an emotion. However, in *De oratore* Cicero comments:

> For nothing in oratory, Catulus, is more important than to win for the orator the favour of his hearer, and to have the latter so affected as to be swayed by something resembling a mental impulse or emotion … for men decide far more problems by hate, or love, or lust, or rage, or sorrow, or joy, or hope [*spes*], or fear, or illusion, or some other inward emotion, than by reality, or authority, or any legal standard, or judicial precedent or statute. (*De or.* 2.42.178 [Sutton and Rackham, LCL])

Hope is clearly listed in the same category as other emotions. Cicero repeats this in *De or.* 2.50.206 in which he also infers that hope is inspired in the audience when some future benefit is held before them (*si proponitur spes utilitatis futurae*).[107] That one can be swayed by hope suggests that, like other emotions, hope influences behaviour.[108] Aristotle links hope to ethical action by commenting that one may endure pain in the present because of the hope that one's actions will end in good (*Eth. eud.* 2.8.12, 1224b15–20; cf. Cicero, *Tusc.* 3.25.61).[109] Seneca too recognises that hope motivates one towards attaining valued goods (*Ep.* 82.18).[110]

We can also reference Philo who in *De mutatione nominum* 30.161–4 discusses the relationship between hope (ἐλπίς), joy (χαρά),

---

[106] Cf. Aristotle, *Mem. rem.* 449b27–8; *Rhet.* 2.12.8, 1389a21.

[107] Aristotle likewise links hope to the good. For Aristotle this type of hope produces confidence, particularly in the young; see *Rhet.*2.12.8–9, 1389a18–31.

[108] Aritsotle's *Rhet.* 2.5.14, 1383a5–8 indicates that hope is motivational, for where there is no hope for the distressed person there is no deliberation or action.

[109] For Aristotle, this expectation is accompanied by pleasure, which shows that hope matches Aristotle's definition of emotions, which are accompanied by pleasure and pain, and affect judgements (*Rhet.* 2.1, 1378a19–21).

[110] However, Seneca does not present this as a positive state of affairs.

grief (λύπη), and fear (φόβος). Philo, as we have seen, uses Stoic conceptions about the emotions, but sometimes modifies them. He reveals a Stoic understanding of distress and fear –distress arises when evil is present; fear when it is expected – and explains hope and joy along similar lines – hope is the expectation of good; joy occurs when good is present.[111] Philo draws a sequential link between hope and joy. Hope via its anticipation comes before joy, just like fear comes before distress. Thus, Philo describes hope as 'joy before joy' (ἐλπὶς χαρὰ πρὸ χαρᾶς, 30.163) because it tastes the good before-hand.[112] In doing so, hope recommends the object to the soul, which sounds like the Stoic movements of the soul towards good. Thus, Philo places hope (ἐλπίς) firmly on the emotional map alongside Stoic primary emotions: χαρά, φόβος, and λύπη.[113]

The above proves that we can be reasonably confident that hope was classed among the emotions in the ancient world.[114] We can also come to a simple demarcation of hope: hope has as its object a future good that is evaluated as beneficial to the person, and, given its asso-ciation with desire and benefits, it encourages pursuit of the object.

In general, the Stoics do not talk positively about hope.[115] The main issue is that hope causes one to look outside of oneself for something. As such, it is an acknowledgement that one is in lack and signals discontentment. Both of these aspects, reliance on external goods and discontentment, are not appropriate to a life

---

[111] Here we would expect βούλησις alongside χαρά, not ἐλπίς.

[112] Cf. Aristotle, *Rhet.* 1.11.9, 1370b.

[113] Strictly speaking, as Graver points out, Philo makes ἐλπίς a προπάθεια (a pre-emotion that occurs before the full emotion). However, there is no evidence that Stoicism made such a move. As we have seen in Cicero, hope is treated as a full emotion. The reason the concept of a προπάθεια was developed by Stoicism was to explain why the Stoic philosopher could appear to be experiencing a passion but was in fact not. The idea of a προπάθεια allowed a time gap in which the philosopher could decide whether to assent to the impression that had caused the προπάθεια. Assent would then determine whether the full emotion occurred. However, what this tells us, if Philo wants to treat ἐλπίς as a προπάθεια, is that hope was a psychological phe-nomenon that to the ordinary person resembled an emotion. For more on Philo's use of προπάθεια see M. Graver, 'Philo of Alexandria and the Origins of the Stoic Προπάθειαι', *Phronesis* 44 (1999): 300–25, note particularly 312–16 for discussion on joy and hope.

[114] This is not to say that they did not recognise that it requires sophisticated cogni-tive abilities. For example, Aristotle comments that humans are the only animals that have hope or expectation of the future (*Part. an.* 3.6, 669a18–20).

[115] Aristotle presents hope as more suited to the young who have less experience of life (*Rhet.* 2.12.8–9, 1389a18–31), which might suggest that he thinks it more fool-hardy. However, it could be that the young think themselves to have more 'future' and therefore tend towards hope unlike the old (*Rhet.* 2.13.12, 1390a6–9).

lived according to nature in which one should accept all that befalls and seek to cultivate only virtue, which is within the control of the person (cf. Seneca, *Ep.* 72.7–9; Cicero, *Tusc.* 5.12.36; Epictetus, *Fragment* 30–31). The most outspoken is Seneca who prefers living in the present. For Seneca, if you cease to hope you will cease to fear, because fear follows on the heels of hope.[116] A mind that looks towards the future is unsettled, but 'the present alone can make no man wretched' (*Ep.* 5.7–9 [Gummere, LCL]; cf. 101.9–10). In fact, to have real joy one must avoid hope, which makes one troubled through goading one towards something (*Ep.* 23.2–3; cf. 59.14). We find a marked difference to the Stoic perspective on hope when we turn to the use of hope in the LXX.

Hope in the LXX

The terms ἐλπίς and ἐλπίζω occur frequently in the LXX, particularly in the Psalms. Therefore, the following is an adumbrated picture that highlights the salient points. First, as with fear, God is the primary object of hope (Pss 9.10–11; 13.6; 15.1 etc.) and God's people (the righteous) are marked as those who hope in him. Hence, hope signals trust in God over trust in any other power (Ps 117.8–9; *Pss. Sol.* 17.33–4). Consequently, hoping in God means declaring him to be your god (see Ps 30.15).[117] Furthermore, hoping in God is presented as the permanent posture of the righteous (Ps 70.14). The positioning of the righteous person through unwavering hope provides the grounds for her confidence that she will be helped by God and experience the good, often vindication (Ps 25.1–3). Psalm 33.9–10, a psalm evidently known by the author of 1 Peter (cf. 2.3), provides a good example of how hope is related to fear of God and his goodness:

> γεύσασθε καὶ ἴδετε ὅτι χρηστὸς ὁ κύριος·
> μακάριος ἀνήρ, ὃς ἐλπίζει ἐπ' αὐτόν.
> φοβήθητε τὸν κύριον, οἱ ἅγιοι αὐτοῦ,
> ὅτι οὐκ ἔστιν ὑστέρημα τοῖς φοβουμένοις αὐτόν.

> Taste and see that the Lord is good;
> blessed is the man who hopes in him.

---

[116] In *Ep.* 82.18 Seneca depicts hope and fear pulling a man in in different directions and causing him to be in turmoil. Such emotions cannot lead to virtue, because virtue comes from the actions of a soul at harmony with itself.

[117] Cf. Pss 15.1–2; 85.2; 90.2; Isa 25.9.

Fear the Lord, his holy ones
because there is no lack for those who fear him.

With an acceptance of God's goodness, it makes sense for the
psalmist to exhort others to hope in God, because hope looks to
the good.[118] But, likewise, they are to fear God, because there is no
lack in God. Thus, both fear and hope orientate one towards God
in anticipation that one's positioning in relation to him will result in
one's benefit.[119] Sirach 2.9 provides a parallel, saying:

οἱ φοβούμενοι κύριον, ἐλπίσατε εἰς ἀγαθὰ καὶ εἰς εὐφροσύνην
αἰῶνος καὶ ἔλεος.

Those who fear God, hope for good things, and for eternal
gladness and mercy.

In the context, the reason for their hope is that God has proved himself faithful to previous generations, he is compassionate, merciful,
and saves in times of trouble (Sir 2.10–11). Therefore, hoping in God
is rooted in an understanding of God's character and actions (cf. Pss
12.6; 20.1–8; 32.22; 129.6–8; 142.8; 146.11). Those who fear God
and hope in him stand in assurance that he is for them (Ps 32.18–22).

In both Psalm 33 and Sirach 2 the close association of fearing
God and hoping in him is demonstrated. This is a common link.[120]
From our exploration of fear we can appreciate why. Fearing God
recognises his power and that he has control over the good. These are
the very same attributes that make hope in God appropriate. If God
has mastery over the good then he is the only one in whom one can
hope, because hope seeks the good. Therefore, fear of God and hope
in him are necessarily interrelated but they have slightly different
valences: though both result in the good, hope is more noticeably
positive and motivates *towards* something. Furthermore, hope, more
than fear, reveals a person's dependence on something outside of
himself, in this instance God. Moreover, hope's dependence reveals
power differences, with God being the able party. Consequently,
hoping in God is a recognition of his power to help, particularly

---

[118] Cf. *Pss. Sol.* 5.8–11 where God's ability to provide is the reason the poor can
hope in him; see also Pss 35.8–10; 144.15.

[119] A number of texts promise benefits and success for those who hope in God; see
Pss 20.6–8; 39.5; 145.5–10; Jer 17.7–8; *Pss. Sol.* 17.38–9. Sometimes hope versus lack
of hope in God is given as the reason for why one group is successful over against
another (2 Chr 13.18).

[120] See Pss 32.18; 39.4; 146.11; Prov 14.26; Sir 34.13–15.

when his people hope in him for their salvation (Pss 7.2; 16.7; 21.4–6; 61.8–9; 85.1–3; Isa 51.5–6; *Pss. Sol.* 15.1).[121] When this salvation is from other powers, hope shows an evaluative perception that God's power is greater than one's foes (Pss 26.1–3; 55.5, 11; 60.4; 2 Macc 15.6–8). As such, those who hope in God, because he delivers them, trust that they will not be shamed (Pss 21.6; 24.20; 30.2; 70.1).[122]

Sirach 2.9 (quoted above) reveals that hoping in God results in other positive emotional states such as gladness and rejoicing (cf. Pss 30.7–8; 63.11; Bar 4.22).[123] Furthermore, because their hope causes them to expect God's goodness they have no fear of evil (Pss 55.4–5, 12; Jer 17.7–8; cf. *Pss. Sol.* 8.31–3). In fact, Psalm 90.9–10 declares that it is precisely *because* the psalmist has made God his hope that no harm will come to him. As such, hope is paralleled to having confidence (πέποιθα), and is linked to security and safety (Pss 15.9; 31.10; 56.2; 72.27–8; 90.1–5; Ezek 28.26–7). Because the righteous person's hope is based on an eternal stable and powerful God, her hope takes on an eternal enduring quality (Pss 51.10; 130.3; Isa 26.4; Wis 3.1–4; *Pss. Sol.* 17.1–3). But, in this type of hope there is an implicit requirement that the person exhibit fidelity: enduring hope is demonstrated in enduring faithfulness. Thus, there is an indication that hope should be followed by certain behaviour. For example, Psalm 36.3 asks the people to hope in God and do good (ἔλπισον ἐπὶ κύριον καὶ ποίει χρηστότητα).[124] Such behaviour, conditioned by hope, promises blessings (Ps 36.3–5). However, these happen because of God's agency. The person simply hopes in God and acts in line with God's ways, but God is the one who brings what is hoped for (ἔλπισον ἐπ' αὐτόν, καὶ αὐτὸς ποιήσει, 36.5).

Conversely, the hope of the ungodly – those who hope in someone or something other than God (cf. Ps 30.7) – will be destroyed (Prov 10.28; 11.23).[125] The fact that the ungodly's hopes can be destroyed

---

[121] In these passages we also frequently see God depicted as their refuge and help. Ps 36.40 declares that God saves the righteous precisely *because* they hope in him; cf. Ps 90.14; Dan 3.95.

[122] Again, frequently, the foundation for their hope is God's mercy.

[123] That Ps 41.6 and 12 suggest hoping in God as a remedy for a disquieted soul indicates that hope is considered a tranquil state.

[124] Cf. Sir 2.6. There are also instances where hoping in God is linked to keeping his commandments; see Ps 77.5–8; Prov 22.17–19. Conversely, those who despise instruction have vain hopes and unprofitable labours (Wis 3.11).

[125] Cf. Prov 11.7, which declares that the hope of a righteous man will not be destroyed.

shows that they are vain (cf. Ps 39.5), fragile, and temporary (Wis 5.14; Sir 34.1). Those who have such empty hopes can expect that harm will come to them (Isa 30.12–14; 31.10; 47.10; Jer 13.25–7; 17.5–6; Wis 13.10). Here the LXX shows the faultiness of the ungodly person's perspective: the ungodly put their hope in something because they expect it to bring them good, when, in reality, their misplaced hope will result in the opposite, harm. Lying beneath this is a rhetoric of power. The unrighteous person's hopes are futile and can be easily damaged because she is trusting in something that does not have the power to provide what she seeks.[126] This is not true of those that hope in God, who has ultimate power to provide all that is required.

Thus, for the LXX, hope is not just a positive emotion but a necessary state of being. Hoping in God is a declaration that you are aligning yourself with him and that he is the one you seek, knowing that he is the sole source of the good. Hope is certainly not turbulent or problematic; it is a sure emotional posture towards God based on his unchanging attributes, particularly his ultimate power and his mercy towards his people. With this understanding, we can turn to the author's use of hope in 1 Peter.

Hope in 1 Peter

Terms for hope (ἐλπίς/ἐλπίζω) appear only five times in the letter (1.3, 13, 21; 3.5, 15). However, to say that hope is used infrequently is not to say that is has a limited function. In the opening sections of the letter it arises at significant points: it occurs in the opening verse of the letter body (1.3) and then forms an inclusio for the second paragraph (1.13–21). One gets the impression by this placement that, like joy, hope is important for the outlook of the letter.[127] We will address the author's use of hope in two sections. First, we will investigate the perspective set in 1.3–21, and then, second, we will look at 3.5 and 3.15 in which hope is linked to praxis and witness.

---

[126] Cf. Jer 2.37, which draws out the connection between hope and attainment of goods. However, because God has rejected Egypt and Assyria (those in whom Israel hoped) Israel will not prosper through them; cf. Ezek 29.13–16.

[127] Brox, *Petrusbrief*, 61; E. Cothenet, 'Le realisme de l'esperance chrétienne selon 1 Pierre', *NTS* 27 (1981): 564–72, at 564.

A Living Hope that Expects God's Favour: 1.3, 13, 21

After the epistolary prescript, 1 Peter opens with (1.3):

Εὐλογητὸς ὁ θεὸς καὶ πατὴρ τοῦ κυρίου ἡμῶν Ἰησοῦ Χριστοῦ ὁ κατὰ τὸ πολὺ αὐτοῦ ἔλεος ἀναγεννήσας ἡμᾶς εἰς ἐλπίδα ζῶσαν δι' ἀναστάσεως Ἰησοῦ Χριστοῦ ἐκ νεκρῶν,

> Blessed be the God and father of our Lord Jesus Christ, the one who according to his great mercy has begotten us anew into a living hope through the resurrection of Jesus Christ from the dead,

This first contextualisation of ἐλπίς is foundational for our understanding of hope in the rest of the letter as it provides the framework in which Christian hope is to be understood.[128] First, the verse starts with the action of God. It is God who, because of his great mercy, has brought the believer into a new state of being that is characterised by living hope (εἰς ἐλπίδα ζῶσαν).[129] Second, God has done this through the resurrection of Jesus Christ. Therefore, Christian hope, as presented by the author, cannot be separated from God's merciful act in Christ; it is tied to Christ's death and resurrection.[130]

It is obvious that the believer is the subject who has hope, but who is the object and what are they hoping for? 1.3 does not answer these questions explicitly. Is the object God, Christ or something else? The fact that 1.3–5 is particularly theocentric (see Chapter 5) suggests that God is the intended object. This would follow LXX usage. In the LXX God was the object of hope because of his attributes and actions. Therefore, it is fitting that our author introduces hope into a context in

---

[128] Here I see hope as an active emotional stance (Schlosser, *Pierre*, 62), not, against Goppelt, 'that which is hoped for'; Goppelt, *I Peter*, 83; see also Cothenet, 'Le realisme', 565.

[129] Scholars disagree about why 1 Peter describes hope as living. It could be to contrast Christian hope with the vain hopes of the non-believer, or the 'dead hope' of their previous life; see Achtemeier, *1 Peter*, 92, 95; cf. Michaels, *1 Peter*, 19; Jobes, *1 Peter*, 84. However, contra Michaels, it is more likely that their hope is 'living' because it has been effected through Christ's resurrection. Thus, their hope has in view and shares in Christ's resurrection life, hence its animated character; see Feldmeier, *Peter*, 69–70. For Schlosser, due to being linked with the act of regeneration, 'living hope' moves towards meaning simply 'eternal life'; Schlosser, *Pierre*, 63. 1 Peter does not describe hope as living, against Holloway, because of a parallel with the 'better hope' or 'sweeter hope' of the mystery cults; see Holloway, *Coping*, 143–4.

[130] Achtemeier comments that the link between hope as living and the resurrection of Christ is unique to 1 Peter; Achtemeier, *1 Peter*, 95.

which God's characteristic of mercy, his role as Father, and his powerful actions of raising Christ and begetting the believer anew are in view. It is not clear from the noun ἀνάστασις that God is the agent in Christ's resurrection. However, our queries about hope's object and whether God raised Christ are resolved in 1.21 when the author declares that the believers, through Christ, believe

εἰς θεὸν τὸν ἐγείραντα αὐτὸν ἐκ νεκρῶν καὶ δόξαν αὐτῷ δόντα,
ὥστε τὴν πίστιν ὑμῶν καὶ ἐλπίδα εἶναι εἰς θεόν.

in God the one who raised him [Christ] from the dead and gave him glory, so that your faith and hope might be in God.[131]

In 1.21 God is explicitly the object of the believers' hope (cf. 3.5) and the reason given for this is that God raised Christ from the dead and gave him glory.[132] Therefore, in 1.3 we see the same contextualisation of hope as in 1.21: God is the object of hope due to his action in Christ.[133] To display God as the object of hope tells the audience, through hope's evaluative content, to look to God for some good or fulfilment of need and to recognise their own deficiency. Second, it infers that God has the capacity to provide the good needed. With this emotion, the author again reminds the audience of God's role in their flourishing. Moreover, in 1.13 the author commands the audience to hope entirely on God.[134] In doing so, every other object of hope is negated and the believers' dependence on God is emphasised.

So, what good is the audience expectant that God will provide for them? Put differently, what are the believers to hope for? It could be that 1.4–5 provides the content of their hope.[135] In which case, the believers hope for an unfading inheritance, God's protection, and their ultimate salvation. However, the problem with this

---

[131] With Achtemeier, contra Elliott, I do not take the absence of the article before ἐλπίδα to indicate that it should be viewed as the predicate, which would result in the translation 'your faith is hope in God', but rather it is stylistic, 'with the τήν before πίστιν understood also to apply to ἐλπίδα'; Achtemeier, *1 Peter*, 133; Elliott, *1 Peter*, 379.

[132] Cf. Achtemeier, *1 Peter*, 133.

[133] Cf. Michaels, *1 Peter*, 19–20 who supports God's agency in 1.3; see also Achtemeier, *1 Peter*, 92; Elliott, *1 Peter*, 330, 333.

[134] Cf. Schelkle, *Petrusbriefe*, 44–5 who comments that hope must be entire, there can be nothing undecided in their hope.

[135] Michaels reads it this way when he sees 'hope' as indicating the content (objective) rather than the state of anticipation (subjective); thus, 1.4–5 further expands the content of the objective hope; Michaels, *1 Peter*, 19; cf. Goppelt, *1 Peter*, 85.

is that each benefit is introduced by the preposition εἰς, which also precedes ἐλπίδα ζῶσαν and, thus, stylistically, the benefits and the living hope are put on the same plane: all are consequences of being begotten anew.[136] Further, our discussion on joy has revealed that these benefits are perceived to be, at least in part, a present reality, so, they cannot be hoped for because hope looks towards a future good. Thus, 1.3 does not express clearly the content of the believers' living hope. However, 1.13 is illuminative. It commands:

τελείως ἐλπίσατε ἐπὶ τὴν φερομένην ὑμῖν χάριν ἐν ἀποκαλύψει Ἰησοῦ Χριστοῦ.

hope completely on the grace which will be brought to you at the revelation of Jesus Christ.[137]

The believers are to hope for grace (χάρις). The preposition ἐπί could suggest that grace is the object of hope.[138] However, the fact that χάρις is described as 'being brought to you' (φερομένην ὑμῖν) means that an additional agent is required. Therefore, it makes more sense to see God as the object of hope and as the agent who brings grace.[139] This also fits with hope's future orientation. Grace is hoped for because it is yet to be revealed at Christ's coming revelation.[140] Receiving this grace will result in the fulfilment of the believers' salvation and inheritance, and given the example of Christ, their vindication (cf. 1.5, 9).[141]

Now we can see how hope in God and fear of God provide two parts of the same picture. The revelation of Christ in 1.13 points towards God's final judgement, and 1.17 reminds the audience that they are to fear God as judge in expectation of that day. It is at this

[136] See Achtemeier, *1 Peter*, 92; Schlosser, *Pierre*, 62. Even if new birth is only into hope and inheritance, my argument stands; see Jobes, *1 Peter*, 84.
[137] With Achtemeier, Elliott, and Feldmeier, against Windisch and Michaels I read τελείως as referring to ἐλπίσατε not νήφοντες; Windisch, *katholischen Briefe*, 55; Michaels, *1 Peter*, 55. See Achtemeier, *1 Peter*, 118–19; Elliott, *1 Peter*, 356; Feldmeier, *Peter*, 99. I also take φερομένην though a present participle to have future force due to the reference to the future event of Christ's revelation.
[138] See Michaels, *1 Peter*, 56.
[139] Cf. Achtemeier, *1 Peter*, 119.
[140] Cf. Michaels, *1 Peter*, 56; De Waal Dryden, *Theology*, 100; Thurén, *Argument*, 106–7. This is not to say that all references to grace in 1 Peter are future (cf. 1.2; 5.12).
[141] Thus, Michaels is right to say that 'Peter's "living hope" is more comprehensive than simply being raised individually as Jesus was raised. It includes that but encompasses everything that the Christian community expects as its future divine vindication'; Michaels, *1 Peter*, 20; cf. Goppelt, *I Peter*, 107. For some, grace becomes equivalent to salvation; Cothenet, 'Le realisme', 89; Schlosser, *Pierre*, 89.

point of judgement that the believer stands before God in both fear
and hope because God is the only one that can bestow or withhold his
favour, favour with which her flourishing is bound. She can depend
on nothing else. Yet, the weight falls on hope, with fear of God being
sandwiched between two strong references to hoping in God (1.13, 21).

But what is the basis for the believers' hope? For Achtemeier, ἐπὶ
τὴν φερομένην ὑμῖν χάριν gives the grounds of hope.[142] But, grace
cannot be what is hoped for *and* the basis of hope. Instead, we need
to come full circle back to 1.3. It is God's mercy towards the believer
demonstrated in the Christ-event that is the basis for hope.[143] As
Feldmeier succinctly comments concerning biblical hope: 'Such a
hope is not founded upon the unstable foundation of human expectation and fears but on the certainty of the trustworthiness of God;
it bases itself *not on something* that one wishes to obtain or avoid
but *on God, the basis and content of hope.*'[144] God's character – his
mercy and justice – and past actions support their future expectation.
Through Christ, God's mercy has begotten them anew, and now they
understand themselves to be God's people, marked by his mercy
(2.10). If they remain faithful to God they can expect that he will
act favourably towards them at the point of judgement.[145] Then, they
will experience the goodness of his grace in full.[146] This is striking,
because it means that the basis of the believers' hope is God's own
affection towards them.[147] Yet, it is also God's power that enables
hope.[148] The resurrection and glorification of Christ demonstrate
God's power and authority and therefore the Christ-event becomes
a grounding rationale for why hope in God is fitting (1.21).[149] This

---

[142] Achtemeier, *1 Peter*, 119; cf. Elliott who reads 1.13 similarly; Elliott, *1 Peter*, 356.

[143] Because Elliott interprets 1.13 as indicating Christ's historical appearance, he
sees the believer's present experience of grace, rather than God's mercy, as the basis
of hope, and therefore hope looks towards the final consummation of that grace;
Elliott, *1 Peter*, 357. For Schelkle ἔλεος is God's salvation deed in Christ; Schelkle,
Petrusbriefe, 27. But this is the action that results from God's mercy. Like in the LXX,
ἔλεος indicates his steadfast covenant love and faithfulness; see Jobes, *1 Peter*, 82.

[144] Feldmeier, *Peter*, 67 (emphasis original).

[145] Cf. Jobes, *1 Peter*, 110.

[146] In this understanding sits the background that in biblical tradition God's mercy
'is a prominent characteristic of God's goodness towards His people'. It expresses an
'intimate relationship' between God and his people; Elliott, *1 Peter*, 331.

[147] Cf. Feldmeier, *Peter*, 64–5 for the uniqueness of this in the ancient world.

[148] Elliott emphasises confidence in God's power as a key component of hope in 1
Peter; Elliott, *1 Peter*, 334–5.

[149] Cf. Michaels who notes that the tone of 1.3–5 in comparison to 1.2 is that of
God's power; Michaels, *1 Peter*, 24. For Cothenet, the Christian can hope because
they can already celebrate God's victory. Everything is done in principle, it is just
waiting for consummation; Cothenet, 'Le realisme', 565.

attribute of power is important, as hope depends on God having the capacity to act for the believers to bring about their good.[150] Thus, the powerful resurrection of Christ becomes the guarantee of the believers' future.[151]

Furthermore, there is an expectation that those who align themselves with Christ through faith will share in Christ's glorification (4.13; 5.1). As Feldmeier comments, 'God has revealed himself in the fate of Christ as the one who can and will transform the lowness, suffering, and death of those who belong to him into triumph, glory and eternal life.'[152] Therefore, as God acted for Christ, so he will act for the faithful believer.[153] We see this relationship between God's grace and the believers' glorification clearly stated in 5.10:

ὁ δὲ θεὸς πάσης χάριτος, ὁ καλέσας ὑμᾶς εἰς τὴν αἰώνιον αὐτοῦ δόξαν ἐν Χριστῷ ὀλίγον παθόντας αὐτὸς καταρτίσει, στηρίξει, σθενώσει, θεμελιώσει.

The God of all grace, the one having called you into his eternal glory in Christ, after you have suffered a little while, he will restore, secure, strengthen, and firmly establish you.

This glorification is 'in Christ' and therefore requires the believers' association with him. What is notable here is the wealth of securing terms that are used. Their hope in God for his grace will lead to their glorification and future security. Notably, it is God's agency that brings about the goods. Here, we must remember that hope, by looking to another for the good, recognises one's own lack. Therefore, the author's statement that they should hope completely on God for his grace (1.13) divests the audience of any power over its own situation.[154] For their eternal security, their only hope is God and Christ (1.9). As such, they are required to live a life of utter dependence.

Before moving on to discuss the next occurrences of hope in 1 Peter, there are still two matters to explore. First, how does hoping in God relate to the mind (διάνοια) and being sober (νήφω)? Lastly, can hope and faith be differentiated?

---

[150] It is therefore not surprising that in 3.15 the believers' hope comes after their acceptance of Christ as their Lord.

[151] Schelkle, *Petrusbriefe*, 28; Jobes, *1 Peter*, 109.

[152] Feldmeier, *Peter*, 120.

[153] Cf. Elliott, *1 Peter*, 379.

[154] Likewise, it cuts 'all cords of security to false gods'; De Waal Dryden, *Theology*, 100.

In 1.13 the exhortation to hope (ἐλπίσατε) is the main verb after two other actions: girding up the loins of the mind (ἀναζωσάμενοι τὰς ὀσφύας τῆς διανοίας ὑμῶν) and being sober (νήφοντες). Sequentially, the aorist participle ἀναζωσάμενοι occurs before ἐλπίζω, and the present participle νήφοντες happens concurrently.[155] Thus, the audience has to prepare their minds; then, in a state of soberness they can hope fully.[156] This reveals that, for the author, hope is not a fleeting fancy but occurs when one has clear thinking. True hope is based on having the right perspective on reality.[157] From hope's future orientation, object, and content, we can appreciate that their outlook is to be eschatologically orientated, centred on God, anticipating God's coming grace because of Christ.[158] This perspective sets the tone for the following paraenesis (1.14–17).[159] It is the emotion of hope that directs the reader to what should be valued in their sober judgements.[160] Consequently, hope is necessary for conditioning the believer's behaviour.[161] As Piper comments, behaviour springs from hope that sees the value of the coming grace, for 'we inevitably conform our behaviour to the future we desire most of all to enjoy'.[162]

This orienting aspect of hope helps us see how it relates to faith: hope sets the destination, but faith (or faithfulness) provides the map and the means. How we read πίστις and πιστεύω, whether as faith or faithfulness, determines how we interpret its interrelationship with hope. It appears that in 1 Peter both senses are meant, as

[155] See Achtemeier, *1 Peter*, 118.
[156] Therefore, I read the participles as imperatival rather than indicating that the audience are already in a state of readiness; see Thurén, *Argument*, 106–7. However, this sequential reading is not affected if, as Achtemeier (following Daube) suggests, the participles are not strictly imperatival but instead reflect more 'the kind of people who can benefit from such an imperative [ἐλπίσατε]'; Achtemeier, *1 Peter*, 117–18.
[157] Cf. Achtemeier, *1 Peter*, 95; Feldmeier, *Peter*, 100–1. Michaels argues that διάνοια 'has in view not the natural human intellect but a capacity that is theirs by virtue of their redemption in Jesus Christ', as opposed to the ignorance of their former way of life. Thus, it means their new Christian understanding; Michaels, *1 Peter*, 54.
[158] Cf. Schelkle, *Petrusbriefe*, 44; Jobes, *1 Peter*, 110.
[159] For Michaels, 1.16–17 makes explicit the 'ethical content' of hope, which is holiness and fear of God; Michaels, *1 Peter*, 52.
[160] Thus, Holloway correctly recognises that the author aims to reorient the believer's hope 'away from the present age ... toward an apocalyptic future' and in doing so to make the values of the future world central. According to Holloway, this perspective enables the audience to emotionally distance itself from a problematic domain to a new apocalyptic one. This is an instance of 'psychological disidentification', which is a recognised coping strategy; Holloway, *Coping*, 156–9.
[161] Cf. Feldmeier, *Peter*, 96.
[162] J. Piper, 'Hope as the Motivation of Love: 1 Peter 3.9–12', *NTS* 26 (1980): 212–30, at 216.

belief is always turned into action.[163] Therefore, hope tells the audience what goal to have and who is significant for the attainment of that goal. Faith, as belief in the gospel about Christ, provides the worldview in which this contextualisation of hope makes sense.[164] Faithfulness – the action of fidelity to God in Christ – provides the means to attain the goal hoped for. In terms of what it looks like in real life, active hope is essentially the same as active faith, that is, faithfulness.[165] Both have to be enduring to reach the desired eternal outcome.

This link between hope, faith, and faithfulness leads us to the remaining two instances of hope in 1 Peter.

Hope as a Declaration of Allegiance: 1 Peter 3.5, 15

The next reference to hope comes in the household code material addressed to the wives (3.1–6). The holy ancient female exemplars are held up as those who hoped in God (αἱ ἐλπίζουσαι εἰς θεόν, 3.5). In this usage, hoping in God becomes a defining marker along with holiness.[166] This intimates two further things: first, that such people are pleasing to God (cf. 3.4) and, second, that hoping in God distinguishes you from others that do not. As such, hoping in God defines his people. Here we see echoes of the LXX idea that hoping in God is declaring God to be your god. Another similarity with LXX usage is that hoping in God is directly linked to behaviour. The holy wives hope in God and therefore adorn themselves with an attitude of heart that results in submissive behaviour.[167] From the context this is paralleled with doing good (ἀγαθοποιέω; 3.6). If this is the case, this use of ἐλπίζω reveals that hoping in God is an emotional stance that shows allegiance (faithfulness) and is worked out in behaviour.

The last occurrence of hope terminology appears in 3.15, where the author says:

---

[163] Cf. Achtemeier, *1 Peter*, 132 who interprets πιστοὺς εἰς in 1.21 as active trust.

[164] Cothenet thinks that faith and hope should be kept distinct. Faith relates to the past action of the resurrection of Christ, whereas hope looks to future glory; Cothenet, 'Le realisme', 567.

[165] Cf. Goppelt, *1 Peter*, 108.

[166] It could be that the author wants us to understand hoping in God as a dimension of their holiness; Achtemeier, *1 Peter*, 215.

[167] As Horrell comments, the inner attitude of the heart is displayed in a way of life; Horrell, 'Fear', 415.

ἕτοιμοι ἀεὶ πρὸς ἀπολογίαν παντὶ τῷ αἰτοῦντι ὑμᾶς λόγον
περὶ τῆς ἐν ὑμῖν ἐλπίδος.

be ready always to answer anyone who asks you for an
account concerning the hope within you.

Here, ἐλπίς covers the whole content of the believers' defence. We
know from our previous discussion that what is causing conflict is
the believers' association with Christ and their resultant Christian
behaviour (3.16).[168] Therefore, for the author, the believers' 'hope'
is a full explanation of why they have such an allegiance and conduct.[169] As Achtemeier comments, one might expect the author to
say 'faith' here. Achtemeier concludes, 1 Peter uses hope, because
' "hope" describes for our author the characteristic element of the
Christian life'.[170] This is true, but there is more to it than this. The
use of hope makes sense when we understand what is contained
in hoping in God. Hope provides the orientation toward a particular object (God) and looks towards particular goods (grace)
and desired ends (salvation, inheritance, establishing, vindication).
This gives information about what should be valued (one's relationship with God) and in turn promotes particular behaviour (belief in
and fidelity to God demonstrated in obedient behaviour). Thus, as
Achtemeier comments concerning 1.3, 'hope ... functions as the content of the Christian life'.[171] Consequently, to explain their hope is
not only to confess Christ as Lord (cf. 3.15a) but is to open up for the
accuser a whole way of seeing the world. This emotional orientation
distinguishes them from the rest of society.[172] As noted in Chapter 6,
this confrontation of worldviews is the cause of persecution but also
a window for witness. The explanation of their hope is a significant

[168] Due to space, I will not enter the debate about whether a courtroom situation
is in view here. The general position has been against this. However, more recently,
others have argued in favour of it being a likely possibility; see Holloway, *Coping*,
202–5; Williams, *Persecution*, 275–97; Horrell, 'Fear', 425–8.

[169] Cf. Achtemeier, *1 Peter*, 232–3. Achtemeier confirms that explaining their hope
is a declaration of allegiance when he says that 3.15b defines how the Christian is to
acknowledge the Lordship of Christ.

[170] Achtemeier, *1 Peter*, 233.

[171] Achtemeier, *1 Peter*, 95; cf. Windisch, *katholischen Briefe*, 70.

[172] Therefore, I agree with Michaels and Achtemeier that ἐν ὑμῖν probably means
'among you' and thus indicates the shared Christian hope that marks them as
Christians rather than hope being located 'in' the individual; Michaels, *1 Peter*, 188–9;
Achtemeier, *1 Peter*, 233–4; cf. Jobes, *1 Peter*, 230.

part of such witness.[173] Therefore, in both 3.5 and 3.15 hope is a declaration of allegiance. As such, it produces and makes sense of particular behaviour. Because of this, hope becomes important for the maintenance of Christian praxis and the possibility of Christian witness.

In the course of exploring fear and hope, we have pulled out some implications of the author's use of these emotions. However, we are yet to outline the sociological and therapeutic outcomes of his rhetoric. To this we can now turn.

Implications for the Believer

Both fear and hope direct the audience towards God. Furthermore, both fear and hope emphasise God's power over the good. Fear warns that God has the power to harm, and hope gives assurance that because of Christ he is willing to act mercifully. Because both emotions are future orientated they anticipate outcomes that have not occurred yet and so cause the believers to consider their present actions in light of future expectations. Fear seeks avoidance of harm, and hope encourages pursuit of the object that promises the good.[174] The net effect of both is that hope and fear spur the believers toward seeking allegiance to God. All this sits within an understanding of a cosmic reality in which God is the ultimate power, judge, and final arbiter of the fate of the believer. But, at the same time, he is the God who has demonstrated his mercy through Christ and begotten the believers into a new existence.

Recognising God as the most significant power and the only hope shapes the believers' perspective on other figures of power in their lives. By revaluing the power dynamics with the other and by disregarding the goods that the other has mastery over, the author is radically changing the audience's perspective of the structuring of reality, including its value systems.[175] Consequently, the norms that uphold these structures can also be questioned. As such, encouraging fear of God and hope in him alone, while negating fear of the other, psychologically releases the believers to behave in ways

---

[173] Piper even argues that such hope can give the reason for going one stage further in being able to bless their persecutors; Piper, 'Hope', 217.

[174] As Feldmeier recognises, hope moves one 'to imagine the future and so to plan'; Feldmeier, *Peter*, 66.

[175] Through his specific contextualisation of hope the author has also highlighted which goods are to be valued. In this case, it is God's grace that leads to other benefits: salvation, glorification, and security.

considered deviant to Greco-Roman society. Negating fear asks the believers to see their relationship to society differently. Whereas previously they were subordinate members who acted out of fear of their persecutors, now they live by different norms – those aligned with fear of and hope in God. Through encouraging this emotional stance, the author creates space for the believers to have a new group identity: they are those that fear and hope in God.[176] Consequently, the author's use of fear and hope has the potential to reshape the audience's allegiances and sense of identity.

We have also become aware that fearing God places boundaries on the believers' lives and that hoping in God is a declaration of aligning oneself with him. Both are demonstrated in behaviour that conforms to God's holiness. In such a way, these emotional stances draw a dividing line between the believer and the other that is made obvious in conduct (ἀναστροφὴ ἐν φόβῳ versus ματαία ἀναστροφή, 1.17–18).[177] From the believers' perspective, despite being defamed for their Christianity, they can recognise that, in fact, the non-believer is deviant and that the believer is on the right path. Because they have chosen to align themselves with God, they can expect that he is on their side and will act favourably towards them. This is explicitly put forward in 3.12, which quotes Psalm 33.16–7:

> ὅτι ὀφθαλμοὶ κυρίου ἐπὶ δικαίους
> καὶ ὦτα αὐτοῦ εἰς δέησιν αὐτῶν,
> πρόσωπον δὲ κυρίου ἐπὶ ποιοῦντας κακά.

> because the eyes of the Lord are upon the righteous
> and his ears [open] to their prayer,
> but the face of the Lord is against those who do evil.

This is why the author can also say to the audience πᾶσαν τὴν μέριμναν ὑμῶν ἐπιρίψαντες ἐπ' αὐτόν, ὅτι αὐτῷ μέλει περὶ ὑμῶν (Cast all your anxiety on him, because he cares for you; 5.7, NRSVA). With this perspective, fear and hope produce confidence and absence of turmoil (see μηδὲ ταραχθῆτε, 3.14).[178] The believers, who were no doubt some of the weakest in society, do not have to perceive of themselves

---

[176] Cf. Feldmeier, *Peter*, 68.

[177] Achtemeier supports this division when he comments that holiness 'is separation from former culture for God that entails certain behavior appropriate for this situation'; Achtemeier, *1 Peter*, 121, 123–4; cf. Elliott, *1 Peter*, 361–2.

[178] As Aristotle noted, confidence can be produced by our own strength against the foe, or if a powerful figure is on our side (*Rhet.* 2.5.17, 1383a20–5).

as downtrodden or at the mercy of the fearsome oppressor. If, as argued, living in fear of and hope in God displaces the mastery of the other and affirms that one's flourishing is dependent on one's relationship with God, then the believer can have psychological fortitude in the face of abuse.[179] The believers know that they are deliberately choosing their behaviour in line with eternal reality, not because they are dominated by an oppressive human power, but because they are aligning themselves with God, in the trust that such faith/faithfulness will end in good. These are not disempowered, anxious individuals. True, they are subordinates in human society and will remain so, but they are active players in their own eternal destinies.[180] Having said that the believers have agency over their present orientation and action, hope reminds the believers of their deficiency and that, when it comes to eternal outcomes, they are utterly dependent on God.[181]

Whereas for the Stoics hope was unstable and a misplaced longing, for the believers their hope in God's mercy and justice is secure.[182] This is because, like in the LXX, hope is made secure by its object – God – and is grounded in events that have already happened.[183] As such, dependency is not unstable but an anchor. The goods to which the believer looks are in part already present, but are still yet to be fulfilled. However, the fact that they have been initiated gives the believers assurance that their hope is not vain.[184] Again, the fact that their hope and fear are reactions to an eternal reality means that they can become consistent dispositions regardless of circumstance. Moreover, fearing God as a just judge will also help them trust that he will reward their faithfulness and call their abusers to account. Thus, they do not need to repay evil for evil (2.23; 3.12; 4.19).[185]

---

[179] For Brox, the letter's presentation of lack of fear in the face of abuse displays the early phase of the development of the virtue of fearlessness in the face of formidableness, which is later praised in martyr literature; Brox, *Petrusbrief*, 159.

[180] Thus, I find Bird's continual representation of the audience as hopeless, isolated, silent victims problematic; Bird, *Abuse*, 121–3. However, this does not stop me from agreeing with Bird that as modern readers we need to be conscious of how we use these texts in creating paradigms for women generally and those suffering abuse today.

[181] Elliott rightly comments, 'believers confidently trust and entrust themselves to God (4:19), not only in the present but until life's end'; Elliott, *1 Peter*, 380.

[182] Cf. Feldmeier, who notes that 1 Peter's 'high theological valuation of hope … stands in marked contrast to the evaluation of hope in … Hellenistic culture'; Feldmeier, *Peter*, 65.

[183] Schlosser, *Pierre*, 62–3.

[184] Cf. Schelkle, *Petrusbriefe*, 28.

[185] Thurén, *Argument*, 206.

Conclusion

It is clear from the above discussion that 1 Peter's use of fear and hope is closer to the LXX contextualisation of emotions than the Stoic idealisation. Whereas for the Stoic both fear and hope are problematic emotions because they allow another to have mastery and look outside of the self for the good, for the author of 1 Peter they are necessary states. This is because fear and hope have been affected by having God as their object. Instead of being turbulent, fear of God is positive, sets necessary boundaries, and provides vital information about how to live in such a way as to avoid harm. Likewise, hope orientates the person, displays where the good lies, and who has power to bestow it. Both fear and hope aim to shape the recipients' goals and as such are directive of their behaviour, encouraging fidelity to God. This emotional stance goes hand in hand with negating fear of the other. By discounting negative fear, the believers are released from assessing their current position in relation to the other. Via this rhetorical manoeuvre the author shifts the believers' view of themselves and the structures of power within their worldview. The consequence is that the link between the self, the other, and necessary goods is severed, and subsequently, a way is paved for potential deviance. The believers' present situation is not radically altered, but fear and hope in God do give the believer confidence that they are on the path to flourishing, even in the face of oppression. With conformity and deviance in mind, we can turn to the final emotion under investigation: shame.

8

APPROPRIATE AND INAPPROPRIATE SHAME

In this final exegetical chapter we will explore the last emotion: shame.[1] It is not new to recognise that honour and shame language appears in 1 Peter. Two works have addressed this directly: first, John Elliott's short article, 'Disgraced Yet Graced', and, second, Barth Campbell's monograph, *Honor, Shame, and the Rhetoric of 1 Peter*.[2] Elliott takes as his starting point sociological work on honour and shame cultures, whereas Campbell opts for a rhetorical approach but includes sociological theory throughout. However, neither adequately details the importance of *shame* language in the letter. Campbell, in particular, focuses on honour, and so, for example, in 4.16 where the author says 'but if [you suffer] as a Christian, do not be ashamed', the shame terminology is read by Campbell in the positive as a bestowal of honour.[3] I agree that honour terms are important in the letter for affirming, theologically and rhetorically, the positive identity of the audience. However, the shame terminology functions in its own right, and, therefore, warrants its own investigation.[4]

---

[1] An abridged version of some sections of this chapter along with certain methodological ideas present in Chapter 2 above have been previously published in K. M. Hockey, '1 Peter 4.16: Shame, Emotion and Christian Self-Perception', in *Muted Voices of the New Testament: Readings in the Catholic Epistles and Hebrews*, ed. Katherine M. Hockey, Madison N. Pierce, and Francis Watson (London: Bloomsbury T&T Clark, 2017), 27–40. Content is reprinted here with permission from Bloomsbury T&T Clark.

[2] J. H. Elliott, 'Disgraced Yet Graced: The Gospel according to 1 Peter in the Key of Honor and Shame', *BTB* 25 (1995): 166–78; Campbell, *Honour*.

[3] Campbell, *Honor*, 213.

[4] There has been much scholarship on honour and shame as a socio-cultural phenomenon in the ancient world. However, I will not enter this discussion. I am interested in shame as an *emotion* and its function within the discourse of the letter. This will require sensitivity to socio-cultural dynamics, but, I hope, in keeping the argument clear of this secondary discussion, that the function of the emotion can stand prominently in view.

Elliott highlights various terms that relate to honour and shame in 1 Peter. Three terms are placed within the 'shame' family: καταισχύνω (2.6; 3.16), αἰσχύνω (4.16), and αἰσχροκερδῶς (5.2).[5] The latter adverb refers to shameful greed, and therefore highlights a quality of behaviour rather than an emotion per se. Thus, καταισχύνω and αἰσχύνω will be the focus of our investigation.[6] We will start by locating shame within the emotional terrain, first using Stoic theory and then moving to the LXX.[7] In order to do this, we need to include the cognate noun αἰσχύνη to our list of terms.

Locating Shame

αἰσχύνη in Stoicism

As noted in Chapter 7 (p. 180), αἰσχύνη is grouped under fear. So, we can expect shame to carry the components of fear outlined in the previous chapter. Andronicus defines shame as follows:

Αἰσχύνη δὲ φόβος ἀδοξίας.

Shame is fear of ill repute/dishonour. ([*Pass.*] 3 = SVF 3.409)[8]

As a type of fear, shame relates to an expected harm, in this instance, dishonour. Thus, shame evaluates dishonour negatively as detrimental. From fear's action-tendency, we can infer that shame presents dishonour as something to avoid. In ancient honour–shame cultures honour was the highest commodity and one did not want to be without it, that is, dishonoured.[9] By grouping αἰσχύνη under the πάθος fear, Stoicism labels αἰσχύνη irrational and excessive. Presumably, like all passions, it is possible for shame to be based on a faulty judgement that wrongly assesses what is honourable and dishonourable and thus motivates the person incorrectly.[10] Lastly,

---

[5] Elliott, 'Disgraced', 174–5.

[6] Both verbs can have the sense of 'to be shamed' and to 'feel ashamed'; see 'αἰσχύνω' and 'καταισχύνω' in BDAG (30, 517); cf. LSJ (43, 892).

[7] I have chosen not to address honour in 1 Peter because honour is not categorised as an emotion in the ancient world. Though both honour and shame can be ascribed from the outside, it seems that honour does not reflect the same kind of internal emotional state as shame. Honour instead is a good that can be attained; it is a commodity not an emotion; cf. Graver, *Stoicism*, 157–8. For Aristotle, for example, the opposite to shame is shamelessness, not honour; see Konstan, *Emotions*, 99.

[8] Cf. Diogenes Laertius 7.112 = SVF 3.407; Stobaeus, *Ecl.* = SVF 3.408.

[9] Cf. Cicero, *Tusc.* 2.24.58–9; Elliott, 'Disgraced', 168–9.

[10] αἰδώς is the counterpart εὐπάθεια.

whereas fear has an obvious future orientation, the temporal aspect of shame is less clear. We can see this from Aristotle's definition:

ἔστω δὴ αἰσχύνη λύπη τις ἢ ταραχὴ περὶ τὰ εἰς ἀδοξίαν φαινόμενα φέρειν τῶν κακῶν, ἢ παρόντων ἢ γεγονότων ἢ μελλόντων.

> Let shame [aiskhynē] be [defined as] a sort of pain and agitation concerning the class of evils, whether present or past or future, that seem to bring a person into disrespect. (*Rhet.* 2.6, 1383b12–14, trans. Kennedy)[11]

Aristotle's definition is fuller than Andronicus' and highlights aspects of shame not obvious in the Stoic delineation. First, shame is concerned with certain evils (τῶν κακῶν). It is not clear what τῶν κακῶν refers to. Freese (LCL) translates τῶν κακῶν as 'misdeeds'. This is supported by Aristotle's use of ἔργα to introduce the type of vice-ridden actions indicated by τῶν κακῶν (*Rhet.* 2.6, 1383b). Furthermore, Aristotle goes on to list behaviour that would be so categorised.[12] Therefore, we can conclude that wrong actions are what bring someone into disrepute, and thus are productive of shame.[13] Subsequently, a virtuous person would not feel shame because he would not exhibit behaviour that would instigate it (*Eth. nic.* 4.9, 1128b21–2). Misdeeds that cause shame can be one's own or the wrongful actions of one's associates (cf. *Rhet.* 2.6, 1383b15–18, 1384a9–11, 1385a37–9). However, the actions that reveal a person's deficiency are considered most shameful (*Rhet.* 2.6, 1384a13–15; cf. Seneca, *Ep.* 95.9). In both of these cases the object of shame is the self, either as an individual or as a member of a group. If Aristotle is correct, then shame, more clearly than any emotion investigated thus far, highlights a person's behaviour, categorising it negatively.[14]

---

[11] Aristotle uses both αἰσχύνη and αἰδώς to refer to types of shame. In *Eth. nic.* 4.9, 1128b10–12 he defines αἰδώς as φόβος τις ἀδοξίας. Thus, for Aristotle, like the Stoics, shame can exhibit qualities of fear in that it is anticipatory. For more on the relationship between αἰσχύνη and αἰδώς see Konstan, *Emotions*, 93–9.

[12] For Aristotle, the wrongful actions are due to faults of character such as cowardice, injustice, and licentiousness; cf. Epictetus, *Diatr.* 3.26.1.

[13] See Konstan, *Emotions*, 100–1. Cf. Nemesius, *De Natura Hominis* 20 (SVF 3.416), who links shame with shameful deeds. Though Nemesius is fourth century, he follows Stoic groupings, placing shame under fear, and also speaks of shame as depressing (καταδύω). He, however, does distinguish between shame (αἰσχύνη) and self-respect (αἰδώς), which he argues the ancients wrongly used interchangeably. For Nemesius, αἰδώς is concerned with loss of reputation, αἰσχύνη focuses on actions.

[14] For Epictetus, one can be ashamed on account of both thinking (ἐνθυμούμενος) and doing (ποιῶν) (*Diatr.* 2.8.14).

If we follow this reasoning, shame is deeply tied to the norms of a given cultural group. For, how can one assess that behaviour is deviant without having some standard to evaluate it by? The culture in which one lives, and more importantly, to which one subscribes provides the framework for categorisation. Thus, shame views the self from this socio-cultural perspective.[15] As Taylor comments: 'in experiencing one of these emotions [pride, humiliation, shame, and guilt] the person concerned believes of herself that she has deviated from some norm and that in doing so she has altered her standing in the world. The self is the "object" of these emotions, and what is believed amounts to an assessment of that self.'[16] Even though the self is shame's object, the other is significant for the occurrence of shame. Taylor explains that shame requires an audience, 'for feeling shame is connected with the thought that eyes are upon one'.[17] She also highlights that *how* one is seen is important. It is not enough that there is a 'seeing' audience, there has to be a 'judging' one.[18] Only through seeing oneself from the other's critical viewpoint does the person recognise the deviant nature of her behaviour.[19] The other's reproach (or expected reproach) produces a sense of shame (cf. Seneca, *Ep.* 94.44). Of course, one has to value the audience for shame to occur. Aristotle recognises this when he comments that one only feels ashamed before those one esteems and therefore whose opinion one cares about (*Rhet.* 2.6, 1384a21–5 cf. 2.6, 1384b23–6; *Eth. eud.* 3.7.3, 1233b26–9; Epictetus, *Diatr.* 3.9.7).[20] The individual may care about the other's judgement purely for the sake of status, or she may desire to appear honourable because she needs the esteem of the other to secure necessary goods (*Rhet.* 2.6, 1384b27–31). Therefore, honour can be the good in itself, or it can be the route to other benefits. Shame fears losing either of these goods, and thus, like fear, gives power to the other.[21] Furthermore, if honour is esteem in the eyes of the other and to be dishonoured is an evil, then the other has the capacity to harm the person.

[15] Cf. G. Taylor, *Pride, Shame, and Guilt: Emotions of Self Assessment* (Oxford: Clarendon Press, 1985), 54.
[16] Taylor, *Pride*, 1.
[17] Taylor, *Pride*, 53; cf. Konstan, *Emotions*, 103.
[18] Taylor, *Pride*, 60, 64–5.
[19] Taylor, *Pride*, 58; cf. Epictetus, *Diatr.* 4.1.18.
[20] Cf. Elliott, 'Disgraced', 168.
[21] In this instance, power does not necessarily indicate authoritarian status; shame can be instigated by the opinion of a rival, equal, or fellow group member.

Exposure is also a key aspect of shame. Aristotle comments:

καὶ τὰ ἐν ὀφθαλμοῖς καὶ τὰ ἐν φανερῷ μᾶλλον· ὅθεν καὶ ἡ παροιμία, τὸ ἐν ὀφθαλμοῖς εἶναι αἰδῶ. διὰ τοῦτο τοὺς ἀεὶ παρεσομένους μᾶλλον αἰσχύνονται καὶ τοὺς προσέχοντας αὐτοῖς, διὰ τὸ ἐν ὀφθαλμοῖς ἀμφότερα.

They are also more ashamed of things that are done before their eyes and in broad daylight; whence the proverb, 'The eyes are the abode of shame'. That is why they feel more ashamed before those who are likely to be always with them or who keep watch upon them, because in both cases they are under the eyes of others. (*Rhet.* 2.6, 1384a33–1384b1 [Freese, LCL])

For shame to occur, one's faults being *revealed* for what they are is crucial.[22] The miscreant action alone does not necessarily produce shame, but shame is generated when the fault is exposed.[23] Having said this, the fear that they will be exposed to one's detriment can lead to anticipatory shame.

Modern theorists, such as Taylor, have demonstrated the complex relationship between the self and the other evidenced in feeling shame. For Taylor, shame is an emotion of self-assessment that makes one aware of one's standing in the world.[24] For an honour–shame culture it is not so easy to distinguish between self-esteem and public esteem. If honour is the only way to know one's value then loss of honour inevitably means loss of self-value and identity. In such a culture 'a person can assess himself only in terms of what the public thinks of him'.[25] Put differently, shame sees the self with the eyes of the other.[26] The other here is specifically the 'honour-group' to which one subscribes and whose norms one judges oneself by.[27] Moreover, to feel shame one has to *accept* the judgement of the self from the viewpoint of the other.[28] This means seeing oneself as

---

[22] Conversely, shamelessness does not care about exposure. One is willing to parade before people actions or attitudes that others might consider faults; see Cicero, *De or.* 2.62.233.
[23] For Epictetus, the examining eyes can be internal, for the god who lives within watches everything, even one's thinking (*Diatr.* 2.8.9–14).
[24] Taylor, *Pride*, 1, 53.
[25] Taylor, *Pride*, 55; cf. Elliott, 'Disgraced', 168.
[26] Taylor, *Pride*, 57.
[27] Taylor, *Pride*, 55.
[28] Taylor, *Pride*, 56–7.

deviant and devalued. Therefore, shame does not just evaluate one's actions, it makes a judgement on the self.

In Greco-Roman thought, feeling shame can have a positive function because it guides someone towards correct conduct (Seneca, *Ep.* 10.2; Cicero, *Tusc.* 4.20.45). Shame itself is not good, but an ability to *feel* shame is, because it shows a regard for norms and an understanding of norm transgression.[29] Consequently, shame performs both an ethical and a social function because desiring to avoid dishonour motivates one to live within the norms of the community.[30] However, Seneca does temper such compliance by recognising that one may choose to endure shame if the goods obtained by the disgraceful action are valuable enough (*Ep.* 81.27–9).[31]

So, we can conclude that shame is fear of dishonour. It evaluates dishonour as detrimental to flourishing and encourages avoidance of ill-repute. Dishonour is brought about by the person's own misdeeds and, therefore, shame discourages the person from pursuing deviant actions and promotes adhesion to defined norms. Shame has the self as the object but assesses the self through the norms of the critical 'seeing' other. Consequently, shame not only evaluates one's actions, but also judges the self and therefore shapes one's self-perception and identity. Moreover, to feel shame shows the value placed on the opinion of the other. As such, the other, in both establishing norms and providing honour (and goods dependent on honour), is given power over the flourishing of the individual. With this in mind, we can turn to the LXX use of shame.

Shame in the LXX

The use of shame in the LXX shows similarities with what we have discovered from Greco-Roman material thus far. First, shame is fitting when someone (or a select group) has acted badly (Sir 5.13–14; 20.26; 41.17–42.18).[32] However, the primary action that causes shame is disobedience to God. Baruch 1.15–18 says:

Τῷ κυρίῳ θεῷ ἡμῶν ἡ δικαιοσύνη, ἡμῖν δὲ αἰσχύνη τῶν προσώπων ὡς ἡ ἡμέρα αὕτη, ἀνθρώπῳ Ιουδα καὶ τοῖς

---

[29] Cf. Cicero, *De or.* 1.28.130.
[30] Cf. Seneca, *Ep.* 25.2–3; Aristotle, *Eth. eud.* 3.1, 1229a13–14, 1230a16–21.
[31] For Seneca, such behaviour indicates misplaced values.
[32] See Sir 41.17–42.18 for a list of which actions someone should and should not be ashamed of.

κατοικοῦσιν Ιερουσαλημ καὶ τοῖς βασιλεῦσιν ἡμῶν καὶ τοῖς ἄρχουσιν ἡμῶν καὶ τοῖς ἱερεῦσιν ἡμῶν καὶ τοῖς προφήταις ἡμῶν καὶ τοῖς πατράσιν ἡμῶν, ὧν ἡμάρτομεν ἔναντι κυρίου καὶ ἠπειθήσαμεν αὐτῷ καὶ οὐκ ἠκούσαμεν τῆς φωνῆς κυρίου θεοῦ ἡμῶν πορεύεσθαι τοῖς προστάγμασιν κυρίου, οἷς ἔδωκεν κατὰ πρόσωπον ἡμῶν.

And you shall say: The Lord our God is in the right, but there is open shame on us today, on the people of Judah, on the inhabitants of Jerusalem, and on our kings, our rulers, our priests, our prophets, and our ancestors, because we have sinned before the Lord. We have disobeyed him, and have not heeded the voice of the Lord our God, to walk in the statutes of the Lord that he set before us. (NRSVACE)[33]

Theses verses highlight communal shame and that shame occurs when wrong actions are seen by another.[34] Here, it is the Lord before whom (ἔναντι κυρίου), that is, in whose sight, they have sinned (cf. Jer 2.26). In the LXX, other humans can also take the place of the observing other. For example, Sirach 41.17–19 lists father, mother, ruler, judge, friend, even the whole assembly (συναγωγή) as people before whom one can be ashamed. Thus, as Aristotle recognised, Sirach highlights figures who are esteemed or close associates. Sirach 41.17–19 also reveals that actions deemed shameful can be specific, e.g. sexual immorality (πορνεία), or general, e.g. lawlessness (ἀνομία) or unrighteousness (ἀδικία). Moreover, like in Greco-Roman thought, shame can occur because of the *reproach* of another (Pss 43.14–16; 68.7–8).

The idiom 'shame of the faces' (αἰσχύνη τῶν προσώπων) in Baruch 1.15 (cf. 2 Chr 32.21; 2 Esd 9.7; Ps 43.16; Dan 9.8) suggests the conspicuity of their fault.[35] The open demonstration of shame is often graphically described through its correlation with bodily exposure (Jdt 9.2; Nah 3.5–7; Isa 20.4; 47.3; Ezek 16.37; 22.10). However, shame can also be depicted as covering or clothing the person (1 Macc 1.28; 3 Macc 6.34; Pss 34.26; 70.13; 108.29; 131.18; Jer 3.25). Such language indicates, in symbolic terms, that shame alters the person's identity: she wears it like a garment before all (including herself).

---

[33] Cf. Gen 2.25; *Pss. Sol.* 9.6; Jer 3.25; 22.22; Ezek 36.32; Dan 9.7–8.
[34] See 1 Kgdms 20.30; 3 Kgdms 18.19; Prov 19.13; Sir 22.3–5; Hab 2.10 for shame by association.
[35] It could be that something like blushing is meant here; cf. Cicero's definition of shame in *Tusc.* 4.8.19.

It is clear from Baruch 1.15–18 and Sir 41.17–19 that particular norms are operating. In both Baruch and Sirach (cf. Sir 42.2) these norms are God's statutes. In the Baruch citation there is an added emphasis on God's righteousness (δικαιοσύνη). God's inherent righteousness means his judgements are correct and, therefore, where he apportions shame, it is fitting. From this it naturally follows that for the obedient there is the promise that they will not be shamed (Sir 24.22; cf. Isa 29.22; 45.16–17; 49.23; 54.4–5). Subsequently, freedom from shame becomes part of the identity of God's people.

At points, God's people appear to be shamed on account of belonging to God (Ps 69.6–8; Dan 3.33). But, those who experience shame because of such allegiance maintain trust in God's righteousness and hope that their accusers will instead be shamed (Dan 3.40; 1 Macc 4.31–2; cf. Pss 34; 68; 88; 118.30–1). It is their righteousness and God's justice that provides the basis for their expectation that they should be shame-free (Ps 118.80; Sir 51.18). The LXX also shows occasions when a godly individual will adhere to God's ways despite public shame. For example, the Suffering Servant of Isaiah refuses to turn away from shame (Isa 50.6). Yet, again, this is turned into a promise that because God is his help he will not be disgraced (Isa 50.7). Thus, we have two perspectives in Isaiah 50: one is the human view; the other is God's truthful reality. In the former the servant is shamed, but in the latter he is not. What sets the two perspectives apart are the norms the servant is assessed by. Isaiah 50.8–9 makes this clear when the servant asks who is able to judge him when the Lord is his help.

Conversely, those who oppose God and his people will be shamed (Pss 118.78; 128.5; 131.18; Isa 41.11; Mic 7.10; Nah 3.4–7; 3 Macc 6.34), as will those who trust in idols (Ps 96.7; Isa 42.17; 44.9–11; 45) or someone other than God (Isa 30.1–5; cf. Prov 29.25; Isa 20.5–6). Again, those who follow God can plead with him to maintain his righteous judgements by requesting that those who revel in evil are shamed (Pss 24.1–3; 34.4, 24–8; 39.14–17; 70.13; 108.28–9). Subsequently, shaming can be seen as part of God's judgement on both Israel and her enemies due to disobedience (Ps 82.14–19; Isa 47.3–4; Ezek 7.10–19).[36] Therefore, shame is generally presented negatively in the LXX. However, we do see, as in the Greco-Roman discussion, that to be without a sense of shame is problematic (cf. Prov 9.13; Sir 29.14). Sirach 29.14 even suggests that a person

---

[36] In Ps 82.18 the shaming is eternal; cf. Isa 45.17; Dan 12.2.

without a sense of shame cannot be a good man (ἀνὴρ ἀγαθός). It must be presumed that this is for the same reason outlined above: a sense of shame shows the ability to recognise norms and deviant behaviour.

Therefore, shame in the LXX shows similarities to the Greco-Roman philosophical understanding. The primary difference is that the most significant observing other is God. It is God who sets the norms and it is his judging eye that determines whether shame is fitting.[37] For both the LXX and Greco-Roman philosophers, a life aligned with correct norms – for the philosophers this is virtue, for the LXX it is God's statutes – can expect to be without shame. For the LXX audience, the expectation of no shame can have an eschato-logical dimension: it will not be shamed even into eternity. With this foundation laid, we can turn to the use of shame in 1 Peter.

Shame in 1 Peter

The use of shame language in 1 Peter will be addressed in two sections: first, its application to the believer, second, to the non-believer.

No Shame in Associating with Christ: 1 Peter 2.4–8; 4.14–16

The first occurrence of a shame term comes in 2.6:

> διότι περιέχει ἐν γραφῇ·
> ἰδοὺ τίθημι ἐν Σιὼν λίθον
> ἀκρογωνιαῖον ἐκλεκτὸν ἔντιμον,
> καὶ ὁ πιστεύων ἐπ' αὐτῷ οὐ μὴ καταισχυνθῇ.

> For it stands in scripture,
> See, I am laying a stone in Zion
> a chosen and honoured cornerstone,
> and the one believing in him with certainly never be (a)shamed.

Verse 2.6 derives from Isaiah 28.16 (LXX), acting as a bridge between 2.4–5 and 2.7–8.[38] The quotation follows the stone imagery

---

[37] Cf. Elliott, 'Disgraced', 167.
[38] Scholars are uncertain about which LXX manuscript form is used by the author; see Michaels, *1 Peter*, 103; Achtemeier, *1 Peter*, 150–2, 159; Elliott, *1 Peter*, 424. Commentators note that ὁ πιστεύων ἐπ' αὐτῷ οὐ μὴ καταισχυνθῇ is similar to καὶ τὰ

in 2.4–5.[39] It repeats the value ascribed to the stone in 2.4 but also develops the thought by making central the role of belief. To agree with Michaels, the 'thrust of the quotation ... comes in the last clause' and thus the weight is on the negation of shame.[40] From 2.3–4 we know that the stone is Christ. Consequently, the phrase ὁ πιστεύων ἐπ' αὐτῷ identifies the Christian believer.[41] Therefore, we can determine that the object of shame here is the believer. As such, the believers are being asked to appropriate the promise that they will certainly not be (a)shamed (οὐ μὴ καταισχυνθῇ). The double negation οὐ μή makes this emphatic. As Brox recognises, this quotation is intended to encourage the audience, but, as we shall see, it does more than this.[42] At this point, it is also necessary to identify three key elements brought together in this quotation: (1) two persons – Christ and the believer; (2) the act of believing; and, (3) the final outcome – not being shamed. We will explore the relationship between these aspects. However, first, we need to decide how to understand καταισχύνω.

I have translated καταισχυνθῇ as (a)shamed. I have opted for this open translation to show that the strict dichotomy between shame as a social status and shame as an emotional experience is misleading; καταισχύνω can cover both objective categorisation and subjective feeling.[43] Furthermore, as discussed above, with shame, the identity and emotions of the individual are closely bound to their group identity and group status. It is problematic to isolate completely being shamed by the community (a passive act and social status) from the loss of identity that the person would experience and, therefore, from the subsequent emotional response of being ashamed.[44] Thus, if an individual identifies with a group and is shamed by that

---

πρόσωπα ὑμῶν οὐ μὴ καταισχυνθῇ in Psalm 33 (v. 6), which has just been quoted (2.3) and will be referenced again in 3.10–12; Selwyn, *St. Peter*, 157–8; Michaels, *1 Peter*, 98, 103; Jobes, *1 Peter*, 145.

[39] The stone imagery links the three scripture quotations used by the author (Isa 28.16; Ps 117.22; Isa 8.14). Though other New Testament passages also use these 'stone' citations as messianic (Matt 21.42; Mark 12.10; Luke 20.17; Rom 9.33), 1 Peter's combination is unique; Michaels, *1 Peter*, 94; see also Goppelt, *1 Peter*, 138–9.

[40] Michaels, *1 Peter*, 103. Achtemeier agrees, but does not go on to discuss the negation of shame here, save to say that the people built through trust in God will be honoured; Achtemeier, *1 Peter*, 160.

[41] The ὑμῖν οὖν in 2.7 emphasises this; cf. Michaels, *1 Peter*, 94–5.

[42] Brox, *Petrusbrief*, 101.

[43] Cf. Goppelt, *1 Peter*, 145. BDAG (517) highlights the subjective emotional aspect of καταισχύνω when it lists 1 Peter 2.6 as an instance when shame includes disappointment.

[44] See Jobes, *1 Peter*, 231 for an example of applying this false dichotomy.

group, then they will both be shamed and *feel* ashamed. This is not the case if the individual does not identify with the group or accept its judgements. In this instance, it is possible that the person could be shamed socially, that is, in the eyes of the other, but have no internal emotional sense of shame. Thus, in order to recognise both the objective status and the emotional experience, I have translated καταισχυνθῇ as 'be (a)shamed'.

Having established that the believers are promised that they will not be (a)shamed, we have to ask the question, who is doing the shaming? Put differently, whose are the critical eyes? There are three options: (1) a human group; (2) God; or, (3) a combination of the two. The first category could encompass humanity as a whole or be a specific socio-cultural group. Given that the reference to shame occurs via a scriptural quotation, it is likely that the LXX conceptual framework, in which God's viewpoint is the primary concern, has been absorbed by the author. This would follow παρὰ θεῷ in 2.4 because παρά 'followed by the dative denotes "in the sight or judgement of someone"'.[45] Thus καταισχυνθῇ is another divine passive (see οἰκοδομεῖσθε (2.5), ἐγενήθη (2.7), ἐτέθησαν (2.8)),[46] which indicates that God's critical judgement is intended.[47] Our exploration of fear revealed that God is the primary judge of action. It is therefore sensible that God should be the judge of whether the believers' actions should result in shame or honour.[48] From this perspective, 2.6 likely refers to the future judgement suggested in 1.13 and 1.17, and, hence, the negation of shame becomes an eschatological outlook.[49] This is supported by Michaels' comments that not being (a)shamed is equivalent to the positive expectation that the believers will experience vindication when Christ appears (cf. 1.7).[50]

Framing Expectations

But what is the reason for the author's confident declaration that the believers will be without shame before God? We have seen that shame is appropriate where there is a transgressing of norms and, therefore, that in the LXX, where there is obedience there will be no

---

[45] Elliott, *1 Peter*, 410.
[46] Cf. Elliott, *1 Peter*, 413, 427.
[47] Cf. Jobes, *1 Peter*, 152–3.
[48] This is in accordance with standard Israelite and early Christian theology; Elliott, *1 Peter*, 427.
[49] Cf. Schelkle, *Petrusbriefe*, 60.
[50] Michaels, *1 Peter*, 104; cf. Schlosser, *Pierre*, 125.

shame. 1 Peter follows this reasoning. However, in 2.6 the believers' lack of shame is on account of their believing in the stone, Christ.[51] On this one act of belief alone the emphatic declaration of 2.6 rests. Logically, this infers that the audience's obedience to God, which negates shame, is its belief in Christ. This is emphasised by the adjoining positive statement that to them, the ones believing, belongs honour (ὑμῖν οὖν ἡ τιμὴ τοῖς πιστεύουσιν).[52] This supports our statement in the previous chapter that, for 1 Peter, the primary act of obedience is putting one's faith in Christ.[53] In 2.7–8 the author shows that the non-believer is judged by the same framework.[54] Thus, Elliott is right in asserting that '[T]he author declares ... one's relations to Jesus Christ to be the ultimate determinant of honor and shame.'[55] The non-Christians are categorised as the unbelieving (ἀπιστοῦσιν, 2.7) who are disobedient (ἀπειθοῦντες, 2.8).[56] Consequently, the unbelieving are deviant specifically because of their disregard for the word (ὁ λόγος, 2.8), which, for 1 Peter, is the gospel about Christ (cf. 1.25).[57] The result for the non-believer is stumbling and falling over the stone. Such stumbling may infer shaming. Campbell certainly reads it this way because of its obvious comparison with the honour of the believer.[58] Furthermore, Campbell notes that honour and shame themes here are not 'just about eternal destinies' but present

---

[51] Thus, with Michaels, ἐπ' αὐτῷ should be translated 'in him' not 'in it' because it refers to Jesus Christ not only a metaphorical foundation; Michaels, *1 Peter*, 104. Consequently, in 2.6, the object of trust/belief is Christ rather than God; see Elliott, *1 Peter*, 426.

[52] I read τιμή as the subject of the clause rather than an adjective referring to the value of Christ (see NRSV, NIV). Thus, τιμή applies to the believers (cf. 1.7). For agreement see Campbell, *Honor*, 85–7; Kelly, *Epistles of Peter*, 93; Michaels, *1 Peter*, 104; Achtemeier, *1 Peter*, 160–1; Feldmeier, *Peter*, 133; contra Brox, *Petrusbrief*, 101.

[53] Where πιστεύω means not just cognitive assent but active trusting followed by faithful behaviour.

[54] See Kelly, *Epistles of Peter*, 93; Achtemeier, *1 Peter*, 160.

[55] Elliott, 'Disgraced', 173.

[56] According to Selwyn, unbelief is more than the 'suspense or refusal of intellectual assent; it connotes a revolt of the will'; Selwyn, *St. Peter*, 164. That ἀπιστέω appears only here in 1 Peter suggests that the act of belief or unbelief is central to the author's argument at this point. This type of contrast between two groups where the stigmatised can compare themselves favourably to the other is a type of emotion-focused coping strategy; see Holloway, *Coping*, 122–3.

[57] In 1 Peter ἀπειθέω 'exclusively describes refusal of the proclamation of salvation'. See 4.17: τί τὸ τέλος τῶν ἀπειθούντων τῷ τοῦ θεοῦ εὐαγγελίῳ; (cf. 3.1, 20); Feldmeier, *Peter*, 134; cf. Elliott, *1 Peter*, 433. Thus, the unbelieving denotes anyone who rejects the gospel. It does not designate the Jews, contra Windisch, *katholischen Briefe*, 61.

[58] Cf. Campbell, *Honor*, 84, 94–5 who lists προσκόμματος, σκανδάλου, προσκόπτουσιν under shame terminology; see also De Waal Dryden, *Theology*, 121, 125. For Elliott, the rock causes offence rather than shame, because Christ violates the social or moral code; Elliott, *1 Peter*, 432.

honourable/dishonourable status.[59] However, though the believers do appear to have a present honoured status before God, the framework established seems to be emphasising eternal realities, particularly if we hold God to be the ultimate judge. Therefore, in 2.6–8 the author has established a framework that enables the believer to understand the consequences of their response to Christ: faith equals no shame but rather honour; disobedience means disaster.[60] This framework is God ordained (εἰς ὃ καὶ ἐτέθησαν, 2.8).[61] Thus, Brox is probably right that the purpose of 2.7–8 is not to threaten the unbeliever, but to confirm for the believers that they are on the right path.[62] Like in the LXX, the recipients can see themselves as obedient and therefore expect that God, in his justice, will not allow them to be shamed. Moreover, if shame anticipates the harm of dishonour, then we can understand that, by negating shame, the author is promoting trusting in Christ as something that will certainly not bring harm to the believer. This statement in the negative reinforces the positive assertions of hope and joy that allegiance to God brings the good.[63]

This line of argument is bolstered by the value language that pervades 2.4–8. There are a number of terms in this passage that ascribe honour to both Christ and the believer. Christ is chosen (ἐκλεκτός) and honoured (ἔντιμος) by God (2.4, 6).[64] This reality is to be determinative for the believer's own value system. In fact, it is specifically recognising Christ's value that distinguishes the believers from others.[65] Those that do not believe reject (ἀποδοκιμάζω, 2.4, 7) Christ.[66] Here we can see, as Elliott acknowledges, the contrast

---

[59] Campbell, *Honor*, 95.

[60] These outcomes should be read soteriologically; see Jobes, *1 Peter*, 153–4.

[61] To agree with Elliott, the 'Petrine formulation is no reference to divine predestination of nonbelievers to condemnation (and of believers to salvation). That which is "set" or established by God is the stumbling … resulting from not heeding the word, rather than disobedience itself … Or to express it differently, it is the result of disobedience that is foreordained, not the decision itself'; Elliott, *1 Peter*, 434; cf. Schlosser, *Pierre*, 126–8; Campbell, *Honor*, 93.

[62] Brox, *Petrusbrief*, 102. However, this also means that the negative counterpoint outcome of disobedience provides a warning to the believer; Thurén, *Argument*, 127–8.

[63] Brox, *Petrusbrief*, 95; Michaels, *1 Peter*, 98; Achtemeier, *1 Peter*, 153. In fact, 2.3 has already shown that the believer has tasted that the Lord (Christ) is good.

[64] For support for translating ἔντιμος as honoured rather than precious see Selwyn, *St. Peter*, 159; Goppelt, *I Peter*, 137; Elliott, *1 Peter*, 411, 426.

[65] Cf. Achtemeier, *1 Peter*, 160.

[66] Here, to agree with Achtemeier, those who reject Christ are the author's 'contemporaries … who reject the gospel, rather than the rejection Christ suffered at the time of his crucifixion'. In Christ's rejection the believers may also see their own experience; Achtemeier, *1 Peter*, 154–5; Elliott, *1 Peter*, 410; Jobes, *1 Peter*, 146.

between the 'human and divine assessments of the "stone"'.[67] On account of accepting the value of Christ, the believers become God's people and find themselves similarly chosen and honoured.[68] Moreover, the believers can understand that by uniting with Christ, who is the living stone, they are able to become living stones and therefore partake in Christ's identity and life.[69] Evidently, the absence of shame sits in a larger matrix of value. If the believers have the right perspective and the right values they will have the correct response to objects within their reality. In this instance, they will value Christ and association with him. As a result, they will choose to tie themselves to Christ by obediently believing in him.[70] On account of their alignment with God's values and norms, like the righteous person of the LXX, they can trust that they will not be shamed. Instead, the climax of 2.9–10 triumphantly affirms their honour and special status.[71] Consequently, the author establishes that belief in and allegiance to Christ means agreement with God's norms but unbelief and rejection reveals deviance. This foundation is important for interpreting the occurrence of shame language in 4.16.

Shaping Self-Assessment

In 4.14–16 the author says:

> εἰ ὀνειδίζεσθε ἐν ὀνόματι Χριστοῦ, μακάριοι, ὅτι τὸ τῆς δόξης καὶ τὸ τοῦ θεοῦ πνεῦμα ἐφ' ὑμᾶς ἀναπαύεται. μὴ γάρ τις ὑμῶν πασχέτω ὡς φονεὺς ἢ κλέπτης ἢ κακοποιὸς ἢ ὡς ἀλλοτριεπίσκοπος· εἰ δὲ ὡς χριστιανός, μὴ αἰσχυνέσθω, δοξαζέτω δὲ τὸν θεὸν ἐν τῷ ὀνόματι τούτῳ.[72]

---

[67] Elliott, *1 Peter*, 410; cf. Selwyn, *St. Peter*, 158–9; Brox, *Petrusbrief*, 97.

[68] See Achtemeier, *1 Peter*, 152. The τιμή of 2.7 is expanded in 2.9. See Michaels, *1 Peter*, 107–10 who notes the present and future aspects of the believers' honour.

[69] Elliott, *1 Peter*, 413; Feldmeier, *Peter*, 135.

[70] The binding of the believer to Christ is emphasised by the incorporation of the believers into a new body: a spiritual house that offers spiritual sacrifices to God through Christ (2.4–5). As Michaels rightly comments, in 2.4–10 the author is teaching the Gentile audience about 'their new identity in relation to Christ'; Michaels, *1 Peter*, 94–5; cf. Feldmeier, *Peter*, 134; Jobes, *1 Peter*, 148–9. The use of ἅγιος (2.5) to describe the new community confirms that it is marked by obedience.

[71] Feldmeier, *Peter*, 132.

[72] See Achtemeier, *1 Peter*, 303; Elliott, *1 Peter*, 796; David G. Horrell, 'The Label Χριστιανός (1 Pet. 4.16): Suffering, Conflict, and the Making of Christian Identity', in *Becoming Christian*, 164–210, at 179–81 for why, due to manuscript evidence and context, ὀνόματι is to be preferred over μέρει (NA28). Contra Michaels, *1 Peter*, 269–70.

If you are reproached for the name of Christ, you are blessed, because the spirit of glory and of God rests on you. But do not let anyone among you suffer as a murderer, thief, wrongdoer, or as a meddler; but if as a Christian, do not be ashamed, but glorify God in this name.

Here the author directly addresses the audience's own subjective emotional stance.[73] The use of αἰσχύνω in the passive can mean to be dishonoured, but more commonly refers to the feeling of shame.[74] 1 Peter 4.16 explicitly links this sense of shame to suffering as a Christian (ὡς χριστιανός).[75] Thus, here, the author addresses the believers' emotional understanding of their current persecution. From outlining what his negation of shame tells us, we can unfold some of the rhetorical advantages of his manoeuvre.

First, we know that the object of shame is the self. Therefore, through using this emotion, the author is primarily seeking to shape the audience's *self-perception*. It has been established above that shame is occasioned by the awareness that one has deviated from an accepted norm, and that this deviance has been (or will be) exposed to a judging other(s) whose opinion one cares about because of the other's ability to affect one's attainment of goals. We can now unpack these ideas with regard to the audience.

In 4.14–16 both actions and associations are in view. The Christians are suffering on account of their connection with Christ as the phrases ὀνειδίζεσθε ἐν ὀνόματι Χριστοῦ (4.14) and ὡς χριστιανός (4.16) highlight.[76] Moreover, their suffering as a Christian

---

[73] Cf. Mark 8.38; Phil 1.20; 2 Tim 1.12; Michaels, *1 Peter*, 269; Elliott, *1 Peter*, 794–5. Contra Achtemeier who sees αἰσχύνω as referring to denying one's faith rather than a subjective feeling; cf. Brox, *Petrusbrief*, 221–2. Here, Achtemeier misses the connection that it is the subjective feeling of shame that leads towards the actions of denial (see discussion below); Achtemeier, *1 Peter*, 314.

[74] See 'αἰσχύνω' in BDAG (30), which lists 1 Peter 4.16 under 'to have a sense of shame, be ashamed'.

[75] It is commonly recognised that this verse provides one of the oldest references to the term 'Christian' (cf. Acts 11.26; 26.28). According to Feldmeier, it provides the earliest reference to the 'stigmatization and criminalization ... connected to this designation'; Feldmeier, *Peter*, 227. For Brox, this criminalisation is one of the chief causes of the believer's shame; Brox, *Petrusbrief*, 221. See Horrell, 'Χριστιανός', 165–76 for the origins of the term.

[76] Cf. Matt 10.22 (and parallels: Mark 13.13; Luke 21.17); Luke 6.22; Michaels, *1 Peter*, 264. I see πάσχω rather than ὀνειδίζω as the implied verb in 4.16a. See Elliott who argues that ἐν ὀνόματι Χριστοῦ means 'because you belong to, are affiliated with, Christ'; Elliott, *1 Peter*, 780–1. Horrell's comments on the etymology of χριστιανός suggest that the designation specifically indicates dependence on or allegiance to Christ; Horrell, 'Χριστιανός', 165–6.

is contrasted with suffering as a murderer (φονεύς), thief (κλέπτης), wrongdoer (κακοποιός), and meddler (ἀλλοτριεπίσκοπος). It is not-able that these terms attribute an identity to the person.[77] It does not say, on account of murder, theft, doing evil, meddling, but as a murderer, thief, meddler, or wrongdoer. This is not to divorce identity from action because out of these identities flow actions: a murderer kills; a thief steals; and, a Christian believes in Christ and demonstrates her allegiance by doing good (cf. 2.6–7; 3.16; 4.19). For the author, the criminal identities and actions should rightly warrant shame, but not being a Christian.[78] Thus far, we can simply conclude that the author is exhorting the audience not to be ashamed of its Christian name or identity.[79] However, there are further implications to this. First, shame categorises the believers' behaviour as a devi-ation from accepted norms.[80] Thus, by denying shame, the author is declaring that being associated with Christ is appropriate, not mis-creant behaviour. To be ashamed of their Christian identity would be to agree that there is something wrong in their allegiance and that reproach is fitting. However, the author refutes this. Furthermore, by removing shame, the author also negates the harm that shame would fear, whether this is the harm of dishonour or the loss of goods that dishonour might bring. From the author's perspective, there is no true negative outcome of being associated with Christ. In refusing shame, the author is again asserting the value of Christ for the believer.

In addition, we saw above that shame requires a critical other. Who is the judging other in 4.16? The idea of reproach (4.14) and suffering (4.13, 15) in this context emphasises the relationship between the believer and the hostile human other. Therefore, the observing others are the members of the believers' surrounding society.[81] Consequently, it is this society's critical assessments that are

[77] Achtemeier, *1 Peter*, 309.

[78] According to Holloway, shaming was both a 'component of social stigma', but also 'an important and well-developed part of the Roman penal system'. Thus, shaming 'drew a line between acceptable and unacceptable behaviour'; Holloway, *Coping*, 225.

[79] However, Horrell has shown that this is not such a simple point after all, for 1 Peter 4.16 'represents the earliest witness to the crucial process whereby the term [χριστιανός] was transformed from a hostile label applied by outsiders to a self-designation borne with honour'; Horrell, 'Χριστιανός', 165.

[80] If Horrell is right that χριστιανός was a form of stigma, then the label itself discredits the person 'in terms of the wider society's values and assumptions'; Horrell, 'Χριστιανός', 198.

[81] This is supported by Michaels' observation that where χριστιανός is used in the New Testament (Acts 11.26; 26.28) it appears 'to reflect the viewpoint of the Jewish

being scrutinised by the author's use of shame language. Moreover, because the others' evaluations are based on the norms and values of their culture (norms and values to which the believers previously subscribed), the author, by denying shame, is also refusing to allow this cultural framework to provide the standards for the believers' behaviour and identity. The result is that the negative opinion of the hostile other is devalued and the supporting norms are torn down.[82] From the other's perspective, the Christians' behaviour contradicts established norms and thus they should rightly be (a)shamed.[83] Phrases such as ἐν ὀνόματι Χριστοῦ and ὡς χριστιανός suggest that merely being associated with Christ was enough to warrant shaming.[84] As Elliott comments; '[T]he derogatory label [χριστιανός] was … a tool in the arsenal of nonbelievers for demeaning the honour and impugning the moral character and reputation' of the Christians.[85] Such reproach was likely intended to correct the believers' wayward behaviour. However, in negating shame, the author counters the other's viewpoint and assessment. In fact, he declares the exact opposite: suffering on account of Christ reveals that they are blessed and that the glory and spirit of God is upon them.[86] Here, like in 2.4–8, an alternate system of value is promoted. From God's perspective, because of their obedient trust in Christ, Christians are chosen, have glory, and are blessed. Shame is certainly not fitting for the believers. Instead, they should glorify God with their name, Christian.[87] Thus, the system of worth established in 2.4–8 is at work here too. The author is actively highlighting contrasting perspectives: God's and the hostile other's. The latter sees Christ and those associated with

and pagan outsiders toward those who followed and worshipped Jesus'; Michaels, *1 Peter*, 268; cf. Achtemeier, *1 Peter*, 313; Horrell, 'Χριστιανός', 167–9. Moreover, ὀνειδίζω 'is the standard term for abuse and public shaming' and therefore fits with reproach by other humans; Elliott, *1 Peter*, 775, 778–9.

[82] Cf. Elliott, *1 Peter*, 795. Thus, there is more taking place here than simply breaking with the social principle of syncretism; see Goppelt, *1 Peter*, 328.

[83] Areas of perceived deviance could include disrespect for civil or domestic order, marital norms, even criminal behaviour; Elliott, 'Disgraced', 170.

[84] Cf. Schelkle, *Petrusbriefe*, 125.

[85] Elliott, *1 Peter*, 791–2.

[86] For Holloway this is a clear example of an 'emotion-focused' coping strategy, where the author seeks 'to regulate the internal psychological effects of stigma and stigma-related outcomes'. One way of doing this is restructuring one's self-concept; Holloway, *Coping*, 122, 226.

[87] There is disagreement about what ἐν τῷ ὀνόματι τούτῳ (4.16) refers to. Here I agree with Goppelt that the phrase refers to the name Christian, rather than Christ; see also Brox, *Petrusbrief*, 222; Horrell, 'Χριστιανός', 181–2. However, such a sharp distinction is perhaps unnecessary if we recognise that their Christian identity comes precisely through their association with Christ; see Goppelt, *1 Peter*, 328.

him as worthy of shame, the former see Christ and the believers as honoured.[88]

Implications for the Believer

We are now in a position to discuss the implications of the author's negation of shame. The most important sociological consequence is the change in the relative importance of the critical other. The believers were previously part of their surrounding society, and would have understood their identity in relation to it. Furthermore, they would have shared the view of reality and adopted the standards of the socio-cultural group into which they had been socialised. However, the Christ-event has caused them to have a radically new view of reality and has brought a new framework of norms centred on God's will. Through denying shame, the believer is being asked to see the world, including her behaviour and her status, no longer through the critical eyes of her previous society. As such, the importance of the hostile other's opinion is denied. Instead, negating shame suggests that another viewpoint (God's) provides truth and is of greater significance. Subsequently, God's critical eyes usurp the assessments of the other.[89]

This displacement of the other also affects the believers' sense of group belonging. Instead of evaluating themselves from the perspective of their previous group, they now have a new 'honour-group', which is God and his people (2.10). Such a revaluing of the others' opinion is seeking to affect the believers' desire to be associated with the other. If the outsiders' judgements and their supporting norms are misguided, and subsequently their behaviour is deviant and leads to calamity, why would one want to be part of this group? Therefore, by denying shame, the author is encouraging an emotional detachment from their previous society and relationships. This is particularly the case given that the label χριστιανός represents 'a label associated not with a facet of person identity ... but with a feature of social identity arriving from group membership'.[90] Thus, by denying shame, the believer is encouraged to value attachment to this membership. Furthermore, as we have recognised previously, where the other is revalued, the emotional response to him/her is altered. Here negating shame asks the believer not to care so strongly about the

---

[88] Cf. Elliott, *1 Peter*, 781.
[89] Thus, 4.17 immediately reminds the audience of God's judgement.
[90] Horrell, 'Χριστιανός', 199.

opinion of the other and therefore the other becomes less important to the believer.[91] One can assume that over time this will reduce the strength of bonds between the believers and their society and will strengthen new in-group bonds.[92] Subsequently, a new desire for belonging based on a different view of reality is fostered. Hence, it is precisely because of their desire to associate with God through Christ that the believers stand alienated from their previous socio-cultural groups.[93] Horrell comments:

> An ironic and surely unintended consequence … of the outsiders' hostile labelling of believers as Χριστιανοί is that it confirms and increases the salience of *this* aspect of the insiders' shared social identity, increases the extent to which this facet of their identity defines their commonality and sense of belonging together, increases, indeed, their sense that *this* badge is the one they must own or deny in the face of hostility.[94]

Thus, once again, allegiance to Christ is promoted. This time, through negating shame, the author asks the audience to internalise a reality in which such allegiance is considered the only right route to flourishing.

This is supported by the fact that denying shame removes the other's power to harm. If dishonour is an evil in itself and can lead to other negative consequences, then to care about the evaluation of others and to seek to be honoured in their eyes gives the other power. If one looks to humans for the good (e.g. honour) then shame and reproach become a hindrance to one's attainment of goals. Thus, shame becomes a means of social control.[95] So, in order to reduce this, presumably detrimental, social conditioning, the author needs to remove the audience's sense of shame. Instead,

---

[91] Such disidentification is typical when one's value domain has been replaced; see Holloway, *Coping*, 126–7.

[92] Awareness of their communal identity is 'an essential element in their coping with the abuse of outsiders and presenting a collective front of resistance'; Elliott, *1 Peter*, 444. This corporate belonging is particularly notable in 2.4–10; see Goppelt, *1 Peter*, 139–40; Feldmeier, *Peter*, 132; Campbell, *Honor*, 91.

[93] Feldmeier recognises the believers' sociological detachment when he comments that, 'Election connects with God, but at the same time separates one from the world around and so creates a distance, indeed, a tension with fellow human beings'; Feldmeier, *Peter*, 132. That 2.4–10 polarises the believer and unbeliever (see Brox, *Petrusbrief*, 95; Schlosser, *Pierre*, 126), is likely to lead to social and eventually emotional detachment.

[94] Horrell, 'Χριστιανός', 202.

[95] Elliott, 'Disgraced', 173.

he must foster allegiance to Christ. For, if one's allegiance to Christ is most important, then reproach from other humans on account of him is insignificant and one is psychologically distanced from the influence of the other. In the framework of 2.4–8 and 4.14–16, the author reminds the audience that the only judgement that counts is God's because he has final control over the good and bestows lasting honour.[96] That the believers are able to glorify God through their Christianity (4.16), infers that in their response to persecution God's honour is also at stake.

If, by denying shame, the author is asking the audience to see reality differently and to live by new norms and goals, then there will be ethical consequences. When the believers value too highly the opinion of the other, and allow themselves to feel shame, then shame will shape their behaviour. This is because shame's action-tendency drives a person towards avoidance of dishonour.[97] Elliott acknowledges this, commenting that public shaming was 'designed to demean and discredit the believers in the court of public opinion with the ultimate aim of forcing their conformity to prevailing norms and values'.[98] Such an emotional stance is likely to encourage cultural assimilation, even defection from the faith.[99] However, by nullifying shame, the author is also eliminating its action-tendency and any associated behaviour. Consequently, through denying shame, which shows a reordering of values and a revaluation of the importance of the other for obtaining goals, the ethical behaviour of the believer is also influenced, and adhesion to Christian norms is promoted. Shame, as an emotion that focuses on the believers' behaviour, is particularly useful for achieving this ethical end.

Finally, we move to the therapeutic consequences of neg-ating shame. For someone to feel ashamed they have to accept the judgement of the critical observer about his/her behaviour and iden-tity. Therefore, to deny shame is to tell the audience not to accept this self-assessment. They are not to see themselves as disobedient and deviant, and therefore neither as shameful nor devalued.[100] Horrell has argued, using Lipp's work on stigmatisation, that the bold

---

[96] Cf. Elliott, *1 Peter*, 782.

[97] Achtemeier sees desire for avoidance intimated in this passage, but links avoidance with the pain of suffering rather than the specific harm of dishonour; Achtemeier, *1 Peter*, 314.

[98] Elliott, 'Disgraced', 170.

[99] Cf. Windisch, *katholischen Briefe*, 78; Schelkle, *Petrusbriefe*, 125; Schlosser, *Pierre*, 263.

[100] Cf. Elliott, *1 Peter*, 795.

wearing of the label Christian could be a type of self-stigmatisation, which 'stands as a challenge to the wider society to change its negative judgement towards the stigma'.[101] Though this may be a secondary social outcome, the bold wearing of the label Christian can only occur if the believers' own assessment of their Christian identity is correctly formed. It is the emotional refusal of shame that establishes an inner challenge to the pressure of societal norms. The shame language focuses on the believers' own assessment and seeks to effect within them a new self-perception that is based on God's perspective on account of Christ, not the views of society. The believers are not to accept the miscreant label, but are to see themselves as obedient children (1.14). We can see a parallel here with the perspective of Christ in Hebrews 12.2 where Christ despises the shame of the cross and is ultimately honoured by God. Therefore, likewise, in the face of persecution, by refusing shame, the author gives the audience a positive, godly, self-assessment of their identity and behaviour.

So, we can see that the two uses of shame language (2.6; 4.16) play an important role in the discourse of the letter. Through this emotion language, the author asks the believers to hold to a different system of value and to judge themselves by different norms. He promises that trusting in and association with Christ will end in the good and downplays membership of their former community. The audience is encouraged to adopt God's perspective and to recognise that his observing eyes are the most important. Subsequently, the opinion of the other is revalued, and the believers are released from conforming their behaviour to the other's expectations. Consequently, the believers are able to form new group bonds and live out their Christian behaviour with a positive sense of self.

We can now move to the last use of shame in 1 Peter. However, this time it applies to the non-believer.

The Shame of the Non-Believer: 1 Peter 3.16

We have seen that the author makes the fate of the individual dependent on their response to Christ, where belief and trust in Christ demonstrate obedience and lead to honour, but rejection of Christ is disobedience and results in shame. In 1 Peter 2.8 this was

---

[101] Horrell, 'Χριστιανός', 206.

conveyed in the metaphor of stumbling over the stone. However in 3.15b–16 the accuser's shame is made explicit:

ἕτοιμοι ἀεὶ πρὸς ἀπολογίαν παντὶ τῷ αἰτοῦντι ὑμᾶς λόγον περὶ τῆς ἐν ὑμῖν ἐλπίδος, ἀλλὰ μετὰ πραΰτητος καὶ φόβου, συνείδησιν ἔχοντες ἀγαθήν, ἵνα ἐν ᾧ καταλαλεῖσθε καταισχυνθῶσιν οἱ ἐπηρεάζοντες ὑμῶν τὴν ἀγαθὴν ἐν Χριστῷ ἀναστροφήν.

be ready always to answer anyone who asks you for an account concerning the hope within you, but do so with gentleness and fear, having a good conscience, so that those who denounce your good manner of life in Christ may be ashamed by that for which you are spoken against.[102]

What is striking is that it is the accusers' response to and treatment of the believers that is the cause of their shame, not their direct response to Christ. In these verses two contrasting patterns of behaviour are highlighted: the unbeliever is depicted as speaking against (καταλαλέω) and threatening/abusing (ἐπηρεάζω) the believer, but the believer has good 'in Christ' conduct. The author then declares that the cause of the believers' denunciation – their good in Christ behaviour – is the very thing that will cause the abuser to be (a)shamed.[103]

---

[102] The phrase ἐν ᾧ καταλαλεῖθε is awkward, specifically the second-person plural καταλαλεῖσθε. A number of manuscripts (א A C) show the variant καταλαλουσιν υμων ως κακοποιων, which makes more obvious sense and conforms to 2.12. However, see Michaels, *1 Peter*, 183–4 for why καταλαλεῖσθε is to be preferred. Explanation of my translation is below.

[103] That P⁷² has αισχυνθωσιν instead of καταισχυνθῶσιν reminds us of the joint subjective and objective experience of shame. Selwyn and Bigg argue that καταισχυνθῶσιν could take the accusative ἀναστροφήν. Therefore, the believers' conduct would be what shames the accusers; Selwyn, *St. Peter*, 194; Bigg, *Epistles of St. Peter*, 159. However, Michaels provides a counter argument, noting that there is only one parallel text that uses the passive of καταισχύνω with an accusative, and no text that uses οἱ ἐπηρεαζόντες without an object. Instead Michaels asserts that that we should read ἐπηρεάζω in 3.16 as related to ἀναστροφήν (cf. Luke 6.22) and therefore the accusers denounce the believers' good conduct; Michaels, *1 Peter*, 183, 190. Michaels, with Brox, Achtemeier, and Elliott, reads ἐν ᾧ as temporal meaning 'when'; Brox, *Petrusbrief*, 161; Achtemeier, *1 Peter*, 236; Elliott, *1 Peter*, 630. Feldmeier offers a different translation: 'so that those who insult your good lifestyle in Christ will become ashamed through just that by which you are slandered'. Feldmeier gives no explanation of his translation, but it appears that Feldmeier agrees with Michaels in taking ἀναστροφήν as the accusative of ἐπηρεάζω but reads ἐν ᾧ not as temporal but as indicating the cause for slander, which is symmetrically their Christian conduct; Feldmeier, *Peter*, 192; cf. Bigg, *Epistles of St. Peter*, 159; Dubis, *1 Peter: A Handbook*, 62, 104–5; Goppelt, *I Peter*, 239, 46; Schlosser, *Pierre*, 207. Dubis likewise argues that ἐν ᾧ in 3.6 'connotes reference'. BDAG (725–6.1.b. α) supports this, listing 1 Peter 2.12 and 3.16 as examples of a concealed demonstrative, so that ἐν ᾧ should be rendered 'in

Thus, we see a clear reversal: the 'shamer' will in fact be shamed by the same actions they denounce. Subsequently, these conflicting 'shames' – the shaming of the Christians versus the accusers' shame – reveal that there are not just two patterns of behaviour, but two competing systems of reality. The non-believers are assessing the believers' actions by their worldview and judging it deviant. However, the author, by saying that the opposition will be shamed, presents a different perspective with different standards. In attributing shame, the author categorises the non-believers' behaviour as divergent, whereas he labels Christians' conduct as good (ἀγαθός). It is clear by the phrase συνείδησιν ἔχοντες ἀγαθήν (3.16), which recalls συνείδησιν θεοῦ in 2.19, that the framework relied upon to categorise behaviour is God's will.[104] Again, we see that norms based on an understanding of God are juxtaposed with society's values.

Moreover, that a consciousness of God (3.16) and God's will (3.17) bookmark the use of shame language recommends that the critical eyes in 3.16 are God's. Elliott comments that 'conscience' should be understood as 'sensitivity to and mindfulness of the evaluation of significant *others* that guided moral behaviour' in a group-orientated society. He goes on to say: 'For the early Christians, it was God who represented the most "significant other."'[105] Elliott's comments support my position that God is the critical other whose judgement determines who should be (a)shamed. However, it is not clear whether shame is a present outcome or if it is eschatological. A number of scholars take the latter (cf. 2.12): if the non-believers persist in their slander they will ultimately be shamed. As such, slander is read as not just a rejection of the believers, but more importantly as a rejection of God.[106] However, Achtemeier thinks that shaming could be an 'immediate matter' that occurs when the accusers become aware of the truth of the Christians' behaviour. This, for Achtemeier, is occasioned by the Christians' explanation of their actions.[107] The verbal account may provide an opportunity

---

that in which'. The variant reading supports the outcome of Feldmeier's and Dubis' position as καταλαλουσιν υμων ως κακοποιων smooths καταλαλεῖθε by supplying the content ('they speak against you as evil doers'). This could indicate that the copyists read ἐν ᾧ as referring to that for which they are spoken against rather than being temporal. Thus, the result is that what the non-believers are shamed by is the very same focus of their accusation. I find Feldmeier's and Dubis' translation persuasive and therefore follow their reading.

[104] See Achtemeier, *1 Peter*, 236.
[105] Elliott, *1 Peter*, 630.
[106] Michaels, *1 Peter*, 190–1; Elliott, *1 Peter*, 632–3.
[107] Achtemeier, *1 Peter*, 236–7; see also Brox, *Petrusbrief*, 162; Feldmeier, *Peter*, 197.

for truth to be communicated, but in 3.16, 2.12, and 2.15 it appears to be the good conduct itself that is efficacious.[108] It could be, as I argued in Chapter 5 (pp. 156–61), that the believers' continued good conduct in the face of persecution points towards a different worldview and thus confronts the non-believer with a new reality. A present aspect to 'shaming' would fit with this reading as it would allow shame to have the useful corrective function that the ancient philosophers acknowledged. On this occasion, the 'exposure' of shame would be experienced by the nonbeliever. Such an awareness of their deviance could cause the non-believers to re-think the basis for their own assessments. If the non-believers were to be ashamed of their behaviour, then they would be accepting the judgement that they in fact are deviant, which in turn would require an acceptance of the Christian reality. Thus, to be (a)shamed could emotionally move the other from opposition towards acceptance of Christ.[109]

The implications for the believers of 3.16 align with those of the shame language in 2.4–8 and 4.14–16 (see above). However, 3.16 goes beyond 4.16. In 4.16 the opinion of the other is dismissed but no mention is made of the opposition's behaviour. In 3.16 the abuser's viewpoint and subsequent treatment of the believer is, by the application of shame, firmly displayed as wrong. Verse 3.16 also suggests that the believers' obedience to Christ not only affects their own fate but has the potential to communicate to the other. Verse 4.16 encouraged the believers to be distanced emotionally from their previous society and to have a positive view of their Christian identity, but 3.16 suggests that this emotional stance is not to remove interaction with their society. In fact, quite the opposite, when they are questioned about their hope (3.15) they are to give a lived response that engages the accuser. Their lack of shame allows this confident response.

Conclusion

We have seen that the author of 1 Peter uses shame language in two ways. First, when applied to the believers, it is negated and thus declared ill-fitting. However, when it comes to those who reject Christ and abuse the believers on account of their Christianity,

---

[108] Cf. Feldmeier, *Peter*, 196; Schlosser, *Pierre*, 205.

[109] Cf. Dubis, who sees in 3.16 a 'missiological motive' in the shaming; Dubis, *1 Peter: A Handbook*, 113; Contra Michaels who sees 2.12 and 3.16 as showing opposing outcomes; Michaels, *1 Peter*, 190; cf. Elliott, *1 Peter*, 630–1.

shame is indeed appropriate. From having a better understanding of shame we have discovered that the shame language is being used to categorise behaviour negatively or positively. In doing so it is also exposing the judgements of the critical other and the norms that the others' assessments are based on. Whether shame is affirmed or negated by the author gives credence to or removes the validity of the others' judgement. Second, this also makes a statement about the value of the worldview the judgement relies on with the effect that the Christian reality is presented as truth. Furthermore, the affirmation and negation of shame has been used to promote being concerned about God's opinion instead of the assessment of the other. This also, by implication, removes the power of the other over one's attainment of goals. All this sits within the understanding that obedience, which is acceptance of Christ, will lead to the good, but rejection of Christ results in calamity, including shame. In this framework, the believer is seen as obedient and the non-believer deviant. Thus, the believers can see their association with Christ positively, rather than accepting shame's assertion that they are devalued and miscreant. All of this requires an inner emotional transformation. To reject shame, the believers have to be internally shaped by the Christian worldview so that they can evaluate themselves and the other differently. Their new perspective on reality should breed a positive sense of self and give an affirmation that they are on the path to flourishing. As we have seen, this emotional outlook leads to other sociological and ethical outcomes. Most notably, the action-tendency of shame (avoidance of dishonour) is also negated, allowing Christian behaviour and cohesion to be maintained.

Having now explored each emotion, we can turn to the synthetic task of determining what our investigation means for 1 Peter's rhetorical and social strategy.

9

CONCLUSION

This book has aimed to demonstrate what can be gained by taking a more informed look at the role of emotions in 1 Peter's rhetorical discourse. Such a full-scale exploration of emotions in a New Testament epistle has not been attempted before. Therefore, it was necessary to establish a theoretical and methodological framework for the investigation. This involved two key elements: (1) being theoretically informed about emotions, and (2) being historically and culturally sensitive in the application of emotion theory. The first required engaging with recent developments in emotion studies that have advanced (or corrected) our modern assumptions about emotions. The second meant exploring ancient Greco-Roman philosophical and rhetorical theory on emotions along with LXX material.

A Working Methodology

My theoretical position on emotions, which provided the foundational assumptions for the following exegesis, was outlined in Chapter 2. It acknowledged that emotions are composite affective processes. However, because this investigation was interested in emotion terms in an ancient text, only the aspects of stimulus (object), cognitive appraisal (evaluation), and action-tendency were deemed relevant. Consequently, we established that, first, emotions have an intentional object ('intentional' means as interpreted by the person). Second, emotions are evaluative judgements that highlight an object's goal relevance. Moreover, each emotion has a characteristic appraisal, which, when applied to an object, says something about that object. Furthermore, because emotions are concerned with goals, they are dependent on one's values, which are in turn shaped by worldview. Thus, to understand the occurrence of an emotion in a given context we need to appreciate the wider value system in which the emotion's rationale makes sense. Lastly, an emotion's judgement produces an action-tendency. Consequently, emotions are drivers for action. Therefore, we arrived at a set of questions to ask when encountering an emotion term in 1 Peter: What is the emotion's object? What evaluation does the emotion communicate? What does the emotion's contextualisation reveal about how the author is presenting reality? What does this indicate about the values and worldview of the author? Lastly, how does the use of this emotion influence action? In addition, because the use of emotions is occurring in a rhetorical context we had to recognise that 1 Peter's presentation of emotion is both idealised and intended to influence its audience. Consequently, it was considered pertinent to question the implications for the audience of the author's use of emotion.

We also acknowledged the cultural boundedness of emotions, and that we cannot assume to understand automatically an emotion in an ancient text. Instead, we must be historically and culturally sensitive. Furthermore, we delineated that emotions can be approached at three levels: (1) general theory of emotion; (2) definition of each emotion; and (3) contextualisation of and rationale given to each emotion. Therefore, in order to be culturally sensitive at every level of discussion the book proceeded as follows: Chapters 3–4 focused on level 1 and revealed that there is in fact a close fit between ancient theories of emotion and recent developments in emotion studies, thus underlining that the above exploratory questions are not anachronistic but are useful heuristic tools. The connections and ideas revealed through them are not purely modern constructs but exist in the ancient mind also. In the exegetical chapters (5–8) levels 2 and 3 were operative. Before investigating emotions in 1 Peter, we defined each emotion using Greco-Roman, mostly Stoic, philosophical theory. This provided the basic characteristics of each emotion, especially what appraisal is encoded in the emotion term. However, in using the philosophical literature we were also aware of the third level of discourse, appreciating that philosophical discussion is nuanced and affected by its own worldview. Such awareness was necessary for two reasons: first, it made sure that the Stoic philosophical worldview was not accidently imposed on to 1 Peter; second, it provided a useful point of comparison that allowed the contours of 1 Peter's own position to be further illuminated. For the latter, the LXX material was also helpful. We discovered that the LXX used terms conventionally, that is, they followed the basic definitions as we came to understand them, but the contextualisation of emotions and the rationale underlying their use was different to Stoic theory.

It became evident that 1 Peter's use of emotions is closer to the LXX than to Stoic usage. Consequently, this study has provided a working methodology for investigating emotions in any New Testament text that is both theoretically informed and historically sensitive.

A Composite Picture

Emotions not only depend on worldview for their evaluative judgement, but, dynamically, they can be used by a given culture to build a worldview. This happens through 'feeling rules' ('emotional regimes'). The emotions allowed/encouraged or disallowed/discouraged in given contexts and of particular objects build up a picture of reality, and in doing so position the person and tell her what is behaviourally expected. Using emotions to build or enforce a worldview is precisely what 1 Peter is doing. As an authoritative communication, it aims to shape rhetorically the recipients' interpretation of their world through applying emotion terms in particular contexts. The positive or negative presentation of each emotion creates an emotional regime for the believers, which subsequently produces the boundaries for their understanding of self and other. We have looked at each emotion individually. It is now necessary to pull the findings together into a composite whole.

The emotions of joy (χαρά), distress (λύπη), fear (φόβος), hope (ἐλπίς), and shame (αἰσχύνη) were found to highlight only a few figures within the audience's world: God, Christ, the hostile other, and the self. This is unsurprising given that the letter is written to a Christian community undergoing persecution for its faith. Thus, these persons are those significant to this occasion. Therefore, by highlighting these characters and applying (or denying) certain emotions to them the author is ensuring that the figures are placed correctly within the audience's worldview. Furthermore, by using certain emotions he is saying something specific about that object, and, importantly, highlighting that figure's relevance to the audience's flourishing. In doing so, he is attempting to shape the believers' value system and affect their goals, which should then influence their behaviour.

God and Christ

We discovered that joy (1.6), hope (1.3, 13, 21; 3.5, 15), and fear (1.17; 2.17–18; 3.2, 16) are all shown to be appropriate responses to God. Both joy and hope relate to the good. Joy is appropriate when the good is present; hope anticipates a future benefit. Therefore, by applying these emotions to God, the author is explicitly highlighting the value of God for the audience's present and future flourishing. In 1.3–6 God is the good to be rejoiced in and is the author of other present goods to which the believers have access through Christ's resurrection. That God is the object of rejoicing and that these goods (inheritance, protection, salvation) are described in eternal terms lifts the believers' perspective beyond their current circumstances. Through the contextualisation of the emotion, the author encourages the audience that the good found in God is not dependent on, nor can be affected by, their present persecution. Whereas joy tells the audience of their present position, hope reminds the audience of their dependence on God for the future. 1.3–21 exhorts the audience to hope on God's grace at the time of Christ's revelation. Thus, hope reminds the audience that the story has not finished yet. If they are to secure their eternal future, God is their only hope. He is the sole person to whom they should look. This is because, as joy reveals, he is the source of all good. Hope, more than joy, speaks of the power of God in relation to the believers. Hope acknowledges the believers' lack of ability to provide the good for themselves and looks to another agent. In doing so, it invests God with power. Moreover, to ask the audience to hope completely in God removes all other possible agents and makes God the sole concern. Therefore, through the use of hope and joy, the author has highlighted God as the primary figure of importance for securing the good, both in the present and future.

I have discussed joy and hope with minimal reference to Christ. However, this is not truly representative of the outlook of the letter. Christ likewise can be rejoiced in (1.8) and is central to the believer's present hope. In 1.3–5 the position in which the believers now stand, which includes having hope, has occurred through the resurrection of Christ, and 1.8 affirms that they can rejoice in Christ because their faith in/faithfulness to him assures them that they are obtaining their salvation. Moreover, in 1.21 the author roots the believers' hope in God's action of raising Christ from the dead. Consequently, it is important to remember that the author's presentation of God as the one to be rejoiced and hoped in sits in the narrative context of God's deed in Christ. Therefore, Christ is also presented as valuable and made central to the believers' flourishing.

Lastly, in 1.17 the believers are exhorted to fear God. Fear anticipates future harm, and thus is used by the author to sound a note of warning. The context in which fear of God is fitting is his role as judge. Consequently, the author uses fear to focus the audience towards a future anticipated event – God's eschatological judgement – but, through fear's evaluation, colours that event with uncertainty. The uncertainty of outcome pushes the audience to deliberate about their present conduct, knowing that choices in the present will affect the final outcome. As with hope, fear highlights power dynamics and reminds the believers that God has control over their good; not only can he bestow it, but he can withhold it. Therefore, once again, being in favourable standing with God is presented as necessary for an assured future.

Joy, hope, and fear therefore seek to shape the believers' goals by presenting God as the route to and determiner of their present and future flourishing. God stands alone in this category, and, as a result, the believers' relationship to God through Christ becomes of highest importance. The outcome is that allegiance to God is fostered. We see the value placed on faithful allegiance to God and Christ most markedly in the exhortation to rejoice in sharing in Christ's sufferings (4.13). Only when one sees aligning oneself with God through doing good as of highest value can one appreciate that to suffer on account of this allegiance can be rejoiced in because it reveals one's faithfulness to God and Christ.

The Hostile Other

The other is not to be a cause of distress (1.6), nor to be feared (3.6, 14). Moreover, the hostile believer is presented as someone for whom shame is fitting (2.7–8; 3.16). Through the author's application of these emotions, he is asking the audience to revalue the importance of the other and also (re)positioning the other within the believers' worldview. In 1.6–7 the author works hard to give the hearers a new interpretation of their present trials. By showing that such trials can only prove the genuineness of faith, the author removes the evaluation that trials are harmful and therefore seeks to minimise the audience's distress. In showing that persecution does not cause the believers any lasting harm he also negates the power of the hostile other. To be distressed by the trials means that the believers are emotionally internalising the reality that the other's actions are detrimental to their flourishing and therefore the believers' behaviour will be influenced by the other. However, the author militates against this by highlighting that trials cannot really harm if they serve to prove faith in/faithfulness towards God. Instead, when trials do so, they result in praise, glory, and honour. Thus, where distress wants to make the hostile others prominent for the audience's interpretation of events, reducing distress serves to sideline them. Consequently, the hostile other becomes a less powerful and less significant figure in the audience's worldview. The negation of fear is a more explicit attack in the same vein. As noted above, fear recognises the power of the other to harm and makes the other master over one's flourishing. However, by negating fear of the other, the author pulls down this evaluation. In doing so he makes a statement about the relative power of the other. No longer is the hostile other, whether that be a master or husband, to be seen as pre-eminently powerful over the believer. The other cannot be, because he cannot truly harm. Instead, fear of God requires that all other powers, and therefore all other fears, be re-evaluated.

Furthermore, by revealing the unbelievers' shame, the author goes one stage further: the hostile other is shown to be not only less significant, but deviant. The non-believers' rejection of Christ and abuse of the Christian is deemed a violation of norms and therefore worthy of shame. The use of this emotion tells the audience that the non-believers' behaviour is miscreant, and presents the believers' surrounding society as collectively devalued. Thus, by shaming the 'shamers' the author also questions the validity of the norms on which the other's rejection of Christ and behaviour towards the believers are based. As such, through his application of shame, the author challenges the worldview that sees the reproach of believers as justified.

The Believer

Because the majority of emotions in 1 Peter are presented as the audience's emotions, each emotion, while saying something about the object, has also, as we have noted, communicated something to the audience about their positioning in relation to the object. The last emotion, shame, which has the self as the object, completes the picture. Through the negation of shame the author categorises the believers as obedient and acceptable. Their obedience is evident in their belief in Christ; this act alone shows alignment with God's norms. Furthermore, the audience is promised that because they have chosen to join themselves to Christ by believing in him, they will be honoured. Moreover, the author, through his use of shame, asks the believers to value God's opinion rather than the hostile other's, and to see themselves from God's perspective. For it is only by this true understanding of reality that they will perceive their own identity and place in the world. To deny shame is to affirm the positive identity and secure positioning of the believer.

I have not yet recounted the implications of the above presentation of reality. However, we must now turn to this, and as we do so,
we will be able to reveal what the exploration of emotions in 1 Peter
suggests about the author's rhetorical and social strategy.

Implications for the Believer and 1 Peter's Social Strategy

After working through the author's use of each emotion in 1 Peter a
number of implications for the audience have been suggested. These
can be broadly grouped into three areas: ethical, sociological, and
therapeutic.

Emotions and ethics cannot be separated because emotions,
through their evaluation of an object's goal congruence, drive
action. This is the most significant reason for engaging emotions.
The author will struggle to move his audience towards behavioural
ends unless he shapes its emotional orientation. Thus, as the ancient
rhetoricians recognised, because each emotion has an associated
action-tendency, emotions have to be selected and used carefully
to achieve the desired outcome. Therefore, by using joy to present
God as the source of good, the author can encourage conduct that
maintains a relationship with God. Hope, likewise, motivates behaviour that pursues God's favour. But, how does one know which
behaviour is appropriate to achieve this end? First, throughout the
letter the author reveals norms of Christian behaviour, either specifically in directive commands and negative vice lists, or more generally
in the call to do good. Second, and more importantly, doing good is
modelled on an understanding of God's holiness. At this point, fear
of God becomes useful, because it sets the boundaries for behaviour
and helps the believer to determine which actions in the present will
lead to future good. Concurrent with the promotion of emotions
like joy, hope, and fear of God, is the negation of other emotions,
which, likewise, aims to influence conduct. By reducing the distress
of trials the author also diminishes the associated action-tendency
of avoidance, and so conditions his audience's behaviour. Similarly,
fear seeks to avoid harm. But if the harm of the other is negated,
then the believers will no longer deliberate about their behaviour
in response to the other. Instead, their fear and awareness of God
alone will drive their conduct. Lastly, the author's use of shame
pushes the audience in the same ethical direction. It categorises the
believers' Christian behaviour as good and honourable, and therefore encourages the maintenance of this behaviour. The declaration
that the non-believers' actions warrant shame has the same end result

but functions through a note of warning. As a result, we can see that if we are to understand how the author is positioning the audience to act, we have to understand his use of emotions. It appears quite clearly that the author is encouraging the audience towards exclusive allegiance to Christ and God, and away from behaviour that is determined by other human relationships.

This leads us to the sociological consequences of the author's use of emotions. If the author, through his contextualisation of emotions, has presented the hostile other in a revalued capacity where the other has become less significant to the audience, then this is likely to reconfigure the believers' emotional ties to their surrounding society. If they accept reality as presented by the author, then they necessarily absorb a different value system and different norms. In doing so, they move away from their previous worldview and into a new one. This brings, as we have seen, a new positioning of objects in their worldview, and therefore starts to affect the believers' perception of the society from which they have come. In the case of shame, it actively marks outside society as misguided and deviant. In the case of fear and hope, the author challenges previous conceptions of worth, but also perceptions of power and, therefore, subsequently, societal structure. Previous figures of power are repositioned and the audience, who are mostly subordinates, is given a positive assessment of its positioning in the world. That they are those who should rejoice in God and not be ashamed of their Christian identity tells the believers that they are in a privileged, honoured position. As the believers live out their new worldview, it will inevitably lead to clashes with their previous society. In fact, it is their emotional orientation toward God that differentiates the believers from those around them. It is thus likely that ties to previous society will weaken, and new in-group bonds will be strengthened. However, the points of conflict between the believer and non-believer can, though perhaps not often, provide an opportunity for the hostile other to encounter the new reality of the believer and be won over to the faith. As the believers explain their hope they open up for the other a whole way of seeing the world. Therefore, the letter hints towards the promise that as they live in accordance with Christian reality they may even be able to transform aspects of their social world.

Therapeutically, the author moves the audience towards a positive and stable outlook on their present situation. Joy, because its focus is on the eternal (both God and the goods he bestows on the believer through Christ), allows the believers' emotional life to be stable. None of this reality – the reality that is producing the believers' joy – can be altered by their present persecution. Because the good to which joy looks is enduring, so is their joy. In fact, their joy is depicted as glorified and effervescent (1.8). Furthermore, they will be able to rejoice exceedingly at the revelation of Christ (4.13). It is this overarching reality, to which joy points, that is able to temper their present distress. The audience can be assured that to choose faithfulness to God is the best course of action. In addition, hope, which is based on God's deed in Christ, assures the believers that their faithful allegiance has a set trajectory towards vindication. Consequently, despite persecution, the author encourages the believers to be confident in their Christian position and behaviour. Moreover, through the author's use of joy in conjunction with his presentation of Christ, the believers can adopt a perspective whereby they can even rejoice in their suffering when it is on account of their allegiance to Christ. As such, suffering for being a Christian no longer becomes a demoralising event, but is affirmative of one's true identity and purpose. Furthermore, that the believers have actively chosen to align themselves with Christ invests the recipients with the capacity to actively choose their own destiny. Therefore, overall, it appears that the author's use of emotion aims to give the audience confidence and to reduce the inner turmoil caused by persecution.

Why is it important for the author's rhetorical strategy that he endeavours to shape the audience's emotional life? The answer is that using emotions enables the author to move beyond issuing prescriptive commands. Through seeking to shape the emotions he is working at a deeper formative level that, though it includes cognitive aspects and is not devoid of reasoning, involves a more fundamental shaping and orientation of the self. This internal orientation is more than accepting certain statements as facts; it is an internalisation of a new way of seeing the world and an acceptance of one's place within it. In this way, the author's use of emotion comes closer to encouraging the believers to assume dispositional states. This is, in fact, more effective than issuing individual commands, because it means that the disposition to act in a certain way can be carried into numerous, varied situations. To learn to rejoice and hope in or fear God prepares the person to prefer particular ends and therefore to select the right course of action accordingly. By shaping the believers' emotional life he can make sure that this formation of the person is deep and long-lasting. Moreover, this does not just happen at an individual level, but, by establishing an emotional regime for his audience as a whole, he can determine community expectations and shape the collective response to circumstances. If the audience adopts this emotional regime collectively it leads to a shared group perspective. As such, everyday experiences can take on new meaning and new prototypical scenarios for emotions are created, for example suffering becomes an occasion for joy when it would previously not have been. Subsequently, a new corporate understanding of the Christian life is produced, and as the individual aligns with this emotional regime she finds herself firmly placed within the community and discovers more about both her identity and how to behave. This emotional regime becomes distinctive of the group and, through fostering a different evaluation of objects within the world, it demarcates this community from others. Their distinctive identity is shown both in their emotional response to events and by the behaviour that their emotional dispositions produce, both of which may appear obtuse to outsiders who do not share the same way of seeing the world. Thus, if the author wants to orientate and shape the individual and the community so that they consistently pursue a certain course and have a distinctive identity, he has to engage the believers' emotions.

So, what are the implications of our investigation of emotion for understanding 1 Peter's social strategy? Here we can enter what has become known as the Balch–Elliott debate. The now classic debate between Balch and Elliott was initiated by the publication of their individual monographs that appeared in the same year and reached opposite conclusions with regard to 1 Peter's social strategy.[1] Balch's monograph, *Let Wives Be Submissive*, focused on the household code section of 1 Peter (2.18–3.7) with particular emphasis on the exhortations towards wives (3.1–6). After surveying comparative discussion of household conduct among Greco-Roman writers, Balch concludes that the form of 1 Peter's address (and other New Testament household codes) has its roots in Aristotle's discussion of household management (οἰκονομία).[2] He highlights that the concern for rightly ordered households was not simply a matter of private interest but was of great importance to society as a whole. Any group that subverted the patriarchal order by encouraging insubordination/emancipation of wives or slaves was a socio-political threat. He goes on to show how eastern cults like those of Dionysus

---

[1] Balch, *Wives*; Elliott, *Home*. The debate was continued in a 1982 SBL seminar. The papers were then subsequently revised and published. See J. H. Elliott, '1 Peter, Its Situation and Strategy: A Discussion with David Balch', in *Perspectives on First Peter*, ed. Charles H. Talbert, NABPR Special Studies Series 9 (Macon, GA: Mercer University Press, 1986), 61–78; Balch, 'Hellenization/Acculturation in 1 Peter', in *Perspectives on First Peter*, ed. Charles H. Talbert, NABPR Special Studies Series 9 (Macon, GA: Mercer University Press, 1986), 79–101.

[2] See Balch, *Wives*, 23–62; 'Hellenization', 81.

and Isis were considered highly suspicious and problematic, not to mention immoral. In this environment, other eastern religions such as Judaism and Christianity could easily be subject to the same accusations. Therefore, since the Roman aristocracy prized the proper ordering of and submission within households, writers such as Josephus provided an apology (*Against Apion*) to demonstrate that Jewish teaching supported the proper ordering of the household and, consequently, was not a socio-political threat.[3] Balch interprets the function of the household codes in 1 Peter in the same vein.[4] Thus, the material is designed to encourage the believers to 'conform to the expectations of Hellenistic-Roman society' with regard to proper subordination and aims to maintain harmony in the household in order to reduce persecution and slander by proving that the believers are in fact obedient citizens.[5] For Balch, the command to 'do good' means to meet societal expectations by accepting 'their role in the socio-political system'.[6] In this way, he sees 1 Peter as encouraging acculturation to surrounding society.[7] However, in *Wives*, Balch does maintain that the letter does not go as far as encouraging the worship of the master's/husband's gods and keeps open the possibility that the wife might convert her husband through submissiveness.[8] Therefore, the behaviour exhorted in the household code of 1 Peter arises from a drive to reduce persecution by means of acculturation.

Elliott considers 1 Peter in its entirety. For Elliott, the key to understanding the social strategy of the letter is to appreciate the significance of the terms πάροικος and οἶκος τοῦ θεοῦ, especially 'the social realities to which they point'.[9] Rather than being metaphorical, Elliott considers πάροικοι to be a technical term designating the political-legal status of the recipients as 'resident aliens'. Such a group was in a vulnerable socio-political position[10] and was

---

[3] Balch, *Wives*, 65–76; cf. Balch, 'Hellenization', 90–3.
[4] Balch later argues: 'First Peter, written by a Hellenistic Jewish Christian author from Rome "to the exiles of the Dispersion" in Asia Minor (1 Pet. 1:1), continues the acculturation process in the Hellenistic Jewish diaspora'; Balch, 'Hellenization', 90–1.
[5] Balch, *Wives*, 86–8; see wider argument (81–109).
[6] Balch, *Wives*, 109; cf. 87–8.
[7] Balch, *Wives*, 119. In a later essay, Balch asserts that such an accepting of Hellenistic social values is 'in tension' with both Jewish tradition and the early Jesus movement with regard to their view on slaves and women respectively; see Balch, 'Hellenization', 81, 96–8.
[8] Balch, *Wives*, 85, 99, 105; cf. Balch, 'Hellenization', 87 where Balch notes that 1 Peter rejects some patterns of behaviour present in Greco-Roman society (e.g. 1 Peter 1.18; 4.3–4).
[9] Elliott, *Home*, 14.
[10] Elliott, *Home*, 24–6, 35–7.

frequently the target of 'social suspicion, censure and animosity'.[11] However, it was the addressees' 'religious allegiance, with the exclusiveness that such allegiance required, which had incited the suspicion and hostility of their neighbors'.[12] As the elect people of God, the believers had separated themselves from society and cut 'past familial, social and religious ties'.[13] For Elliott, the suffering the Christians were experiencing because of their religious exclusiveness posed a threat to the internal cohesion of the sect and had the potential to lead to defection.[14] However, unlike Balch, Elliott does not think that social conformity is what is being espoused by 1 Peter as the correct response to hostility, since this would have 'resulted in the loss of the distinctiveness and exclusiveness to which the sect owed its existence'.[15] For Elliott, 'Social conformity is … precisely the trend which 1 Peter was designed to counteract.'[16] Instead, the social conflict that occasioned 1 Peter could be used positively as an opportunity to reaffirm group boundaries, emphasise key loyalties, and reassert group distinctiveness and status.[17] Therefore, in the face of opposition, the letter communicates to its audience a theological rationale for why the believers should foster internal cohesion along with separation from outsiders, maintaining their faithful solidarity with God, Christ, and each other.[18] For Elliott, the primary language used to support this is the identification of the community as the household of God. The household language and its range of associated terms 'supplied powerful social, psychological and theological symbols for depicting … Christian conversion and cohesion, the commonality of Christian values and goals, and the distinctive character of communal Christian identity'.[19] In such a household the alienated πάροικοι could find their desired home.[20]

Given the preceding investigation into the function of emotions in 1 Peter, it may now be obvious that I find more sympathy with

---

[11] Elliott, *Home*, 68–9.
[12] Elliott, *Home*, 73.
[13] Elliott, *Home*, 75.
[14] Elliott, *Home*, 84.
[15] Elliott, *Home*, 84. Using the sociologist Bryan R. Wilson, Elliott categorises the letter's recipients as a 'conversionist sect', which offered the alienated 'the prospect for a communal experience of salvation in a brotherhood of love' (77; cf. 74–8). This conversionist sect had its own values and ideals that would have been at odds with those of surrounding society (78).
[16] Elliott, *Home*, 111; cf. 75.
[17] Elliott, *Home*, 112–15; see also discussion on election (120–7).
[18] See Elliott, *Home*, 132–49.
[19] Elliott, *Home*, 223; cf. 165–237.
[20] Elliott, *Home*, 233.

Elliott's position than Balch's.[21] However, I would not want to argue that 1 Peter's pushes for such a radical separation from society as Elliott seems to narrate[22] since the letter does continue to ask the believers to engage with their socio-cultural environment. It is as members *within* their current non-Christian household that the slaves and wives are addressed.[23] However, I would not go as far as Balch to say that the letter encourages acculturation if by this we mean that its ethics are driven primarily by acceptance of Greco-Roman cultural values.[24] In this way, I would want to agree with Elliott that the community has its own values, which are shaped by the will of God and the example of Christ's obedience.[25] Having said this, as discussed above (pp. 201–2; cf. pp. 158–61), the letter does allow for behaviour that would have been acceptable to Greco-Roman society, but such an ethic is oriented by the believer's stance towards God not a care for accommodating to the outsider.[26] It is necessary at this point to note the advances of scholars like Horrell, who have shown using resources from postcolonial studies that the tensions between conformity and resistance are more complex and varied than the Balch–Elliott debate allows, particularly when aspects such as the dominance of the Roman Empire are taken into consideration. For example, it is possible for 'communication and action to subtly and

[21] However, I do not find Elliott's argument concerning the literal political-legal interpretation of πάροικος convincing, nor do I consider the 'household of God' to be the defining metaphor.
[22] For example, Elliott claims that the Christian community was 'set apart and disengaged from the routine affairs of civic and social life'; Elliott, *Home*, 79.
[23] See Balch, 'Hellenization', 84. As such, I do not agree with Elliott that the focus of the household code is life within the household of God; Elliott, *Home*, 231 (cf. 'Situation', 65–6).
[24] After arguing for 1 Peter's ethic of acculturation, at the end of his 1982 essay Balch provides a short section on what would have maintained the *boundaries* of the Christian community. His answer to this question is the story of Christ. It is this *mythos* that is important: a *mythos* rather than any *ethos* provided the 'key identity symbol'. Here, Balch seems to want to allow acculturation at a practical level, but not at a symbolic. I find this difficult to agree with. How can one absorb an over-arching story that includes its own value system to such an extent that it becomes identity defining and, yet, be driven in one's behaviour by the values and opinions of an entirely different worldview? Surely, if the mythos is what is boundary defining and boundaries are most obviously seen in praxis, then it is the values revealed by this foundational story that will drive behaviour. Thus, Balch inadvertently adds weight to the argument that it is an orientation towards God and Christ that proves both forma-tive and normative, first emotionally and then behaviourally. Balch, 'Hellenization', 98–101; cf. Elliott, 'Situation', 76–7.
[25] Elliott, *Home*, 128.
[26] Cf. Elliott, 'Situation', 73; cf. Williams, *Good Works*, 246–7, 257–60.

changeably weave resistance into what is in various other respects a discourse of conformity and obedience'.[27] Horrell concludes:

> [T]he author of 1 Peter calls his readers to conform as far as is possible to the standards of goodness expected by the powerful: honouring the emperor, submitting to masters and husbands, living such innocent lives to negate all criticism ... Yet at the same time ... it would be wrong to characterize the author of 1 Peter as someone who promotes a life of conformity and acquiescence to Rome among the converts in Asia Minor. There are a number of respects in which he encourages a stance of what might be called distance and resistance.[28]

For Horrell, such indicators of distance and resistance include: the narrative of the believer's positive identity, which is founded on the scriptures and God of Israel and calls into question the political claims of the Empire; the proud wearing of the label Χριστιανός, which subverts any implication of criminality; and the line drawn by the letter, which determines that Caesar can be honoured but not worshipped. For Horrell then, the author's stance is one in which 'resistance and conformity are combined in a nuanced yet clear position': polite resistance.[29]

It is of note that in the debate concerning 1 Peter's social strategy little attention has been given to the emotions.[30] This is problematic

---

[27] D. G. Horrell, 'Between Conformity and Resistance: Beyond the Balch-Elliott Debate Towards a Postcolonial Reading of 1 Peter', in *Becoming Christian: Essays on 1 Peter and the Making of Christian Identity*, LNTS 294 (London: T&T Clark, 2013), 218.

[28] Horrell, 'Between Conformity and Resistance', 236–7.

[29] Horrell, 'Between Conformity and Resistance', 237–8; cf. 222–35. See also M. Volf, 'Soft Difference: Theological Reflections on the Relationship between Church and Culture in 1 Peter', *Ex Auditu* 10 (1994): 15–30. Like Horrell, I would want to reject Lauri Thurén's stance in *Rhetorical Strategy* (see pp. 12–14) that the letter addresses two different audiences in one – the passive and the active members – and therefore exhibits a tendency towards both cultural assimilation and separation. As Horrell argues, 'This "solution" not only fails to give a coherent account of the letter's strategy but also depends on the implausible idea that different audiences could and would be specifically addressed and challenged by the bits of the letter that related to the author's perceptions of their needs.' It is more preferable to assume, as the letter seems to reveal, a consistent directive and orientation; see Horrell, 'Between Conformity and Resistance', 214.

[30] For example, Balch notes that the wives are exhorted not to fear 'those who might injure' but instead are to fear God. However, he does nothing further with these ideas, which occur within the household code section of the letter and should surely impact upon his discussion; Balch, *Wives*, 95.

because emotions are both deeply tied to cultural norms and prescriptive for behaviour. Thus, through understanding them we can see how the author is orientating his audience (i.e. towards what values and symbols) and also what behaviour is being promoted. These are the very points on which the Balch–Elliott debate hinges. From our investigation, it is apparent that the author's use of emotion is seeking to establish a different framework of values based on God's character and his action in Christ. Moreover, time and time again, the emotions direct the audience towards God, and position God and Christ as of primary importance in the audience's worldview, presumably in order to mould the believers' behavioural response. The hostile other, conversely, is continually displaced and either devalued or revalued. Furthermore, the author's use of shame language poses a frontal attack on society's assessments of the believers and, as such, challenges the norms and assumptions of surrounding society. The suggestion that the author wants the audience to acculturate to surrounding society cannot be reconciled with this evidence. Thus, as noted above, this investigation finds more sympathy with Elliott. However, I find that, in fact, Torrey Seland's position is the most compelling. Seland challenges the Balch–Elliott debate, and suggests that the discussion starts from the wrong point. For, in reality, the believers were already acculturated to their previous society, but what they are in need of is socialisation into the new Christian community, including its ideologies and symbols.[31] In agreement with Seland, my investigation into emotions has convinced me that *this* is what the letter is aiming at. The emotional rhetoric of 1 Peter asks the audience to move towards internalising a new view of reality, a reality that has a new set of values, norms, narrative, and symbols. The believers' emotional internalisation of this reality is a necessary stage in the socialisation process if the believers are to fully accept and identify with their new Christian worldview and community.[32] Through their internal acceptance of this reality the believers will be able to carry an outlook that consistently informs their priorities and consequently their ethics. Put differently, through a new emotional

[31] T. Seland, *Strangers in the Light: Philonic Perspectives on Christian Identity in 1 Peter*, BInS 76 (Leiden: Brill, 2005), 168–72. Therefore, any alienation is a result of their conversion, not, contra Elliott, a specific displaced status they had before conversion; see Horrell, 'Between Conformity and Resistance', 226; cf. Volf, 'Soft Difference', 17–19.
[32] Of course, members of the audience will be at different stages of the socialisation process. For some, the ideas presented by the letter may be new; for others, they will serve as a reminder.

regime, the author enables the audience to be fully incorporated into the reality revealed in Christ. As Horrell comments, the believers are located within a new 'identity-defining narrative which offers a fundamentally different perspective on their existence'.[33] Of course, the second question of how they are to relate to their previous community does inevitably follow, but this is a *secondary* question.[34] If the socialisation process has been effected successfully, then aspects of this process such as one's new emotional orientation will necessarily put boundaries on behaviour and interaction. Consequently, our investigation into emotions has revealed that 1 Peter's worldview aims to produce a desire to be in allegiance with God through Christ because of a belief that such allegiance is the only way to flourish as a human, even if it leads to suffering.[35] In asserting this worldview through his use of emotions the author can make sure that the audience is equipped to navigate its world correctly. This may at points mean that the audience exhibits behaviour also considered 'good' by external society, but on other occasions it may require outright deviance. Their Christian outlook and its associated goals and values are what determine behaviour, and this will *secondarily* impact upon their relationships. Therefore, it is allegiance to God that is most important, not (non)conformity or assimilation/separation as social principles in themselves.

Moving Forward

It is evident that taking a theoretically informed look at the use of emotions in 1 Peter has enabled us to assess the rhetoric of the author in a fresh light. As such, it has extended and given greater depth to work previously done by Petrine scholars in this area. Through exploring a number of emotions, this investigation has taken a broader approach to pathetic persuasion than Campbell's work, *Honor, Shame and the Rhetoric of 1 Peter*. It has also rejected the importing of ancient rhetorical categories on to the text exhibited in Campbell's work, and has sought to understand how emotions work through the discourse of the letter as a whole rather than in

---

[33] Furthermore, this new narrative that the believers internally carry may, as Horrell suggests, give the audience a new sense of 'dislocation and distance' from their society; Horrell, 'Between Conformity and Resistance', 227–9.

[34] Cf. Volf, 'Soft Difference', 19.

[35] Thus, as Volf correctly asserts, Christian identity is forged positively through promoting allegiance to something. Its starting point is not the rejection of external culture; Volf, 'Soft Difference', 20.

isolated passages. In such a way, it has been possible to highlight the thoroughgoing importance of emotions in persuasion across the letter, drawing parallels between and collating the evidence from emotions that occur in different sections of the letter's argument. This wider approach can more readily lead on to larger scale discussion, for example, about what the author thinks it means to flourish as a human, or how the early Christian communities sought to use emotions to establish a distinctive Christian culture.

We noted at the outset that Thurén's *Argument and Theology in 1 Peter* does acknowledge that emotions are motivating and his analysis implicitly recognises the logic of emotions. However, where Thurén has expressed the importance of emotion in persuasion and has only started to make steps towards appreciating the role of emotions in 1 Peter in influencing the audience's behaviour, this study has provided an in-depth and full-scale analysis of emotion's function. The theoretical insights provided by modern emotion theory, which this investigation has utilised, have provided a fresh set of heuristic questions not utilised by previous scholars of 1 Peter, such as Thurén or Martin. These directing questions have enabled us to draw new connections between emotions, objects, goals, values, worldview, and actions not hitherto articulated, and therefore also to identify the fundamental connection between emotions and ethics. Furthermore, through being aware of the complexity of conversation about emotions and the various levels at which this can take place, this study has sought to move beyond simply talking about emotional arousal – often overtly or implicitly coloured by the interpreter's own cultural understanding of emotions – towards a greater awareness of the varieties of the exegetical task that are open to us when we approach emotion terms in an ancient text. As such, with an awareness of the levels of conversation, it has shown how ancient philosophical and rhetorical material on emotion can be used sensitively to help us have a better historically and culturally informed understanding of the ideas encoded in an emotion term and then, comparatively, what the author's distinctive contextualisation of this emotion reveals. Consequently, one significant step forward this study has taken is to appreciate that emotion terms themselves contain logical communicative content and, therefore, that it is possible to unpack what their communication means for our understanding of the text and the implications of this for the letter's recipients, especially for their ethical, social, and therapeutic lives. Where Thurén has noted the importance of fear and joy for the ideological structure of 1 Peter's argument, this investigation has suggested that emotions play a much more significant role in the letter. It has been able to demonstrate how the author has moved beyond using emotions to 'moralise' or 'judge' events to using emotions to place an entire eschatological worldview before his audience's eyes by applying familiar emotions to new scenarios.[36] As such, it has demonstrated that the letter seeks to internally shape the recipients in order to effect within them a deep and lasting internal orientation, which would likely prove more effective in determining behaviour than prescriptive commands alone.

In terms of previous readings of 1 Peter, the above exegesis has shown how being more aware of emotions can pinpoint where a cursory reading of emotion terms has led to errors, such as what the author is encouraging the audience to rejoice in, or the place of trials and suffering in the life of the Christian. In the case of fear, a better understanding of emotions has highlighted where our modern sensibilities regarding emotions may cause us to dampen the intended force of 1 Peter's language. Furthermore, with the emotion of shame, it has shown how the assessment of a person's social status without recourse to her internal emotional understanding of her identity is problematic. Thus, this study has demonstrated that investigating emotions in the New Testament epistles opens up new avenues for discussion, and can even provide corrective tools. Moreover, it has shown that if we really want to understand an author's worldview and/or his ethics we must take account of the emotions.

In the foregoing investigation, we have only started to scratch the surface of exploring emotions in the New Testament. We have not even covered every emotion in 1 Peter, leaving love and the absence of anger untouched. Consequently, there remains plenty of scope for investigating emotions, whether that be in other New Testament texts individually or comparatively across texts. My hope is that this book has provided both a working methodology by which this can be accomplished, and evidence of the value of such an investigation.

[36] See Lutz, *Unnatural*, 10.

APPENDIX

Chronology of the Leading Stoics

The following information is taken from Tiziano Dorandi, 'Chronology', in *The Cambridge History of Hellenistic Philosophy*, ed. Keimpe Algra et al. (Cambridge: Cambridge University Press, 2005), 31–54, at 50–4; F. H. Sandbach, *The Stoics*, 2nd ed. (Bristol: Bristol Press, 1989), 7; D. Sedley, 'The School from Zeno to Arius Didymus', in *The Cambridge Companion to The Stoics*, ed. Brad Inwood (Cambridge: Cambridge University Press, 2003), 7–32; and C. Gill, 'The School in the Roman Imperial Period', in *The Cambridge Companion to The Stoics*, ed. Brad Inwood (Cambridge: Cambridge University Press, 2003), 33–58, at 33–8. Those listed in bold indicate the heads of the Stoic school in Athens. Where there is disagreement in dating the below follows Dorandi and Gill.

The Founder

Zeno of Citium (born 334/3, died 262/1 BCE)

Early Stoicism

Aristo of Chios (contemporaneous with Zeno)
Dionysius of Heraclea (born 330–325 BCE)
Cleanthes of Assos (born 331/0, becomes Scholarch 262/1 BCE, died 230/29 BCE)
Persaeus of Citium (born 307/6, flourished 260–256 BCE, died 243 BCE)
Sphaerus of Borysthenes (born *c*.285)
Chrysippus of Soli (born 280–276 BCE, becomes Scholarch 230/29, died 208–204 BCE)
Zeno of Tarsus (Scholarch *c*.208–205 BCE)
Diogenes of Seleucia/Babylon (born *c*.230 BCE, died *c*.150–140 BCE)

269

Middle Stoicism

Antipater of Tarsus (becomes Scholarch *c.*150–140 BCE, died 130/29 BCE)

Panaetius of Rhodes (born 185–180 BCE, becomes Scholarch 129/8 BCE, died 110/09 BCE)

Hecato of Rhodes

Mnesarchus and **Dardanus** (born *c.*170 BCE, joint heads *c.*110/09 BCE)

Posidonius of Apamea (born *c.*135–130 BCE, died 55–50 BCE)

Athenodorus (late first century BCE)

Arius Dydimus (late first century BCE)

Roman Stoicism

Seneca the Younger (1 BCE–65 CE)

Musonius Rufus (*c.*30–100 CE)

Epictetus (*c.*50–130 CE)

Hierocles (active around 120 CE)

Marcus Aurelius (b.121 CE, Emperor 161–180 CE)

BIBLIOGRAPHY

Primary Sources

All English Bible translations are from:
www.biblegateway.com. Accessed 27 November 2015.

All Greek New Testament quotations, unless otherwise stated are from:
Nestle-Aland Novum Testamentum Graece 28. Stuttgart: Deutsche Bibelgesellschaft, 2012.

LXX quotations are from:
Septuaginta: Edito altera. Rev. ed. Stuttgart: Deutsche Bibelgesellschaft, 2006.

Aeilus Herodianus. 'Περὶ ὀρθογραφίας'. Vol. 3.2 in A. Lentz, *Grammatici Graeci*, 407–611. Leipzig: Teubner, 1870. Repr. Hildesheim: Olms, 1965. Accessed 23 October 2015. http://stephanus.tlg.uci.edu.ezphost.dur.ac.uk/inst/browser.

Andronicus Rhodius. *Andronici qui fertur libelli Περὶ Παθῶν (De affectibus)*, pt. 1. Translated by X. Kreuttner. Heidelberg: Winter, 1884: 11–21. Accessed 2 December 2015. http://stephanus.tlg.uci.edu.ezphost.dur.ac.uk/inst/browser.

Aristotle. *Art of Rhetoric*. Translated by J. H. Freese. Loeb Classical Library 193. Cambridge, MA: Harvard University Press, 1926.

The Athenian Constitution. The Eudemian Ethics. On Virtues and Vices. Translated by H. Rackham. Loeb Classical Library 285. Cambridge, MA: Harvard University Press, 1935.

De Anima. Translated by W. D. Ross. Oxford: Clarendon Press, 1961 (repr. 1967).

De Anima. Translation with Introduction and Notes by Hugh Lawson-Tancred. Penguin Classics. London: Penguin Books, 1986.

Eudemian Ethics. Translated and edited by Brad Inwood and Raphael Woolf. Cambridge Texts in the History of Philosophy. Cambridge and New York: Cambridge University Press, 2013.

Nicomachean Ethics. Translated by H. Rackham. Loeb Classical Library 73. Cambridge, MA: Harvard University Press, 1926.

Nichomachean Ethics. Translation (with Historical Introduction) by Christopher Rowe. Philosophical Introduction and Commentary by Sarah Broadie. Oxford: Oxford University Press, 2002.

On Rhetoric. A Theory of Civic Discourse. Translation with Introduction, Notes and Appendices by George A. Kennedy. 2nd ed. New York and Oxford: Oxford University Press, 2007.

On the Soul. Parva Naturalia. On Breath. Translated by W. S. Hett. Loeb Classical Library 288. Cambridge, MA: Harvard University Press, 1957.

Parts of Animals. Movement of Animals. Progression of Animals. Translated by A. L. Peck and E. S. Forster. Loeb Classical Library 323. Cambridge, MA: Harvard University Press, 1937.

[Cicero]. *Rhetorica ad Herennium.* Translated by Harry Caplan. Loeb Classical Library 403. Cambridge, MA: Harvard University Press, 1954.

Cicero. *Brutus. Orator.* Translated by G. L. Hendrickson and H. M. Hubbell. Loeb Classical Library 342. Cambridge, MA: Harvard University Press, 1939.

On Duties. Translated by Walter Miller. Loeb Classical Library 30. Cambridge, MA: Harvard University Press, 1913.

On Ends. Translated by H. Rackham. Loeb Classical Library 40. Cambridge, MA: Harvard University Press, 1914.

On the Nature of the Gods. Academics. Translated by H. Rackham. Loeb Classical Library 268. Cambridge, MA: Harvard University Press, 1933.

On the Orator: Books 1–2. Translated by E. W. Sutton and H. Rackham. Loeb Classical Library 348. Cambridge, MA: Harvard University Press, 1942.

On the Orator: Book 3. On Fate. Stoic Paradoxes. Divisions of Oratory. Translated by H. Rackham. Loeb Classical Library 349. Cambridge, MA: Harvard University Press, 1942.

Tusculan Disputations. Translated by J. E. King. Loeb Classical Library 141. Cambridge, MA: Harvard University Press, 1927.

Diogenes Laertius. *Lives of Eminent Philosophers, Volume II: Books 6–10.* Translated by R. D. Hicks. Loeb Classical Library 185. Cambridge, MA: Harvard University Press, 1925.

Dionysius of Halicarnassus. *Critical Essays, Volume I: Ancient Orators. Lysias. Isocrates. Isaeus. Demosthenes. Thucydides.* Translated by Stephen Usher. Loeb Classical Library 465. Cambridge, MA: Harvard University Press, 1974.

Epictetus. *Discourses, Books 1–2.* Translated by W. A. Oldfather. Loeb Classical Library 131. Cambridge, MA: Harvard University Press, 1925.

Discourses, Books 3–4. Fragments. The Encheiridion. Translated by W. A. Oldfather. Loeb Classical Library 218. Cambridge, MA: Harvard University Press, 1928.

Marcus Aurelius. *Marcus Aurelius*. Edited and translated by C. R. Haines. Loeb Classical Library 58. Cambridge, MA: Harvard University Press, 1916.

Philo. *Every Good Man Is Free. On the Contemplative Life. On the Eternity of the World. Against Flaccus. Apology for the Jews. On Providence.* Translated by F. H. Colson. Loeb Classical Library 363. Cambridge, MA: Harvard University Press, 1941.

On Abraham. On Joseph. On Moses. Translated by F. H. Colson. Loeb Classical Library 289. Cambridge, MA: Harvard University Press, 1935.

On the Cherubim. The Sacrifices of Abel and Cain. The Worse Attacks the Better. On the Posterity and Exile of Cain. On the Giants. Translated by F. H. Colson and G. H. Whitaker. Loeb Classical Library 227. Cambridge, MA: Harvard University Press, 1929.

On the Creation. Allegorical Interpretation of Genesis 2 and 3. Translated by F. H. Colson and G. H. Whitaker. Loeb Classical Library 226. Cambridge, MA: Harvard University Press, 1929.

On Flight and Finding. On the Change of Names. On Dreams. Translated by F. H. Colson and G. H. Whitaker. Loeb Classical Library 275. Cambridge, MA: Harvard University Press, 1934.

On the Special Laws, Book 4. On the Virtues. On Rewards and Punishments. Translated by F. H. Colson. Loeb Classical Library 341. Cambridge, MA: Harvard University Press, 1939.

Questions on Genesis. Translated by Ralph Marcus. Loeb Classical Library 380. Cambridge, MA: Harvard University Press, 1953.

Plato. 'Charmides'. Translated by Rosamond Kent Sprague. In *Complete Works*, edited by John M. Cooper, 639–63. Indianapolis, IN and Cambridge: Hackett, 1997.

'Laws'. Translated by Trevor J. Saunders. In *Complete Works*, edited by John M. Cooper, 1318–616. Indianapolis, IN and Cambridge: Hackett, 1997.

'Phaedo'. Translated by G. M. A. Grube. In *Complete Works*, edited by John M. Cooper, 49–100. Indianapolis, IN and Cambridge: Hackett, 1997.

'Republic'. Translated by G. M. A. Grube and C. D. C. Reeve. In *Complete Works*, edited by John M. Cooper, 971–1223. Indianapolis, IN and Cambridge: Hackett, 1997.

'Timaeus'. Translated by Donald J. Zegyl. In *Complete Works*, edited by John M. Cooper, 1224–91 Indianapolis, IN and Cambridge: Hackett, 1997.

Plutarch. *Moralia, Volume VI: 439a–523b.* Translated by W. C. Helmbold. Cambridge, MA: Harvard University Press, 1962.

Quintilian. *The Orator's Education, Volume II: Books 3–5.* Edited and translated by Donald A. Russell. Loeb Classical Library 125. Cambridge, MA: Harvard University Press, 2002.

The Orator's Education, Volume III: Books 6–8. Edited and translated by Donald A. Russell. Loeb Classical Library 126. Cambridge, MA: Harvard University Press, 2002.

Seneca. *Epistles, Volume I: Epistles 1–65.* Translated by Richard
   M. Gummere. Loeb Classical Library 75. Cambridge, MA: Harvard
   University Press, 1917.
   Epistles, Volume II: Epistles 66–92. Translated by Richard M. Gummere.
   Loeb Classical Library 76. Cambridge, MA: Harvard University Press,
   1920.
   Epistles, Volume III: Epistles 93–124. Translated by Richard M. Gummere.
   Loeb Classical Library 77. Cambridge, MA: Harvard University Press,
   1925.
   *Moral Essays, Volume I: De Providentia. De Constantia. De Ira. De
   Clementia.* Translated by John W. Basore. Loeb Classical Library 214.
   Cambridge, MA: Harvard University Press, 1928.

Compilations of more than one ancient author:
Kidd, I. G. *Posidonius. Volume III. The Translation of the Fragments.*
   Cambridge Classical Texts and Commentaries Series 36. Cambridge:
   Cambridge University Press, 1999.
Long, A. A. and D. N. Sedley. *The Hellenistic Philosophers. Volume 1:
   Translations of the Principal Sources with Philosophical Commentary.*
   Cambridge: Cambridge University Press, 1987.
Long, A. A. and D. N. Sedley. *The Hellenistic Philosophers. Volume 2: Greek
   and Latin Texts with Notes and Bibliography.* Cambridge: Cambridge
   University Press, 1987.
von Arnim, H., ed. *Stoicorum veterum Fragmenta.* 4 vols. Leipzig: Teubner,
   1923–38.

Secondary Sources

Achtemeier, Paul J. *1 Peter: A Commentary on First Peter.* Hermeneia.
   Minneapolis, MN: Fortress Press, 1996.
Atherton, Catherine. 'Hand Over Fist: The Failure of Stoic Rhetoric'.
   Classical Quarterly, New Series 38 (1988): 392–427.
Averill, James R. 'The Social Construction of Emotion: With Special
   Reference to Love'. In *The Social Construction of the Person*, edited
   by Kenneth J. Gergen and Keith E. Davis, 89–109. Springer Series in
   Social Psychology. New York: Springer-Verlag, 1985.
Balch, David L. 'Hellenization/Acculturation in 1 Peter'. In *Perspectives on
   First Peter*, edited by Charles H. Talbert, 79–101. National Association
   of Baptist Professors of Religion Special Studies Series 9. Macon,
   GA: Mercer University Press, 1986.
Balch, David L. *Let Wives Be Submissive: The Domestic Code in 1 Peter.*
   The Society of Biblical Literature Monograph Series 26. Atlanta,
   GA: Scholars Press, 1981.
Bammel, E. 'The Commands in I Peter II.17'. *New Testament Studies* 11
   (1965): 279–81.

Barton, Stephen C. ' "Be Angry But Do Not Sin" (Ephesians 4:26a): Sin and the Emotions in the New Testament with Special Reference to Anger'. *Studies in Christian Ethics* 28 (2015): 21–34.

Barton, Stephen C. 'Eschatology and the Emotions in Early Christianity'. *Journal of Biblical Literature* 130 (2011): 571–91.

Barton, Stephen C. 'Spirituality and the Emotions in Early Christianity: The Case of Joy'. In *The Bible and Spirituality: Exploratory Essays in Reading Scripture Spiritually*, edited by Andrew T. Lincoln, J. Gordon McConville, and Lloyd K. Pietersen, 171–93. Eugene, OR: Cascade Books, 2013.

Barton, Stephen C. 'Why Do Things Move People? The Jerusalem Temple as Emotional Repository'. *Journal for the Study of the New Testament* 37 (2015): 351–80.

Baumert, Norbert. *Koinonein und Metechein – synonym? Ein umfassende semantische Untersuchung.* Stuttgarter biblische Beiträger 51. Stuttgart: Katholisches Bibelwerk GmbH, 2003.

Bechtler, Steven Richard. *Following in His Steps: Suffering, Community, and Christology in 1 Peter.* Society of Biblical Literature Dissertation Series 162. Atlanta, GA: Scholars Press, 1998.

Berger, Peter L. and Thomas Luckmann. *The Social Construction of Reality: A Treatise in the Sociology of Knowledge.* New York: Doubleday & Company, 1966. Repr., New York: Anchor Books, 1967.

Betz, Han Dieter. *Galatians: A Commentary on Paul's Letter to the Churches in Galatia.* Hermeneia. Philadelphia, PA: Fortress Press, 1979.

Bigg, Charles. *A Critcal and Exegetical Commentary on the First Epistles of St. Peter and St. Jude.* The International Critical Commentary. Edinburgh: T&T Clark, 1901.

Bird, Jennifer G. *Abuse, Power and Fearful Obedience: Reconsidering 1 Peter's Commands to Wives.* Library of New Testament Studies 442. London: T&T Clark, 2011.

Brennan, Tad. 'The Old Stoic Theory of Emotions'. In *The Emotions in Hellenistic Philosophy*, edited by Juha Sihvola and Troels Engberg-Pedersen, 21–70. Dordrecht: Kluwer Academic, 1998.

Brennan, Tad. *The Stoic Life: Emotions, Duties, and Fate.* Oxford: Oxford University Press, 2005.

Brox, Norbert. *Der Erste Petrusbrief.* Evangelisch-Katholischer Kommentar zum Neuen Testament 21. Zürich: Benziger Verlag, 1979.

Campbell, Barth L. *Honor, Shame, and the Rhetoric of 1 Peter.* Society of Biblical Literature Dissertation Series 160. Atlanta, GA: Scholars Press, 1998.

Cavanaugh, Lisa A., Keisha M. Cutright, Mary Frances Luce, and James R. Bettman. 'Hope, Pride, and Processing During Optimal and Nonoptimal Times of Day'. *Emotion* 11, no. 1 (2011): 38–46.

Classen, Carl Joachim. *Rhetorical Criticism of the New Testament.* WUNT 128. Tübingen: Mohr Siebeck, 2000.

Cooper, John M. 'Posidonius on Emotions'. In *The Emotions in Hellenistic Philosophy*, edited by Juha Sihvola and Troels Engberg-Pedersen, 71–111. Dordrecht: Kluwer Academic, 1998.

Cothenet, E. 'Le realisme de l'esperance chrétienne selon 1 Pierre'. *New Testament Studies* 27 (1981): 564–72.

Dalton, William Joseph. *Christ's Proclamation to the Spirits: A Study of 1 Peter 3:18–4:6*. 2nd ed. Analecta Biblica 23. Rome: Editrice Pontificio Istituto Biblico, 1989.

Daube, David. 'κερδαίνω as a Missionary Term'. *Harvard Theological Review* 40 (1947): 109–20.

de Villiers, J. L. 'Joy in Suffering in 1 Peter'. In *Essays on the General Epistles of the New Testament: 11th Meeting of Die Nuwe-Testamentiese Werkgemeenskap van Suid-Afrika, 1975*, edited by W. Nicol, 64–86. Neotestamentica 9. Pretoria: NTWSA, 1975.

de Villiers, Pieter G. R. 'Love in the Letter to the Galatians'. In *The Bible and Spirituality: Exploratory Essays in Reading Scripture Spiritually*, edited by Andrew T. Lincoln, J. Gordon McConville, and Lloyd K. Pietersen, 194–211. Eugene, OR: Cascade Books, 2013.

De Waal Dryden, J. *Theology and Ethics in 1 Peter: Paraenetic Strategies for Christian Character Formation*. WUNT 2.209. Tübingen: Mohr Siebeck, 2006.

Dixon, Thomas. ' "Emotion": The History of a Key Word in Crisis'. *Emotion Review* 4 (2012): 338–44.

Dixon, Thomas. *From Passions to Emotions: The Creation of a Secular Psychological Category*. Cambridge: Cambridge University Press, 2003.

Dorandi, Tiziano. 'Chronology'. In *The Cambridge History of Hellenistic Philosophy*, edited by Keimpe Algra, Jonathan Barnes, Jaap Mansfield, and Malcolm Schofield, 31–54. Cambridge: Cambridge University Press, 2005.

du Toit, A. B. 'The Significance of Discourse Analysis for New Testament Interpretation and Translation: Introductory Remarks with Special Reference to 1 Peter 1.3–13'. *Neotestamentica* 8 (1974): 54–79.

Dubis, Mark. *1 Peter: A Handbook on the Greek Text*. Baylor Handbook on the Greek New Testament. Waco, TX: Baylor University Press, 2010.

Dubis, Mark. *Messianic Woes in First Peter: Suffering and Eschatology in 1 Peter 4:12–19*. Studies in Biblical Literature 33. New York: Peter Lang, 2002.

Elliott, John H. *1 Peter: A New Translation with Commentary*. The Anchor Bible 37B. New York: Doubleday, 2000.

Elliott, John H. '1 Peter, Its Situation and Strategy: A Discussion with David Balch'. In *Perspectives on First Peter*, edited by Charles H. Talbert, 61–78. National Association of Baptist Professors of Religion Special Study Series 9. Macon, GA: Mercer University Press, 1986.

Elliott, John H. *A Home for the Homeless: A Sociological Exegesis of 1 Peter, Its Situation and Strategy*. Philadelphia, PA: Fortress Press, 1981.

Elliott, John H. 'Disgraced Yet Graced: The Gospel according to 1 Peter in the Key of Honor and Shame'. *Biblical Theology Bulletin* 25 (1995): 166–78.

Elliott, Matthew. *Faithful Feelings: Emotions in the New Testament*. Leicester: Inter-Varsity Press, 2005.

Erler, Michael and Malcolm Schofield. 'Epicurean Ethics'. In *The Cambridge History of Hellenistic Philosophy*, edited by Keimpe Algra, Jonathan Barnes, Jaap Mansfield, and Malcolm Schofield, 642–74. Cambridge: Cambridge University Press, 2005.

Estrada, Bernado. 'The Last Beatitude: Joy in Suffering'. *Biblica* 91 (2010): 187–209.

Everson, Stephen. 'Epicurean Psychology'. In *The Cambridge History of Hellenistic Philosophy*, edited by Keimpe Algra, Jonathan Barnes, Jaap Mansfield, and Malcolm Schofield, 542–59. Cambridge: Cambridge University Press, 2005.

Feldmeier, Reinhard. *The First Letter of Peter: A Commentary on the Greek Text*. Translated by Peter H. Davids. Waco, TX: Baylor University Press, 2008.

Friesen, Steven J. 'Poverty in Pauline Studies: Beyond the So-Called New Consensus'. *Journal for the Study of the New Testament* 26 (2004): 323–61.

Frijda, Nico H. 'Varieties of Affect: Emotions and Episodes, Moods, and Sentiments'. In *The Nature of Emotion: Fundamental Questions*, edited by Paul Ekman and Richard J. Davidson, 59–67. New York and Oxford: Oxford Univesity Press, 1994.

Frijda, Nico H., Peter Kuipers, and Elisabeth ter Schure. 'Relations Among Emotion, Appraisal, and Emotional Action Readiness'. *Journal of Personality and Social Psychology* 57 (1989): 212–28.

Gage, John T., ed. *The Promise of Reason: Studies in the New Rhetoric*. Carbondale and Edwardsville: Southern Illinois University Press, 2011.

Gill, G. 'The School in the Roman Imperial Period'. In *The Cambridge Companion to The Stoics*, edited by Brad Inwood, 33–58. Cambridge: Cambridge University Press, 2003.

Goppelt, Leonhard. *A Commentary on I Peter*. Edited by Ferdinand Hahn. Translated by John E. Alsup. Grand Rapids, MI: William B. Eerdmans, 1993. Translation of *Der Erste Petrusbrief*. Göttingen: Vanhoeck & Ruprecht, 1978.

Graver, Margaret. 'Philo of Alexandria and the Origins of the Stoic Προπάθειαι'. *Phronesis* 44 (1999): 300–25.

Graver, Margaret R. *Stoicism and Emotion*. Chicago: University of Chicago Press, 2007.

Harker, Andrew. 'The Affective Directives of the Book of Revelation'. *Tyndale Bulletin* 63 (2012): 115–30.

Hart, Roderick P. and Suzanne Daughton. *Modern Rhetorical Criticism*. 3rd ed. London and New York: Routledge, 2016.

Hockey, Katherine M. '1 Peter 4.16: Shame, Emotion and Christian Self-Perception'. In *Muted Voices of the New Testament: Readings in the*

Catholic Epistles and Hebrews, edited by Katherine M. Hockey, Madison N. Pierce, and Francis Watson, 27–40. London: Bloomsbury T&T Clark, 2017.

Holloway, Paul A. *Coping with Prejudice: 1 Peter in Social-Psychological Perspective*. WUNT 244. Tübingen: Mohr Siebeck, 2009.

Horrell, David G. 'Aliens and Strangers? The Socio-Economic Location of the Addressees of 1 Peter'. In *Becoming Christian: Essays on 1 Peter and the Making of Christian Identity*, edited by David G. Horrell, 100–32. Library of New Testament Studies 394. London: T&T Clark, 2013.

Horrell, David G. 'Between Conformity and Resistance: Beyond the Balch-Elliott Debate towards a Postcolonial Reading of 1 Peter'. In *Becoming Christian: Essays on 1 Peter and the Making of Christian Identity*, edited by David G. Horrell, 211–38. Library of New Testament Studies 394. London: T&T Clark, 2013.

Horrell, David G. 'Fear, Hope, and Doing Good: Wives as a Paradigm of Mission in 1 Peter'. *Estudios Bíblicos* 73 (2015): 409–29.

Horrell, David G. 'The Label Χριστιανός (1 Pet. 4.16): Suffering, Conflict, and the Making of Christian Identity'. In *Becoming Christian: Essays on 1 Peter and the Making of Christian Identity*, edited by David G. Horrell, 164–210. Library of New Testament Studies 394. London: T&T Clark, 2013.

Horrell, David G. 'The Product of a Petrine Circle? Challenging an Emerging Consensus'. In *Becoming Christian: Essays on 1 Peter and the Making of Christian Identity*, edited by David G. Horrell, 7–44. Library of New Testament Studies 394. London: T&T Clark, 2013.

Hort, F. J. A. *The First Epistle of St Peter 1.1–2.17: The Greek Text with Introductory Lecture, Commentary and Additional Notes*. London: Macmillan, 1898. Repr. Eugene, OR: Wipf & Stock, 2005.

Jobes, Karen. H. *1 Peter*. Baker Exegetical Commentary on the New Testament. Grand Rapids, MI: Baker Academic, 2005.

Kelly, J. N. D. *A Commentary on the Epistles of Peter and of Jude*. Black's New Testament Commentaries. London: Adam & Charles Black, 1969.

Kendall, David W. '1 Peter 1:3–9'. *Interpretation* 41 (1987): 66–71.

Kendall, David W. 'The Literary and Theological Function of 1 Peter 1:3–12'. In *Perspectives on First Peter*, edited by Charles H. Talbert, 103–20. National Association of Baptist Professors of Religion Special Studies Series 9. Macon, GA: Mercer University Press, 1986.

Kennedy, George A. *New Testament Interpretation Through Rhetorical Criticism*. Chapel Hill: University of North Carolina Press, 1984.

Klassen, William. 'Coals of Fire: Sign of Repentance or Revenge?'. *New Testament Studies* 9 (1963): 337–50.

Konstan, David. *The Emotions of the Ancient Greeks: Studies in Aristotle and Classical Literature*. Toronto: University of Toronto Press, 2006.

Kraftchick, Steven J. 'Πάθη in Paul: The Emotional Logic of "Original Argument"'. In *Paul and Pathos*, edited by Thomas H. Olbricht and

Jerry L. Sumney, 39–68. Society of Biblical Literature Symposium Series 16. Atlanta, GA: Society of Biblical Literature, 2001.

Lampe, Peter. 'Affects and Emotions in the Rhetoric of Paul's Letter to Philemon: A Rhetorical-Psychological Interpretation'. In *Philemon in Perspective: Interpreting a Pauline Letter*, edited by D. François Tolmie, 61–77. Beihefte zur Zeitschrift für die neutestamentliche Wissenschaft 169. Berlin: De Gruyter, 2010.

Lazarus, Richard S. 'Cognition and Motivation in Emotion'. *American Psychologist* 46 (1991): 352–67.

Lazarus, Richard S. 'Hope: An Emotion and a Vital Coping Resource Against Despair'. *Social Research* 66 (1999): 653–78.

Lazarus, Richard S. 'Progress on a Cognitive-Motivational-Relational Theory of Emotion'. *American Psychologist* 46 (1991): 819–34.

Lazarus, Richard S. 'The Stable and Unstable in Emotion'. In *The Nature of Emotion: Fundamental Questions*, edited by Paul Ekman and Richard J. Davidson, 79–85. New York and Oxford: Oxford University Press, 1994.

Lazarus, Richard S., James R. Averill, and Edward M. Opton Jr. 'Towards a Cognitive Theory of Emotion'. In *Feelings and Emotions: The Loyola Symposium*, edited by Magda Arnold, 207–32. New York: Academic Press, 1970.

Lewis, Charlton T. and Charles Short. *A Latin Dictionary. Founded on Andrews' Edition of Freund's Latin Dictionary. Revised, Enlarged, and in Great Part Rewritten by Charlton T. Lewis and Charles Short*. Oxford: Clarendon Press, 1879.

Liebengood, Kelly D. *The Eschatology of 1 Peter: Considering the Influence of Zechariah 9–14*. Society for New Testament Studies Monograph Series 157. Cambridge: Cambridge University Press, 2014.

Lincoln, Andrew T. 'Communion: Some Pauline Foundations'. *Ecclesiology* 5 (2009): 135–60.

Long, A. A. 'The Socratic Legacy'. In *The Cambridge History of Hellenistic Philosophy*, edited by Keimpe Algra, Jonathan Barnes, Jaap Mansfield, and Malcolm Schofield, 617–41. Cambridge: Cambridge University Press, 2005.

Longenecker, Bruce W. 'Exposing the Economic Middle: A Revised Economy of Scale for the Study of Early Urban Christianity'. *Journal for the Study of the New Testament* 31 (2009): 243–78.

Lutz, Catherine A. *Unnatural Emotions: Everyday Sentiments on a Micronesian Atoll & Their Challenge to Western Theory*. Chicago: University of Chicago Press, 1988.

MacDonald, Michael J., ed. *The Oxford Handbook of Rhetorical Studies*. Oxford: Oxford University Press, 2017.

Mack, Burton L. *Rhetoric and the New Testament*. Guides to Biblical Scholarship. New Testament Series. Minneapolis, MN: Fortress Press, 1990.

Martin, Troy W. *Metaphor and Composition in 1 Peter*. Society of Biblical Literature Dissertation Series 131. Atlanta, GA: Scholars Press, 1992.

Martin, Troy W. 'The Present Indicative in the Eschatological Statements of 1 Peter 1:6, 8'. *Journal of Biblical Literature* 111 (1992): 307–12.

Martin, Troy W. 'The Rehabilitation of a Rhetorical Step-Child: First Peter and Classical Rhetorical Criticism'. In *Reading First Peter with New Eyes: Methodological Reassessments of the Letter of First Peter*, edited by Robert L. Webb and Betsy Bauman-Martin, 41–71. Library of New Testament Studies 364. London and New York: T&T Clark, 2007.

Martin, Troy W. 'The Voice of Emotion: Paul's Pathetic Persuasion (Gal 4:12–20)'. In *Paul and Pathos*, edited by Thomas H. Olbricht and Jerry L. Sumney, 181–202. Society of Biblical Literature Symposium Series 16. Atlanta, GA: Society of Biblical Literature, 2001.

Mesquita, Batja. 'Emotions Are Culturally Situated'. *Social Science Information* 46 (2007): 410–15.

Michaels, J. Ramsey. *1 Peter*. Word Biblical Commentary 49. Nashville, TS: Thomas Nelson, 1988.

Millauer, Helmut. *Leiden als Gnade: Eine traditionsgeschichtliche Untersuchung zur Leidenstheologie des ersten Petrusbriefes*. Europäische Hochschulschriften 23. Frankfurt: Peter Lang, 1975.

Moffatt, James. *Love in the New Testament*. London: Hodder & Stoughton, 1929.

Moors, Agnes. 'Theories of Emotion Causation: A Review'. *Cognition and Emotion* 23 (2009): 625–62.

Moors, Agnes, Phoebe C. Ellsworth, Klaus R. Scherer, and Nico H. Frijda. 'Appraisal Theories of Emotion: State of the Art and Future Development'. *Emotion Review* 5 (2013): 119–24.

Morgan, Teresa. 'Is *Pistis/Fides* Experienced as an Emotion in the Late Roman Republic, Early Principate, and Early Church?'. In *Unveiling Emotions II: Emotions in Greece and Rome: Texts, Images, Material Culture*, edited by Angelos Chaniotis and Pierre Ducrey, 191–214. Heidelberger Althistorische Beiträge und Epigraphische Studien 55. Stuttgart: Franz Steiner Verlag, 2013.

Morrice, William G. *Joy in the New Testament*. Exeter: Paternoster Press, 1984.

Mulligan, Kevin and Klaus R. Scherer. 'Toward a Working Definition of Emotion'. *Emotion Review* 4 (2012): 345–57.

Nauck, Wolfgang. 'Freude im Leiden: Zum Problem einer urchristlichen Verfolgungstradition'. *Zeitschrift für die neutestamentliche Wissenschaft und die Kunde der älteren Kirche* 46 (1955): 68–80.

Nussbaum, Martha C. *The Therapy of Desire: Theory and Practice in Hellenistic Ethics*. Martin Classical Lectures, New Series 2. Princeton, NJ: Princeton University Press, 1994.

Nussbaum, Martha C. *Upheavals of Thought: The Intelligence of Emotions*. Cambridge: Cambridge University Press, 2001.

Ogereau, Julien M. 'A Survey of Κοινωνία and Its Cognates in Documentary Sources'. *Novum Testamentum* 53 (2015): 275–94.

Olbricht, Thomas H. and Jerry L. Sumney, eds. *Paul and Pathos*. Society of Biblical Literature Symposium Series 16. Atlanta, GA: Society of Biblical Literature, 2001.

Oxford Dictionary (Online). Accessed 26 November 2015. www.oxford dictionaries.com/definition/english/joy.

Patera, Maria. 'Reflections on the Discourse of Fear in Greek Sources'. In *Unveiling Emotions II: Emotions in Greece and Rome: Texts, Images, Material Culture,* edited by Angelos Chaniotis and Pierre Ducrey, 109–34. Heidelberger Althistorische Beiträge und Epigraphische Studien 55. Stuttgart: Franz Steiner Verlag, 2013.

Perelman, Chaim and Lucie Olbrechts-Tyteca. *The New Rhetoric: A Treatise on Argumentation*. Translated by John Wilkinson and Purcell Weaver. Notre Dame, IN: University of Notre Dame Press, 1969. Originally published as La Nouvelle Rhétorique: Traité de l'Argumentation. Press Universitaires de France, 1958.

Piper, John. 'Hope as the Motivation of Love: 1 Peter 3.9–12'. *New Testament Studies* 26 (1980): 212–30.

Ramelli, Ilaria L. E. and David Konstan. 'The Use of Χαρά in the New Testament and its Background in Hellenistic Moral Philosophy'. *Exemplaria Classica: Journal of Classical Philology* 14 (2010): 185–204.

Riis, Ole and Linda Woodhead. *A Sociology of Religious Emotion*. Oxford: Oxford University Press, 2010.

Sandbach, F. H. *The Stoics*. 2nd ed. Bristol: Bristol Press, 1989.

Schelkle, Karl Hermann. *Die Petrusbriefe: Der Judasbrief*. 3rd ed. Herders Theologischer Kommentar zum Neuen Testament 13 Fasz. 2. Freiburg: Herder, 1970.

Schlosser, Jacques. *La Première Épître de Pierre*. Commentaire biblique: Nouveau Testament 21. Paris: Les Éditions du Cerf, 2011.

Schückler, Georg. 'Wandel im Glauben als missionarisches Zeugnis'. *Zeitschrift für Missionswissenschaft und Religionswissenschaft* 51 (1967): 289–99.

Sedley, D. 'The School from Zeno to Arius Didymus'. In *The Cambridge Companion to The Stoics,* edited by Brad Inwood, 7–32. Cambridge: Cambridge University Press, 2003.

Seland, Torrey. *Strangers in the Light: Philonic Perspectives on Christian Identity in 1 Peter*. Biblical Interpretation Series 76. Leiden: Brill, 2005.

Selwyn, Edward Gordon. *The First Epistle of St. Peter: The Greek Text with Introduction, Notes and Essays*. London: Macmillian, 1946.

Sihvola, Juha and Troels Engberg-Pedersen, eds. *The Emotions in Hellenistic Philosophy*. The New Synthese Historical Library 46. Dordrecht: Kluwer Academic, 1998.

Solomon, Robert C. *The Passions: Emotions and the Meaning of Life*. Indianapolis, IN: Hackett, 1993.

Sorabji, Richard. 'Chrysippus – Posidonius – Seneca: A High Level Debate on Emotion'. In *The Emotions in Hellenistic Philosophy*, edited by Juha Sihvola and Troels Engberg-Pedersen, 149–69. Dordrecht: Kluwer Academic, 1998.

Sumney, Jerry L. 'Paul's Use of Πάθος in His Argument Against the Opponents of 2 Corinthians'. In *Paul and Pathos*, edited by Thomas H. Olbricht and Jerry L. Sumney, 147–60. Society of Biblical Literature Symposium Series 16. Atlanta, GA: Society of Biblical Literature, 2001.

Taylor, Garbriele. *Pride, Shame, and Guilt: Emotions of Self Assessment.* Oxford: Clarendon Press, 1985.

Thurén, Lauri. *Argument and Theology in 1 Peter: The Origins of Christian Paraenesis.* Journal for the Study of the New Testament Supplement Series 114. Sheffield: Sheffield Academic Press, 1995.

Thurén, Lauri. *The Rhetorical Strategy of 1 Peter: with Special Regard to Ambiguous Expressions.* Åbo: Åbo Akademis Förlag, 1990.

Tong, Eddie M. W. 'Differentiation of 13 Positive Emotions by Appraisals'. *Cognition and Emotion* 29 (2015): 484–503.

Volf, Miroslav. 'Soft Difference: Theological Reflections on the Relationship between Church and Culture in 1 Peter'. *Ex Auditu* 10 (1994): 15–30.

von Gemünden, Petra. *Affekt und Glaube: Studien zur historischen Psychologie des Frühjudentums und Urchristentums.* Studien zur Umwelt des Neuen Testaments 73. Göttingen: Vandenhoeck & Ruprecht, 2009.

Voorwinde, Stephen. *Jesus' Emotions in the Gospels.* London: T&T Clark, 2011.

Wassmann, Claudia. 'On Emotion and the Emotions: A Comment to Dixon, Mulligan and Scherer, and Scarantino'. *Emotion Review* 4 (2012): 385–86.

Welborn, L. L. 'Paul and Pain: Paul's Emotional Therapy in 2 Corinthians 1.1–2.13; 7.5–16 in the Context of Ancient Psychagogic Literature'. *New Testament Studies* 57 (2011): 547–70.

Wierzbicka, Anna. *Emotions Across Languages and Cultures: Diversity and Universals.* Studies in Emotion and Social Interaction. Cambridge: Cambridge University Press, 1999.

Williams, Travis B. *Good Works in 1 Peter: Negotiating Social Conflict and Christian Identity in the Greco-Roman World.* WUNT 337. Tübingen: Mohr Siebeck, 2014.

Williams, Travis B. *Persecution in 1 Peter: Differentiating and Contextualizing Early Christian Suffering.* Supplements to Novum Testamentum 145. Leiden: Brill, 2012.

Windisch, Hans. *Die katholischen Briefe.* 2nd Rev. ed. Handbuch Zum Neuen Testament 15. Tübingen: J. C. B. Mohr (Paul Siebeck), 1930.

Wisse, Jakob. *Ethos and Pathos from Aristotle to Cicero.* Amsterdam: Adolf M. Hakkert, 1989.

ANCIENT SOURCES INDEX

Greco-Roman Authors

Aetius
    4.12.1–5 = SVF 2.54, *62*, *63*
    4.12.2 = SVF 2.54, *62*
    4.21.1–4 = SVF 2.836, *58*
Andronicus
  [*Pass.*]
    1 = SVF 3.391, *68*, *107*, *180*
    2 = SVF 3.414, *109*
    3 = SVF 3.409, *207*, *227*
    6 = SVF 3.432, *110*, *181*
Anonymous Stoic Treatise
  SVF 2.131, *72*
Aristotle
  De an.
    1.1, *63*
    2.2, *58*
    3.3, *63*
    3.7, *66*
    3.9, *65*
    3.10, *65*
  Eth. eud.
    2.1.11, *78*
    2.2.4, *61*
    2.2.4–5, *58*
    2.8.12, *208*
    2.11.7–9, *79*
    3.7.1–10, *81*
    3.7.3, *229*
    8.1.5, *70*
  Eth. nic.
    2.5, *58*
    2.6, *81*, *82*
    3.7, *66*
    3.9, *74*
    3.11, *66*
    3.12, *69*
    4.9, *228*
    6.2, *66*
    6.12, *79*
    7.1, *82*

Rhet.
  1.1.1–2, *86*
  1.2.4, *90*
  1.2.5, *90*, *92*
  1.2.6, *90*
  1.2.7, *97*
  2.1.4, *92*
  2.1.8, *92*
  2.1.9, *97*
  2.2–3, *98*
  2.4, *98*
  2.5, *98*, *180*, *181*, *182*
  2.6, *98*, *228*, *229*, *230*
  2.7, *98*
  2.8, *99*
  2.9, *99*
  2.10, *99*
  2.11, *99*
Calcidius
  220 = SVF 2.879, *58*, *59*
[Cicero]
  Rhet. Her.
    1.2.3, *94*
    1.5.8, *98*
    2.31.50, *97*, *98*
    3.11.19, *95*
    4.43.55–6, *94*
Cicero
  Acad.
    2.21, *63*
  De or.
    1.5.17, *91*
    1.12.50–1, *95*
    1.12.53, *96*
    1.32.146, *86*
    1.46.202, *96*
    1.51.220, *97*
    1.51.220–2, *86*
    1.51.223, *96*
    2.9.35, *96*
    2.27.114, *91*
    2.42.178, *208*

25.9, *114*
25.19, *114*
26.4, *212*
28.16, *234*
29.22, *233*
30.1–5, *233*
30.12–14, *213*
31.10, *213*
32.11, *115*
35.1–2, *114*
35.10, *113, 116*
40.29, *116*
41.10, *185*
41.11, *233*
41.13, *185*
41.16, *114*
42.17, *233*
44.9–11, *233*
45, *233*
45.16–17, *233*
47.3, *232*
47.3–4, *233*
47.10, *213*
49.13, *114*
49.23, *233*
50.6, *233*
50.7, *233*
50.8–9, *233*
50.10–11, *115*
51.5–6, *212*
51.11, *113, 116*
51.13, *185*
54.4–5, *233*
54.14, *185*
59.18–19, *184*
61.10, *114*
63.17, *185*
65.13–14, *113, 114*
65.19, *114*
Jeremiah
2.26, *232*
3.25, *232*
10.5, *185*
13.25–7, *213*
15.18, *113*
16.4–9, *115*
17.5–6, *213*
17.7–8, *185, 212*
25.10, *115*
26.28, *185*
39.40, *184*
49.11, *183*
Baruch
1.15, *232*
1.15–18, *231, 233*
4.22, *212*

4.30–4, *115*
4.33–4, *113*
Lamentations
1.22, *113, 116*
Ezekiel
7.10–19, *233*
16.37, *232*
16.43, *113*
22.10, *232*
28.26–7, *212*
Daniel
3.17, *185*
3.33, *233*
3.40, *233*
3.50, *113*
4.37, *184*
5.17–19, *183*
6.19, *113*
9.8, *232*

New Testament

Matthew
5.11–12, *147*
10.25, *147*
Mark
13.9–13, *147*
Luke
6.22–3, *123*
John
15.18–20, *147*
16.1–4, *147*
Romans
6.1–11, *150*
Hebrews
12.2, *246*
12.7–11, *169*
1 Peter
1.1, *46, 47, 48, 117, 129*
1.2, *133*
1.3, *121, 122, 146, 194, 213, 221, 253*
1.3–5, *16, 118–19, 122, 123–4, 125, 127, 134, 137, 254*
1.3–6, *254*
1.3–9, *117, 118, 154, 172, 175, 190*
1.3–12, *117, 124*
1.3–21, *213, 214–20*
1.4, *121*
1.4–5, *121*
1.5, *121, 122, 130*
1.6, *10, 16, 105, 253, 255*
1.6–7, *144, 255*
1.6–8, *105, 106, 116–41, 155*
1.6–9, *117*
1.7, *174, 236*
1.7–9, *192*

impulse, 58, 61, 64–6, 67–8, 69, 71, 74, 76, 77, 78, 80, 84, 90, 97, 171, 208
indifferents, 71, 72–3, 87
inheritance, 121, 124, 190, 215, 216, 221

joy, 16, 105–29, 136–41, 142–5, 173–6, 207, 208, 209, 212, 238, 253–4, 259, 260
  characteristics of, 108
  contextualisation of, 114–15, 116, 117–19, 124–5, 143–5, 154–5, 173, 175, 254
  definition of, 107, 209
  enduring, 128–9, 138, 140, 258–9
  glorified, 138–9, 259
  in Greco-Roman sources, 106–11
  as identity marker, 115, 125–6
  in the LXX, 111–13, 114–15, 116
  object of, 108, 110, 114–15, 117, 121–6, 128, 135–7, 138, 139, 144–5, 254
  subcatergories of, 109–10
  subject of, 114–15, 117, 118
judgement, *see* appraisal

Kennedy, George A., 11, 12
Kraftchick, Steven K., 6

Logos, 6, 12, 17, 25, 67, 89, 90
Lutz, Catherine, 32–3, 35

Martin, Troy W., 17–18, 120, 267
mastery, *see* power

nature, 82
  contrary to, 65, 69, 81, 181
  living in accordance with, 57, 65, 80, 81, 85, 210
Nauck, Wolfgang, 10
Nussbaum, Martha C., 27, 28, 30, 33

Object, 26, 29, 59, 62, 64, 88, 239, 251, 267
  -directedness, 15, 27, 29, 30, 37, 38, 40, 45, 69, 75, 84, 85, 92, 93–4, 97, 105, 179, 221
  intentional, 27, 29, 38, 251
  salience of, 27, 28, 30, 39, 200, 251, 253, 257
  typical, 97, 99, 100, 114, 181–2, 184, 210
opinion, 63, 65, 71–2, 82, 83, 85, 92, 107, 108, 131, 227
Other, the, 17, 40, 140, 203, 204, 205, 225, 243, 253, 257
  conflict with, 153, 160, 221, 262

conversion of, 157–8, 160, 164–5, 199, 221–2, 249, 258, 261
detachment from, 126, 128, 135, 140, 165–6, 176, 200–2, 204–5, 222–3, 242, 243–5, 246, 249, 255–6, 258, 262, 265
hostile, 51, 130–1, 134, 135, 140, 143, 155, 157, 158, 200, 204, 205, 242, 243, 255–6, 258, 265

pain, *see* distress
passion(s), 19, 20–1, 24, 64, 67, 78, 80, 81–2, 83, 87, 183
  definition of, 60–1, 67–9
  four primary Stoic, 60–1, 88, 106, 111, 179
  irrationality of, 61, 67, 69–70, 81, 107, 179, 180, 196, 227
pathos/pathē, 5, 6, 12, 17, 23, 56, 58, 60, 88, 89–90, 207, 227
  and judgement/appraisal, 91–4, 95
  as *pistis*, 89–91, 100
  and rhetorical style, 87, 88, 94–6
persecution
  of believer(s), 50–1, 120, 123, 129–31, 135, 142, 144, 158, 166, 200, 206, 221, 240, 245, 249, 253, 255, 259, 261
pleasure, 60, 61, 65, 73, 74, 82, 107, 108, 111
power, 32, 131, 179, 181–2, 185, 186, 189, 190, 192, 195, 197–8, 199, 200, 201–2, 203, 204–5, 206, 211–13, 215, 217–18, 222, 224, 225, 229, 231, 244–5, 250, 254, 255, 256, 258
pre-emotions, 83
proper functions, 79–80, 181, 196

reason, 24, 25, 58, 61, 67, 69, 70, 71, 76, 78, 79, 80, 81, 82, 83, 84, 85, 91, 95, 97, 108, 110, 111, 196
rhetorical criticism, 3, 5, 10, 11–18
  and 1 Peter, 99–100
  ancient, 11, 17–18, 266
    failure of Stoic rhetorical theory, 87–9
  modern, 13, 14, 45
rhetorical strategy
  of 1 Peter, 12–13, 259–60

salvation, 114, 118, 119, 121, 137–8, 163, 164, 165, 166, 190, 191–2, 193, 212, 215, 216, 221, 254
Seland, Torrey, 265
self
  positioning of, 37, 38, 105, 155, 182, 185, 196, 230, 253, 259

acculturation, 131, 159, 201, 202, 206, 245, 261, 263, 265
action(s), *see* behaviour
action-tendency, 15, 18, 26, 31, 38, 39, 40, 64–6, 69, 71, 74, 75, 80, 84, 85, 96, 105, 207, 251, 252, 257
  of distress, 108, 131–2, 139, 140, 257
  of fear, 180, 182, 183, 193–4, 203, 205–6, 222, 257
  of hope, 209, 211, 222, 257
  of joy, 108, 127, 257
  of shame, 227, 231, 245, 250
affect/affection(s), 19, 20–1, 24, 25, 58, 70, 81, 82, 207, 217, 251
agency, 28, 77–9, 83, 85, 212, 215, 224, 254
allegiance, 124, 140, 151, 152–4, 155, 159, 161, 162, 166, 169, 172, 174, 176, 185, 194, 198, 199, 200, 204, 205, 213, 218, 220, 221, 222, 223, 224, 233, 238, 239, 241, 244, 245, 246, 250, 255, 258, 259, 262, 266
apatheia, 81, 83, 85, 179, 182, 196
appearances, 72, 73
appraisal, 8, 14, 15, 26, 28–9, 30, 31, 32, 37, 38, 39, 40, 45, 59, 66, 67–9, 70, 74, 76, 79, 80, 84, 85, 96, 100, 105, 116, 139, 207, 219, 251, 253, 257
  alteration of, 14, 38, 132–5, 139, 140, 154–5, 171–2, 176, 205, 241–3, 246, 249, 255–6, 260
  of distress, 108, 131, 132–5, 139
  of fear, 180, 181, 182, 198, 204, 255, 256
  of hope, 208, 209, 215
  of joy, 108, 126, 127, 128, 137, 175
  propositional content of, 28, 33, 39, 40, 75, 92, 96, 100, 108, 179, 198, 251, 252
  of shame, 227, 229, 230, 231, 250
  theory, 28–9, 33

assent, 15, 58, 61, 65, 66–9, 74, 75, 76, 77–9, 83, 85
  faulty, 71
assimilation, *see* acculturation
association, *see* allegiance
audience
  location of, 47–8
  shaping of, 91, 92, 97, 100, 138, 139, 140, 155, 189, 193, 223, 240, 250, 253, 259, 265, 268
  situation of, 50–1
  social make-up of, 48–50

bad, *see* goods, harm(s)
Balch, David L., 13, 260–1, 263
Balch–Elliott debate, 12, 260–2, 263, 265
Barton, Stephen, 7–9, 18
behaviour, 24, 26, 39, 45, 77, 78, 79, 81, 85, 93, 100, 108, 134, 171, 208, 220, 252, 253, 259, 267
  of believers, 8, 14, 17, 50, 126, 131, 138, 139, 149, 155, 168, 172, 173, 179, 189, 191, 192–3, 195, 196, 197, 204, 206, 219, 221, 222, 225, 236, 238, 242, 243, 245–6, 248, 250, 253, 255, 257–8, 259, 260, 265, 266
  in fear, 187, 190, 191, 193, 198–202, 204, 205
  doing good, 147, 149, 152, 153, 154, 155, 156, 157–61, 163, 164, 166, 168, 169, 170, 172, 175, 176, 190, 199, 201, 203, 204, 205, 220, 241, 247, 248, 249, 255, 257, 261, 266
  holy, 158, 190, 199, 204
belief, *see* faith(fulness)
believer(s)
  flourishing of, 126, 127, 137, 139, 140, 176, 190, 200, 205, 215, 217, 224, 225, 244, 250, 253, 254, 255, 256, 266, 267
  identity of, 8, 50, 118, 119, 147, 150, 152, 155, 159, 160, 174, 176, 179,

For EU product safety concerns, contact us at Calle de José Abascal, 56–1°,
28003 Madrid, Spain or eugpsr@cambridge.org.

www.ingramcontent.com/pod-product-compliance
Ingram Content Group UK Ltd.
Pitfield, Milton Keynes, MK11 3LW, UK
UKHW020323140625
459647UK00018B/1980